THE FINAL CHALLENGE

The Final Challenge

The American Frontier
1804–1845

❦

DALE VAN EVERY

Quill
William Morrow
New York

Library of Congress Cataloging-in-Publication Data

Van Every, Dale, 1896–
The final challenge.

Bibliography: p.
Includes index.
1. West (U.S.)—History—To 1848.   2. Frontier and pioneer life—West (U.S.)   3. United States—Territorial expansion.   I. Title.
F592.V3   1988   978'.02   88-8928
ISBN 0-688-08256-4 (pbk.)

Printed in the United States of America

First Quill Edition

1 2 3 4 5 6 7 8 9 10

Foreword

One of the most noteworthy contributions to American historical writing in recent decades is brought to completion in this volume. In four panels Mr. Van Every has painted a panorama of the progress of the frontier from 1763 to 1845, the period in which it played a dominant part in the shaping of the continent. For sheer human interest, for color and drama, his comprehensive history is hard to match; not a page is lacking in vigor and hardly a chapter in suspense and excitement. This final record, reaching from the days of Lewis and Clark to those of Marcus Whitman and Jason Lee, is as rich in adventurous episodes and picturesque personalities, all carefully depicted, as its predecessors. But the whole work has values reaching well beyond drama and color.

The first three volumes of Mr. Van Every's series can be read, and have been read, primarily as a sweeping story of perils surmounted by courage and hardships conquered by endurance; with chapters of social history—that is, descriptions of life, manners, and ideas on the frontier—intermingled with the narrative. This fourth volume continues the theme, but enriches it by new elements. As an epos of the frontier, Mr. Van Every's story is romantic in detail and generous in temper, reminding us at times of Theodore Roosevelt's less expert *The Winning of the West*. Some critics might complain that the frontier daring was more frequently recklessness, the hardihood more often streaked with brutality, and the morals and manners cruder and more squalid than the author suggests. But Mr. Van Every's work is lifted above mere romantic writing by two virtues: the depth of its comprehension that the movement of the frontier was a great central force—perhaps *the* central force—in the forging of the nation, and the originality of its separate insights.

Recklessness, brutality, greed—the frontier certainly had them. But what Mr. Van Every rightly presents is an irresistible folk movement responsible to powerful democratic impulses rather than to materialistic appetites; the impulses of men and women striving for a fuller, freer, juster life in a plastic environment, where they could found all their institutions, political, religious, and cultural, upon the bedrock of self-government. This conception of the frontier movement lifts it to a higher level and invests it with a fuller significance. And as the story proceeds, the author's interpretive insights, though unobtrusive and in the first three volumes so well absorbed into the rapid narrative that some readers may miss them, are novel and illuminating. The work has realism in the larger sense for all its romantic aspects and trappings.

The first volume, *Forth to the Wilderness,* dealing with the years of the struggle of Britain 'and France for North America, demonstrated the validity of the author's bold claim that the most momentous event in early American history, apart from the Revolution, was the crossing of the Appalachian mountain barrier by white settlement. This feat was achieved by a small body of pioneers who struggled across two hundred miles of a tangled mountain barrier into a dangerous wilderness against the opposition of every European power, every Indian nation, their own government, powerful land companies, fur-trading organizations, and all conservative citizens. Here we find memorable personalities: not only the familiar Washington, Wolfe, and Amherst, but also John Stuart, Henry Bouquet, Sir William Johnson, George Croghan, and John Forbes, with Pontiac foremost among the red foes. Then in *A Company of Heroes,* treating the years 1775–1783, Mr. Van Every gave readers a side of the Revolution too easily ignored. Here again we met Washington and Sir William Johnson. Here we saw George Rogers Clark as the central figure in the seizure of the Old Northwest, and arrayed against him the still more striking Joseph Brant of the Iroquois, protégé of Johnson and champion of the British cause.

But the true heroes and heroines of both books, in Mr. Van Every's pages, were not the famous leaders. They were the ordinary men and women who first braved every peril to establish themselves byond the mountains and then underwent almost incredible dangers and hardships, during the border wars of the Revolution, to maintain their exposed position. They did maintain their foothold, and enlarged it. This opened the way for the settlers' encounter of the terrifying post-Revolutionary crises, a story told with vigor by Mr. Van Every in his *Ark of Empire,* which brought the story of the frontier down to 1803. This pivotal chapter in the history of the rise of the infant nation is set in a time of dire perils, some overt, some insidious. The British had fastened on the region northwest of the Ohio River, and the Spanish on the region to the southwest. Both were powerful; both found allies among traitorous Americans as well as Indian tribes. The onslaughts of the savages resulted in some heavy defeats for American arms. But the leadership furnished by Washington, Adams, and Jefferson, and the stubborn valor of the frontier folk, made both Northwest and Southwest integral parts of the republic. As the author says with insight, it was really love of self-government that preserved the settlers from yielding to the British or the Spanish. The key to the feat, he remarks in another insight, had been not so much their own indomitability as the example they set for others perhaps less fitted to meet the rigors of the frontier struggle. But wherever we place the credit for the achievement in holding and peopling the lands up to the Mississippi and beyond, it was an achievement crucial to American nationalism, for they had attached this part of the West "so firmly to the United States that there could be no question of Americans having become one nation occupying the major portion of the continent."

Sweep and insight are not dependent upon the labored minutiae of scholarship; they are independent of it. They rest upon a combination of vision and style, two words which comprehend many virtues. A larger discovery of new truths can sometimes be made from the careful digestion of old sources, or from reading between the lines in old texts, than from long toil in dusty archives. Mr. Van Every's method is much that of Parkman, with one vital difference. Parkman's history of the struggle of Britain and France for the mastery of North America was written at a time and upon a subject which offered him little in monographic support. Mr. Van Every found instead a vast wealth of published histories, biographies, special studies, personal narratives, and well-edited official documents, which cover his principal topics so completely that he needed little if any supplementary material. His has been a task of digestion, interpretation, and imaginative revivification rather than of fresh discovery. If not so formidable in unknown areas as that of Parkman—who, after all, stands unapproached in his field—it was formidable in a different way. It is no small tribute to say that by industry combined with insight and imagination he has made his segment of the past relive to a degree which will command the attention of scholars and general readers alike.

This fourth volume not only extends the previous narrative, but to a considerable extent sums up the significance of the whole well-rounded history. It is much richer in generalizations than its predecessors; it is more reflective, and it profits from the fact. Altogether Mr. Van Every enables us to see the history of the frontier from the days of Wolfe and Washington to those of Sutter and Frémont in at least two novel or ill-appreciated aspects: as an important part of the history of democracy, and a vital part of the history of national feeling and sense of destiny. He shows that frontier energy came from the people, whose march westward was an irresistible self-generated force that paused at no obstacle. It had an urgency that defied every effort, foreign or domestic, to impede it; it conquered every geographical and climatic obstacle with the same inner compulsion. It moved at first on narrow fronts, finding channels like river valleys; once across the Appalachians, its fronts broadened; but always it moved. The frontier of the Old Northwest was very different from the frontier of the Old Southwest—and Mr. Van Every clearly defines the differences; never mind, the frontier rolled on in both regions. Everywhere the family in this mighty Anglo-Saxon advance (differing in this respect from the early French and Spanish advance) was more important than the individual.

Everywhere, in the irresistible occupation of the continent on a line of march three thousand miles east to west, the frontier folk moved in advance of the government, first British and later American. Everywhere in this movement of self-generated force they defied the Indian, the Frenchman or Spaniard, and the home-bred conservatives, with equal sternness. It was their obstinate pressure which laid hold upon lands, from Florida to California, that but for their brash settlement would have passed into foreign hands. And everywhere they took their half-unconscious but conquerable love of democratic autonomy, and their ability to erect what Mr. Van Every calls "the edifice of fully-functioning self-government," an attribute central to the growth of Americanism as well as America. It is a mighty story, and the country is fortunate to have it so ably rendered.

ALLAN NEVINS

Contents

MAPS

THE FINAL CHALLENGE

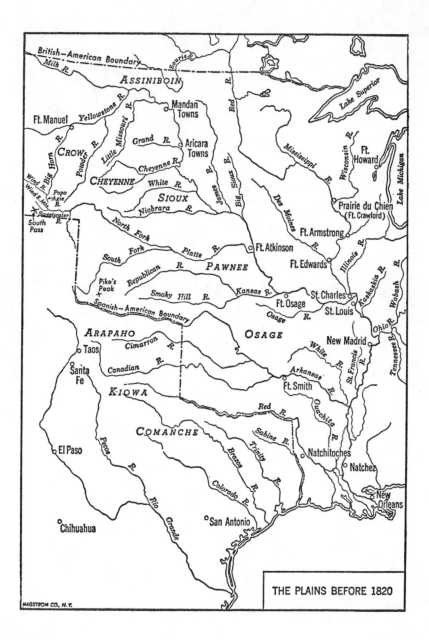

THE PLAINS BEFORE 1820

I

ॐ

New Country

THE HALF COMPANY of American troops marched up the slope
from the waterfront to the clapboard-porticoed, squared-log,
shake-roofed government house in St. Louis, the provincial capital
of Upper Louisiana. The plenipotentiaries of three nations exchanged greetings, credentials, and acknowledgments. The banner
of Spain inched down from the staff to be replaced by that of
France. Drums beat. Cannon in the little fort on the hill above
fired a salute. The following day, in a repetitive ritual, the flag of
France was lowered and the flag of the United States raised. By
these diplomatic processes of the 9th and 10th of March, 1804, the
United States, a republic so young that its federal government had
existed but 15 years, had been endowed with sovereignty over the
valley of the Missouri, an immense, wild region stretching from the
Ozarks to the Canadian Rockies.

Seldom in the history of international relations has possession of
so vast and valuable a territory passed in a single transaction, and
certainly never has so great a prize been transferred among three
nations in the span of 24 hours. Every aspect of the proceedings

3

was singular. The Spanish lieutenant governor who was delivering the title deeds, Charles Delassus, had been born a Frenchman. The commissioner of France who accepted title for France on the first day was Captain Amos Stoddard of the Army of the United States. On the second day French Commissioner Amos Stoddard handed the reins of government to American Governor Amos Stoddard. Of the inhabitants viewing with mingled emotions the swift variations in their allegiance to Spain, to France, to the United States, the few Spanish-born were officials or soldiers. The slight majority of the population who were technically Spanish citizens were recent American settlers who had accepted that citizenship in exchange for permission to own land. The longer established French residents had moved across the Mississippi from the Illinois in the 1760's to escape British dominion, only now to be overtaken by American dominion.

These French residents had somewhat more reason to regard this as their country than did their Spanish and American neighbors. They had been here longer and since their arrival they had confidently expected its reclamation by France. They had been heartstricken when the fulfillment of their hopes gave way overnight to the rule of still a third alien power. In his reassuring address to the inhabitants, Stoddard defined the miraculous political formula which had invested the new republic with such a growth potential as no other nation has ever enjoyed:

> You will perceive, that you are divested of the character of subjects, and clothed with that of citizens. You now form an integral part of a great community, the powers of whose government are circumscribed and defined by charter . . . You may soon expect the establishment of a territorial government . . . From your present population, and the rapidity of its increase, this territorial establishment must soon be succeeded by your admission as a State into the Federal Union. At that period, you will be at liberty to try any experiment in legislation, and to frame such a government as may best comport with your local interests, manners and customs; popular suffrage will be its basis.

Among the witnesses to the ceremonies there could have been

no man who watched with an interest so intense as Captain Meriwether Lewis, cocommander of the expedition then encamped on what had been until that day the American bank of the Mississippi. Not only had the west bank now become American but along with it the banks of every farthest western tributary of the most extensive river system in the world. Lewis knew that within weeks he would set out to proclaim to wild nations in distant and mysterious regions never before visited by white men the American sovereignty that was being proclaimed here.

President Thomas Jefferson, whose secretary Lewis had been, had been astounded the previous summer by the notification that the emissaries he had dispatched to Europe to buy Florida from Napoleon had instead bought Spain's claim to an indeterminate expanse of country stretching westward from the Mississippi no man knew how far. Great as was his exultation that he had been privileged to add so vast a territory to his country's domain, he had been troubled by a number of misgivings, not the least of which was his private opinion that he had irresponsibly exceeded the powers vested in the presidency by the Constitution. He had also been acutely disturbed by the realization that he had no faintest idea, aside from the obvious immediate value of the right to use the Mississippi, of just what it was that he had bought.

The persistent mystery still shrouding the continent's western interior had sprung from the extraordinary eccentricities of the New World's occupation by white men. Possession of the temperate belt between what is now the Canadian border in the north and the Mexican border in the south, eventually to become the continent's most populous and prosperous area, had paradoxically been the last to be sought. The first white men to cross the Atlantic, the gold-seeking Spaniards, had elected instead to assail the region most difficult of all to penetrate. With fierce and implacable energy they had within the first half century after Columbus scaled the mountain ramparts of Mexico and overthrown the Aztec empire, the most formidable of all Indian nations. Propelled by the momentum of that first surge, Spanish explorers had ranged widely in search of more gold, De Soto from the Savannah to the Arkansas, Coronado from the deserts of Sinaloa to the plains of Kansas, and Cabrillo northward from Mexico along the California coast to beyond Cape Mendocino. But after that first dynamic half century, the flame of Spanish energies burned lower and Spaniards thereafter concentrated on defending from their envious rivals the treasure they had already won.

Throughout this period of Spain's explosive occupation of the West Indies and Mexico and for more than another half century, the primeval calm of the northern seven eighths of the continent had remained undisturbed by white men. It was not until 1607 that the first permanent English settlement was founded at Jamestown and 1608 that the French were established at Quebec. There followed no strong impulse to consummate white occupation of the temperate middle belt for an other century and a half. With fur traders and missionaries leading the way, the French pushed their dominion rapidly westward across the northern third of the continent, reaching the farthest shores of the Great Lakes before the English had crossed the Delaware, but they were much slower in asserting a sustained interest in the great central valley below the Lakes. They had been on the St. Lawrence 110 years before they capped their tentative exploration of the Mississippi with the settlement of New Orleans in 1718. The English continued for another 50 years to remain absorbed in the development of their seaboard settlements, founding their thirteenth colony, Georgia, in 1733. It was not until 1769 that English settlers first crossed the Appalachians into the central valley, the same year that Spain was nervously undertaking the occupation of California as a precaution against the Russian advance southward along the Pacific coast from Alaska.

But this long delay in the start of the English-speaking people's westward movement had represented a gathering of forces. Time and circumstance had provided for the emergence on the American colonial frontier of a unique breed of men and women peculiarly adapted to meet the challenge of any wilderness. With a sudden burst of energy fully comparable to the original Spanish occupation of Latin America, this American frontier people seized upon the Ohio Valley. Though opposed by fiercer Indian resistance than white men ever encountered elsewhere, within 25 years after their first crossing of the mountains they had established their domination over the entire Ohio basin. Yet swift as had been this sudden spurt in their progress westward from the Atlantic, they were just beginning to cross the Mississippi at the very end of the third century after Columbus.

As a consequence of these singularities distinguishing the white occupation of North America, the western half of what is now the United States was in 1804 still represented on the map by a space as blank as that marking central Africa. Frenchmen had known the Mississippi since 1673, Spaniards the Rio Grande since 1535, Englishmen the Saskatchewan since 1766, and traders of all three nations had carried their intermittent contacts with Indians as far west as the northward bend of the Missouri and as far north as its great westward bend. But of that tremendous area beyond the Missouri lying directly west of the United States, the major part of Mr. Jefferson's purchase, not much more was known than when Columbus sailed.[1]

This age-old veil of ignorance was about to be rent by rude and vigorous hands. When the first American frontiersmen crossed the Mississippi, their contemplation of the stupendous mystery was like

[1] After Coronado in 1540, Villasur's 1720 expedition apparently reached the Platte before being overwhelmed by the Pawnee, the Mallet brothers traveled from the Missouri to the Rio Grande in 1739, Verendrye's sons in 1742 visited the Bad Lands and Black Hills of the Dakotas and by some scholars have been presumed to have sighted from a distance either the Wind River or the Big Horn ranges of the Rockies, and Escalante in 1776 circled from Santa Fe through southern Colorado and southern Utah. But these events had been so narrowly and imprecisely reported that they had not added appreciably to established geographical knowledge. The 1806 map prepared by John Cary, a careful and scientific cartographer, in summing up for the New Universal Atlas what was actually known at the time, included no detail whatever between the north-south stretch of the Missouri and the Pacific coast. The Lewis map of 1804, published in A New and Elegant General Atlas, Philadelphia, ventured to supply more detail and as a result had the Platte rising in northeastern Nevada, the Missouri in southeastern Oregon and Sioux Indians occupying southern Idaho. Maps as late as those of Rector and Roberdeau in 1818 and Finley in 1826 showed the rivers of California rising in southern Utah and western Colorado. The Gallatin map of 1836 was the first to make due allowance for the interior drainage of the Great Basin or to suggest any general comprehension of the geographical complexities of the immense region between the eastern face of the Rockies and the western face of the Sierras.

applying a spark to gunpowder. They were moving with the impetus that had carried them through the five hundred miles of battle-scarred forests immediately behind them. They and their fathers and grandfathers had known no impulse so strong as to seek to be first in any new country. They had been hardened by long and bitter experience with the demands of survival in a wilderness, with hardships and vicissitudes, with deprivations and disappointments, with many defeats as well as many victories. They were supremely fitted for this final challenge.

They sensed immediately that the Missouri River, stretching four weeks' travel time westward, then ten weeks' northward, then westward again to be lost to sight in a distance that baffled conjecture, was the key to the great mystery. They were familiar with mighty rivers. The Ohio had provided the principal way by which they had come as far and as fast as they had. They had sailed it and its tributaries in every sort of craft from a two-log raft to a forty-man keelboat. But nothing more sharply emphasized the difference between this new country lying to the west and the country through which they had already passed than the difference between the two rivers. The Ohio had been helpfully ready to bear them in the direction that they were going. It had invited the lonely canoes of the firstcomers and those who had continued to come had been able to float down it on huge flatboats capable of carrying whole communities. The Missouri offered none of these advantages. For such passage as it afforded it exacted a painful price. From now on the river-borne way west prescribed a perpetual battle against its current, a constant struggle with its vagaries. Yet, as much as had the Ohio, it appeared a gateway, and what seemed at first the only gateway to the new country.

The lower river offered immediate signs and portents heralding the remarkable nature of that country. The theme most often reiterated was that this was the threshold of a land where everything was larger, wilder, fiercer. At its mouth the Missouri thrust the comparatively clear and placid Mississippi against its eastern bank with the brute impact of its thick dark current laden with mud, decaying vegetation, and uprooted trees. In flood time the terrible river threshed about its valley like a demented monster, changing its course by miles, devouring and reproducing islands, carrying away whole forests along its banks. Sand bars and mud flats miles long moved erratically downward with the current, altering the river's main channel from day to day.

This display of violence was accompanied by as striking a display of fertility. Every new sand bar sprouted immediately with the green of willow and poplar. The river bottom's sycamore, walnut, cottonwood, and linden reached gigantic size. Grass on the valley slopes grew to six and eight feet and weeds to fifteen. Wild grapes, currants, plums, cherries, papaws, persimmons, walnuts, pecans, hickory nuts, acorns abounded. The river harbored enormous catfish, and adjacent pools, lagoons, and streams teemed with trout, bass, perch, and pike. Seasonal migrations of pigeons, geese, duck, cranes, swans, pelicans, and gulls darkened sky and water with their limitless numbers. The multitude of deer, bear, elk, and turkeys in the bordering forests seemed as inexhaustible. No aspect of the lower river's fertility was so extravagant, however, as the suggestion of an even more unbridled fecundity above. Each spring's flood waters were crested by the floating carcasses of thousands of buffalo, the victims of the thawing ice as heedless herds had attempted to cross the river's upper reaches. The wheeling clouds of buzzards attending this manifestation of the abundance of life in the region beyond testified as graphically to the prevalence there of death.

To such men as the first Kentuckians and Tennesseans to reach the lower Missouri a land so distant and unknown as this new country beyond beckoned with an irresistible appeal. They had penetrated the defiles of the eastern mountains and kept on down the Ohio and the Tennessee with the urgency of men whose attention was constantly on the horizon ahead. This horizon had suddenly receded into an incomprehensible distance. They could not rest until they had determined how far, until what had been unknown had been to them made known. What awaited them was, in fact, a land infinitely more strange and wonderful than they could have dreamed.

First and most astonishing among the novelties awaiting their discovery was the revelation of the great plains. A racial stock conditioned through hundreds of generations to the lush, varied, and limited landscape of western Europe and eastern America was in no way prepared for this sudden emergence into flat, empty, and increasingly arid space. Striking out for the first time into this boundless and treeless open was an experience as perturbing as when the first primitive navigator lost sight of land. On this sea of grass distances stretched so far and remained so featureless that the same judgment and patience was demanded as that of a mariner. Impressions without precedent continued to multiply. The adventurer who had left behind him every scene with which he had ever been familiar was required to divide his attention between the highest and lowest of concerns. He must study the stars in the heavens to know his direction and detect on the ground at his feet the dried buffalo dung which provided the only fuel for his fire.

To the man who had known only the land of his forebears with its forests and hills, streams and meadows, orderly sequence of seasons and weather, his first venture out upon the plains was an entry into another world. His courage and confidence were at once diminished. Distance and loneliness emphasized his insignificance. He was made to feel the more vulnerable by never being able from moment to moment to know what to expect from any quarter. Weather changes were sudden, complete, and totally unpredictable. The temperature could vary in hours from blazing hot to freezing cold. Across this endless open expanse rushed winds of appalling velocity. Winter blizzards transported arctic cold hundreds of miles southward in a day. In their blinding blasts death waited at the end of the next step or the next minute. Summer thunderstorms brandished a fury made more sensational by intimacy. Denied the attraction of hilltops or trees or other projections from the surface of the earth, the generation of thunderbolts gathered energy in everlowering storm clouds until the lightning began to strike straight downward into the ground. Wild fires attained the proportions of hurricanes. Once started, whether by lightning or Indian hunters, they roared across the plains at the speed of the wind. Each season thousands of square miles were blackened. For men and animals overtaken in their path there was no escape. The one end to each successive conflagration was the onset of the next general rain.

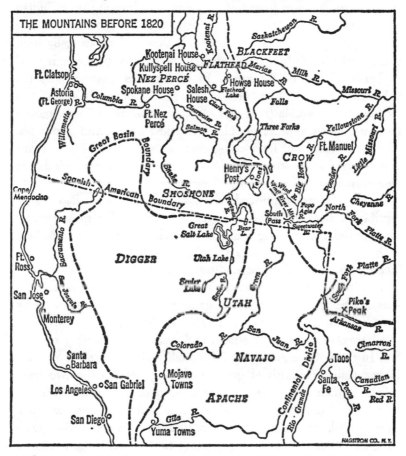

These extremes of nature's violence that characterized the plains were balanced by one reward which to any man bred a hunter from childhood was more than sufficient. These broad grasslands were occupied by the greatest accumulation of game known in historic time. Deer, elk, and antelope grazed in incalculable herds. In many areas they had been so seldom hunted that they regarded the approach of man with unconcern and often, moved by simple curiosity, even advanced to meet him. It was the buffalo, however, that contributed the supreme quest for any hunter. Their size, their temper, their fierce appearance, and their number combined to make them the most prized of all game, and hunting them Indian fashion on horseback was soon recognized as the most exhilarating of all sports. In the eastern woodlands they had occasionally been encountered in herds of hundreds. On these plains they congregated in herds of tens of thousands. In midsummer mating time the bellowing conflicts of embattled bulls shook the earth and stirred clouds of dust visible from afar. At times enormous herds, moved by some sudden obscure impulse, embarked upon blind stampedes, taking no account of intervening obstacles such as ravines or rivers and continuing for scores of miles in a wild onrush as irresistible as an avalanche.

As the venturer continued westward, the plains swelled imperceptibly higher and turned progressively drier. The grass became shorter and sparser. Sagebrush and dwarf pinon appeared along with low hills, deeply eroded gullies, and outcroppings of rock. There also appeared in astounding numbers the great bear of the mountains, at first known as the white bear or the yellow bear and later as the grizzly bear. Of all game animals ever confronted by hunters in North America the grizzly was the most dangerous by its size, ferocity, readiness to attack, and near invulnerability to gunfire. In spite of the increasing inhospitality of the climate, on these higher plains all kinds of game, including notably the two most valued, buffalo and beaver, became even more plentiful than in the longer grass country. There were slopes and hills from which a wide outlook was possible and often as far as sight could distinguish the entire vista was black with grazing buffalo while the diminishing streams were so thick with beaver that the most cursory trapping could quickly gather what would amount to a fortune were the catch to be got safely to St. Louis.

Eventually there lifted above the western horizon a shadowed blue and white apparition. Confused and half-understood Indian reports had long since led white speculation to refer to the hypothetical western mountains as the "stony mountains" or the "rocky mountains" or the "snowy mountains" or the "shining mountains." The first white men to enter them were not long in realizing why the Indian accounts had seemed so garbled. No amount of the most careful description could have made their nature comprehensible. They were not one great north-south mountain chain but a labyrinth of a hundred ranges sprawled as haphazardly as a dropped fistful of jackstraws. Within the compass of this mountainous disorder was every sort of geographic contrast. Cool green mountain valleys were but an hour's climb from sun-blistered deserts, sapphire fields of dewy camas blossoms as near to blackened lava wastes. In the higher recesses of the many ranges were blue glaciers, perpetual snow, ice-cold rivers, crystalline lakes, leaping waterfalls, verdant forests, and gracious meadows, while spread everywhere about their lower slopes were dreary and desiccated fans and flats of sagebrush, sand, dust, and alkali.

The mountains which from the plains had seemed so distant a goal were, when reached, to prove to be but another threshold. From a first sight of the mountains to a first sight of the western ocean stretched a distance twice as great as that from the bend of the Missouri to the mountains. In that bewildering region that intervened waited many more wonders—mile-deep canyons, inland seas, deserts ever more extensive, and rockbound rivers seasonally choked with salmon from the depths of the remote Pacific. Beyond this vast and unforeseen expanse loomed suddenly another rampart of snow-capped mountains, more precipitous and far less passable than the Rockies. And beyond this final barrier waited still another world in which to the north lay the fabled region of Oregon with the continent's heaviest rainfall and tallest forests and to the south the legendary marvels and incongruities of California.

Of all the successively discovered attributes of this new, spectacular and enigmatic country none was so impressive as the immensity of its distances. Journeys across it had to be considered in terms not of days and weeks but of months and years. When the frontier people had crossed the eastern mountains and thereafter had kept restlessly on and on what they had been continually seeking had been what they themselves termed elbowroom. In the new country now opening before them this they had unmistakably found.

II

۞

New Indians

AMID ALL THE ANTICIPATION with which the Kentuckian or Tennessean newly arrived on the Missouri speculated upon the nature of the strange new country suddenly opening before him nothing so engaged his interest as his speculation upon the kind of Indian that might prove to inhabit it. Evaluation of Indians was a field in which he was an expert. Indian behavior had been a study to which since childhood he had applied himself with constant diligence. Indian hostility had impinged upon every facet of his life from planting and harvesting to courting and begetting. For 50 years the Indian had been his people's mortal adversary. He and his father and his father's father had had to hold himself perpetually on guard against the possibility that from any thicket an Indian might spring upon him, that upon any dawn he might awaken to the tumult of an Indian assault on his cabin. His lifelong conflict with the Indian had been a struggle decided by wits and skills as much as by strength and valor. Concealment, ambush, surprise, and strategem had been prevailing tactics. It had been a war fought in the obscurity of forest shadows in which decisive movements and

15

actions had remained invisible. He was already beginning to sense how different might prove the conditions under which he was to confront these new Indians in the endless and naked spaces of this new country. He was also beginning to guess that these western adversaries might prove as different from the eastern Indians with whom he had been so painfully familiar as was the one country from the other. The greatest of these differences, as would shortly appear, was the result of their having so far escaped subjection to contact with white men. Ahead awaited the historic last instance of a first encounter between the two races.

Upon no people had ever been inflicted an alien invasion so bewilderingly catastrophic as that visited upon the eastern Indian by the original advent of white men. The intruders had materialized without warning out of mysterious ocean distances which in Indian conception stretched beyond the limits of the world. They were an unaccountable race of whose existence the Indian had had no previous intimation. Everything about them was as repellent as it was terrifying. They were grotesquely hairy, unwholesomely pallid creatures as outlandish in aspect as the more monstrous spectors of Indian mythology. They came in great winged craft which compelled the very winds to their service. They were clad in steel, armed with fire, rode huge beasts. From the moment they landed they were belligerently aggressive, unnaturally bent upon rapine and enslavement. Resistance appeared futile. They had sprung not only out of a distant land but out of a still distant age. Morally they were more savage than their victims but their overwhelming physical superiorities stemmed from a material culture a hundred generations more advanced than the Indian.

The difficulties weighing upon every attempt to cope with so formidable an intrusion had been insuperable. Resort to war or diplomacy alike had failed to contain the invaders' perpetually increasing demands. It had from the outset been made apparent that any hope of successful resistance depended on resort to the white man's infinitely superior tools and weapons. Yet this recourse was self-defeating. Commerce with the white man exposed the Indian to a still more lethal weapon—the white man's diseases. Smallpox,

typhus, cholera, syphilis, and tuberculosis had spread from the seacoast into the interior to devastate nations which had yet to sight a
white man. A population capable of erecting the enormous earthen
temples and fortifications of the eastern Mississippi Valley was soon
reduced to a fraction of its former numbers. The military requirements of defense nevertheless forced the survivors to seek to possess
guns. The necessary trading associations progressively disrupted
tribal disciplines, inculcated acceptance of white values, and developed an Indian without the virtues or vitalities of either race.
Indian courage and determination had not been lacking during
this long decline. In the area between the Atlantic and the Mississippi there had been two hundred years of wilderness war in which
Indians had won many victories and the white inhabitants of the
border had suffered untold miseries. Still the tide had continued to
run but the one way. The whites had continually expanded the area
of their occupation while their population had increased until by
the time of the final eastern Indian military downfall in 1794 they
outnumbered the Indians east of the Mississippi by more than 40
to 1. It had been from the beginning an invasion against which no
defense could have proven sufficient.

The western Indian had meanwhile been spared all of this.
He had enjoyed, in particular, one enormous advantage over his
eastern brother. The eastern Indian had been enabled to gain the
gun only through suffering in the process from the fatal proximity
of the white man. The western Indian, on the other hand, had
gained the horse generations before he had ever been obliged to
have any dealings whatever with the white man. It had, moreover,
been an even greater gain. The eastern Indian had found his condition as hunter and warrior to be immensely improved by possession of the gun for which he had paid so mortal a price. The
condition of the Indian of the far western plains and mountains
had been totally revolutionized by acquisition of the horse which
had come to him as a free gift.

Before he became a horseman he had been dwarfed by the vast
distances among which he lived. He had been forced to depend
upon his dogs and his women for the transport of his few posses-

sions. Pursuit of the buffalo, deer, elk, and antelope upon which he relied for food was more often than not unsuccessful. Game migrations ushered in periods of starvation during which he dug frantically for roots and rodents. Existence was a laborious and desperate and never-ending struggle for bare survival. All was miraculously changed by the advent of the horse. As by the waving of a wand the Plains Indian had suddenly been made the complete master of his environment. The distances were no longer oppressive. The herd movements of game were no longer disasters. The horse owner could range as widely as he pleased. He could outrun any prey. His wealth was unlimited, for the countless buffalo had been made so available that he could consider them his cattle. His life had been filled to overflowing with rewards.

The horse was unknown in the Americas until brought across the Atlantic by the white man. Various theories have been advanced to account for the phenomenally successful spread of horse culture among the western Indians. One, long and widely held, presumed that strays from the 1540 expeditions of De Soto and Coronado propagated wild herds which the Indians eventually learned to capture and domesticate. More recent examination of the evidence has called attention to a number of factors that make this explanation seem less likely. It was Spanish military custom to use only stallions for campaign service.[1] The Indians of the Coronado-De Soto period regarded Spanish horses as no less hostile than Spanish soldiers and were as intent on killing stray horses as stray Spaniards. There is no indication that anywhere along the continent-girdling routes of the two expeditions were there for the next several generations Indians in possession of horses or Indian tradition connected with the existence of wild horses. When Juan de Oñate undertook the colonization of New Mexico in 1598, he found no horses in use by Indians and no wild herds, though one of his expeditions ranged to the northeast across the Arkansas. The first Frenchmen on the Mississippi in the 1670's heard reports of Indians to the west who rode horses but found none along the river. La Salle first saw

[1] For example, of the nearly 600 horses carried on Coronado's muster roll only two were mares.

Indians with horses in southeast Texas. Farther north the earliest French encounters with Indians who had horses occurred well west of the Mississippi on the Red and the Missouri, indicating, as had La Salle's experience, a source to the west and southwest. The absence of horses north of the Rio Grande when New Mexico was colonized and their first appearance near the Gulf and the Mississippi nearly a century later would seem to dispose of the supposition that there could have been any connection between the De Soto and Coronado expeditions and Indian adoption of the horse.

It would seem, therefore, much more likely that the Spanish horse of the Spanish rancher in Mexico was the progenitor of the Indian horse of the plains and mountains. The Spanish livestock industry was extended rapidly northward in the latter half of the sixteenth century until by 1600 it had reached the upper Rio Grande at Santa Fe. On great haciendas from central Mexico northward the domestic horse herds had multiplied and large numbers of Indians had been employed as herdsmen. Adjacent wild tribes had ample opportunity to become familiar with horse management. A central purpose of every Indian raid during the almost continual Spanish-Indian border warfare of the late sixteenth century became the procurement of horses. Intertribal trade and wars accelerated the process by which the novel improvement became available to more distant nations. The Comanche of northwest Texas, confirmed raiders of the Mexican frontier, appear to have been the first nation north of the Rio Grande to take full advantage of the horse. They had been poor, ugly, weak, and despised but possession of the horse soon made them the most feared of all Plains Indians.

In the great Pueblo Revolt of 1680 hundreds of Spanish horses were taken by Indians at one swoop. Indian acquisition of the horse was presently further expedited by the development of wild herds. Horses that had been stampeded and scattered during a hundred years of raids, pursuits, and engagements found an environment so favorable in the plains of western Texas, Oklahoma, and Kansas[2] that by the end of the eighteenth century they were beginning to

[2] For the convenience of reader and writer alike, the names of modern states often will be used to indicate localized areas of the early west.

rival the buffalo in number. Trade, theft, and war had meanwhile continued to carry realization of this extraordinary and readily available advantage to an ever-widening circle of more distant Indians. Horse culture spread east and southeast from the Comanche area, but even more rapidly northward along the eastern flank of the Rocky Mountains. The Verendryes in 1740 found great numbers of horses among the Indians of the Black Hills region at a time that they were still unknown among the Mandan on the Missouri. With the Utah and Shoshone as middlemen the horse spread most rapidly of all northward along the Green and Snake rivers west of the continental divide. The Indians of the upper Columbia had had horses for at least three generations before the appearance of Lewis and Clark.[3]

In this leap to the back of a horse the western Indian had transformed his entire existence. The immense expanse across which he had trudged painfully on foot had suddenly become his pasture. Powers of which he had not dreamed were now at his command. No aspiration seemed longer impossible. History has often noted the significance of the transition when men on foot became men on horseback. Once mounted, the previously scorned natives of Asian and Arabian deserts were able to embark upon world conquests. Every society has considered the cavalier a being in every respect superior to the plodding peasant. Military tactics through the ages have revolved about the maneuvers of horsemen. In the case of the Indian, the transition was made the more striking by the circumstance that his whole life centered upon his enterprise as hunter and warrior in an environment that placed an exceptional premium upon mobility. In both of his principal pursuits the horse

[3] Eastern Indians, particularly in the south, were beginning to make considerable use of horses by the middle of the eighteenth century. They were obtaining them by theft from eastern white settlements and by a rapidly developing trans-Mississippi trade in horses with the western Indians. The Chickasaw and Choctaw, whose range bordered the Mississippi, became notable horse breeders. The trade in horses spread northward. When George Rogers Clark invaded Illinois in 1778 he was specially directed by Governor Patrick Henry of Virginia to buy "Spanish" stallions, considered to be superior to American stock, for the Governor's breeding farm, and when James Robertson visited Clark in 1780 he took care to bring back with him to the Holston a string of these coveted western horses.

gave him gigantic new stature. He was even granted time to perfect his achievement. When the western Indian was beginning to ride, his eventual white adversaries were only beginning to press inland along the far-off coasts of the Atlantic.

By the time the first white traders had approached the edges of the plains, the "horse Indians," as they were termed by their envious eastern Indian neighbors, had developed self-sufficiency and self-confidence. The buffalo was everywhere available providing abundant food and shelter which the horse enabled them to make use of at whatever time and place they elected. They felt little need of the white man's trade goods, except as novelties or supplements to their arrays of ornaments. Even the gun had value for them mainly as a status symbol. On horseback the rapidity with which arrows could be discharged from a bow made it more effective than a muzzle-loading gun either in hunting buffalo or in engaging mounted enemies.[4]

After acquiring the horse the Indians of the plains developed a spirit as fierce and proud as a primitive people has ever evidenced. Success as a mounted hunter and warrior demanded all the capacities of an expertly conditioned athlete. Regard for physical dexterity and headlong valor was elevated to the fervor of a religion. The ease with which subsistence could be provided offered leisure in which the hunter-warrior could seek expression for his overweening self-esteem. Quilled and beaded garments, necklaces of bear claws, devices mounted with the heads and horns of animals, fearsome designs painted on face and body, zebra-striped shields, and towering eagle-feather headdresses featured an excess of self-adornment so sensationally picturesque that it became accepted the world over as the universal image of the American Indian. The same instinct for self-justified self-glorification led to incredibly brutal rites manifesting the importance attached to fertility and

[4] In later nineteenth century clashes with mounted white men this superior effectiveness of the bow continued to hold until the invention of the Colt revolver with an equal rapidity of fire restored the balance. An arrow could be discharged from a bow at one- or two-second intervals (compared to the 20 to 30 seconds required to reload a gun) at a sufficient velocity to drive it entirely through the body of a buffalo.

virility. Male sexual prowess was celebrated in grotesquely obscene ceremonies, and in prolonged dances young men tore the flesh from their bones to prove their conquest of pain.

The value set upon physical fitness extended among the Indians of the northern plains to what amounted to a cult of cleanliness. The ease with which their buffalo-skin tepees could be dismantled and transported permitted a frequency of movement which escaped the accumulation of filth ordinarily associated with primitive towns. Fragrant grasses and herbs were prized adjuncts in the arrangement of hair and apparel. Camp sites were invariably on streams and communal bathing was as general as among South Sea Islanders. From earliest childhood both sexes were expert swimmers. High therapeutic value was attached to a sweat bath followed by a cold plunge. In winter, holes were chopped in the ice to provide an uninterrupted opportunity for bathing.

In the tremendous expanse of the trans-Mississippi west there were, of course, many variations in Indian manners, pursuits, and capacities. The way of life of some nations presented a nearly total contrast to the attainments of the mounted nomads of the plains. These other types of Indians ranged from the seagoing boatmen of the northwestern rain belt, to the fisheaters of the Columbia basin, to the miserable diggers of the central deserts, to the pueblo dwellers of the southern deserts. The distinction among western Indians most significant to the first trans-Mississippi frontier was that between the agricultural nations inhabiting the better watered region east of the plains and the roving, buffalo-hunting nations immediately to the west.

Most of these nearer and more sedentary Indians occupied the banks of the Missouri where they lived in permanent towns composed of large, substantial, dome-shaped houses constructed of beam-supported earth. Like the Indians of the eastern forests, they depended only partially on hunting and for their major food supply relied heavily on the cultivation of corn and garden crops. They were the last western Indians to gain horses but when they did they at once began eagerly to embark upon seasonal hunting excursions into the buffalo country, thus adding conflict with the Plains Indians to their former quarrels with their nearer neighbors. The River Indians inhabiting the lower Missouri had been first to experience contact with white traders. As early as 1724 the French had established a considerable trade as far inland as the northward bend of the Missouri, and by 1740 trespassing English traders from South Carolina were crossing the Mississippi. As a result of these early white associations, the nearer nations below the Platte had by 1804 been reduced by disease to beggary and impotence.

A similar fate awaited the upstream River Indians. Living in permanent towns on the shores of a waterway accessible to white transport they were as vulnerable to the processes of white intrusion as had been the Indians of the Connecticut, the Delaware, or the Ohio. Their settled and communal way of life permitted the accumulation of possessions and cultivated an appetite for the manufactured articles offered by traders. Competition for trade excited new and deadlier wars with their neighbors. Every acceptance of trade was a new invitation to disease and drunkenness while every rejection of trade raised a new threat of military intervention. The Missouri on which they lived provided the avenue by which civilization probed a thousand miles deep into what remained in every other respect an unaltered wilderness. The River Indians were foredoomed.

The wild free nomads of the plains had a fairer hope. Before them had opened a more favorable opportunity than had ever been accorded other Indians on the continent. They could escape the proven dangers of contact with whites as long as they wished, for they had ample space in which to keep their distance and the buffalo offered an inexhaustible supply of everything required to maintain the highest Indian standard of living. They were not threatened by the inexorable year-by-year and mile-by-mile advance of the white settlement line that had dislodged the eastern Indians, for the white settler after crossing the Mississippi was pausing in puzzled frustration at the western margin of the eastern woodlands. Their towns were not menaced by the punitive destruction so often visited upon eastern Indian towns for they were more mobile than any white military expedition that could be launched against them. In the immense and secure expanses across which the Plains Indians roamed at will they could look forward with what appeared to be fully justified confidence to their children's children continuing to enjoy the same freedom.

So complete was their assurance of invulnerability, indeed, that they felt free to indulge in any excess without considering the consequences. The extraordinary military advantages of the horse in conjunction with the bow demanded employment, and the one employment available was in conflict with fellow Indians. The still distant white man appeared to offer no threat whatever. Military satisfactions could instead be sought with impunity in wars with Indian neighbors. These were waged with never-tiring interest and spirit. The buffalo exceeded by a thousandfold the number required for Indian need, yet all Indians perpetually strove to deny hunting opportunities to all other Indians. Indian horse herds had increased far beyond practical Indian needs, yet the favorite occupation of every Indian warrior was the theft of other Indians' horses. To consider itself in a permanent state of war with all of its neighbors and with many peoples more distant became for every nation of the plains an essential part of its way of life. When harassment of nearer enemies palled, excursions of many hundreds of miles could be undertaken to deliver surprise attacks upon distant victims whose paths might not ever otherwise have crossed those of the assailants. In the century after white men first appeared on the Missouri, many more western Indians fell in engagements with each other than with white men. The earlier white men who had meanwhile wandered out on the plains were by most Indians regarded as entertaining curiosities, often welcomed as friends, and occasionally adopted as respected members of the community.

The constant conflict among the Plains Indians developed the mounted warrior into an ever more formidable fighting man. Most later military observers considered Indian horsemanship and tactics permitted them to maneuver and strike much more effectively than white cavalry. Another consequence of this chronic state of intertribal war, however, was an interest in trade that might not otherwise have so soon developed. War with River Indians, Canadian Indians, and Mexican Indians who already possessed guns led to a recognition by the Plains Indians of the gun's value as a defensive weapon. This experience, plus a desire to deny rivals the fancied advantages of trade, led to casual and irrational acceptance of traders' overtures. Trade began to penetrate the plains and mountains at a far earlier date than might have been the case had the region enjoyed internal peace. But the eventual effect of these two threats to the Indian defense position, intertribal war and dependence on trade, were not apparent for generations after white men had appeared on the Missouri. The Plains Indian continued to appear invulnerable.

A third Indian weakness, likewise not apparent to Indians or white men of the time, was inherent. The most distinctive feature of the Indian population of the plains and mountains was its extreme sparsity. The tendency toward an increase that had set in when the acquisition of the horse had so much improved living conditions had been counteracted by the casualties of intertribal war. The primary objective of every internecine attack was to kill men and steal horses but young women and boys were frequently seized as slaves. Many were traded to eastern nations where they turned up in appreciable numbers as far east as the towns of the Iroquois in New York and the Cherokee in the Carolinas. It was the rapid and uncertain movements of the Plains Indians and their unexpected appearances in widely separated locations that gave an impression which led to so many overestimates of their numbers. For mutual protection they ordinarily moved in groups of at least 50 families. At the beginning of the nineteenth century their actual total number probably averaged a density that allowed an area of more than 2500 square miles for each such band. So few were they compared to the space in which they wandered that the appearance of a human being among the herds of game and the cloud shadow patterns moving across those endless vistas was the rarest of occurrences. Many contemporary observations support this conclusion. The first white men to reach many areas reported wild animals so unaccustomed to danger from man that it must have been many seasons since they had been disturbed by Indian hunters. When Lewis and Clark became in 1805 the first white men to ascend the Missouri to its mountain headwaters, they traveled more than 1200 miles along its upper reaches through the heart of the buffalo country which the Indians of the plains were the most accustomed to frequent without sighting an Indian from April 11th to August 13th. When white trappers began to infest the mountains in the 1820's, they occasionally encountered Indians but it was a common experience to wander, hunt, and camp for weeks and months at a stretch without being troubled by any reminder that Indians existed. Many of the ponderous and slow-moving wagon trains of the 1840's crawled across the plains to see their first wild Indians sociably camped about the trading post at Fort Laramie and crawled on through the mountains for many more weeks to see their next at Fort Bridger or Fort Hall.

To the first American frontier people who began settling on the lower Missouri in the 1790's the new Indians to the west awaiting their further advance were still no more than names. The few Indians in the foreground were the remnants of a native population that had been reduced to insignificance by earlier white associations. They posed little threat to a frontier stock accustomed to the depredations of Iroquois, Shawnee, Wyandot, Miami, and Cherokee.

The nearest of the more formidable western nations was the Osage, occupying the area between the lower Missouri and the middle Arkansas. They were an enterprising, pugnacious, relatively sophisticated, and totally unprincipled people who constantly interfered by war and diplomacy in the affairs of other nations but had generally sought amicable relations with first the French and then the Spanish. There had been times in the past when in their anxiety to extend their influence they had dispatched military expeditions to points as distant as Green Bay, Detroit, or Natchez and they were forever at war with their immediate neighbors. Their principal towns were sufficiently remote to have spared them so far from serious epidemics in spite of their early and considerable contact with whites.

The next nearest important Indians were the Pawnee whose restless existence was centered about permanent towns on the lower Platte some 700 miles up the Missouri from the westernmost white settlement. Since acquiring the horse the Pawnee had extended their interest in hunting and war over an ever-widening range. During the intervals before and after planting and harvest time they roved across the central plains, westward to the Rockies and from the headwaters of the Cheyenne to the headwaters of the Pecos. They had been generally friendly to whites, especially white traders, but were perpetually at war with all other Indians of the plains, particularly the redoubtable Comanche and Sioux. Early white observers were shocked by the annual fertility rite of the Pawnee in which a captive girl, after being hailed as queen during days of festivity, was put to death in order that the anointment of the seed by her blood might assure the growth of the corn about to be planted.

Some familiarity with the more distant Indians of the northward stretch of the Missouri had been gained from accounts brought back by the occasional St. Louis trader who had ventured so far. Some hundreds of miles above the Platte were the Sioux, the most numerous and powerful of all western Indians, who ranged from the upper Mississippi to far west of the Missouri. They had formerly lived in the forests of northern Wisconsin and eastern Minnesota where they had been harassed by the attacks of Lake Indians who had been able to gain guns from the French earlier than had the Sioux. Their westward drift had been accelerated when they had gained horses. They were adapting themselves with great gusto to all the demands and rewards of a buffalo-hunting existence and meanwhile driving the former Indian occupants from their westward path. Their trade needs had long been served by British traders from the Lakes and they therefore were seldom inclined to cultivate the favor of St. Louis traders. Their favorite device was to embarrass their upstream neighbors by turning back traders attempting to ascend the river.

Next above were the Aricara who had been driven northward when the Sioux had pressed westward. They lived in permanent riverbank habitations which tended to become less elaborate as

Sioux hostility forced them to make successive moves. The Aricara were an incorrigibly disputatious and deceitful nation in whose relations with both other Indians and whites fervid peace professions were customarily employed as a cover for sudden and capricious attacks.

Finally, at the great westward bend of the Missouri, 1600 miles above its mouth,[5] were the famous Mandan. Remote as was their situation they had had contacts with white men earlier than any other far western Indians. French traders from the Canadian north had visited them in the 1730's, English traders, also from the north, since the 1780's, and occasional St. Louis traders had reached them by the 1790's. The Mandan lived in immense circular houses, up to 90 feet in diameter, so commodious that each sheltered several families together with their more valuable horses and so stoutly built that they served as fortifications. Many Mandan were appreciably lighter skinned than other Indians which had led to the circulation of various fanciful theories of their origin, ranging from the assumption that they were a lost tribe of Israel to an assertion that they had descended from a pre-Columbian colony of Welshmen. Their communal bathing habits, their promiscuous sex customs, and their excessively cruel ceremonies fascinated and astonished all white visitors.

Of the Indians of the farther plains the early settlers on the lower Missouri knew little beyond hearsay. Much had been heard of the Comanche to the southwest of the Osage who for two centuries had been the scourge of the Spanish borderlands, occasionally extending their raids as far into Mexico as Durango. Northwest of the Comanche toward the slopes of the Rockies were said to range two other considerable nations, the Kiowa and the Arapaho. Of the Indians of the northwest plains, the Cheyenne, the Crow, and the Blackfeet, the most typical and notable of all Plains Indians, nothing beyond the vaguest rumor was yet known.

---

[5] Estimates of early nineteenth-century river distances can only be approximate. Continued erosion materially altered the river's course, and therefore the distance from point to point, before the first government surveys made exact determinations.

This was the new country and these were the new Indians with which the advancing frontier people were about to be confronted. A prodigious expansion of distances, a stupendous alteration in climate, and Indians emboldened by a swiftness of movement that enabled them always to choose the time and place for battle posed enormous and unfamiliar difficulties to further advance. Nothing that the frontier people had learned in the half century of conflict which had distinguished their progress from the eastern mountains to the Mississippi had prepared them for the unforeseen problems they now must solve. An examination of their success in adapting to these changed conditions in time to rise to this final challenge is the principal object of this book.

III

❦

The Frontier of 1804

THE WESTWARD MOVEMENT of the American frontier had never, since the first crossing of the mountains in 1769, been a general advance of the line of settlement. It had always been a single spear thrust westward. The ferocity of Indian resistance from central New York to the Mississippi in the north and from western North Carolina to the Mississippi in the south had for a quarter of a century confined the westward extension of settlement to the corridor between the Ohio and the Tennessee. In 1804 after nearly a million people had crossed the mountains, the western frontier still was the same deep salient with its eastern shoulders still in the Catskills of New York and the Great Smokies of North Carolina. Nowhere had it approached either the Great Lakes or the Gulf. Its tip, however, had crossed the Mississippi in the narrow area in the center about the mouth of the Ohio. The frontier had become more than ever a spear thrust westward.

The major developments in that thrust had been the frontier people's first lodgment in Kentucky after they had cleared the way by the Shawnee War of 1774, their defense of that lodgment against the British-Indian assaults of the Revolution, their establishment of a secondary 1780 lodgment in Tennessee, their maintenance of their twin wilderness perimeters in the face of the post-Revolutionary Indian attacks promoted by Great Britain in the north and Spain in the south, the national government's eventually successful military intervention in 1794, and, finally, the totally unplanned and unexpected opening of the trans-Mississippi west by the Louisiana Purchase.

During the 20 years of continuous Indian war, the successful defense of every stockade had been a turning point, and the readiness of every isolated family to remain in danger a victory. But the great turning point and the decisive victory had been Anthony Wayne's 1794 overthrow of the Western Indian Confederation at Fallen Timbers. It had marked the national government's first successful assumption of responsibility for the west and had been followed by Great Britain's grudging evacuation of the Lake posts and Spain's equally grudging opening of the Mississippi, the two foremost deterrants to western expansion. The Indian peace Wayne was able to dictate threw open south central Ohio to immediate occupation. The effect was galvanic. In the ten years after 1794 the population of Ohio increased from a few scattered settlements along the river to 120,000. Elimination of the Indian danger likewise stimulated migration from the east to the older settlements of Kentucky and Tennessee. During the same ten-year period Kentucky's population increased by 170,000 to 300,000 and Tennessee's by 100,000 to 170,000.

The movement into southern Ohio had widened the salient along its northern flank. By 1804, the outer settlement line ran roughly from the bend of the Ohio north of Pittsburgh to the mouth of the Miami west of Cincinnati. Expansion along the salient's southern flank had meanwhile been less striking. The aggressions of the southern Indians had ceased following Fallen Timbers, but Spain's possession of the Gulf coast had continued to cast doubt upon the region's economic future. There was a tendency for landseekers to float down the Mississippi to the American settlements in the Natchez area rather than to push directly southward across the Tennessee into what was still Indian country. By 1804 the population of the combined Alabama-Mississippi area still did not much exceed 20,000.

The outer settlement line in the west had at no stage represented a static situation. It had rather resembled a partially smothered explosion. Its day-to-day conformation had always been the momentary consequence of a complex of conflicting pressures as the resistance exerted by Indians and foreign powers sought to contain the inclination of the border inhabitants to continue to reach for new land. In 1804 the half million inhabitants of Kentucky and Tennessee constituted an enormous accumulation of such pressure. All were recent settlers who were already accustomed to movement. All had crossed the mountains to improve their condition and most were persuaded that further improvement was possible. The ferment in this yeast of restlessness was supplied by the leaven of original frontier people, the firstcomers for whom the perpetual urge to move on to new scenes and new experiences had by now become a way of life.

The major population pressure along the settlement line of 1804 was northwestward across the Ohio toward the fertile valleys of the Wabash and the Illinois. Indian reluctance to withdraw persisted but Indian military power had been broken at Fallen Timbers. From now on, as fast as the spread of settlement required new land, new cessions would be extorted and new Indian withdrawals compelled. This northwestward advance was to continue until the 1816 admission of Indiana and the 1818 admission of Illinois had succeeded Ohio's 1803 admission and was to keep on for the next two generations to the headwaters of the Mississippi.

In this advance the first ventures into each new strip of wilderness were in almost every instance by the same hardy stock that had been first on the Monongahela and the Watauga in 1769, on the Kentucky in 1775, and on the Cumberland in 1780. The same kind of frontier family cleared the same kind of corn patch and built the same kind of one-room cabin and suffered the same kind of hardships. The Indian danger had lessened but other dangers had not. The chief reliance of these settlers of the outermost frontier was still on hunting and trapping, and the depletion of game had made subsistence in the edges of the wilderness more precarious than it had been before. As the following wave of more substantial settlers and town builders caught up with them they again moved on. They had from the beginning been too poor to buy land or to hire lawyers to dispute titles and, in any event, most of them pre-

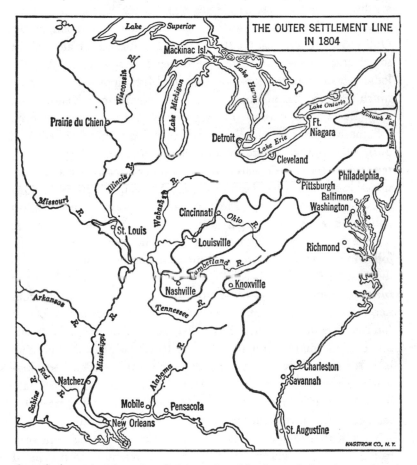

THE OUTER SETTLEMENT LINE IN 1804

ferred the primitive simplicities of a life free of the demands of normal society. The successive movements of Abraham Lincoln's family across Kentucky and Indiana into Illinois well illustrated this historic process.

The northwest population pressure was important as an eminently successful fulfillment of the inspired plan promulgated in the Northwest Ordinance. It did not, however, represent a dramatic new extension of American dominion. It was a reasonably orderly and signally promising occupation of territory already in the possession of the United States. The so far much less considerable southwest pressure was of greater significance in that it was inexorably to lead within 15 years to American annexation of the Gulf coast and Florida. Of the greatest significance of all was the so far scarcely noticeable pressure directed westward. In 1804 the lodgment of frontier people west of the Mississippi had not yet by much exceeded the numbers of the first lodgment in Kentucky in 1775. But it was to prove as pregnant with future consequences.

Some hundreds of American citizens had crossed the Mississippi during the 15 years before the Louisiana Purchase in 1803 suddenly restored to them their status as American citizens. The first considerable settlement had been in George Morgan's short-lived colony at New Madrid in 1789.[1] Morgan had withdrawn when Spanish authorities established a garrison and restricted his land-selling scheme but many of his colonists had remained. In each of the following years some scores of American families had migrated to the west bank of the Mississippi and the nearer reaches of the lower Missouri. Almost all had come from the Kentucky-Tennessee frontier, many after an intervening experimental residence in the French communities of Vincennes, Kaskaskia, and Cahokia. Spain, as one phase of its frantic effort to avert the threat to Spanish dominion inherent in the advance of the main American frontier, had alternately invited and prohibited the entrance of American settlers into Spanish territory. Neither official position had made perceptible difference. In either event the newcomers kept on coming.

They were exhibiting a fundamental attitude of the American frontiersman. He had never paid respectful attention to provincial boundaries, state boundaries, national boundaries, or racial boundaries. Good land and good hunting appeared to him equally worth seeking wherever they might be found. Legal considerations were

[1] See Chapter 9 of Dale Van Every's *Ark of Empire* for an account of the Morgan venture.

of importance only in those instances when they could be physically enforced, just as Indian opposition had meaning only when given positive effect by military action. In crossing the mountains the frontiersman had flouted every existing law. In crossing the Mississippi he swore allegiance to Spain in exchange for land grants with as little compunction. If pressed he did not balk at promising to become a Catholic. To push on into new country and new hunting and a new set of experiences and adventures had become for him a sufficient allegiance and a sufficient religion. George Rogers Clark, the greatest of all frontiersmen, perfectly exemplified this attitude. In his compulsive desire to widen the prospects open to all westerners he had neither hesitated to offer to become a Spanish citizen in return for the right to found an American colony in Spanish territory nor to accept a French major general's commission for the purpose of taking New Orleans for France. The frontiersman, when his outward callousness to patriotic principle was assailed by his contemporaries, refused to admit disloyalty to his country. He took it for granted that whatever his ventures sooner or later his country would catch up to him. He considered himself an American and proposed wherever he went to remain an American. It followed that the alien land upon which he settled would in time likewise become American. His lifelong experience with the advance of the American frontier had made this seem to him a process as certain as tomorrow's sunrise. The eventual result of every later American settlement in Spanish territory, even in regions as remote as Texas, New Mexico, and California, was to prove how justified was his assumption.

The American settlers in Missouri had not so long to wait. By Napoleon's dictate they had scarcely ceased to be Spanish citizens before they became once more American. They had been getting along amicably with their French neighbors, had been suffering little interference from Spanish officials, and had been left largely to their own devices in their own communities. There had been enough local Indian trouble to require the erection of stockades in every more isolated community. Game was as plentiful as it had once been on the Ohio. So far their frontier experience in this foreign country had been a repetition of their former frontier experience in their own. This it continued to be.

Upon declaration of American sovereignty they immediately took the inevitable next step which demonstrated their frontier to be as unmistakably American as had been any that they had previously held in Kentucky or Tennessee. Captain Amos Stoddard of the United States Army raised the flag at St. Louis March 10, 1804, Congress on March 26th placed what is now Missouri within the jurisdiction of what was then Indiana Territory, and on October 1st Governor William Henry Harrison of Indiana Territory arrived to institute territorial government. The settlers, however, had already met in convention to protest the exercise of authority over them from points as distant and as uninformed of their needs and desires as the Wabash and the Potomac. On September 29th the convention had memorialized Congress with the settlers' demand for a redress of grievances and a greater measure of self-government. The leopard had not changed his spots. They were conforming to the invariable frontier pattern according to which every new settlement as almost its first action asserted its democratic self-sufficiency. They were carrying on the tradition established by the Watauga Association, the Boonesborough Convention, the Cumberland Compact, and the long series of Kentucky conventions demanding statehood. Insistence upon self-government had from the American frontier's inception proved its strongest resource and had been the impulse that most distinguished it from the less vigorous colonization efforts of other peoples. This newest American frontier was demonstrating the same vitality.

It was a vitality ignited in a people by the extraordinary demands made upon them and developed by their growing realization that they had proved fully capable of meeting those demands. It had required a foolhardy excess of self-confidence to undertake the first crossing of the mountains into a remote wilderness. The hazards had proved more terrifying than the boldest among them had anticipated. The discovery that nevertheless they were capable of surmounting such hazards had developed a sense that their self-confidence was justified. To men who had survived such perils it seemed only natural to consider themselves their own masters, to admit the sanction of no other authority than their own will. Common experiences, common needs, common perils, and common demands had placed upon a rabble of individual adventurers a common stamp which had made them a distinctive and recognizable new kind of people—the frontier people. In the successive surges, venture by venture, stockade by stockade, battle by battle, of the westward movement, the total undertaking had likewise become a coherent and continuing process dependent upon the repetition of proven methods, devices, and adaptations. The frontier people had come to know where they were going, how to get there, and what they wanted when they did.

In this continuing process the individual was of great importance but certain personal relationships at the roots of the social order were of greater. The family was the social and economic unit upon which all else depended. Only by the division of labor possible in the family could the individual's need for food, clothing, and shelter be effectively supplied. The pressures of Indian resistance presently produced a larger social unit that became almost as important as the family. The perpetual Indian threat made the survival of a family altogether unlikely except through resort to the shelter of a stockade. Defense of a stockade required the co-operation of several families. The enforced intimacies of stockade existence encouraged intermarriage among the associated families, and the stockade period lasted long enough to develop this interrelationship of family groups into a pattern of mutual loyalty and dependence that amounted to clanship. The partnership of interrelated families produced other functional advantages than those connected directly with defense. Greater numbers working in co-ordination permitted a more efficient division of labor. The man better adapted to the practice of blacksmithing, or leatherworking, or cabinetmaking, or boatbuilding, or horse training, or of any of the other skills upon which the community's welfare relied, could become a specialist in his craft. Numbers likewise greatly facilitated the group's successive westward moves. Younger sons and nephews could be spared to the search for and investigation of new locations, however distant.

The old station could be held until the new was securely established. Development of the frontier clan, as a complement to the basic functioning of the frontier family, became a significant factor in the continuity of the westward movement and the homogeneity of the people making it. A clearer light on this continuity and homogeneity may be cast by a glance at the former frontier experiences of four of the first such clans to cross the Mississippi.

The Bledsoe and Neely families had been inhabitants of the most exposed frontier since the 1760's and neighbors since they had settled together on the Holston. Anthony, Isaac, and Abraham Bledsoe and James and William Neely had been among the first long hunters to range westward across Tennessee and Kentucky. All had served in the Shawnee War of 1774 and the Cherokee War of 1776. William Neely had been with James Robertson's overland party which founded the first settlement on the Cumberland and in the immediate Indian onslaught was one of the first to be killed. Isaac Neely had been with John Donelson's river party which had reached the Cumberland after running a gauntlet of Indian attacks for hundreds of miles. Isaac Bledsoe's Station had been established in the new colony's first year. In the ensuing years of Indian war seven Bledsoes were killed. When the Bledsoe-Neely clan made its fourth westward move by crossing the Mississippi into Spanish territory in 1797, its members had had 30 years of strenuous and unremitting experience with the problems of frontier survival. They were familiar with all the difficulties and were in a position to make a fully informed estimate of what they conceived to be the advantages.

The Byrd-Gillespie clan had had as rigorous a preparation for their trans-Mississippi venture. Amos Byrd had grown up on the Watauga. The Gillespie family had come to the Watauga so early that one of the passes over the Blue Ridge from the Yadkin acquired the name Gillespie's Gap. After participating in the border campaigns that so much distinguished the Holston frontier during the Revolution, the associated families had settled in the Iron Mountain-Big Cane Creek district near what is now Knoxville and was then the border most of all exposed to southern Indian depredations. In 1788 Gillespie's Station had been overwhelmed during that year's great Indian invasion in one of the major disasters of frontier history. Every man was killed and 28 women and children carried away captive. The Byrds and Gillespies had had as much occasion as had had the Bledsoes and Neelys to be made acutely aware of all they were undertaking in electing once more to take a position on the outermost frontier.

The Ruddle-Hinkston-Conway clan had been inseparably associated with the foundation of Kentucky. Joseph Conway had been born on the Greenbrier frontier when it was the most remote and exposed of all settlements. Among his later Kentucky experiences had been once to have been scalped and left for dead and at another time to have been carried off to Detroit as one of the Ruddle's Station captives. John Hinkston had built one of Kentucky's first stations on the Licking in 1776, had been forced to abandon it for lack of defenders by that winter's Indian invasion, had rebuilt it in 1777 in association with Isaac Ruddle, and after its destruction in 1780 had rebuilt it a third time. Isaac Ruddle had commanded one of the two companies of Holston militia led to Kentucky's relief by John Bowman in 1777 and had remained to found Ruddle's Station with the assistance of Hinkston and Conway. In 1780 it had fallen to the Indian invasion under Colonel Henry Bird when, for the only time in frontier history, Indians had succeeded in transporting cannon from Detroit for use against Kentucky stockades. Of the station's 200 inhabitants more than half had been butchered and the remainder carried into captivity. The arrival of the Ruddles, Hinkstons, and Conways at the Missouri frontier in the early 1790's had represented another reinforcement by the most hardened and seasoned pioneer stock.

The most noted of the frontier clans to make the westward move across the Mississippi before 1800 had been the Boone-Bryan-Van Bibber-Callaway group of families. Daniel Boone's frontier career had been crowded with distinctions. He had blazed the Cumberland Gap trail to Kentucky which later became known as the Wilderness Road. He had been the first settler to take his family to Kentucky. In innumerable encounters with Indians he had been twice wounded and twice captured. His sons, James and Israel, and his brother, Edward, had been killed. The Bryans had moved in the 1760's from the Valley of Virginia frontier to the Yadkin where they had become neighbors of the Boones. Daniel Boone's wife, Rebecca, was a Bryan. Bryans had been members of Daniel Boone's first Kentucky party. Joseph Bryan, his son-in-law, had established the Kentucky station which withstood the famous Indian siege preceding the Battle of Blue Licks. John Van Bibber had been a long hunter in Kentucky whose roving had included a canoe trip down the Mississippi to have a look also at New Orleans. Upon his return he had become one of the surveyors in Kentucky prior to the Shawnee War. Isaac Van Bibber had been killed at Point Pleasant. A daughter of Peter Van Bibber had married a son of Daniel Boone. The Callaway family had been prominent in the defense of the frontier since the period of the French and Indian War. Richard Callaway had been one of the frontier's representatives, along with John Sevier, James Robertson, Isaac Shelby, and Daniel Boone, at the Sycamore Shoals purchase of Kentucky from the Cherokee, had participated in the foundation of Boonesborough, and had been killed by Indians in 1780. The Callaway girls, Frances and Elizabeth, had, in the company of Daniel Boone's daughter, Jemima, been the first white women captured by Indians in Kentucky. The last of this notable clan's westward moves had been to the Femme Osage River where they had established the westernmost American settlement on the Missouri. Daniel Boone at the age of 65 had felt the same impulse to be first in a new country that he had in 1773. Once more he was at the very tip of the spear thrust westward.

The former experiences of these earliest trans-Mississippi settlers indicate how compulsive was the inclination of the original frontier people to remain in the vanguard of the westward movement. The years of peril and disaster through which they had struggled had not dulled but rather sharpened their impulse to risk new hazards. The frontier mechanics and motives involved in the trans-Mississippi move were illustrated by some of the details of the Boone enterprise. Boone's sons had gone ahead in 1796 to select a site and establish the station. Daniel Boone had followed in 1799 with the stock and the main party, which included related Callaways, Van Bibbers, and Bryans. Though patriarch of the clan he had not come in quest of wider or more fertile lands. He had begun at once to devote every winter to trapping and every summer to hunting. He had soon lost title to his land, as he had so often before in Kentucky, by his neglect of legal technicalities and his failure to cultivate. He had not come in search of improved opportunities to sow and reap but of new opportunities to enjoy the wilderness. He had undoubtedly been made to feel completely at home when, in what could have been anything from his fiftieth to his hundredth brush with Indians, the Osage in 1802 had robbed him of his winter's fur catch. He had had an identical experience with the Shawnee 33 years before in Kentucky. The family group continued after 1804 to make intermittent moves westward up the Missouri while Daniel Boone continued to hunt and trap each season until well into his eighties, ranging so widely that he was reputed once to have sighted the Rocky Mountains.[2]

These Kentuckians and Tennesseeans represented the kind of people who had come to the edge of the strange, vast new country to the west and were approaching contact with the still mysterious new Indians who inhabited it. The new difficulties which awaited them were of prodigious complexity but they had been prepared for the test by the monstrous difficulties with which they had formerly dealt. In the raw new settlements dotting the Missouri wilderness energies were being generated capable of striking across any distance, however immense, and coping with any adversary, however dangerous. Among these restless and irrepressible people were gathering impulses that were soon to reach across plains and mountains and deserts to the Western Ocean and to claim for their country Oregon, Texas, and California.

[2] There was evidence in the Boone family of a second generation transition to more average pursuits. His son, Daniel Morgan, had become sufficiently prosperous by 1796 to own slaves and later operated a gristmill and a saltworks. Another son, Nathan, became a merchant and later entered the army in which he rose to the rank of lieutenant colonel. Both sons, however, were accomplished hunters, woodsmen, and Indian fighters. The pioneering tendency also persisted. Daniel Morgan Boone became a first settler of Kansas and a grandson, A. G. Boone, an early settler of Colorado.

IV

༚

Lewis and Clark

JEFFERSON WAS NOT ONLY the third president of the United States but also the third president of the American Philosophical Society, and his interest in its affairs was exceeded only by his interest in his country's. The range of his intellectual curiosity was extraordinary, even in a period when scholars everywhere were intrigued by any bit of new information concerning the nature of the physical world. Among all the facets of his scientific inquisitiveness nothing had so captured his imagination as the mystery shrouding the geography of interior North America. This was not a recent interest. His boyhood guardian had been Dr. Thomas Walker, the first explorer of Kentucky, and that great frontiersman's stories had stirred in him a desire to know more about the west which had never flagged and had never been satisfied.

The central puzzle of North American geography was still entangled with the age-old search for the presumed Northwest Passage from Europe to Asia. When Columbus sailed the Atlantic, it had been considered the way to the east. The disconcerting barrier of an intervening continent forced a search for some passage through or around it, and it soon became apparent that this way to the west could only lie somewhere to the north of Florida and Mexico. Balboa had no sooner discovered how near was the Pacific beyond the 35-mile-wide Isthmus of Panama than other Spanish explorers were making the more painful discovery that the west coast of North America extended not only at least two thousand miles northward from the isthmus but also two thousand miles westward. The full dimensions of the problem were revealed when Magellan's circumnavigation and the Manila galleon's itinerary had given practical confirmation to the vastness of the ocean stretching between that west coast and the Orient.

The disclosure of these unwelcome geographical truths served, however, only to make the need for the Northwest Passage more obvious. Once it were located it would shorten the westbound voyage from Europe to China by 7500 miles. So rewarding a hope was not one to be easily cast aside. Geographers continued to assume the existence of a waterway across North America somewhere north of the region once traversed by De Soto and Coronado and to its western approaches the mythical name Strait of Anian was applied. This fiction persisted through generations of mapmakers. The French discoverer of Canada, Jacques Cartier, assumed Indian reports of the Great Lakes to be references to the Western Ocean. Seventy-five years later Samuel Champlain clung to the same illusion until he himself reached the shore of unsalty Lake Huron in 1615. When the French trader-explorer, Jean Nicolet, reached the western shore of Lake Michigan in 1634, he took with him a brocaded mandarin robe so that he might be suitably garbed in case he encountered high-ranking Chinese officials. When Thomas Batts and Robert Fallam became in 1671 the first Englishmen to discover water flowing westward, New River in southwest Virginia, they reported the impression that they had glimpsed the Pacific at the farther end of an Allegheny mountain valley. Long after the French had become familiar with the shores of the Great Lakes and the course of the Mississippi the belief still persisted that not far west of the St. Lawrence system of waterways extending westward from the Atlantic lay the eastern tip of a similar system extending eastward from the Pacific. The new English commander at Mackinac, Robert Rogers, in 1766 dispatched an overland expedition to seek this Northwest Passage. The effort barely crossed the upper Mississippi but it produced one lasting result. In a book written by the party's coleader, Jonathan Carver, he referred to Indian reports of a great "River of the West" to which, striking some obscure chord in his imagination, he applied the name "Oragon."

The advancement of knowledge to be gained by a penetration of the continent's unknown interior continued increasingly to appeal to Jefferson. In a 1783 letter to George Rogers Clark relative to a shipment of mammoth bones from Kentucky's Big Bone Lick he wishfully suggested that Clark consider a trans-Mississippi exploration, though he admitted "I doubt whether we have enough of that kind of spirit to raise the money." In those first years after the Revolution neither the government nor individuals had funds to spare for such luxuries as scientific exploration. During his ministry to France new fuel was added to Jefferson's fire by conversations in Paris with John Ledyard. That ebullient Connecticut adventurer had been with the great English navigator, James Cook, on his epoch-making 1778 voyage of Pacific discovery which had, when supported by Captain George Vancouver's 1789-93 surveys, forever disposed of the Strait of Anian by ascertaining that the northwest coast of North America stretched unbroken from California to Bering Strait. In Jefferson's estimation Cook's determinations only gave added importance to the exploration of a central overland route. After his return to become Secretary of State he attempted in 1793, in his capacity as vice president of the Philosophical Society, to enlist the French naturalist, André Michaux, for a project "to explore the country along the Missouri, and thence westward to the Pacific ocean." The Society voted to solicit subscriptions to support the effort[1] but Michaux instead became involved in the Genêt conspiracy.

By the time Jefferson became president accelerated discoveries in other areas of the continent had made exploration of the central

---

[1] Among the subscribers were Washington, Hamilton and Jefferson, with Washington's contribution of $25 the most considerable on the list.

route west seem ever more urgent. The English trader-explorers, Samuel Hearne and Alexander Mackenzie, had reached the frozen shores of the Arctic at the mouths of the Coppermine and Mackenzie rivers, eliminating the last vestiges of the ancient illusion that there could be a Northwest Passage around the northern coast of North America. In 1793 Mackenzie had made the first transcontinental crossing since Cabeza de Vaca's in 1535, this one as far to the north as the other had been to the south. Scaling the mountains enclosing the headwaters of the Peace River, he had reached the Pacific on an arm of Queen Charlotte's Sound. Remarkable as had been his feat and avid as had been the scientific interest attracted by it, the excessive ruggedness of his route had denied it practical importance. Of the utmost practical importance, on the other hand, had been the discovery the year before by a Yankee shipmaster, Robert Gray, of the mouth [2] of the fabled River of the West to which he gave the name of his trading vessel, *Columbia*. Here, at last, was a substitute for the Strait of Anian.

These several geographical discoveries had added tremendous new significance to the central route west. Somewhere in the unknown region presumably shared by the headwaters of the two great rivers, the Missouri and the Columbia, seemed to lie the last remaining possibility that there might be a Northwest Passage. An associated commercial discovery had further emphasized this significance. Cook's voyage had revealed to the western world what only the Russians had previously realized: The sea otter of the northwest coast provided the richest fur trade ever known. Adventuresome shipowners in England and New England had rushed to take advantage of the opportunity. A single voyage around the Horn by a ship with trade goods for the Indians of the northwest coast, then on to China with a cargo of sea-otter skins, then back to home port with tea and silk, could make a notable fortune. Were the overland route to prove shorter and more serviceable, as seemed theoretically likely, this flow of wealth could be tapped at its source. There was meanwhile every chance that English traders

[2] The river's estuary had been masked from the notice of earlier coasting mariners, including Cook, by a prevailing barrier of shoals and fog.

from Montreal or Hudson Bay would soon be reaching the Pacific by way of the Saskatchewan. Exploration of the Missouri-Columbia route had become more than urgent. It had become imperative.

Jefferson's scientific interest in the geographical mystery had been further excited by the successive achievements of the English explorers. His impatience was restrained during the early months of his presidency only by the continuing threats of war with England, Spain, and France that culminated in Napoleon's reach for New Orleans and Jefferson's celebrated diplomatic duel with the dictator. It was, nevertheless, at the height of this final crisis that he decided that he could wait no longer. Once more he precipitated another of the great moments in American history. On January 18, 1803, he laid a secret message before Congress proposing a semi-surreptitious American exploration beyond the Mississippi. He was committed to initial secrecy by the circumstance that the territory which must first be crossed was under the flag of France and the provincial administration of Spain. He sought to get around this international difficulty by the public pretense that only scientific research was envisaged, though he was privately bent on supporting the American claim to the Columbia implicit in Gray's discovery of its mouth. To disarm the opposition of less imaginative congressmen he pointed to the trade advantages that were possible. Congress authorized an expenditure of $2500. Jefferson embarked happily upon the drafting of instructions detailing the multitude of zoological, botanical, and anthropological questions to which he hoped his explorers would bring back answers. His appetite for information was omnivorous. He was particularly interested in the unknown Indians of the farther west. His requests for data on them ranged from reports on their pulse rates at various times of day and night to what they used for laxatives.

The nature and scope of the project were revolutionized by the July revelation of the Louisiana Purchase. The venture was no longer subject to the sufferance of foreign powers. It had become a public and official enterprise with no further need to conceal its major objectives. Additional funds were made available. The expedition's manpower was increased and its responsibilities enormously enlarged. Upon the original purposes of scientific exploration and trade advantage had been superimposed the vastly greater purpose of asserting American sovereignty over the immense region which had suddenly become United States territory. This was more than a formal gesture. Armed opposition was possible, not only from Indians but from foreign powers. The border conflict with England and Spain which had blazed so long east of the Mississippi had been reignited in the limitless expanses of the farther west. The boundary disputes with both promised now to extend all the way to the Pacific. In the north British traders from the Great Lakes and Lake Winnipeg were already spreading anti-American animosities among Indians as far to the southwest as the Pawnee. In the south Spain was indignantly denying the validity of the Louisiana Purchase and preparing military expeditions to enforce the claim that the borders of New Spain extended north of the Platte. The explorers about to plunge into the unknown would have need also to serve as soldiers, lawgivers, and conquerors.

Among all of Jefferson's inspired services to his country none was more inspired than his selection of personnel for this unprecedented undertaking. He had had himself no frontier experience but his imagination had made the frontier a part of his being. He realized instinctively that this was a task that could be entrusted only to frontiersmen. To command of the expedition he appointed his 28-year-old secretary, Meriwether Lewis, whose essential qualifications Jefferson described in a letter to Dr. Benjamin Rush as "brave, prudent, habituated to the woods & familiar with Indian manners and character." All subsequent recruiting he left to Lewis' informed discretion. Lewis was of a Virginia family which had had many early associations with frontier affairs. His uncle and guardian, Colonel Nicholas Lewis, had commanded a regiment in the Cherokee War of 1776. Meriwether had been an accomplished hunter since the age of eight, had in his boyhood known Indian alarms on the Georgia border, and had for seven years served in the army on the western frontier. His first move was to invite his friend, 32-year-old William Clark, whose qualities he had learned to appreciate during their service under Anthony Wayne, to become his cocommander. The unmatched success of their collaboration was forecast by the warmth of Lewis' message. Were Clark to participate in the expedition's "fatiegues . . . dangers . . . and honors," he wrote, "believe me there is no man on earth with whom I should feel equal pleasure in sharing them." Clark, youngest brother of George Rogers Clark, came of the most distinguished of all frontier families. George had saved the west during the Revolution. William was henceforth to preside over the west's advance beyond the Mississippi for the next 35 years.

The two young captains[3] were immediately agreed on the recruiting of the kind of men they considered they needed. Clark's terse definition of what they wanted was "robust helthy hardy young men." Lewis described their needs as for "good hunters, stout, healthy, unmarried men, accustomed to the woods, and capable of bearing bodily fatigue." What they absolutely required was experienced hunters and boatmen familiar with the wilderness and with Indians. They had notable success in their search. Though most were militarily enrolled as enlisted men[4] all were volunteers and all were individuals. The recruits were as representative of the frontier as were the two captains. Charles Floyd was a nephew of John Floyd, famous as the leader of Kentucky's surveyors in 1774, as cofounder of one of Kentucky's first stations, and as foremost defender, until killed by Indians in 1782, of Kentucky's northern border. John Colter came of a family that had been among the earliest settlers of the Valley of Virginia and then of Kentucky; he volunteered for the expedition as it passed the storied mouth of the Limestone. Patrick Gass had been a companion of the redoubtable Lewis Wetzel on the Pennsylvania frontier. Alexander Willard had been born in New Hampshire but had run away to the frontier in his early youth. The Kentucky brothers, Reuben and Joseph Fields, were regarded as exceptional hunters and woods-

[3] Technically, Lewis' regular army rank was captain and Clark's second lieutenant but at Lewis' insistence their authority and responsibility were considered equal at every stage of the undertaking.

[4] They were paid while on the expedition double the regular army private's rate of $5 per month and assured a land grant upon their return.

men by neighbors who took mere proficiency with rifle, ax, and canoe for granted. John Shields was an expert gunsmith, the most essential of all skills in the wilderness. George Drouillard's [5] father had saved Simon Kenton from the stake and George had been reared by Kenton, a frontier schooling without rival. Two other Frenchmen, Peter Cruzatte and Francis Labiche, were enlisted as boatmen, another, Toussaint Charbonneau, employed as interpreter, and a fourth, Baptiste Lepage, recruited at the Mandan towns. The inclusion of the wilderness-bred Frenchman was reminiscent of the equally successful association of the two nationalities in George Rogers Clark's dramatic 1779 march upon Vincennes. The Indian side of the frontier was not excluded. Charbonneau's young Indian wife, Sacajawea, became the heroine of the expedition. Negroes, either as companions of their migrating masters or as runaways to Indian towns, had always played a significant role in frontier history. That race, too, was represented. Clark took with him his Negro slave, York. The westward journey was a catapulted segment of the frontier with all of the frontier's principal characteristics in microcosm.

Since before the first crossing of the Appalachians frontiersmen had embarked upon amazing ventures as individuals. Their exploits had again and again produced consequences of inestimable value to their country. In now embarking upon this most amazing venture of all they were endowed with an advantage with which they had never before had experience. For the first time they were enjoying the planned encouragement and support of the national government. They were being paid to do what they would have in any event most yearned to do.

Dependence upon frontiersmen assured the success of the expedition, as it had of so many wilderness undertakings in the past. It was not, however, any more than it had ever been before, an unmixed blessing. There had never been a frontier commander who

---

[5] George Drouillard was listed by both Lewis and Clark in their reports and journals as "George Drewyer." Most later commentators have accepted the spelling. Three generations of the Drouillard family had resided in Detroit and Drouillards had taken an active part in wildnerness affairs since before the French and Indian War.

had not been driven near distraction by the difficulty of managing followers so predisposed to restlessness, recalcitrance, and insubordination. The "robust helthy hardy young men" who had been assembled in 1803 winter quarters across the Mississippi from the mouth of the Missouri were no exception to this rule. Lewis and Clark solved the problem by a two-pronged policy. They lived in the closest intimacy with their men, shared every labor, privation, hardship, and danger, took them completely into their confidence, consulted with them on important decisions, treated them as equals and friends. But they punished outright disobedience with ruthless severity. Again and again during the expedition's first few months infractions of discipline as minor as drunkenness drew sentences of fifty or a hundred lashes, after a court-martial upon which sat fellow enlisted men. The need for such rigorous reproval presently passed. The adversities of the tremendous journey soon shaped the party into a closely knit band of brothers guided by a common conviction that they were all for one and one for all.

As special representative of the president, Lewis attended the March flag-raising ceremonies in St. Louis that signalized the transfer to the United States of at least the eastern portion of the territory he had been committed to investigate. The expedition sailed May 14, 1804, from winter camp in a 55-foot, 22-oared keelboat with a large square sail and 2 pirogues, one 6-oared and one 7. There were 29 men in the "permanent detachment" which had been selected during the months of training to participate in the eventual crossing of the mountains. A supplemental party of 7 soldiers and 9 boatmen was to accompany the expedition upriver as far as the Mandan to assist in transport and defense during that phase of the journey when opposition from Indians was considered most likely. Whether or not opposition developed there could be no doubt of how long and laborious an effort was in prospect. Occasionally a favorable wind might permit easier progress but more often the struggle against the current must be waged by hard rowing and poling or by men scrambling and wading along the bank dragging on a towline.

The first stage to the Mandan, 166 days of travel time to the north, was in no sense an exploration. Many traders had worked their way up the Missouri past the mouth of the Platte and many others had reached it overland from the east and north. In 1790 the Spaniard, Jacques D'Eglise, had journeyed all the way to the Mandan from St. Louis. The Spanish governor, Hector de Carondelet, had been so impressed by the importance of the route that in 1794 he had offered a reward of $3000 to the first Spaniard to reach the Pacific Ocean by way of the upper Missouri. In 1796 a Spanish representative, the Welshman, John Evans,[6] had raised the Spanish flag at the Mandan towns. His map of the river, furnished Lewis by Jefferson, was often consulted by Lewis and Clark during their 1804 upriver journey.

Jefferson's firmest injunction had been that the explorers record in the greatest detail all that they observed and experienced. The sergeants and all the men able to write were likewise encouraged to keep diaries. From the moment of the expedition's departure Lewis and Clark kept daily journals in which they set down everything they noticed from the depth of prairie dog holes to the height of cloud formations. They saw the rivers, plains, and mountains of the far west as they once were before civilization had altered every prospect and they described all that they saw with perceptive attention. The volumes of their original journals reporting upon their day-to-day experiences and including each day's observations, measurements, sketches, and maps contribute some of the most fascinating reading in all frontier literature. The reader is privileged to see what they saw through their eyes and to see it at moments when they had no idea what the next moment might reveal. Random excerpts from the early weeks of their journal give some faint indication of the matter-of-fact and yet imaginative flavor of their account:

> Set out at 4 oClock P.M. in the presence of many of the neighboring inhabitants and proceeded under a jentle brease up the Missourie . . . Rained the greater part of the last night . . . Saw a number of Goslings

[6] Evans had come to America to search for the mythical Welsh Indians and had found employment at St. Louis with the Spanish-chartered Missouri Company under the direction of the ex-Northwester, James MacKay.

to day on the Shore, the water excessively rapid, & Banks falling in . . . Set out early, passed a verry bad part of the River Called the Deavels race ground . . . Our hunters killed 7 Deer to day . . . Great numbers of Deer in the Prairies, the evening is Cloudy, our party in high Spirits . . . Camped in a bad place, the Mosquitoes and Ticks are noumerous & bad . . . The Country on each side of the river is fine interspursed with Praries, in which immence herds of deer is seen . . . Great quantity of Summer & fall Grapes, Berries & wild roases on the banks . . . Alexander Willard was brought forward charged with "Lying down and sleeping on his post" . . . do Sentience him to receive One hundred lashes, on his bear back . . . the Storm which passed over an open Plain from N.E. Struck our boat on the starbd quarter, and would have thrown her up on the Sand Island dashed to pices in an Instant, had not the party leeped out on the Leward Side and kept her off . . . left the Perogue with two men and at 200 yards we assended a riseing ground of about Sixty feet, from the top of this High land the Countrey is leavel & open as far as can be seen . . . we beheld a most butifull landscape; Numerous herds of buffalow were seen feeding in various directions; the Plain to North N.W. & N.E. extends without interruption as far as can be seen . . . Great number of Buffalo & Elk on the hill side feeding . . . this senery already rich pleasing and beautiful was still farther hightened by immence herds of Buffaloe, deer Elk and Antelopes which we saw in every direction feeding on the hills and plains . . . below the bend is a butifull inclined Plain, in which there is great numbers of Buffalow, Elk & Goats in view feeding and scipping.

Among the novel sights and impressions enlivening each day of their journey, nothing appeared to them so striking as the incredible extent of the plains of which they were able to catch glimpses whenever they left their boats to climb the benchland enclosing the wooded river bottom.[7] They had hoped upon reaching the Platte

[7] Most of the thousands of names given streams, mountains, and other physical features along their route by Lewis and Clark were later ignored by settlers and mapmakers. The most important of all their terms, however, did survive. East of the Mississippi an area of grassland in a generally wooded country was called

to hold a general conference to impress upon the Indian nations of the area the assumption of American sovereignty. Most Indians of the Platte region, however, were away on their summer buffalo hunt and the two captains were able to address only a few at the camp site thereafter known as Council Bluffs.

Lingering disciplinary problems continued to irritate them. A French boatman, mentioned in the journals only as La Liberty, disappeared while carrying a message to the Indians and was never heard of again. Next a soldier, Moses Reed, attempted to desert. He was recaptured by Drouillard who had been sent in pursuit with Lewis' instructions to bring him back dead or alive. On August 20th the expedition suffered the loss of its most highly regarded enlisted man. Sergeant Charles Floyd died of a sudden illness that was termed "bilious colic" and which could have been acute appendicitis. Clark's journal entry reporting the tragedy said: "This Man at all times gave us proofs of his firmness and Determined resolution to doe Service to his Country and honor to himself after paying all honor to our Deceased brother we camped in the Mouth of Floyds River about 30 yards wide, a butiful evening."

Continuing on upriver they at length approached the country of the Sioux and the critical stage of their 1804 pacification mission. The Sioux practice of robbing traders and warring with their neighbors was to be officially reproved. Inasmuch as the Sioux numbered many thousands of warriors, the 43 men in the Lewis and Clark party did not appear to constitute a show of force calculated to impress them greatly. Upon nearing the southern range of the Sioux, grass fires were set on the plains to advertise the American approach. The first Sioux sighted were of the Yankton tribe, a division of the nation which had had trade relations with St. Louis and was therefore more disposed to be outwardly friendly. Pierre Dorion, an old trader who had been encountered on the

---

prairie. During the early weeks of their passage up the Missouri Lewis and Clark continued to call grassland prairie. But as they began to realize the extent of the treeless expanse to the west "prairie" seemed no longer adequate. They began to use the term "great plains."

river two months earlier, served as interpreter but his helpfulness was handicapped by his knowing much more Sioux than he did English. The Yankton listened respectfully to the formal announcement that they must consider themselves henceforth subject to American rule and as a consequence cease attacks on traders and neighbors.

So far the travelers had met no obstacles more eventful than storms, shoals, and mosquitoes, but their next contact was with the pro-English Teton division of the Sioux. This brought on the crisis that had been anticipated. The Teton scoffed at American pretensions, undertook to prevent the expedition's upriver progress, and attempted to seize Clark when he came ashore to address them. To their astonishment the so greatly outnumbered Americans manifested an instant readiness to fight. Clark drew his sword, companions paddled furiously to his rescue, and the cannon on the keelboat were brought to bear. The episode was a repetition of George Rogers Clark's highhanded defiance of a similarly overwhelming number of Indians at Cahokia in 1778, and his younger brother William described the moment in terms as trenchant as had been those used by George:

> Raised a Flag Staff & made a orning or Shade on a Sand bar in the mouth of Teton River, for the purpose of Speeking with the Indians under, the Boat Crew on board at 70 yards distance from the bar . . . Met in Council at 12 oClock and after Smokeing, agreeable to the usual Custom, Cap. Lewis proceeded to Deliver a Speech which we were oblige to Curtail for want of a good interpreter all our party paraded . . . Envited those Cheifs on board to Show them our boat and such Curiossities as was Strange to them, we gave them ¼ a glass of whiskey which they appeared to be verry fond of, Sucked the bottle after it was out & Soon began to be troublesom, one of the 2nd Cheif assumeing Drunkness, as a Cloake for his rascally intentions I went with those Cheifs which left the boat with great reluctiance to Shore with a view of reconsileing those men to us, as soon as I landed the Perogue three of their young Men Seased the Cable of the Perogue . . . and the 2d Chief was verry insolent both in words and justures declareing I should not go on . . . his

justures were of Such a personal nature I felt My self Compeled to Draw my Sword at this Motion Capt. Lewis ordered all under arms in the boat, those with me also Showed a Disposition to Defend themselves and me, the grand Chief then took hold of the roap & ordered the young Warrers away, I felt My Self warm & Spoke in verry positive terms. Most of the Warriers appeared to have their Bows strung and took their arrows from the quiver. as I was not permitted to return, I Sent all the men except 2 Interpreters to the boat, the perogue Soon returned with about 12 of our determined men ready for any event. this movement cause a no: of the Indians to withdraw at a distance . . . after remaining in this Situation Some time I offered my hand to the 1. & 2. Chiefs who refusd to receve it. I turned off & went with my men on board the perogue . . . We proceeded on about 1 Mile & anchored out off a Willow Island placed a guard on Shore to protect the Cooks & a guard in the boat . . . I call this Island bad humered Island as we were in a bad humer.

The Sioux, accustomed to the ease with which they had intimidated traders, were disconcerted by the expedition's unterrified reaction. For the next ten days, as the little fleet beat its slow way upstream, they assembled on the bank in ever greater numbers, alternating professions of friendliness with new and more threatening demands that it turn back. They possessed the military superiority to annihilate the tiny American force, but it had been made clear that any attack would be met by a resistance that would inflict serious Indian losses and in Indian estimation serious foreseeable losses were seldom acceptable. At length the Sioux were convinced further threats were useless. By their unwavering firmness Lewis and Clark had succeeded in the first of their main missions. They had broken the Sioux blockade and opened the Missouri to American use. The Sioux were to remain difficult for the next three quarters of a century but never again were they to seek to deny navigation of the river.

The expedition kept on northward to the Aricara towns where for the first time the men experienced the personal amenities involved in social contact with an established Indian community which had not been denaturalized by long association with white men. The Aricara had heard of the Sioux' discomfiture and welcomed their guests with every protestation of friendliness. Unlike the nomadic Sioux they lived in permanent houses encircled by fields and gardens and their hospitality was framed by this tranquil and domestic background. The episode was not unlike the visit of a ship's crew to a friendly South Sea island:

> after the Council was over we Shot the air guns which astonished them much, they then departed and we rested Secure all night. Those Indians were much astonished at my Servent, they never Saw a black man before, all flocked around him & examind him from top to toe, he Carried on the joke and make himself more turribal than we wished him to do . . . a curious custom with the Souix as well as the rickeres is to give handsom squars to those whome they wish to Show some acknowledgements to. The Seauex we got clare of without taking their squars, they followed us with Squars two days. The Rickores we put off dureing the time we were at the Towns but 2 hansom young Squars were sent by a man to follow us, they came up this evening, and pursisted in their civilities . . . Those people are much pleased with my black Servent. Their womin verry fond of caressing our men &c.[8]

On October 27th they reached the first of their principal geographical goals, the Mandan towns. This preliminary stage of their journey had taken 23 weeks and had totaled, according to their estimate, 1600 miles. Here they established winter quarters and began making preparations for their great westward dash the following summer. Their official mission here was twofold. They sought to impress upon all Indians with whom they were able to make contact that the United States had assumed possession of the region and expected them henceforth to keep the peace with each other and with traders. Meanwhile, they established amicable relations with resident and visiting English traders, at the same time firmly reminding them that the Missouri had become an

---

[8] The commanders guarded their dignity by evading such overtures but customarily offered no objections to their men taking advantage of them. In every Indian town York was specially favored with these attentions.

American river upon which they might trade only by American sufferance.

In the course of preparing for the resumption of their journey they employed as interpreter Toussaint Charbonneau, a former employee of the North West Company who had lived among the Mandan for the past eight years. He was to prove a poor enough bargain but his young wife, Sacajawea, a Shoshone girl captured by the Minnataree five years before, was to become of inestimable value when it developed that their transmountain route would cross her homeland. The two captains concentrated during the winter on learning what they could from Indians of the geography of the country they were preparing to penetrate. There was not much to learn from the sedentary Mandan but a great deal from their immediate neighbors, the Minnataree,[9] who had long made it a practice to raid and hunt as far west as the mountains. Before they plunged into the unknown, Lewis and Clark by a remarkably judicious appraisal of Indian stories had gained a general idea of the course of the upper Missouri and the Yellowstone and of the location of the falls and the forks of the main river.

The return party with dispatches, records, collections, and Indian ambassadors embarked downriver for St. Louis on the same April 7, 1805, that the permanent detachment set off upriver toward the mountains and the western ocean. The exploring fleet now consisted of 2 pirogues and 6 cottonwood canoes. Sacajawea's recently born baby, Pomp, who soon became the pet of the expedition, had raised the party's total to 32 persons. In sailing west from the Mandan they were launched upon the dramatic stage of their great venture which both leaders had so eagerly anticipated. When only nineteen, Lewis had sought to be included in the projected Michaux expedition. Now, 12 years later, he was at last actively engaged in the exploit of which he so long had dreamed. Clark, like every genuine frontiersman, had from boyhood thought of being first in a

[9] The Minnataree, related to the Crow and also called the Hidatsa and the Gros Ventre, are not to be confused with the other Gros Ventre, sometimes also called the Atsina and the Fall Indians, who were related to the Arapaho and confederated with the Blackfeet.

new country. For both, their lifelong yearnings were being satisfied in a fuller measure than either could possibly have foreseen. They were entering upon scenes never before viewed by civilized man. Before them lay a wilderness infrequently visited in fact by any human being. On April 11th they saw the last Indians they were to see for many months. Three days later they passed the highest point on the river any white man had ever reached. With the exultation of born explorers they realized that they had crossed the momentous line between the known and the unknown.

Their primary concern was with geography. Daily they entered observations in their journal, plotted the mouths of tributaries, extended westward their map of the river. The mouth of the Yellowstone was found where Indian accounts had led them to expect to find it. Here they paused to select a site for the future fort which they assumed would soon be established to keep the peace in a region that had known no law since the beginning of time. They were representing another climactic moment in the amazing westward surge of the American frontier. Just so had George Washington in his winter journey in 1754 selected the site for a fort at the Forks of the Ohio, 1200 miles to the east of this fork of the Missouri.

Each day revealed new scenes never before viewed by people capable of recording what they had seen. Being all inveterate hunters, everybody in the party found among all these novel experiences the greatest cause for astonishment in the prodigious abundance of game and the incredible evidence that the region had been so seldom hunted. Pages of their journals crackle with their marveling:

April 22 . . . I asscended to the top of the cutt bluff this morning, from whence I had a most delightfull view of the country, the whole of which except the vally formed by the Missouri is void of timber or underbrush, exposing to the first glance of the spectator immence herds of Buffaloe, Elk, deer, & Antelopes feeding in one common and boundless pasture . . . walking on shore this evening I met with a buffaloe calf which attached itself to me and continued to follow close at my heels until I embarked and left it . . . April 25 . . . the whol face of the country was covered with herds of Buffaloe, Elk & Antelopes; deer are also abundant, but keep themselves more concealed in the woodland. the buffaloe Elk and Antelope are so gentle that we pass near them while feeding, without appearing to excite any alarm among them; and when we attract their attention, they frequently approach us more nearly to discover what we are, and in some instances pursue us a considerable distance apparenly with that view . . . May 4 . . . in the after part of the day we passed an extensive beautifull plain on the Stard. side which gradually ascended from the river. I saw immence quantities of buffaloe in every direction, also some Elk deer and goats; having an abundance of meat on hand I passed them without firing on them; they are extreemly gentle the bull buffaloe particularly will scarcely give way to you. I passed several in the open plain within fifty paces, they viewed me for a moment as something novel and then very unconcernedly continued to feed . . . May 9 . . . we saw a great quantity of game today particularly Elk and Buffaloe, the latter are now so gentle that the men frequently throw sticks and stones at them in order to drive them out of the way.

As hunters they were presently even more impressed by their experiences with the giant bear of the mountains which they began to encounter many hundreds of miles before they had so much as sighted the mountains. They had listened to awed Indian accounts of the extraordinary ferocity of the monsters but they soon discovered that the half had not been told them:

April 29 . . . I walked on shore with one man. about 8 A.M. we fell in with two brown or yellow bear; both of which we wounded; one of them made his escape, the other after my firing on him pursued me seventy or eighty yards, but fortunately had been so badly wounded that he was unable to pursue so closely as to prevent my charging my gun; we again repeated our fir and killed him . . . it is asstonishing to see the wounds they will bear before they can be put to death . . . May 5 . . . Capt. Clark and Drewyer killed the largest brown bear this evening which we have yet seen. it was a most tremendous looking anamal, and extreemly hard to kill nothwithstanding he had five balls through his lungs and five others in various parts he swam more than half the distance acoss the river to a sandbar, & it was at least twenty minutes before he died; he did not attempt to attack, but fled and made the most tremendous roaring from the moment he was shot . . . May 14 . . . Six good hunters of the party fired at a Brown or Yellow Bear several times before they killed him, & indeed he had like to have defeated the whole party, he pursued them separately as they fired on him, and was near catching several of them one he pursued into the river.

As they kept on westward up the Missouri more hundreds of miles, their progress was occasionally interrupted by sudden fierce storms. Several times they escaped complete disaster by the narrowest of margins in recurrent crises that served to demonstrate Charbonneau's worthlessness and Sacajawea's heroism. Then, on May 26th, they were rewarded by their first glimpse of the distant snow-tipped peaks, rising beyond the horizon, of what they assumed was the main range of the Rockies. A week later they were confronted by a geographical riddle upon their answer to which depended the fate of the enterprise. Due to unusual regional rainfall a river entering from the north, which Lewis named Maria's,[10] appeared equal in volume to the river it joined. It was a dilemma which only explorers can be posed. There was no way to determine certainly which was the real Missouri, and yet were the wrong choice to be made so much time would be lost that the expedition would be unable to withdraw in time to resume its drive toward the Pacific. After days of preliminary investigation, earnest consultation, and rationalization it was decided that the south fork was the true Missouri. Resuming their journey up it, discovery on June 13th of the Great Falls of the Missouri, of which the Minnataree had informed them, proved their choice had been correct.

So far their venture had been an exhilarating success. The fantastically good hunting, their providential escapes from storms and grizzlies, their astute solution of the Marias puzzle, their reassuring discovery of the falls, all seemed to presage continued good fortune. In his eagerness to obtain proof that they had chosen the right river

---

[10] In thus paying homage to one of the romantic episodes in his past, Lewis entered in his journal: "it is true that the hue of the waters of this turbulent and troubled stream but illy comport with the pure celestial virtues and amiable qualifications of that lovely fair one." It is now generally known as Marias.

Lewis had gone on ahead overland. His elation upon making the discovery was evidenced by the ecstatic terms in which he described the spectacle: "The grandest sight I ever beheld ... the water assumes a thousand forms ... flying up in jets of sparkling foam ... from the reflection of the sun in the sprey ... there is a beautifull rainbow produced which adds not a little to the beauty of this majestically grand senery." His mood was so euphoric that he was equally ecstatic about his supper: "My fare is really sumptuous this evening: buffaloe's humps, tongues and marrowbones, fine trout parched meal pepper and salt, and a good appetite." He was not even subdued when the next morning a grizzly, catching him with unloaded gun just after he had shot a deer, chased him into the river.

But this was the end of the expedition's honeymoon with fortune. From here on awaited nothing but toil, trouble, disappointment, and every degree of discouragement short of despair. The first untoward development was Sacajawea's desperate illness. Her brave and cheerful disposition and the endearing antics of her baby had won for both the affectionate regard of every man in the party except her husband. All were oppressed by the fear that she was dying. It was an immense relief when after days of deepening suspense she rallied from her sickness as well as from the repeated bleedings and enormous doses of salts, quinine, and opium administered to her by the distracted captains. Meanwhile, portage past the falls and the building of new canoes had cost a month's hard work. Thereafter the river's course instead of keeping on into the mountains veered to the south. The volume kept dwindling until, upon electing to try the north fork after coming upon Three Forks, they were soon laboriously dragging their canoes over the rockbound shallows of a mountain stream. Their hope that they might find a commercially feasible route between the navigable waters of the Missouri and those of the Columbia was daily diminishing.

So far Sacajawea had been a comfort and an inspiration but in no sense a guide for she had had no previous acquaintance with the stretch of the Missouri between the Mandan and Three Forks along which they had been traveling. Now, suddenly, her knowledge of the country became of supreme importance. She recognized the spot where she had been captured by the Minnataree. They realized therefore that they had come within the range of her people, the Shoshone. All depended on speedily locating and establishing friendly relations with these mountain Indians. If the expedition's westward progress was to continue, horses had to be acquired as transport to replace the canoes which were reaching the limit of their usefulness.

In his anxiety to make contact with the Shoshone, Lewis with three companions went on ahead up the ever narrowing stream. He came upon an Indian trail and twice caught tantalizing glimpses of Indians in the distance. His earnest signals of peaceful intentions failed sufficiently to reassure them. They had been taught by grim experience to regard intruders from the plains as enemies. Suspicious and fearful, they kept eluding him. His increasing exasperation did not prevent his appreciating the moment when on August 12th he crossed the continental divide. He recorded with relish that Hugh McNeal "stood with a foot on each side of this little rivulet and thanked his god that he had lived to bestride the mighty & heretofore deemed endless Missouri." They passed in three quarters of a mile from the rill destined to end in the Gulf of Mexico to another flowing toward the Pacific. The next day Lewis came upon an old squaw too suddenly to permit her time to flee, convinced her that he was white by rolling up his sleeve, and through her finally made contact with a Shoshone hunting camp. By a triumph of sign language diplomacy, after two days of debate he persuaded them to accompany him back to his main party at the canoe camp. They remained edgy and suspicious, seemed repeatedly on the verge of bolting, and the suspense continued until Drouillard shot three deer. Mountain hunting was much inferior to that on the plains and the Shoshone had been desperately hungry. After they had gorged on the meat, Lewis was able to prevail upon them to stay with him a little longer. On August 17th the Indians were again about to scatter when Clark appeared in advance of the main party. With him were Charbonneau and Sacajawea. Fortune beamed briefly once more when it was suddenly realized that the chief of the Shoshone band was Sacajawea's brother with whom she had an affecting reunion. The next day was Lewis' 31st birthday. Sitting astride the continental divide he entered in his diary: "I reflected that I had as yet done but little, very little, indeed, to further the happiness of the human race, or to advance the information of the succeeding generation."

The Shoshone were now devoted friends, glad to sell horses and anxious to help with advice. Their advice was as unimpeachable as it was disheartening. They insisted that there was no passable way west from this headwater of the Missouri to any navigable branch of the Columbia. A probe westward by Clark while Lewis was negotiating for horses confirmed the Indian verdict. But the captains had not come this far to entertain now any impulse to turn back. They ranged desperately northward searching through the mountain labyrinth for some possible way west. They, like their men, had by now been so hardened and seasoned that they could withstand even so fearful a test. Leaders and followers formed as durable a group as has ever been assembled. They crossed and recrossed the continental divide. They starved. They wallowed through snowfields. They encountered strange Indians of whom their Indian informants on the Missouri had never heard. They sickened on diets of dried salmon, boiled roots, and stewed dog. They struggled on until at last they reached navigable water again at the forks of the Clearwater. Here they paused to build canoes. They had succeeded in crossing the mountains from the waters of the Missouri to those of the Columbia but in the light of their principal hope the great achievement had been an inherent failure. Since leaving their canoes on the Missouri they had been grappling with mountains for fifty weary days. Instead of discovering a shorter more direct way to the Pacific, they had discovered that the way was far longer and infinitely more difficult than anybody had presumed. They had no more found the Northwest Passage than had Mackenzie.

Comfortably water-borne again, they traveled down the Clearwater to the Snake, down the Snake to the main Columbia, and on down that great river until November 7th Clark could enter in his journal: "Great joy in camp we are in view of the Ocian, this great Pacific Octean which we been so long anxious to See." After an unexampled display of courage, endurance, ingenuity, and common sense they had accomplished their primary mission. They had crossed the continent to the Pacific by way of the Missouri. Though the route that they had taken across the mountains was never to prove useful, they had attained one objective of measureless value. By entering the Columbia basin from the east they had greatly improved the American claim to the region originally suggested by Gray's discovery of the river's mouth.

After a cheerless winter on the rainswept and fogbound Oregon coast, they still clung to the hope that they might yet find a more passable route connecting the two rivers. As they approached the continental divide on their 1806 homeward journey, they separated in order to make a wider search for more feasible passes. Clark struck southeastward to Three Forks and then over Bozeman Pass to the Yellowstone where he built canoes and descended the river to its mouth. Lewis headed northeastward to Great Falls and then, again dividing his party, essayed an exploratory excursion up the Marias with three men. These diverse explorations served only to confirm the conclusion that there existed no practical route connecting the Missouri and the Columbia. Later explorations were to make it ever clearer that Lewis and Clark had challenged the Rockies in the one area where they were the least passable.

Aside from having his horses stolen by Crow, the most adroit of all plains horse thieves, Clark had an agreeable journey down the Yellowstone, but Lewis suffered two serious misadventures. Well up the Marias he encountered a roving band of eight Blackfeet. Realizing that they outnumbered the white men two to one and accustomed to the ease with which they terrorized their Indian rivals, the Blackfeet undertook to seize the explorers' guns and horses. It was a remarkably ill-advised venture. They were dealing not only with a Lewis but with a Drouillard and two Fields. There were many too few Indians, even though they were Blackfeet. In the brief whirl of action two Indians were killed and it was they who lost their weapons and horses. It was not, however, ground on which the victors could hope to stand. The probability that any number of avenging Blackfoot reinforcements might at any moment appear could not be ignored. Making use of the Indian horses, which were better than his own, Lewis made a hard ride of more than a hundred miles, much of it by moonlight through herds of buffalo, to rejoin the other members of his party on the Missouri. They then resumed their downriver journey toward reunion with Clark. En route, while stalking elk in the willow-shrouded river bottom, Lewis was accidentally shot in the thigh by his hunting companion,

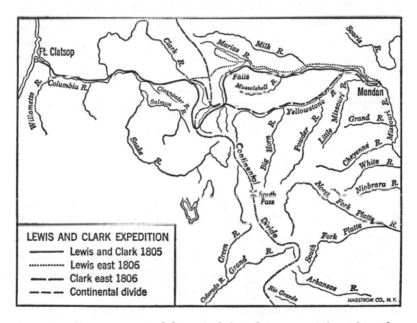

Cruzatte. It was a painful wound but he recovered within the month. In the uncontaminated atmosphere of the plains and mountains few wounds were mortal, and a man who still breathed could hope to survive even after having been mangled by a grizzly.

The day before Lewis and Clark were safely reunited on August 12th, 200 miles below the mouth of the Yellowstone, Clark's party had one of the more significant experiences of the entire journey. They had sighted the first white men they had seen since April 13th of the year before at almost the same spot when, on their westward voyage, they had parted from two French hunters who had accompanied the expedition that far west from the Mandan. It was the identity of these unexpectedly encountered white men that was significant. They were two American trappers, Joseph Dickson, from the Illinois, and Forest Hancock, from Boone's settlement. They had trapped their way up the Missouri the previous winter, had been robbed of their season's catch by the Sioux, had been repeatedly endangered by an outbreak of general war among the Mandan, Minnataree, Aricara, and Assiniboin, and yet were now on their way to try trapping up the Yellowstone. Lewis and Clark had been assumed lost by Indians and traders on the Missouri, but even the presumption that a so much larger and stronger party had failed to survive the perils of the mountains had not dissuaded these two roving young frontiersmen from chancing whatever risks might await them.

Dickson and Hancock were the first representatives to appear in history of that most amazing breed—mountain men. They were the earliest forerunners of the conquerors of the farthest west just as they were the direct successors of the equally individualistic long hunters who had opened the way to Kentucky and Tennessee. They were men of a special type, shaped and conditioned by the demanding experiences of three generations of frontier people. In them long acquaintance with danger had served only to engender a scorn of danger. Their driving compulsion was to roam ever more freely and widely in order to seek new experiences however perilous. It was in keeping with the frontiersman's instinctive point of view that Lewis and Clark were not in the slightest surprised to encounter these two lone wanderers paddling nonchalantly into an unknown distance that stretched before them they neither knew nor cared how far. This frontier attitude was further emphasized when Colter, who had for 27 months been denied the comforts of normal living and for the past 15 months had been suffering the extraordinary hardships of the transmountain journeys, eagerly begged permission to accompany the trappers. The captains made no attempt to point out that he must be out of his mind. They understood his impulse and sympathetically gave him his discharge, on the one condition that no other member of the expedition ask permission to seek a similar latitude. When Colter got into the canoe with Dickson and Hancock, the known number of mountain men had risen to three. Soon there would be hundreds.

Lewis and Clark paused at the Mandan long enough to persuade the principal Mandan chief, Shehaka, more commonly known as Le Gros Blanc or Big White, to accompany them so that he might visit the United States. It was felt that, after being received by Jefferson and having seen for himself the population, wealth, and power of the United States, he would return so impressed that he would devote his people o American interests.

The expedition descended the Missouri at a speed which suggested fortune had tired of placing obstacles in its path. Thirty-four days after leaving the Mandan, Clark reported, "we saw some cows on the bank which was a joyfull Sight to the party and caused a Shout to be raised." Voyagers returning down the Missouri traditionally anticipated the first sight of cattle as the certain signal that they were approaching settled country. The expedition's appearance at the first settlement, the French hunters' hamlet at La Charette, amazed the inhabitants and a number of traders whose boats were moored there:

> Every person, both French and americans seem to express great pleasure at our return, and acknowledged themselves much astonished in seeing us return. they informed us that we were supposed to have been lost long since, and were entirely given out by every person &c.

They reached St. Louis September 23, 1806, 28¼ months after the day their boats had been launched from winter camp and 36½ months after Lewis' departure from Pittsburgh with the keelboat.

In reporting their safe return to Jefferson, Lewis wrote, "with rispect to the exertions and services rendered by this estimable man Capt. Wm. Clark on this expedition I cannot say too much, if, sir, any credit be due to the success of the arduous enterprize in which we have been engaged he is equally with myself entitled to the consideration of yourself and that of our common country."

Credit was unmistakably due. As a physical and moral achievement the undertaking had been a monumental success. To list the immense distances they traversed and the stupendous difficulties they overcame is to record an unbroken series of triumphs. Unfamiliar demands and unnatural problems had been matched by an unfailing display of intelligence, adaptation, and efficiency. Aside from Floyd's death by illness they had completed their prodigious journey without the loss of a single man. As practitioners of the art of exploration they were truly professionals. With regard to the easy passage between the navigable waters of the Missouri and the Columbia which it had been hoped they might discover, Lewis candidly reported to Jefferson that "of 340 Miles land carriage 200 miles is along a good road and 140 over tremendious mountains which for 60 Miles is covered with eternal snows." But theirs had been a more consequential achievement than the relative practicability of a trade route. They had erected a great arch of American sovereignty extending over plains and mountains from the headwaters of the Mississippi to the shores of the Pacific.

V

౿

Aaron Burr

JEFFERSON'S INTEREST in the scientific results of exploration was accompanied by his necessary concern with the conflict between American territorial claims and those of Great Britain in the north and of Spain in the southwest. Great Britain, distracted by the European war with Napoleon, was not disposed to be insistent, but Spain was reaching aggressively for possession of the southern plains. The vast expanses of an uninhabited wilderness separated the two nations' frontiers except on the Sabine River west of New Orleans where a Spanish army confronted a much smaller American force under Brigadier General James Wilkinson, still commanding the Army of the United States in the Jefferson administration as he had in that of Adams and Washington. By midsummer of 1806 the border tension had tightened until the firing of a single shot could provide the incident to precipitate a war which in any event was regarded by most impatient westerners as sooner or later inevitable. The perpetually expansionist west, traditionally antagonistic to Spain since the days of Spain's blockade of the Mississippi and promotion of Indian devastations, welcomed the accelerating drift toward war as affording an opportunity to seize new land in Florida and Texas. Western belligerence was universal and enthusiastic.

Jefferson, informed by the wider perspectives of the presidency and burdened by its responsibilities, remained as reluctant to commit his country to the uncertainties of a foreign war as had been his predecessors, Washington and Adams, when faced by similar crises. Even were the young republic's economic and political structure to prove sufficiently formed to withstand the shocks of war, it had few weapons with which to wage one. An economy-minded Congress had continued to resist the development of a federal military establishment. In 1806 the regular army totaled 175 officers, 2389 soldiers and 12 West Point cadets. The available field strength was scattered in isolated detachments and posts along the 2500-mile arc of the frontier extending along the southern shores of the Great Lakes, down the Mississippi and eastward again along the northern border of Spanish Florida to the Atlantic.

But Jefferson's pacifism, though earnest, was exceedingly tough-minded. In the process of seeking to avoid war he remained determined to relinquish no American territorial claim. His exploring expeditions were calculated flag-showing military probes of the areas in dispute. In 1804, at the President's request, William Dunbar and Dr. George Hunter had conducted private explorations of the Ouachita as far upstream as the great hot springs and had reported their observations to the American Philosophical Society. The next three of Jefferson's expeditions were as officially accredited instruments of national policy as had been Lewis and Clark's.

Lieutenant Zebulon Pike left St. Louis August 9, 1805, in a keelboat manned by 20 soldiers with orders to ascend the Mississippi into the area west of the Great Lakes still dominated by English traders. He changed to smaller craft at the Falls of St. Anthony and went into fortified winter quarters October 16th at Little Falls. During the winter he ranged by sled as far north as Cass Lake which he assumed to be the source of the Mississippi, a principal cornerstone in the still unsurveyed British-American boundary west of Lake Superior. His primary mission, like that of Lewis and

Clark, was to advise the Indians that they were henceforth subject to the United States and to remind English traders that they were operating in American territory. He specifically admonished the Sioux and Chippewa to renounce the traditional state of war which marked their rivalry since in the seventeenth century Lake Indians had gained a temporary superiority over the Sioux by being first in the area to procure guns from the French.[1] Both Indians and traders listened to him indulgently and continued to conduct their affairs much as before. Pike was particularly irritated by the traders' practice of flying the British flag over their posts. When one trader was slow to haul down a British flag, Pike ordered his soldiers to shoot it from the staff. He returned to St. Louis in the spring after having met no outward resistance to his formal assertions of American sovereignty on the upper Mississippi.

There was no such complacence in the southwest where Spain in 1806 was making indignant and determined preparations to oppose American implementation of the Louisiana Purchase. While Pike was preparing to lead a second expedition across the plains to the mountains, Captain Richard Sparks, accompanied by geographer Thomas Freeman, undertook an official exploration of the Red River from Natchitoches. The possibility of Spanish military reaction was foreseen and the operation was guarded by an escort of 37 soldiers under lieutenants John Duforest and Enoch Humphreys. Sparks got around the hundred-mile-long driftwood obstruction of the Red River known as the Great Raft but thereafter was confronted by a Spanish column of such overwhelmingly greater numbers that he had no recourse other than to agree to make a hasty withdrawal.

Not content with having turned back Sparks, Spain that same summer undertook a startlingly aggressive offensive operation. Don Facundo Melgares with an army of 600 dragoons and mounted

---

[1] Everywhere in the wooded area east of the open plains even the most primitive guns were considered militarily superior to bows. Pike, the eager young tactician, noted with the greatest interest the practiced celerity with which the Sioux when exposed to Chippewa gunfire dismounted to dig foxholes, trenches, and earthworks.

militia was dispatched northeastward from Santa Fe to impress the Indians of the southern plains with Spanish military might and to intercept any American expeditions that might be encountered in the disputed area. He held a number of councils with the Comanche, instructing them that they were still as much the subjects of the King of Spain as they had been before the Louisiana Purchase, and he kept on northward as far as the principal Pawnee town on the Republican River. The last Spanish force to range this far had been Villasur's in 1720 which the Pawnee had destroyed, but they were so impressed by Melgares' martial demonstration that they readily accepted Spanish flags and medals, swore allegiance, and promised to turn back any Americans who approached their territory. Melgares had hoped to cut off Lewis and Clark as well as Pike's overland expedition, but supply difficulties required him to withdraw southward after having made no more consequential captures than several American traders.

Though nominally responsible for all military operations, Wilkinson had taken little personal interest in the Missouri and Mississippi explorations in the north, but there was no limit to his personal interest in any project associated with the territorial dispute in the southwest. His secret attachment to Spain had been his chief preoccupation since the days of Kentucky's threatened secession and his usefulness to Spain had steadily increased as he rose in rank in the American regular army. Spanish-American relations had been troubled since the end of the Revolution and he had made a career of attempting in every recurrent crisis to betray his country's interests. He had been for the past 19 years on Spain's secret service payroll and had eventually been granted an annual pension of $2000. As recently as 1804 he had accepted a special payment of $12,000 as added compensation for keeping Spain informed of Jefferson's intentions and advising Spanish authorities on how Florida might be most effectively defended against American invasion. In consonance with his secret Spanish association, Wilkinson planned every detail of Pike's southwestern journey, even to the extent of taking care that Pike was accompanied by his son, Lieutenant James B. Wilkinson, and by one of the general's personal agents, Dr. John H. Robinson. The expedition's mission, as defined by Wilkinson's directives, presented more of the aspects of a military reconnaissance seeking an opportunity to engage in espionage than of a geographical exploration. Pike accepted his peculiar instructions without question. He was a zealous and devoted young officer, dedicated to the professional soldier's basic principle that the direct orders of a superior must be obeyed under all circumstances.

After setting out July 15, 1806, Pike first visited the Osage with whom he held a council at which, as he described the negotiation in his journal, he "explained at large the will, wishes, and advice of their Great Father." Osage proximity to the American frontier inclined them to profess friendliness, but they were so little impressed by Pike's small force of 19 soldiers that it was only with the greatest difficulty that Pike procured from them the horses he needed in order to continue onward into the plains. He next marched northwestward to contact the Pawnee, more distant by some hundreds of miles from the American frontier. They were even less impressed than had been the Osage. Only a few days before they had been visited by Melgares and the contrast in numbers between his army and Pike's half platoon made the American military display appear ludicrous. Mindful of Melgares' instructions, the Pawnee chief, Sharitarish, demanded that Pike turn back, threatening to oppose his further advance by force. Pike recorded that he replied: "I had been sent out by our great father to explore the western country . . . that I should therefore proceed, and that if he thought proper to stop me, he could attempt it, but we were men, well armed, and would sell our lives at a dear rate to his nation." The Pawnee, as disconcerted by what seemed to them so irrational a scorn of consequences as had been the Sioux by the similar Lewis and Clark defiance, elected to stand aside.

Pike struck out southwestward, brazenly following with his 19 the broad trail left on the plains by Melgares' 600. Upon reaching the Arkansas the party separated according to plan. Lieutenant Wilkinson turned eastward toward the safety of the frontier, ostensibly to explore the lower river, while Pike with Dr. Robinson, an interpreter, Baronet Vasquez, and 13 men started upriver toward the mountains and an unrelieved series of disasters. It was the end of October with snow already beginning to dust the high plains and obviously long since too late to contemplate any realistic exploration of the mountain area ahead. Pike, nevertheless, continued doggedly to obey his orders, even though he could no longer have remained unaware that it had been Wilkinson's central intention that he expose his command to capture by the Spaniards. Struggling among the mountains of southeastern Colorado, his party starved for weeks while suffering so severely from below-zero temperatures that several were crippled for life. He had so far been in a borderland claimed by both nations, had several times found and followed Spanish trails but had encountered no Spaniards, and there was no longer hope that he would be challenged in this remote area until the following spring. He therefore made a desperate midwinter crossing of the Sangre de Cristo Mountains to establish a stockade on the upper Rio Grande in what constituted a flagrant invasion of territory that had been admittedly Spanish for the last two centuries.

Pike later maintained, officially, that he had assumed he was on a headwater of the Red River and therefore still in territory claimed by the United States. There was every indication, however, that he knew exactly where he was and had taken the position in compliance with Wilkinson's secret instructions for, when still no Spaniards appeared, Robinson left the stockade and traveled alone on down the Rio Grande, perfectly aware that he was proceeding toward Santa Fe. When he arrived he professed to have come to negotiate the settlement of a private mercantile debt due William Morrison, the great Kaskaskin merchant. Informed by Robinson of the location of the American post, the Spanish governor dispatched a column to make Pike and his men prisoners of war. This phase of Wilkinson's devious and complex design had at last matured. The American trespass had provoked Spain, the capture of Pike had provoked the United States, and the power to decide the issue of war or peace had been placed more than ever in the hands of a border commander who outwardly served one nation and secretly served the other, while hoping to profit by both relationships.[2]

But his device had matured too late to play a significant part in the anticipated unfolding of Wilkinson's over-all plan which had meanwhile been thrust off balance by the rush of events in the United States. While Pike was toiling up the Arkansas toward his scheduled sacrifice, what was presently to be known as the Burr Conspiracy was gripping the nation's attention and appearing for a few weeks to have placed the issue of war or peace beyond the control of either Wilkinson or Jefferson. As Pike waded through snowfields in the shadow of the peak that was to perpetuate his name, Aaron Burr, recent Vice President whose vote for the presidency had exactly matched Jefferson's, was leading his armed followers down the Mississippi as the self proclaimed champion of the west and the eagerly acclaimed advocate of an immediate war with Spain. His flamboyant gamble was to end prematurely in grotesque and humiliating failure, but it was a failure that demands attention because it shaped the course of frontier events for the next half century.

The precise dividing line in Burr's conduct which could have marked a possible distinction between treason and patriotism has been variously viewed and bitterly disputed. His design was in essence a filibustering expedition aimed at an irregular attack in the interest of western expansion upon Spanish borderlands, a direct successor to the earlier and similar projects of George Rogers Clark in 1787, 1791, and 1794, William Blount in 1797, and Alexander Hamilton in 1798. Among the many verdicts that have been rendered on his guilt or innocence by friend and foe in his own

[2] Pike, while a Spanish captive, was taken to Santa Fe, then to Chihuahua, well treated, and finally released on the Sabine border, June 28, 1807. Insofar as his original mission had included an effort to gather useful information on conditions in New Spain, his misadventure had opened to him one great success. As a consequence of his movements and experiences during his four-month captivity he was able upon his return to report in professional detail on Spanish military dispositions, the personalities of Spanish commanders, and the intentions of Spanish governors as well as upon routes, towns, population, wealth, and public opinion.

time and historians since, one at least cannot be challenged. Few men have ever suffered such a catastrophic run of sheer bad luck. After sweeping him to the heights of success at the early age of forty-four, the tide of his fortunes turned suddenly and inexorably. In an uninterrupted series of disasters he missed becoming President of the United States by the margin of a tie vote in the Electoral College, lost political control in his own state as a consequence not of a triumph of his opposition but of the death of his chief enemy, was hounded from public life by the leader of his own party, was branded a traitor by the word of a man whose word was notoriously worthless, was recognized in flight by a backwoods busybody who had never before seen him, achieved a brilliantly successful defense in court only to see the effort result in his final ruin, and lived on for thirty empty years of brooding over the greatness that had so narrowly escaped him.

Those last few months Burr had presided over the Senate had posed him a personal problem without parallel, before or since. He was still Vice President of the United States but he was also under indictment for murder in the states of New York and New Jersey. He had killed Alexander Hamilton in a formally and normally staged duel in defense of his personal honor which Hamilton had scandalously impugned. Still, the public outcry had been astounding. It had soon become apparent that his political career had suffered a blow from which there was little hope it might ever recover. The campaign of 1804 was boiling on toward election day, and he who four short years before had loomed so large on the national scene was a bystander. His own party had declined to nominate him for either state or national office. He had devoted the better part of his forty-eight years to gaining the political heights and he was fiercely unready to be thrust back into oblivion. In public he continued to mind his Senate duties with an outward judicious calm with which even his most carping critics could find no fault. In private he was engrossed in an active, imaginative, and calculating canvass of the possible alternatives open to him. He was not casting about for a substitute for success but for clues to a greater success than he had known before.

Well-meaning friends were urging him to move west and run for Congress from Tennessee. The west, they pointed out, was peopled by a breed of Republicans who considered the extinction of Federalist Hamilton an heroic public service. Burr professed to be heartened by these reports of his popularity in that lively and fastest growing section of the country. But the vista he was already beginning to glimpse was a wider one than standing for Congress from an obscure district in the canebrakes.

Throughout that fall and winter of 1804 he had been very nearly as much the object of general attention in Washington as was the man in the White House. Everyone knew he must be making some plan for his future. Anyone who pretended to keep an eye on the national scene was watching to catch the first intimation of the shape that plan might take. When the first hint came, it should have been revealing. A delegation of indignant Frenchmen from New Orleans had come to Washington to protest the kind of government the United States had imposed upon their city. The Frenchmen's vexation was significant, for New Orleans, the traditional key to the west, was a predominantly French city. What immediately intrigued more thoughtful observers was that the Vice President sought out the visiting Frenchmen, won their confidence, became their champion. Friends had told him that he had become a hero generally in the west. He was making sure that he became a hero in particular to the French inhabitants of New Orleans.

At this early and formative stage the orderly development of his plans for a greater future had been handicapped by a most mundane circumstance. Like so many humbler men, he was in painful need of money. Always unfrugal, he seldom had enough for his immediate needs. To meet the new opportunities he could see opening to him he would need much more. So it had developed that certain diplomatic figures on the Washington scene had gained an earlier and closer insight into the direction of his thinking than did the shrewdest American observer. Anthony Merry, English minister to Washington, was reporting to his government that the Vice President of the United States was prepared to "lend his assistance to his Majesty's government in any manner." This assistance, Merry said, would extend to steps leading to the separation of the west from the United States. Don Carlos Martínez de Yrujo, the Spanish minister, was also reporting to his government. Burr was offering him information involving the United States' patently aggressive intentions with regard to Spanish possessions in Florida and Texas.

These remarkable sidelights were, of course, jealously guarded diplomatic secrets at the time. Burr's defenders, who have tended to outnumber his detractors, have never seriously denied these allegations. They have been content to argue that Burr had no intention of rendering any actual service to England or Spain, that all that he was trying to do was to get money which he needed for purposes which were in themselves essentially patriotic. At any rate, Spanish authorities, who had so long made a practice of advancing secret service money to influential Americans, in the east as well as the west, doled out to him, according to their accounting, some $1500. Merry kept him hopeful and dangling but his government was skeptical, and from England Burr got nothing.

Aside from these unseemly eddies, the main current of Burr's design had by midwinter of 1804 begun to flow in a definite direction and, so far, in rational secrecy. One of his oldest friends was James Wilkinson, whom he had known since they had served together in Benedict Arnold's tragic Quebec campaign. Their paths had separated after the war. Burr had climbed the ladder of New York and then national politics. Wilkinson had gone west to seek his fortune. However, they had kept in touch through the years by way of a continuing correspondence, much of it so confidential that their letters were written in a private cipher. Wilkinson had been in the east that winter in connection with an expected appointment as governor of Upper Louisiana. Since Burr's interest was turning westward it was but natural that he should seek his old friend's counsel. They conferred repeatedly in New York, in Philadelphia, and in Washington.

The picture of the west that was unfolding before Burr's eager gaze was breath-taking, in the light of the new political opportunities for which he was searching. Easterners by the scores of thousands were swarming westward. The purchase of Louisiana had opened almost unlimited horizons. The west had become the section of action, ferment, growth. It promised soon to overbalance the conservative east. Multitudes of lesser men were seeking a fresh start there. Under Wilkinson's experienced guidance he could not have been long in appreciating the central and controlling factor in the western situation. The west was committed to the idea of continued expansion. No one was satisfied with what he had. Men who had left forty acres in Virginia to take up a thousand in Tennessee were already looking toward ten thousand beyond the Mississippi. But already, also, the treeless and uninviting plains across the Missouri were in sight. Therefore, this perpetual expansion which was every westerner's resolve could only continue in the better watered and more fertile portion of the continent, at the expense of Spain in the south and southwest. Every circumstance led back to the same central and controlling presumption. Nothing would suit westerners better than an immediate war with Spain, with Florida and Texas as the prizes. Each week of that Washington winter the great opportunity had seemed to become clearer. Burr was accustomed to the center of the stage. To the west was a far wider stage. All looked so incredibly promising that he burned with impatience to go there to see and judge finally for himself.

On March 2, 1805, his term as Vice President ended, he rose from his President's chair in the Senate for the last time. On April 10th he set out for Pittsburgh on horseback. Wilkinson had left earlier for St. Louis. Light was thrown on the temper of the two friends that spring by their letters to intimates: Wilkinson was referring to his station in St. Louis as "on the high rode to Mexico." Burr, writing to his beloved daughter, Theodosia, was characterizing his arduous western tour with the cryptic comment "the objects of this journey may lead me to Orleans and perhaps further."

From Pittsburgh to New Orleans Burr visited farms, villages, and towns, talked to settlers, merchants, boatmen, army officers, land speculators, hunters, trappers, squatters, men of great influence, and men of none. All were eager to express their views to so eminent a traveler. He was an experienced politician, well able

to sense the public pulse. All that had been told him about the
disposition of the west was proving true. These westerners were a
people perpetually obsessed by the impulse to force their way on
westward.

One highlight of his tour, unappreciated at the moment but to
have tragicomic consequences, was a casual visit on his way down
the Ohio to the manor of Harman Blennerhasset on an island on
the Virginia side below Marietta. Blennerhasset was a wealthy
émigré Irishman who had built this palace in the wilderness in
order, it was said, to enjoy in the greater peace of these primitive
surroundings the companionship of his beautiful young wife who
was also his niece. The exuberant Celt was dazzled by the honor
of entertaining so distinguished a guest. Other highlights were reassuring conferences with Andrew Jackson at Nashville and Wilkinson at St. Louis. And finally there was a colorful sojourn in
New Orleans to cement his relations with his hospitable French
friends.

Everything that Burr had learned had seemed to confirm his
highest hopes. In the west he was still a hero. A border war with
Spain was certain, sooner or later. Increasing Spanish belligerence
made it feasible for the American commander in the field to get it
started at a moment of his own choosing. Wilkinson professed
readiness to do this. The whole west yearned for such a war. Not
only Texas but, with proper guidance, the most of Mexico, as well,
appeared within reach. All that was needed was a leader of national
stature. Burr, providentially, was in a position to become that leader.
It was an office to which he could consider himself elected not by
votes but by destiny.

He rushed back to the seaboard to make personal arrangements
to take advantage of his great opportunity. He was on fire with
confidence and enthusiasm. The very boldness and simplicity of
his design gave it inevitable scope and force. He was taking advantage of a movement of people that had been irresistible since
it first surged over the Appalachians and could be expected to
prove equally irresistible as it continued to surge on westward.

Two frustrating difficulties still stood in his way. The first was time. He had so little. The military crisis on the Sabine might not wait. His opportunity only existed if he seized it at once. He had talked freely in the west. He talked more freely now and to almost whoever would listen. There was, after all, no secret about the possible imminence of a border war. Everybody was talking about that. But in his talk there was more point and bite. He spoke of the treasure house of Mexico that lay beyond the border, as had Cortés to his followers on the beach. To each listener he had an approach with an appropriate appeal. To army and navy officers he spoke of high commands. To United States senators, of proconsulships. To bankers, of profits and investments. To land speculators, of ten-million-acre tracts. To adventurers, of certain fortune.

Burr's defenders have made much of the circumstances that during this winter Jefferson seemed moved to none of the alarm that he proclaimed so violently the following year. He must have gained more than an inkling of the crusade that Burr was preaching so indiscriminately. But he evidenced no concern. He received Burr amicably and once was closeted with him for more than two hours. But he hated Burr too bitterly to wish him new opportunities and he knew him too well to consider him a harmless fanatic. Jefferson's critics have accused him of coldly dealing out rope with which Burr could be trusted to hang himself. It is more likely that Jefferson at this stage saw a passing diplomatic advantage in impressing upon Spain how generally American public opinion favored fighting, if necessary, for American rights in the southwest.

Burr's second difficulty was even more frustrating. He not only had too little time, he had too little money. He needed much more now than he had ever needed before. The essence of his design to lift the border dispute to the level of a conquest of Mexico depended upon the hard core of a personal following which he could control. Even the most modest expeditionary force required a great deal of money. The apparent indiscretion with which he had been broadcasting his intentions sprang from his need to approach literally anybody who might contribute. The principal hope to which he had clung, that the English interest in his project might be matched by a substantial advance of English money, had by now been blasted. He received various dribbles from some of the people who had been listening to him, a little more from his son-in-law, but nothing to begin to measure up to the least that he needed. The most considerable contribution was an unsolicited one from Harman Blennerhasset whom he had all but forgotten.

The glitter of the opportunity that he envisaged made his need for money truly desperate. Yrujo was presently reporting to his government another approach from Burr. This time it was a fantastic proposal to seize Washington. According to Yrujo, Burr professed to have at his beck and call a corps of hard-bitten frontiersmen capable of any exploit he asked of them. The President, the Treasury, the Arsenal, the Navy Yard, would be set upon simultaneously and all taken into temporary custody. Before the country could be fully aroused the adventurers would sail off in their captured naval vessels to take New Orleans and separate the west from the United States. Such a blow at the nation with which Spain seemed certain soon to be at war was represented as worth the advance of a very large sum. The Spanish minister listened, fascinated, but no money was forthcoming. Again Burr's defenders have taken a determined position: Obviously he could have had no slightest intention of attempting any such preposterous coup; he was merely endeavoring to confuse his country's enemy while at the same stroke hoping to gain funds from that enemy for a purpose which would eventually prove to be in his country's best interests.

The spring of 1806 had come. There was no more time. And still no money. And he could wait no longer. With a handful of devoted personal followers, including his lovely daughter and her indulgent husband, he set out for the west on his second and decisive tour. Action, any action, had revived his spirits. At the romantic island in the Ohio they were welcomed by the infatuated Blennerhasset. And here the great design at last took something like coherent shape. With a down payment of $5000, furnished by Blennerhasset, Burr purchased from a group of Kentucky land speculators a tract of 400,000 acres on the Ouachita. His new domain was on the flank of the Spanish frontier where he would be in a strategic position to play his destined part in the forthcoming war. Boats were ordered constructed at Marietta. Recruits signing for the ostensible settlement-founding expedition were required to agree in writing to proceed with it to the Ouachita and there to hold themselves in readiness to resist any Spanish aggression. Arms chests were opened, muskets distributed, drills instituted, and imperial titles, some playful, some in apparent earnest, assigned to various figures in the little band for whom the future was beginning to glow with so bright a shimmer.

Burr hurried on ahead to Kentucky to rally his supporters and enlist more recruits. Here, however, he was harassed by those political animosities which had become so much more virulent since the death of Hamilton. A suspicious United States District Attorney, Joseph Hamilton Daveiss, hauled him before a Kentucky grand jury to charge him with providing the means for "a military expedition and enterprise . . . for the purpose of descending the Ohio and Mississippi therewith, and making war upon the subjects of the King of Spain . . . I have information upon which I can rely that all western territories are the next object of the scheme."

The first Kentucky trial aroused much local excitement, but among the crowds assembling in Frankfort the majority were good western Republicans who denounced the scandal-mongering Federalist United States attorney, while privately applauding Burr's design, if design there was. The jury was discharged for lack of witnesses. That night Frankfort staged a ball to celebrate the prosecutor's discomfiture. Two weeks later Daveiss doggedly petitioned for another grand jury. This time Henry Clay appeared in Burr's defense. All real westerners welcomed Burr's anti-Spanish and pro-war agitation, and there was as yet no distrust of his motives. Again the grand jury returned no true bill, and Burr was free to continue on his way.

However, the Frankfort crowds had scarcely dispersed before the news of Jefferson's proclamation burst upon Kentucky. The President had at last decided the moment had come to show his hand. He wanted Spain confused but he did not want a war. His proclamation declared parties of armed Americans were assembling to make war on a friendly power and called upon all patriotic citizens to confound the undertaking. Having, at long last, taken public alarm, Jefferson blazed with indignation. In characterizing the conspiracy he asserted that it was Burr's purpose "to place himself on the throne of Montezuma and extend his empire to the Alleghanies, seizing on New Orleans as the instrument of compulsion for our western states."

Kentucky, as well as the rest of the country, was astounded by the enormity of the charge but law-abiding elements soon rallied to the President's trumpet call. Even in the west Jefferson's diatribe gained a hearing. Denunciation by a fellow Republican, and that one the most distinguished in the land, even if misguided, had to be taken more seriously than the fuming of a Federalist district attorney. Federal officials and Virginia militia seized as many of Burr's boats as they could lay hands on, arrested some of his adherents, and ravaged Blennerhasset's island.

But Burr himself kept ahead of the hue and cry. After depositing $4000 with Andrew Jackson in Nashville, to pay for some additional boats Jackson had there under construction, he joined his main "expedition" of 13 boats and some 60 men at the mouth of the Cumberland, the same site where in 1794 George Rogers Clark's lieutenant, Colonel John Montgomery, had assembled his force of frontiersmen for a descent on New Orleans. Burr knew now of Jefferson's proclamation but he set sail down the Ohio and on down the Mississippi, still confident that the imminent outbreak of war on the Spanish border would make Jefferson the fool and him the hero.

Meanwhile, in the field with his encamped army facing the aggressive Spanish forces on the Sabine frontier, Wilkinson had on October 11th received Burr's emissaries with Burr's famous cipher letter spelling out his intentions for the information of the American commanding general upon whom so much depended. The exact text of the letter has been disputed. Only Wilkinson, its recipient, custodian, and master of the cipher key, knew exactly what it contained. His version of it varied somewhat from time to time and differed in several particulars from the couriers' understanding of it. But there is no dispute that the gist of it was that Burr was on his way down the Mississippi and the time had come to get on with the war for the good of the west and all concerned.

For ten days Wilkinson entertained Burr's agents and encouraged them to think he welcomed the prospect of becoming the eventual military commander of Burr's conquering army-to-be. Then, on October 21st, his whole attitude suddenly changed. He got off a dispatch to Jefferson which revealed in one explosive blast all that he had so long known about Burr's plans. It had been receipt of this confidential message that had triggered the President's violent proclamation. Wilkinson at the same time initiated a conciliatory negotiation with the Spanish commanders which amounted to a local accession to Spanish boundary claims. He thereupon withdrew the bulk of his forces to New Orleans. The apparently imminent war for Texas had by this decisive action of the American field commander been indefinitely postponed.

In New Orleans Wilkinson was able to excite in Governor William C. Claiborne an outward concern to equal his own. Martial law was proclaimed, known Burr agents arrested, the construction of fortifications undertaken, a call issued for volunteers. The city, Wilkinson insisted, was about to be assaulted by Burr's overwhelming army now on its way down the Mississippi and already literally at the gates. Great public excitement and alarm were aroused, which served to distract people's attention from the disappointing and totally unexpected American retreat from the Sabine. Wilkinson even got off a warning of the incipient civil war to the British authorities at Jamaica.

Reaching Bayou Pierre, Burr was stunned by his first news of Wilkinson's letter to Jefferson and of the extravagant preparations being made by Wilkinson and Claiborne to defend New Orleans against him. A body of Natchez militia, taking their courage in their hands, made a dramatic all-night pull with muffled oars to confront the fearsome invader, ready to sacrifice themselves, if necessary, to delay his onrush. Burr's tiny force sardonically surrendered, after hastily disposing of their arms in the river, and Burr professed to have no idea what all the uproar was about. The sheepish militia returned with their prisoners. The bubble of public apprehension had burst. A Natchez grand jury cleared Burr and denounced the gratuitous public hysteria promoted by Wilkinson and Claiborne.

But Burr remained a military prisoner. He expressed fears for his personal safety if he were to continue long in Wilkinson's custody and contrived an escape through the Gulf coast swamps disguised in old clothes and a floppy white hat. He had hoped to gain the sanctuary of a British ship at Pensacola and leisure to prepare his defense. But his luck which had been so bad took a sharp turn for the worse. He had drawn in his horse before a cabin after nightfall to inquire the way to a nearby plantation where he proposed to spend the night. Nicholas Perkins, a young frontier lawyer, coming to the door, caught a glimpse of the face under the white hat. He had never seen Aaron Burr but something told him that this was he. Perkins routed out the sheriff. After talking to Burr most of the night the sheriff declined to interfere. Perkins rushed to Lieutenant Edmund P. Gaines at nearby Fort Stoddard to insist upon Burr's arrest. The whole countryside protested. Perkins, by now a veritable nemesis, volunteered to take Burr north and Gaines was only too glad to be rid of his embarrassing prisoner. Taking a circuitous route through the back country in order to keep well away from settled communities where the populace might take action to free Burr, Perkins delivered his captive to the authorities in Virginia and went on to Washington to receive the thanks of the President together with a reward of $3331.

Throughout this rigorous journey Burr seethed with indignation. His private papers had been seized, he had been allowed to communicate with no one, he had been treated as unceremoniously as a common criminal. But upon his arrival in Richmond he recovered his morale. The eyes of the country were upon him. He was now to have his day in court and he knew well how to play his part in such an arena. Friends and Republicans and westerners had rallied to his support. The President was being widely condemned for having himself so quickly condemned Burr without a hearing. Vastly encouraged, Burr took charge of his own defense.

The young nation had until then known no such political sensation. It was a state trial not to be exceeded in public interest until the impeachment of Andrew Johnson. The man who had so narrowly missed becoming President and who had so recently been Vice President was being accused of high treason. The President who had gained that highest office at his expense was his foremost accuser. Chief Justice John Marshall of the Supreme Court of the United States was presiding, on account of the importance of the issue, over the Federal District Court for Virginia before which the prisoner had been haled. The principal witness against Burr was the commanding general of the Army of the United States. His defense counsel was headed by Edmund Randolph who had been Governor of Virginia and Washington's Secretary of State. His most vehement and headlong defender, as well as the severest and loudest critic of Jefferson's action, was the rising idol of the west, Andrew Jackson. The prosecution staff included Caesar Rodney, Attorney General of the United States, Colonel George Harvey, United States District Attorney and son-in-law of James Monroe, and William Wirt, special prosecutor personally selected by Jefferson. The grand jury was of unprecedented distinction, being composed largely of men who had been United States senators, governors of Virginia, and members of Congress.

The proceedings against Burr struck an immediate roadblock. Marshall refused to commit the prisoner for high treason and held him on the lesser charge of high misdemeanor. The prosecution thereupon undertook the presentation of the broad outlines of the government's case to the grand jury. These principal charges, few of which were ever to be denied by the defense, dealt with Burr's movements, conversations, and preparations during the period his treason was alleged to have been committed. After hearing the essence of the government case, the distinguished Richmond grand jury indicted Burr for high treason, along with Blennerhasset and five other associates, including Jonathan Dayton, former member of the Constitutional Convention and United States Senator from New Jersey, and John Smith, United States Senator from Ohio. The indictment specifically charged Burr with levying war against the United States at Blennerhasset Island and proceeding down the Ohio with the design of taking possession of New Orleans, all within the District of Virginia and the jurisdiction of the court.

Meanwhile, some of the initial delay in getting the trial under way had been due to the failure of Wilkinson, the government's principal witness, to put in an appearance. Marshall had enlivened the interlude by acceding to the defense's demand that the President be required to lay before the court Wilkinson's dispatch to him and the even more critically significant cipher letter alleged to have been sent Wilkinson by Burr. Marshall issued a subpoena directing Jefferson to appear in person with the two documents. If the purpose was to infuriate Jefferson, the effort was a distinct success. Jefferson heatedly refused to recognize the court's power to summon him. In addition, taking a position with a familiar ring in our own day, he directed officers of his administration to disclose only such army and navy activities as were in the interest of national security.

When at last Wilkinson had arrived, he became the center of almost as much public attention as Burr. His conceivable motives were as much the subject of bitter dispute. Not only in the courtroom but throughout the country there was the same sharp cleavage of opinion, with most Republicans, except for the angry President, holding the view that Burr was being victimized by Jefferson and Wilkinson, and most Federalists countering with the assertion that it was no more than natural for Republicans to be indulgent of treason. But it was more difficult to come up with an intelligible defense for Wilkinson than for Burr. It was uneasily recognized even by his defenders that had he not, at the last moment, turned on Burr the enterprise might have scaled unpredictable heights instead of collapsing into a comic-opera fiasco. To all good westerners, whose views were repeatedly voiced by Andrew Jackson in impromptu public speeches on any Richmond street corner, Wilkinson was of a lower order than Judas Iscariot. The border war with Spain, with all its advantages so obvious to every perceptive westerner, with Texas and possibly Mexico within reach, had been at the brink. All this Wilkinson had thrown away. After leading Burr on to that dreadful and critical last moment, he had fiendishly betrayed him. Wilkinson had himself been a westerner for the last twenty years. What, demanded Jackson, could have led him at this supremely crucial hour for the west to have dashed the west's fondest hopes?

The answer was not an administration secret being wilfully withheld from the court by a headstrong President. Only Spanish governors and ministers could, had they chosen, have enlightened either the court's judgment or the public's curiosity. Their explanation of Wilkinson's motive would have been more damning than Jackson's cruelest jibes. They could have testified that during the years of Spanish-American rivalry on the Mississippi this man who had commanded the Army of the United States under three Presidents had continuously served Spain for money. With the purchase of Louisiana and the necessary abandonment of the last Spanish hope of enticing the American west into the Spanish camp, Wilkinson's usefulness to Spain seemed to have diminished. But with the development of the Sabine boundary dispute his value had skyrocketed again. One source close to the Viceroy of Mexico later intimated that his asking price was $110,000, another that it was $200,000. There is no Spanish account that he received anything at this time, but Yrujo had been able to begin as early as November of 1805 to report to his government details of Burr's dealing with Wilkinson and with other confidants. These reports had been so explicit that they included even the circumstance that Pike's exploring expedition was to be accompanied, apparently without Pike's knowledge, by one of Burr's agents. The worldly Yrujo had his own dismayingly simple explanation of Wilkinson's motive. According to him, Wilkinson's course was obvious in that by betraying Burr he could at one happy stroke secure his own preferment in the United States service while at the same time expecting to gain a greater reward from Spain.

In any event, it was Burr who was being tried, not Wilkinson. Government counsel undertook to develop their case against Burr under the indictment for treason. Almost at once their ship foundered on the rock of Chief Justice Marshall's basic ruling on the admissibility of evidence. He accepted the defense's contention, largely argued by Burr himself, that treason, lacking in American law the person of a king to be assailed, required an act of war. Marshall ruled that the case presented at most an intention to commit an act of war and that that intention could not be considered before the act any more than it could be in murder before the act of killing. Since literally the entire prosecution case depended upon a demonstration of Burr's intentions, the Marshall ruling served to bar the introduction of further government evidence.

The jury's verdict said: "We, the jury, say that Aaron Burr is not proved to be guilty under his indictment by any evidence submitted to us. We, therefore, find him not guilty." Burr objected to the wording of the verdict and Marshall ordered it entered on the record as "not guilty." He was promptly tried again on the lesser misdemeanor charge of organizing a military expedition against a foreign prince with whom the United States was at peace. Marshall again ruled against the admissibility of any evidence bearing on intention. The prosecution asked that the jury be discharged but Marshall refused, and the recorded verdict again became "not guilty."

Burr had had his day in court and won. Jefferson had lost, if not to Burr, at least to Marshall and Jackson. But in a larger sense Jefferson had again overcome his flamboyant rival. In the minds of the majority of his countrymen Burr's reputation was irretrievably damaged. He was never to emerge from the cloud of public disapproval.

Of far greater significance than the degree of his guilt or innocence was the one great tangible consequence of his adventure. Generated by the sudden revelation of new prospects provided by the Louisiana Purchase, the pressures of western expansion were building in 1806 to a certain explosion. The slightest border incident on the Sabine would have led immediately and inexorably to a rush of belligerent, land-hungry westerners into Texas. Burr's ill-advised reliance upon Wilkinson instead furnished that confirmed servitor of Spain with a dramatic cover to distract the west's attention from his acquiescence in Spain's boundary claims. When Wilkinson withdrew from his position on the Sabine to arouse

New Orleans against Burr, he was betraying a greater cause than his old friend's. Burr had afforded him the opportunity to stultify the gathering American advance upon Texas. It became a fateful delay. There was to develop no occasion to resume that advance for another forty years.

VI

ॐ

The Shining Mountains

LEWIS AND CLARK had established an American claim to the
Pacific northwest which fitfully persisted until, after nearly a
half century of suspense, American possession had been recognized
by Spain and Russia and in 1846 finally and formally was acknowledged by Great Britain. Of greater immediate significance was the
reaction of the 1806 frontier to the story Lewis and Clark had returned to tell. It was the vigor and duration of this reaction which
made certain that the long suspense was eventually to end as it did.
Upon hearing any report of distant marvels the average frontiersman's overriding impulse was to set out forthwith to see for
himself. The marvels reported by the returning explorers were
truly prodigious—such an abundance of game as no man had ever
imagined, immense ranges covered with perpetual snow, congregations of monster bear, fortunes in beaver in every creek bottom.
To many men standing on the St. Louis waterfront as Lewis and
Clark disembarked the far-off Shining Mountains were already
beginning to gleam with an irresistible appeal.

From its foundation in 1764, St. Louis had been the center of

a western fur trade which had gradually expanded since Frenchmen
had first penetrated the region in 1719. The town's French inhabitants had for generations been as familiar with trade on the
Mississippi, the Wabash, the Great Lakes, and the farthest reaches
of eastern and central Canada as they were now with it on the
lower Missouri. They had from childhood been adept in the two
skills most required—how to get along with Indians and how to
handle any kind of a boat in any kind of water. The town's
American inhabitants had been as familiar for nearly as many
generations with a more violent frontier. They knew Indians only
as enemies and had had little experience with barter and less
patience with poles and towropes, but as individuals they were unrivaled hunters and trappers. Collaboration of these two comple-
mentary types of wilderness experts could bring to bear upon any
effort a conjunction of proficiencies that left no enterprise apparently
impossible.

All that winter and spring St. Louis boiled with discussion and
argument as men sought to organize ventures to take advantage of
the newly revealed opportunity. Expeditions to regions so distant had previously appeared too costly to be undertaken without
governmental support, but the Lewis and Clark breach of the Sioux
blockade together with their report on the quantity of beaver on
the river's headwaters had opened a profit prospect that invited
private investment. If furnished the initial capital for boats, equipment, and trade goods hundreds of men were eager to go. Of the
many parties assembling four were made important by historic
consequences.[1] The first, organized by Manuel Lisa, a veteran
trader long associated with Francis Vigo, whose opportune advice

---

[1] A fifth which might have been the most historic of all totally escaped contemporary American mention and still remains a fascinating mystery. David Thompson, the English trader-explorer, having crossed the Rockies to etsablish a post
near Lake Windermere in British Columbia, noted in his diary August 13, 1807,
an Indian report that a party of 42 Americans was building "a military post
at the confluence of the two most southern and considerable branches of the
Columbia." A few weeks later he received a letter, dated September 29, 1807,
and signed "Lt. Jeremy Pinch," warning him to cease trespassing on American
territory. No other evidence has come to light suggesting the identity of Jeremy
Pinch, the composition of his party, or the wanderers' eventual fate.

had activated George Rogers Clark's conquest of Vincennes in 1779, was preparing to go all the way to the Yellowstone. The second, under Auguste Pierre Chouteau, a West Point graduate and scion of the family which dominated so much of early St. Louis history, was headed for the Mandan. The third, led by young Pierre Dorion, whose father had long lived among the Sioux and whose mother was a Yankton, was to deliver supplies to the family trading establishment with the Sioux. The fourth was a military expedition under Lieutenant Joseph Kimball and Ensign Nathaniel Pryor, recently a Lewis and Clark sergeant, which had been directed to return a Sioux delegation and the Mandan chief, Shehaka, in safety to their respective peoples.

Lisa was something of an outsider in the St. Louis trading community, being neither Frenchman nor American but a Spaniard of South American descent who had been born in New Orleans. With that driving energy and ruthless purpose that throughout his career made him so many enemies, he was first to be ready to start. Aside from his native abilities Lisa had two enormous advantages. His partner was the uniquely experienced George Drouillard, who had been in the mountains with Lewis and Clark, and his backer was William Morrison, the most powerful mercantile firm in the Mississippi Valley. The other three expeditions decided to join forces to gain the greater safety of numbers. Frederick Bates, acting governor of the Territory of Upper Louisiana since Jefferson's March 3, 1807, removal of Wilkinson as governor, urged Lisa to wait for them so that the combined force might more successfully confront possible Sioux and Aricara opposition to their passage. Lisa, however, determined to wring any advantage of being first upriver, left April 19, 1807, before the others were ready.

He gained the first reward for his intransigence at the Platte. A lone canoeman was sighted paddling downriver. It was John Colter.[2] Having spent the past winter trapping the precise area to which the expedition was proceeding, his extraordinary value to

---

[2] The circumstances under which he had parted from Dickson and Hancock remain unclear. Dickson was known to have survived and later became a prominent settler on the Illinois and Wisconsin frontiers.

it was self-evident. Of his own inclination there might well have been more doubt. Since leaving with Lewis and Clark in the spring of 1804, he had for three interminable years been subjected without intermission to all the rigors, hardships, and dangers of existence in the farthest wilderness. No clearer light could be shed on the typical frontiersman's anxiety lest he miss some opportunity for new adventure than was cast by Colter's ready acquiescence in the proposal that he turn back again toward the mountains.

Lisa had no trouble with the Sioux but the Aricara refused him permission to pass. They were again at war with the Mandan and were bent upon denying supplies to their enemy. Lisa gave a striking demonstration of his talent for managing savages. By marshaling his men and bringing his cannon to bear, he proclaimed his readiness to fight but, at the same time, he cheerfully offered a portion of his trade goods as blackmail while confidentially assuring the Aricara that just behind was a much larger American expedition which would furnish them all they required. They let him pass. He got past the Mandan and the Minnataree by the same shrewd tactics. By November 21, 1807, he was building on the Yellowstone at the mouth of the Big Horn a fort he called Fort Raymond, also known as Fort Lisa and better known as Fort Manuel. This lodgment of private adventurers represented a westward lunge in the westward movement of the frontier that dwarfed all former advances. The nearest American settlement was Boone's, 2000 miles downriver.

The Kimball-Pryor-Chouteau-Dorion expedition got off two weeks later than had Lisa, hoping to overtake him. No one ever overtook Manuel Lisa. At the Sioux, Dorion dropped off and Kimball returned to St. Louis with his portion of the army detachment which was considered no longer needed. Pryor, escorting Shehaka homeward, and Chouteau, planning to establish a trading post at the Mandan, kept on northward with some 50 men. Remembering the Aricara welcome of Lewis and Clark, Pryor had anticipated no difficulty with them. But the Aricara could not be reconciled to the safe passage of their enemy's supplies and their enemy's chief. They interrupted negotiations with a sudden attack in which 4 Americans were killed and 9 wounded and from which the expedition's boats were with the greatest difficulty extricated and withdrawn downstream. Pryor proposed taking Shehaka the rest of the way home by an overland route around the Aricara towns but the old chief, encumbered by his family, discreetly declined. The American commander was therefore obliged to retreat to St. Louis with his undelivered charge, now become a symbol less of American might than of American impotence. This had been the first engagement of the United States Army west of the Mississippi. It had resulted in an Indian triumph and a disastrous lowering of American prestige on the upper river.

While Pryor and Chouteau were retiring disconsolately down the Missouri, Lisa on the Yellowstone was energetically striving to take advantage of the advanced location he had attained. His operation, as did all succeeding his, depended on two parallel processes to gain the returns necessary to the success of a profit-seeking enterprise. Beaver were diligently trapped by the company employees and by free trappers attached to the party. At the same time trade goods were held in readiness to be exchanged for the much larger amount of fur it was hoped could be secured by barter with Indians. The Indians of the region, however, had never before had experience with traders, and it was necessary first to contact them in order to acquaint them with the novel opportunity that had so suddenly opened to them. Colter was selected for this intricate task. Work had scarcely begun on the new fort before he set out on snowshoes to drum up Indian business. In the following months he ran the gauntlet of such a succession of extraordinary adventures as could only have been experienced by an utterly fearless man exposed to the myriad hazards of that country in that time.

Colter had crossed and recrossed the mountains with the Lewis and Clark expedition in summer and fall but now he crossed and recrossed them alone in midwinter.[3] He became the first white

[3] There was testimony to his route in the geographical data he later furnished William Clark which was incorporated in the map accompanying the 1814 first edition of the *History of the Lewis and Clark Exploration* prepared for publication by Nicholas Biddle, Paul Allen, and George Shannon.

man of record to see Wind River, the Absaroka Mountains, Jackson Lake, the Tetons, Pierre's Hole, and many of the wonders of Yellowstone Park. The volcanic area about the sources of the Yellowstone across which he ranged in midwinter was in territory so inaccessible that it was to be seldom visited at any season by later mountain men, who were content to refer to it from a distance as "Colter's Hell," and it was not fully explored until 1870. In the course of his journeying he was so successful in making friends with the Indians whose favor he had been commissioned to cultivate that in 1808 he had assembled some hundreds of Crow and Flathead who had agreed to accompany him to Fort Manuel to trade. The Crow and Flathead, however, were traditionally the bitterest enemies of their neighbors, the Blackfeet. The ultrabelligerent Blackfeet had not been irreparably antagonized by the Lewis engagement in 1806 which they had judged a justified resistance to a brazen robbery attempt, but this effort to provide their principal enemies with a major supply source appeared to them a development in intertribal power politics which they could not tolerate. They fell in overwhelming force upon the Crow-Flathead column near Three Forks. Colter, necessarily participating in the ranks of his new friends, was wounded in the battle. The event was as significant as had been Samuel Champlain's estrangement of the Iroquois in 1609. For the next 23 years, the supremely critical period of British-American rivalry in the mountains, the Blackfeet remained invariably and inveterately hostile to all Americans whenever they were encountered.

After his return to Fort Manuel and recovery from his wound, Colter attempted in the fall of 1808 to establish more amicable relations with the Blackfeet. Again he invaded their territory but this time with more circumspection. With one companion, John Potts, a fellow veteran of the Lewis and Clark expedition, he returned to Three Forks to trap the Jefferson River. He assumed that the appearance of only two men could not be regarded by the Blackfeet as a threat and that negotiations leading to a reconciliation might develop. The Blackfeet descended upon them as had been expected. Colter surrendered with a view to establishing pacific communications. But Potts became confused and attempted to escape. When he was pierced by one arrow, he shot one of his assailants. He was instantly transfixed by innumerable arrows. Whatever chance Colter had had to parley had been lost. To provide sport for his enraged captors he was stripped naked and told to run for his life. Young warriors then pursued him in a competition to determine the most fleet in which the prize was the opportunity for the winner to sink his spear into the back of the fugitive.

The game proved less entertaining than the Blackfeet had anticipated. Colter ran so fast that he outdistanced all of them except one. Though he strained until blood gushed from his nostrils, this one continued gradually to gain until the gap was closing to a distance permitting him to hurl his spear. Colter turned suddenly to confront him which so startled the Indian that he fell, breaking the spear. Colter snatched up the pointed end, killed the Indian, ran on to the riverbank and plunged into the water where he found refuge under a mass of driftwood lodged against an island. Here he could remain submerged and concealed, while still able to breathe through the cracks in the irregular pile. Though the furious Indian search failed to locate him, he found little comfort in his temporary safety for he was haunted by the thought that, since it was standard Indian hunting practice to rely on fire to drive game from cover, they must surely be preparing to set fire to the tangle of dried driftwood extending above the water line. To his infinite relief, the device did not occur to them.

After dark he floated undetected downstream, crept ashore, and set off for Fort Manuel. His bare feet were lacerated by the prickly pear so profuse in the region until they became swollen and bleeding stumps, his nakedness was plagued by the day's heat and the night's cold, and he was progressively weakened by hunger but he made the 300 miles in 7 days. This travel average of more than 40 miles a day would have been in itself a striking achievement for any man on foot, however well he was equipped, shod, and fed.[4]

---

[4] Colter's escape was described in detail in the writings of his fellow trapper, Thomas James, and of the English naturalist, John Bradbury, both of whom

And he had not been subdued by even so harsh an experience. That winter he returned alone to Three Forks to pick up his traps. Again he was jumped by Blackfeet and again he escaped, this time by scaling a cliff. Among companions memorable for daring and hardihood John Colter still stood out.

Lisa returned to St. Louis in August of 1808 to assemble more men and supplies. From now on the tremendous 2000-mile journey to the Big Horn would cease to be regarded as an extraordinary feat. St. Louis was still a frontier village of less than 200 houses but it was stirring with new growth and new energies. The year before, Lewis[5] had been appointed governor of the Territory and Clark, Indian Agent and brigadier general of its militia. Lisa had brought back a respectable cargo of beaver, had left the Yellowstone before Blackfeet hostility had developed, and his report on mountain conditions was optimistically favorable. St. Louis seethed with enthusiasm. Every most influential citizen rushed to share in the apparently widening opportunity. On March 7, 1809, the Missouri Fur Company was organized. Among the 10 partners were Lisa, Clark, Wilkinson's nephew, Benjamin, Lewis' brother, Reuben, Morrison's associate, Pierre Menard, Pierre Chouteau, and Andrew Henry. It was the last who was to contribute the most to the project and to many of its kind which followed. Henry became the expedition's most active field commander and for the next 15 years continued to serve as the foremost leader of mountain enterprises. He had been born on the Pennsylvania frontier during the border wars of the Revolution and from his earliest childhood had known experiences which had prepared him for the brutal responsibilities that would henceforth weigh upon him.

---

heard the story directly from Colter. The attendant circumstances were of course known to everyone then at Fort Manuel.

[5] On October 11, 1809, while en route to Washington, Lewis died by violence in an isolated cabin in a Tennessee canebrake. His great friend, Jefferson, who knew how perturbed Lewis had been by certain criticisms of his official accounts, assumed that it had been suicide. Most evidence indicated murder and robbery.

This first Missouri Fur Company[6] expedition had taken on such proportions that it did not get off until the middle of June. There were so many disagreements among the 350 self-willed recruits that nearly a half deserted or were discharged before reaching the recently established U.S. Army post, Fort Clark, 375 miles up the Missouri, but the party was still so strong that no serious difficulty was expected with the Sioux or Aricara.[7] Anticipating this prospect, Lewis had contracted with the company for the safe delivery of the long-suffering Shehaka. No opposition developed and the Mandan chief was returned to his home September 24, 1809, three years after his departure to see the sights of the United States. It had been hoped that his people would be so impressed by his account that all would understand the value of courting the favor of the United States. Instead, they regarded their chief's stories as totally incredible and after his return he lost most of his influence over them.

The start had been too late to keep on to the Yellowstone and the expedition went into winter quarters at the Mandan. Colter was waiting there and early in the following March guided a party under the command of Menard overland to Fort Manuel and then on to Three Forks where a fort was erected. Travel across the northern plains was exceptionally rigorous at such a season and there had been much added suffering from snowblindness. But Menard had been driven by a double purpose. He needed to reach Three Forks in time to take advantage of spring trapping and he wanted to flaunt the company's defiance of the Blackfeet by establishing a position there in such strength.

Both purposes were defeated. The process of trapping required a dispersal of men to tend scattered trap lines which left them vulnerable to piecemeal attack, while the only response of the Blackfeet to this new invasion of many white men was an un-

[6] A commercial syndicate founded May 5, 1794, The Company for the Exploration of the Country West of the Missouri, had functioned briefly during the Spanish regime.

[7] One of the party was Thomas James who wrote a book about his experiences, *Three Years Among the Indians*, which was eventually published in St. Louis in 1916.

relenting determination to expel them. On one day in mid-April, 5 of the trap tenders were killed and, when a few days later 3 more were killed, one of those lost was the wilderness-wise Drouillard who had survived so many former perils. The Blackfeet made no attempt to assault the fort but their investment of the entire area made trapping impracticably hazardous. At the same time the grizzlies of the region, excited by so much unnatural commotion and perhaps by feeding on the dead, became so much more aggressive that the hard-pressed trappers feared them more than they did the Blackfeet. Maintenance of the post was clearly becoming useless, inasmuch as it could not serve as a workable base for either trapping or trading.

On April 21, 1810, Menard wrote the disastrous news to Pierre Chouteau. Colter took the letter overland to Fort Manuel and then by canoe down the Missouri to St. Louis in the miraculous time of 30 days. Finally back in the settlements after six uninterrupted years in the wilds, he experienced one of those revulsions of feeling to which the hardiest mountain man was occasionally subject. He firmly decided to settle down, became a neighbor of the Boones and married to seal his resolution.

Menard with a portion of the party returned to St. Louis in July of 1810 with the limited amount of furs that had been accumulated. Henry remained at Three Forks making ineffectual efforts either to drive off the Blackfeet or to lure them into peace negotiations. Finally convinced that operations were impossible in Blackfoot country, in the fall he led the remnant of his party southwest over the divide to build a post in Shoshone country on a headwater of the Snake, threafter called Henry's Fork. The new location proved an insufficient answer for it was too remote to keep supplied and was still exposed to threat of attack by the widely ranging Blackfeet. Henry was a businessman as well as a mountain man. In the spring of 1811 he returned to the Big Horn, abandoned that post, and marched overland to join Lisa at a new Fort Manuel at the Aricara. Submitting to the pressures of so many threats and difficulties, the Missouri Fur Company had withdrawn not only from its more advanced posts, on the Snake, at

Three Forks, and at the mouth of the Big Horn, but even from its post at the Mandan. The first organized effort to establish the American fur trade in the mountains had been a ruinous and total failure.

However, a coincidental, utterly disorganized effort was to lead to entirely different consequences. Many of the men with Henry had not been company employees but free trappers able to make their own decisions. Most had declined to accompany the withdrawal and chosen instead to continue to seek their fortunes in the mountains. Their dispersal that fall of 1810 and spring of 1811 had scattered men carrying traps and rifles throughout that great expanse of unknown country between the headwaters of the Missouri and those of the Rio Grande. To those who survived these remarkable wanderings it would remain no longer unknown. There was no governmental or military or fur company head-quarters to which it was their duty to report their findings. They were concerned chiefly with the satisfaction of their own curiosity. But they did contribute materially to the frontier's gradually developing grasp of western geography. The majority of those who set out, singly or in groups of two or three or a dozen or a score, from the company posts being abandoned on the Snake and the Big Horn never again reappeared, but enough of them regained the frontier to add their reports on what lay directly westward across the plains to what had already been learned of the upper Missouri in the far northwest by Lewis and Clark, Lisa, Henry, and Colter. To all later ventures there was thereafter available the counsel of men who had spent years roving through those distant mountains of which so recently nothing whatever had been known. Most of these mountain men of 1810 and 1811 had remained un-identified but the experiences of enough of them gained contemporary notice to establish the pattern of their amazing peregrinations.

Edward Rose, with the special frontier stamp of having been the offspring of a trader and a Cherokee-Negro woman, ranged alone until he was befriended, adopted, and accepted as a principal chief by the Crow, a position that made his favor much sought after by every later mountain enterprise. Edward Robinson, John Hoback, and Jacob Reznor, Kentuckians who were inseparable and only to be distinguished one from the other by the circumstances that Robinson was so much older, 66, and had been scalped in his youth, trapped the headwaters of the Snake, crossed the mountains and the plains to the Missouri, encountered the northbound Astorians,[8] returned with them as far as the Snake and there resumed their trapping. Archibald Pelton, intermittently deranged by his misadventures with Blackfeet and grizzlies, wandered alone northwestward for months before being picked up by the Astorians on the Columbia. Ezekiel Williams with a party of 19 struck south from the Big Horn to trap the headwaters of the South Platte and the Arkansas. The group separated into smaller parties more suited to trapping, some pushing westward over the mountains, some being killed by Indians, some being captured by Spaniards, and some making their way eventually to Santa Fe where they made contacts leading to the establishment of a secondary base for American free trappers and to the initiation of the Santa Fe trade. Williams himself escaped an Arapaho captivity, descended the Arkansas alone in a canoe, trapping en route, was robbed of his furs by the Kansas, and finally reached his home in Boone's settlement in September of 1813, four years after he had left with the Missouri Fur Company expedition.

It was such heedlessly roaming adventurers as Williams and Robinson and Hoback and Reznor and Rose and even Pelton who were the true pacemakers for the American way west. To such men as they the terrors of the mountain—distances, blizzards, duststorms, starvation, Indians, grizzlies—had become familiar and acceptable. It was their reckless irresponsibility that removed the sting from the grievous American repulse at Three Forks. They had transformed a great defeat into a greater victory.

[8] See Chapter VIII.

VII

❦

The Great Earthquake

DURING MORE THAN A HALF century of tribulation the inhabitants of the frontier had grown accustomed to the many long familiar dangers of border existence when, in 1811, they were subjected to a more elemental threat against which there could be no resistance and from which there could be no escape. They were staggered by an earthquake of a severity matching any ever recorded and of a duration never experienced elsewhere. After a number of preliminary shivers and rumblings the first great convulsion came December 11, 1811. This was followed by a series of tremendous quakes December 16th and 17th and by two even greater January 23rd and February 7th of 1812. The earth did not once cease to tremble through all of 1812 and intermittent quivers continued for the next seven years. The center of violence was along the shores of the Mississippi below the mouth of the Ohio, but the radiation outward of gradually decreasing intensity produced occasional shocks that drove people into the open everywhere west of the Appalachians. Residents of New Orleans, Charleston, Washington, and Baltimore were astonished by the repeated tremors which were perceptible as distant as the shores of the Gulf and the Atlantic. Terrified Indians far up the Missouri were counseled by British traders to hold American malice responsible for the unprecedented shaking of the earth. The extent of the earthquake's effect westward across the plains and mountains remains uncertain and it could have been only a coincidence that late in 1812 a series of exceptionally violent shocks destroyed missions in California. That so monstrous and general a phenomenon should have gained so little notice in American history, and none at all in American folklore, is one of the stranger anomalies of our career as a people.

This fading from the public's memory could not have been due to a lack of contemporary evidence bearing on the catastrophe. The earthquake was throughout 1812 a principal topic of conversation in every section of the United States. West of the Appalachians people were almost daily reminded by recurrent shakes which as far east as Frankfort and Cincinnati threw dishes from shelves and made walking difficult. Westerners tended to become inured to the threat, as do villagers on the slopes of a volcano. Alexander Sampson of Little Prairie told of a traveler, who had started up in alarm upon hearing the subterranean rumble, being soothed by his hosts with the comforting assurance that "it was only the earthquake." Letters, diaries, and newspapers of the time were filled with detailed eyewitness accounts. The noted and widely traveled frontier preacher, Timothy Flint, made it his fascinated practice to record the earthquake stories of each locality he visited. Scientific observers of the stature of John Bradbury and John James Audubon wrote at length of their personal experiences. A committee of Congress took hundreds of pages of testimony from survivors as a preliminary to the passage of a relief appropriation for the sufferers, hundreds of whom had lost not only their homes but the land on which their homes stood.[1]

The major loss of life suffered from the initial onset of the earth-

---

[1] The most complete survey of all evidence bearing on the earthquake and its consequences is presented by Myron L. Fuller in "The New Madrid Earthquake" (*U.S. Geographic Bulletin* 494), Washington 1912.

quake was visited upon river traffic. Hundreds of keelboats, barges, and flatboats were as usual on the river. The banks of the Mississippi were strewn for hundreds of miles with the debris of flatboats and their cargoes. Listing of casualties was not possible. The boats had been isolated when wrecked. Most of the voyage from the Falls of the Ohio to New Orleans was through uninhabited country. Friends and families of those lost could only begin to guess the worst when after months the missing had still not returned. Bradbury, then en route from St. Louis to New Orleans with a French boat crew, wrote a vivid account of his experience with the first series of shocks:

> I resolved to wait until morning, and caused the boat to be moored to a small island . . . After supper we went to sleep as usual; and in the night, about ten o'clock, I was awakened by a most tremendous noise, accompanied by so violent an agitation of the boat that it appeared in danger of upsetting . . . the four men who slept in the other cabin rushed in, and cried out in the greatest terror, 'O mon Dieu. Monsieur Bradbury, qu'est ce qu'il y a?' I passed them with some difficulty, and ran to the door of the cabin, where I could distinctly see the river agitated as if by a storm; and although the noise was inconceivably loud and terrific, I could distinctly hear the crash of falling trees, and the screaming of the wild fowl on the river, but found that the boat was still safe at her moorings. I was followed by the men and the *patron*, who, in accents of terror, was still enquiring what it was: I tried to calm them by saying, '*Restez vous tranquil, c'est un tremblement de terre*,' which term they did not seem to understand . . . the perpendicular banks, both above and below us, began to fall into the river in such vast masses, as nearly to sink our boat by the swell they occasioned . . . we consulted together, and agreed to send two of the men up the bank, in order to examine if it had separated from the island, a circumstance that we suspected, from hearing the snapping of the limbs of some drift trees . . . At about nearly half-past two, I resolved to go ashore myself, but whilst I was securing some papers and money, by taking them out of my trunks, another shock came on, terrible indeed, but not equal to the first . . . I went ashore, and found the chasm really frightful, being not less than four feet in

width, and with the bank sunk at least two feet. I took the candle to examine its length, and concluded that it could not be less than eighty yards; and at each end, the banks had fallen into the river . . . Before we completed our fire, we had two more shocks, and others occurred during the whole night . . . I had already noticed that the sound which was heard at the time of every shock, always preceded it at least a second, and that it uniformly came from the same point, and went off in an opposite direction . . . At daylight we had counted twenty-seven shocks during our stay on the island, but still found the chasm so that it might be passed. The river was covered with foam and drift timber, and had risen considerably, but our boat was safe . . . Two men were in the act of loosening the fastenings, when a shock occurred nearly equal to the first in violence. The men ran up the bank, but before they could get over the chasm, a tree fell close by them and stopped their progress . . . We continued on the river till eleven o'clock, when there was another violent shock, which seemed to affect us as sensibly as if we had been on land. The trees on both sides of the river were most violently agitated, and the banks in several places fell in, within our view, carrying with them innumerable trees, the crash of which falling into the river, mixed with the terrible sound attending the shock, and the screaming of the geese and other wild fowl, produced an idea that all nature was in a state of dissolution. During the shock the river had been much agitated, and the men became anxious to go ashore: my opinion was, that we were much safer on the river . . . We did not experience any more shocks until the morning of the 17th, when two occurred; one about five and the other about seven o'clock. We continued our voyage, and about twelve this day, had a severe shock, of very long duration. About four o'clock we came in sight of a log-house, a little above the Lower Chickasaw bluffs.[2] More than twenty people came out as soon as they discovered us, and when within hearing, earnestly entreated us to come ashore. I found them almost distracted with fear, and that they were composed of several families, who had collected to pray together. On entering the house, I saw a bible lying open on the table. They informed me that the greatest part of the inhabitants in the neighborhood had fled to the hills, on the opposite side of the river, for

2 Site of the present Memphis.

safety; and that during the shock, about sunrise on the 16th, a chasm had opened on the sand bar opposite the bluffs below, and on closing again had thrown the water to the height of a tall tree. They also affirmed that the earth opened in several places back from the river. One of the men, who appeared to be considered as possessing more knowledge than the rest, entered into an explanation of the cause, and attributed it to the comet that had appeared a few months before, which he described as having two horns, over one of which the earth had rolled, and was now lodged betwixt them.

Bradbury was well advised in his judgment that it was safer afloat than ashore. The center of greatest disturbance was in the 100-mile radius about the conjunctions of the present states of Missouri, Tennesee, Arkansas, Kentucky, and Illinois. The most considerable settlement in the area was New Madrid which led to the cataclysm being commonly termed the "New Madrid Earthquake." In this region of maximum violence the greater shocks were accompanied either by sounds resembling terrific explosions or by a vast rumbling that culminated in a roar infinitely louder than thunder. They appeared to approach, depending on the observer's location, either out of the northwest or the northeast so that there were sometimes seconds of awful warning that another wave of devastation was about to break. During the severer quakes the earth rose or subsided by many feet. Where forests existed they were leveled in a crashing deluge of splintering timbers. In more open country the surface of the earth could be seen to undulate in regularly advancing waves proceeding at about the pace of a trotting horse. The extreme dislocation of the land's conformation resulted in the emptying of some lakes and the creation of others. The course of streams was altered, in some instances by miles. On one occasion a stretch of the Mississippi flowed northward for several hours. At times day became as dark as night and for weeks the sky was veiled by a yellow haze that hid the sun.

Most terrifying of the earthquake's manifestations were the chasms which opened with sounds described as like tremendous claps of thunder followed by the dimishing cracking and grumbling of a great sheet of ice. Some of these openings were circular holes resembling the vents of small volcanoes from which escaping gases, steam, and water shot high in the air or which emitted glistening black or dead white protrusions of rock from substrata never before exposed to man's view. More often the openings came in the shape of long fissures, some no more than a few feet wide and others as much as thirty. From these yawning cracks, some described as being "as deep as a well" and others as apparently bottomless, erupted sulphureous fumes, upheavals of an ashlike white sand, blasts of carbonized dust, or great geysers of water. These fearful fissures appeared always to open parallel to the advancing waves of each new disturbance and refugees soon learned to run to the nearest prostrate tree that chanced to lie at right angles. To this they clung astride in the hope of saving themselves were another crack to open beneath their feet.

After the first shocks, crowds of stupefied fugitives fled to higher ground to escape the floods, their flight made more difficult by the necessity of bridging chasms en route. Great numbers of equally stupefied wild animals, bear, deer, wolves, panthers, pressed close among them, apparently seeking the unnatural comfort of human companionship. From the vantage of their refuges on ridges and hilltops, which in most areas seemed less subject to distortion than did the lowlands, the survivors watched with dread the continuing devastation below, meanwhile composing themselves for death by frantic hymn singing and prayer meetings. As the passage of days indicated no prospect of relief from the universal danger, most returned to their ruined homes where they remained in dogged defiance of later shocks. There were even accounts of the perseverance of neighborhood merrymakings through recurrent quakes, the dancers resuming the moment that they could again keep their feet.

The total loss of life among people on land was not great according to most contemporary estimates. This was largely due to the limited population of the area of maximum violence, most of which was entirely uninhabited. The few hundred settlers, most occupying the west bank of the Mississippi in southeastern Missouri, lived in one-story cabins the collapse of which could be readily escaped. The more mortal threats to which they were subjected, if they were able to avoid being engulfed by an opening chasm, were by drowning or by falling trees. Their situation had moreover not been so radically altered as would have been the case with a more developed society. Their land had been ruined, but they were a people already accustomed to moving and they moved on to the lower Missouri or the lower Arkansas. The congressional relief act offered them substitute grants of public land though speculators were able to buy up most of the certificates before the distressed settlers were aware of their rights. Within a generation or two nature had healed most of the scars of the earth's torment. Brush had overgrown the deposits of white sand and black dust, the prostrate forests had rotted, the chasms had been filled by erosion, and the displaced lakes and rivers had begun to seem to belong in their new locations. The mitigation of permanent effects and the excitements of the War of 1812 encouraged public forgetfulness. It was not long before settlers were again pushing into the afflicted area. Some 13,000,000 people now live in the region that was then devastated.

In 1811 the west was being agitated by shocks of its own contrivance which produced more significant consequences than did the great earthquake. Since its emergence as an independent and coherent political force in the 1780's, the west's attitude with regard to the nation's foreign relations had been perpetually and impetuously aggressive. Inspired by the initial success of transmountain expansion, the newly arrived Americans in the Mississippi Valley became dedicated to a continuing and accelerating expansion and a willingness to resort to whatever force might prove required to affect it. Presidents Washington, Adams, and Jefferson had by courageous and adroit statesmanship managed to avert the threats of foreign war repeatedly raised by the west's belligerence. The fourth president, James Madison, was not to be so fortunate.

The west's own foreign policy was simple, definite, and direct and took little or no account of the national government's foreign policy. From the outset it had been marked by a determination to risk whatever seemed necessary for the attainment of three supreme objectives: (1) the perpetual acquisition of more territory, (2) freedom of commerce via the Mississippi, and (3) the expulsion or extermination of all Indians. In the judgment of westerners England's apparent opposition to the attainment of these objectives represented an impediment to the west's progress that could only be removed satisfactorily by war with England. The west's reasoning was forthright on all three counts. First, the most available and valuable new territory was in East and West Florida, both in the possession of Spain, England's current European ally, and thus subject to conquest in the event of war. Second, England's interference with American sea-borne commerce, thought in the east to bear most heavily on New England shippers, had produced a ruinous depression in the west where it had been demonstrated that use of the Mississippi was valueless if western cargoes were barred at sea from the world's markets. On the third count the west was the most immediately exercised. People had become convinced that English traders and English authorities in Canada were engaged in the rearming and reactivation of the Indian confederacy overthrown by Wayne in 1794.

It was the development of this presumed Indian menace that brought the west's agitation to the boil of action. The white settlement line had been pushing inexorably into central Indiana and southern Illinois. Since the Treaty of Greenville in 1794, the cession of many more millions of acres of former Indian land had been extorted by bribes or threats of force. William Henry Harrison, Governor of Indiana Territory, a firm believer in the frontier principle of expulsion and/or extermination, was energetically and callously expediting the process. The sullen Indians could only retreat. Numbering only some tens of thousands, they could not hope successfully to resist the pressures of a white population that now numbered more than 7,000,000. It was in this new Indian crisis that Indian despair elevated a new Indian leader, Tecumseh, upon whose shoulders fell the mantle of the two earlier great advocates of Indian unification, Brant and Pontiac.[3]

Tecumseh had been endowed by birth and experience with the

[3] Pontiac had been assassinated by an obscure Indian assailant in Cahokia in 1769. Brant had died of a lingering illness in his Ontario home, November 24, 1807, at the age of 64.

qualifications and incentives to fit him to become the champion of his people. He was a Shawnee, since 1777 the most consistently belligerent of all Indians. The place of his birth had been destroyed by Kentuckians in 1780. The murdered Cornstalk had been his mentor. As a young warrior he had fought in all the border wars of the Revolution and its aftermath. His father had been killed at Point Pleasant. One brother had been killed on the Tennessee border and another at Fallen Timbers.

A third brother had recently emerged from obscurity to become a religious leader of such fervor that Indians hailed him as the long-awaited Prophet. Formerly a drunken ne'er-do-well, he had suddenly proclaimed his enlightenment as the result of a sojourn in the spirit world. His presence at Tecumseh's side helped to attract Indian attention but at the same time distracted it from Tecumseh's purpose. The Prophet preached a doctrine that aroused intense Indian enthusiasm but that was in practice self-defeating. He advocated not only abstinence from white man's liquor and white intermarriage but the abandonment of all tools, utensils, and weapons of white manufacture from calico to guns. He assured his excited hearers that were they to return wholeheartedly to their original state of simplicity and purity they would no longer need weapons for his supernatural powers would prove sufficient to protect them.

Tecumseh's program for Indian salvation was more worldly. Having won general Indian esteem by his record, his eloquence, and his forceful personality, he counseled them to refrain from provocative actions until unification had given them the strength to set up a certain and successful resistance to further American intrusions. The core of his policy, as it had been of Brant's, was his assertion that land cessions granted by factions or minorities of single nations, as had been those recently negotiated by Harrison, were invalid. Only by the consent of all Indians, he argued, could the birthright of all Indians be abridged. With enormous energy he sought to create that degree of Indian unification that was necessary if Indian resistance was to assume force or importance. He or his emissaries visited every Indian nation from the upper Missouri to the Gulf, exhorting them to abjure intertribal hostilities so that they might present a united front to their common white enemy. Meanwhile, Indian delegations streamed to Fort Malden, the British western headquarters at the mouth of the Detroit River. The British government and Governor of Canada Sir James Craig firmly disavowed any official intention of encouraging Indian hostility to the United States, but Indians continued to receive from English traders, agents, and local commanders increasing quantities of guns and ammunition. The revival of the Indian menace which the west had been imagining was beginning to take on potentially serious substance in 1811.

After an angry conference with Harrison at Vincennes on August 15, 1811, Tecumseh departed on a tour of the southern Indians to rally the Creek, Cherokee, and Choctaw to his cause. Taking a calculated advantage of the Indian leader's absence, Harrison moved swiftly to provoke a premature outbreak of Indian belligerence. With a column of 900 regulars and Kentucky militia he ascended the Wabash to camp November 6, 1811, on the outskirts of the Indian town on Tippecanoe Creek in which the Prophet resided. This threat to the intended capital of the budding Indian confederacy represented a challenge that the angered Indians were bound to resent. Denied Tecumseh's counsel, eager young warriors were readily persuaded by the Prophet that his mystic power rendered them invulnerable to gunfire. Stalking their prey through a cold rain, some 700 Indians attacked Harrison's camp before dawn on November 7th in a surprise assault reminiscent of Little Turtle's terrible pounce upon St. Clair 20 years before, almost to the day. Harrison's troops were better disciplined than had been St. Clair's and after sustaining a loss of 62 killed and 126 wounded successfully beat off the attackers by a series of cavalry charges. The issue had been so close, however, that Harrison had no idea he had won a victory and kept his troops laboring for the next 24 hours on breastworks to guard his camp against an expected renewal of the Indian assault. But the Indians were through. They had suffered losses approximating those of the Americans and there had been the added, more crushing casualty that their faith in the Prophet's magic had been destroyed. Eventually informed by scouts that

Prophetstown had been deserted, Harrison hastily burned the place and withdrew to Vincennes. He had succeeded in his planned confirmation of Indian belligerence but he had driven many more Indians to Fort Malden and had laid the long undefended frontier far more open to Indian molestation than it had been before he marched.

The major consequence of the Harrison campaign was the new excitement it pumped into the west's demand for war with England. At Tippecanoe the Indians had proved to be both well armed and excessively bellicose. Were the flow of military suppies from Fort Malden and Tecumseh's reorganization of the Indian confederation to be permitted to proceed unchecked, the mounting danger to the frontier was self-evident. In the west's jaundiced view the fires of British-Indian intrigue demanded prompt quenching before they became an uncontrollable conflagration. There was in the west no Federalist party to provide a political counterbalance to the war faction. The west was unanimously Republican with all of that party's traditional anti-English prejudice. With this predilection superimposed on the bitter memories of the 20 years of English-Indian depredations during and after the Revolution, the west's belligerent impulse became an irrepressible insistence.

The action taken was characteristically direct. When the new Congress assembled in November 1811, senators and representatives from border states and districts took advantage of the balance between northern and southern interests in Congress to seize control of both houses. The brilliant young Kentuckian, Henry Clay, was elected Speaker of the House and soon had made himself the most powerful figure in the national government. His band of fiery followers demonstrated a singleness of purpose that gained them the epithet, the "War Hawks." They bombarded their colleagues in Congress with daily orations demanding war with Britain, the perennial enemy of every American aspiration. The pressure mounted until Madison reluctantly yielded, and the fateful foreign war which his great predecessors had repeatedly succeeded in averting was formally declared June 18, 1812. That summer of 1812, marching over a trembling earth under a yellowed sky, regiments of western volunteers enthusiastically assembled to make good Clay's boast on the floor of Congress "that the militia of Kentucky are alone competent to place Montreal and Upper Canada at your feet."

The year 1811 which had been agitated by the great earthquake, the Tippecanoe campaign, and the rush toward war with England was marked by another more constructive and equally extraordinary event which had a greater bearing on the west's future than any development since the first crossing of the mountains. The first steamboat to appear on western waters was launched at Pittsburgh. The project was directed by Nicholas Roosevelt of New York who had been associated with the inventor, Robert Fulton, and Chancellor Robert Livingston in the institution of steam navigation on the Hudson in 1807. The *New Orleans* was a midget of a hundred tons with a stern paddle wheel driven by a primitive wood-burning engine. But the contraption worked. The novel craft set off down the historic river that had formerly borne the fleets of the mound-builders, the canoes of explorers, traders, and long hunters, the rafts of Indian raiders, the barges of Clark's conquest, the flat-boats of the pioneers, the *Mayflower* en route to Marietta, Spanish war galleys, Wayne's supply convoys, Wilkinson's silver shipments, the skiffs of river pirates, Pittsburgh-built brigantines destined for the open sea, and innumerable keelboats with their chanting crews straining against their poles and towlines. Its passage, attended by an unprecedented clamor of hissing, clanking, splashing, and the intermittent roar of exhaust steam, was a continuing sensation. At Louisville people tumbled from their beds to stare incredulously at the apparition's arrival in the middle of a moonlit night. Low water prevented an immediate passage of the Falls, and in the interim the *New Orleans* essayed an upstream trip to Cincinnati which it managed at the miraculous rate of three miles an hour. With higher water the voyage was resumed, the fearful perils of the earthquake encountered and survived, and New Orleans reached in safety January 13, 1812.

So far in the west's tumultuous history the region's hope of prosperity or even stability had been inhibited by the basic transportation difficulty inherent in its isolation. Cargoes of any burden could be dispatched with ease downriver but shipments upriver could only be achieved at prohibitive cost. This enormous difficulty was removed by the advent of steam navigation. The normal profits of a normal circulation of commerce had been brought within reach. Within a dozen years the blast of a steamboat's whistle had become a sound as familiar as the cry of a night owl. A giant had been unbound.

VIII

༃

The Astorians

THE ACTIVITIES of incorporated private enterprise had from the
beginning played a significant part in the occupation of North
America by English-speaking peoples. The land schemes of the
Ohio Company had precipitated the war with France which had
culminated in the transfer of Canada and the eastern Mississippi
Valley to England. Land-company manipulations of the Iroquois
cession at the first Treaty of Fort Stanwix had opened the way
to the first crossing of the mountains by American settlers into
western Pennsylvania in 1769. Daniel Boone's Kentucky settlement
in 1775 and James Robertson's Tennessee settlement in 1780 had
both been under the auspices of the Transylvania Land Company.
The first Ohio settlement in 1788 had been promoted by the New
Ohio Company. North of the Canadian border where lack of population limited the value of land the forerunning role of private
enterprise had been assumed by fur companies. The Hudson's Bay
Company had been established on the shores of Hudson Bay since
1668 and had before the end of that century begun the penetration
of the interior. The later and more aggressive North West Com-

pany, based in Montreal, had extended its vast system of water transport and intermediate storehouses so vigorously that by 1810 it had advance posts on the western slopes of the Rocky Mountains. Into this westward race of private enterprise there entered in 1810 an American competitor with as bold a design as any ever framed by the long succession of great merchant adventurers who since the discovery had sought to exploit the opportunities unfolding in the New World.

John Jacob Astor had come to the United States by way of London from his native Germany the year after the Revolution to embark upon a career that could have served as the original model for the Horatio Alger story. He was then just 20 but, like so many former hopeful immigrants, was bent upon making his fortune with the least possible delay. During a trans-Atlantic voyage prolonged by storms he had been intrigued by conversations with a fellow passenger who was a furrier. As a result of this recently and accidentally acquired interest in an unknown field, upon arrival in New York Astor began to deal in furs, one of the more important North American exports of the time. So certain was his business acumen in this peculiarly complex branch of merchandising that during the next 20 years he became the richest man in America. His operations required frequent visits to Montreal where he was captivated by the dramatic mechanics of fur gathering in the remote western wilderness and, in partcular, by the swashbuckling character of the men who were engaged in that extraordinary profession.

As a result of this growing interest in the production as distinguished from the marketing of furs, he undertook the organization of an American fur company on a scale capable of competing in the wilderness with the two powerful and long-established English companies. He proposed at one stupendous leap to preempt the Columbia basin before either could become fully established there. To effect this, his grand design included posts on the Columbia and on the Pacific to be jointly maintained by transport overland from the Missouri and by sea around Cape Horn. The land route was a hedge against the risk of interference by British sea power while his supply ships, after picking up furs at the mouth of the Columbia, were in a position to multiply returns by taking advantage of the China trade. Further to bolster his position he even negotiated a contract to supply the Russian posts in Alaska. It was a completely reasoned and fully developed plan which he had ample capital to implement and which promised to set up a timely barrier to the current British advance to the Pacific. Though essentially a commercial project by which he expected to profit, he was agreeably aware that it was serving his adopted country by affording assurance that the flag raised west of the mountains by Lewis and Clark would continue to fly. Jefferson, the most eminent proponent of American westward expansion, heartily approved, and Astor received many expressions of administration and congressional sympathy.

Evidence was pouring in that his great idea had not come to him a moment too soon. That summer of 1810 when he was completing his plans seemed literally the last hour offering hope of successfully reasserting the American claim to the Pacific northwest. Three rival world powers were in a more advantageous position to make good a prior occupation. Great Britain's westward advance appeared the most immediately threatening. The aggressive thrust of the North West Company's trade empire, outdistancing its more orthodox competitor, the Hudson's Bay Company, had repeatedly penetrated the Rockies to the headwaters of the Columbia. The standard bearer of this westward plunge was David Thompson, the great trader-explorer-geographer whose field maps were of such amazing accuracy that in some areas they have not yet been superseded. Thompson had got across the Canadian Rockies to found Kootenai House near Lake Windermere in 1807. After a 2500-mile round trip to his eastern base of supplies at Rainy Lake, along with a series of lateral explorations seeking better passes, by 1809 he had established two posts, Salesh House and Kullyspell House, in what is now western Montana and northern Idaho. After another many-month struggle to bring up more supplies from Rainy Lake, he was on his way back to the Columbia where in January of 1811 he would prepare to descend the river, as soon as weather and Indian hostility[1] permitted, to plant the British flag at its mouth.

The Russian threat was very nearly as imminent. Aleksandr Baranov, the domineering governor of Russian Alaska, had in 1805, with the approval of Nikolai Rezanov, the Chamberlain of the Czar then making an inspection tour of Russia's farthest frontier, dispatched the ship *Juno* to establish a post at the mouth of the Columbia to which Russia's North American headquarters could be transferred from Sitka. The attempt was frustrated by storms and indifferent seamanship and *Juno* took refuge in San Francisco Bay where the expedition's more memorable accomplishment was Rezanov's romantic wooing of Doña Concepción Argüello.[2] Baranov persisted in his determination to extend Russian dominion southward and by 1811 was establishing a temporary base at Bodega Bay on the California coast in preparation for the erection of Fort Ross.

The third claimant, Spain, having earlier occupied California as a bulwark against the Russian threat in Alaska, was equally exercised by the more recent British and American moves and, in spite of having been rebuffed by the British Nootka ultimatum in 1790, continued stubbornly to assert Spanish possession of the Pacific northwest on the basis of prior discovery. The New York merchant was thus not only challenging these international forces but entering the contest at a moment that seemed already too late.

Thoroughly prepared as appeared his over-all design in all its practical details, Astor made one functional mistake that proved a continuing handicap. With the pragmatic judgment of a business-man he concluded that operations so distant that they would be separated by years from communication with his New York headquarters could only be efficiently conducted by men of proven fur-trade experience. The American fur trade seemed a feeble and

---

[1] English traders had also antagonized the Blackfeet by supplying the Flathead.

[2] She waited faithfully for years, finally became a nun and did not learn until 1842 that he had died in Siberia soon after he had left with his ardent promise to return.

irresponsible infant compared to its gigantic English rivals. He therefore staffed his organization with a preponderance of managers and supervisors who were seasoned Montreal traders and for the rank and file of employees depended almost entirely on that class of French-Canadian boatmen who had for generations been accustomed to the lakes and rivers of the Canadian wilderness. It was presently to develop that these opinionated ex-Northwesters and mecurial engagés [3] were less well equipped to deal either with the pressures of an international rivalry or with the plains, mountains, and deserts of the trans-Missouri west than would have been the kind of American frontiersmen who had made such a success of the Lewis and Clark overland journey.

To one feature of the Astor enterprise was attached an historic importance more enduring than the physical accomplishment itself. The operation was chonicled in vivid detail by men who were participants or eyewitnesses. As in the case of Lewis and Clark, we can accompany the Astorians, almost from day to day, and live with them through adventures and vicissitudes so various and violent that they must otherwise have seemed incredible. An Englishman, a Scotsman, a Frenchman, and an American wrote contemporary books about their observations and experiences that have become frontier classics.[4] In addition, the official history of the enterprise, Washington Irving's famous two-volume work, *Astoria*, possesses much of the authority of a firsthand account. He based his narrative on interviews wth most of the survivors, on their diaries, journals, letters, and reports, and on the company's records and papers. Of so many of the river, plains, and mountain occur-

---

[3] French-Canadians hired by fur companies as boatmen, camp tenders and general service laborers were commonly called *engagés*. If experts of long experience, they were sometimes termed *voyageurs*.

[4] Bradbury, John. *Travels in the Interior of America in the Years 1809, 1810, and 1811*. London, 1819. Reprint, Reuben Gold Thwaites, ed. Cleveland, 1904. Ross, Alexander. *Adventures of the First Settlers on the Oregon or Columbia River*. London, 1849. Reprint, Reuben Gold Thwaites, ed. Cleveland, 1904. Franchère, Gabriel. *Narrative of a Voyage to the Northwest Coast of America*. New York, 1854. Reprint, Reuben Gold Thwaites, ed. Cleveland, 1904. Brackenridge, H. M. *Journal of a Voyage up the River Missouri*. Baltimore, 1816. Reprint, Reuben Gold Thwaites, ed. Cleveland, 1904.

rences of the time we can gain but an occasional tantalizing glimpse. With the Astorians we have a clear and satisfying view of the entire picture.

To assure the diligent application of his field managers, Astor had allotted fifty per cent of the company to participating partnerships. Among the more important partners were Alexander McKay, who had been Alexander Mackenzie's lieutenant on both his transcontinental explorations, four other ex-Northwesters, Duncan Mc-Dougal, Donald McKenzie, David Stuart, and Robert Stuart, and one American, Wilson Price Hunt, of New Jersey. Of these principals, Hunt and McKenzie were assigned to the overland expedition and the others to the sea contingent.

Astor's first ship, the 290-ton, 10-gun *Tonquin*, sailed from New York September 8, 1810, convoyed for a time by the frigate *Constitution* to guard the British-born partners aboard from the danger of impressment by British cruisers. Her master, Jonathan Thorn, was a brave and experienced naval veteran of the Tripolitan War but he was also an arrogant disciplinarian of the Captain Bligh stamp. His bitter quarrels during the voyage with his passengers, the equally self-willed partners, gave premonitory warning of the personal dissensions that would continue to haunt all phases of Astor's enterprise. The voyage around the Horn was swift and favorable until, upon sighting the mouth of the Columbia, 8 men were lost in small boats while attempting to take soundings to guide the ship over the bar. Astoria was founded April 12, 1811, and the American flag which had first been planted by Lewis and Clark on the shores of the Pacific was again flying there.

How narrow had been the margin was demonstrated by the July 15th arrival of David Thompson by canoe down the Columbia. He had been constantly engaged in pushing ahead into the unknown since his original apprenticeship to the Hudson's Bay Company at the age of 15 and had been moved to transfer to the North West Company in 1797 by its more aggressive inclination to extend operations westward. It was with understandable chagrin that, after 28 years of service in the forefront of the British fur trade's westward advance, he was forced to realize that he had reached

his ultimate goal just three months too late. During his descent
Thompson had raised the British flag at that great western wilderness crossroads, the junction of the Snake and the Columbia, but in
July David Stuart with a party of Astorians started upriver to
establish posts to compete with the North West Company for the
fur trade of the interior and thus to tighten the American grasp
on the Columbia. Astor's great project was initially a success.

Tonquin had meanwhile sailed north to trade with coastal Indians and in the process to fulfill her discordant destiny. Alexander
McKay, on board in charge of the company's commercial interests,
had had years of dealing with Indians, but Captain Thorn, holding
to his insistence that he was sole master of all matters pertaining to
his ship, refused to heed his advice. The consequence became known
to the horrified Astoria garrison only through reports brought by
friendly Indians. According to this account Thorn, while at anchor
in Nootka Sound, had permitted as many Indians as chose to come
aboard to engage in trade. The natives of the northwest coast had
had 30 years of experience with sea-borne traders and were no
longer awed by white men or their devices.[5] Once an overwhelming
number had come over the side, at a prearranged signal the Indians
whipped out concealed weapons and attacked, killing 18 of the
ship's company of 23. Thorn and McKay were among the first to
fall. Five seamen who had been in the rigging managed to get
firearms from the cabin, drove the Indians from the deck by musket
fire, and by cannon fire sank a number of their retreating canoes.
Considering themselves too few to handle the ship, four of the
survivors attempted to flee that night by small boat but were
overtaken and put to death by torment. The fifth, the ship's clerk,
James Lewis, had been so seriously wounded that he had elected
to remain with the ship. When the next morning the Indians
swarmed over the undefended vessel to complete their looting, the
magazine exploded, presumably by Lewis' design, destroying ship,

[5] These Nootka Sound Indians had in 1803 captured the trading ship *Boston*,
killing all aboard except John Thompson and John R. Jewitt, artisans whose
services they appreciated. The latter after his eventual rescue wrote a book,
Narrative of the Adventures and Sufferings of John R. Jewitt, published at
Middletown in 1815.

canoes and, according to Indian report, some hundreds of Indians. By the loss of *Tonquin* Astoria was left dependent for future supplies on the next year's ship and on the already overdue overland expedition.

Astor had eventually concluded that an expedition across American territory might better be commanded by an American and had therefore assigned that responsibility to Hunt, to the intense dissatisfaction of Hunt's associate, Donald McKenzie, the ex-Northwester. Hunt was resolute and upright but his only frontier experience had been five years of St. Louis storekeeping and he fell short of being entirely fitted to cope with demands that would have taxed the capacities of a Lewis, a Clark, or a Henry. To reach the starting point at St. Louis was an expedition in itself. Most of the summer of 1810 was devoted to canoe travel from Montreal to the Missouri by way of Mackinac, the Wisconsin, and the Mississippi. It was therefore impossible that season to get more than 450 miles up the Missouri to the mouth of the Nadowa where winter quarters were established November 16, 1810. Hunt returned to St. Louis to improve his preparations which had been much impeded by the jealousy of the Missouri Company and local business interests resentful of Astor's invasion of their area.

He had meanwhile recruited another partner, Ramsay Crooks, an ex-Northwester who had for the past two years been engaged in the Missouri fur trade. At Crooks' suggestion his Missouri associate, the American, Robert McLellan, was also offered a partnership. McLellan was a fantastically expert marksman with a breadth of frontier experience that had included service with William Wells' famous corps of scouts during Wayne's campaign but his extreme irascibility much reduced his usefulness. The partnership of another American, Joseph Miller, who had in 1805 resigned a second lieutenancy in the army to turn trapper, had been arranged before Hunt reached St. Louis. The most useful of the Nadowa recruits was John Day, a Boonslick settler, hunter, and trapper who had been a frontiersman from his earliest boyhood. After setting out a second time from St. Louis in the spring of 1811 to regain his winter quarters, Hunt narrowly missed acquiring the most valuable of all recruits. As the keelboat drew away from Boone's settlement, John Colter ran along the bank after it, all but overcome by his impulse to accompany the expedition. Washington Irving effectively describes his temptation:

> Here they met Daniel Boon, the renowned patriarch of Kentucky, who had kept in the advance of civilization, and on the borders of the wildnerness, still leading a hunter's life, though now in his 85th year.[6] He had but recently returned from a hunting and trapping expedition, and had brought nearly sixty beaver skins as trophies of his skill. The old man was still erect in form, strong in limb, and unflinching in spirit . . . The next morning early, as the party were yet encamped at the mouth of a small stream, they were visited by another of these heroes of the wilderness, one John Colter . . . He had recently . . . known . . . dangers and hardships enough to break down any spirit . . . yet with all these perils and terrors fresh in his recollection, he could not see the present band on their way to those regions of danger and adventure, without feeling a vehement impulse to join them . . . Nothing seems to have kept Colter from continuing with the party to the shores of the Pacific but the circumstances of his having recently married. All the morning he kept with them, balancing in his mind the charms of his bride against those of the Rocky mountains; the former, however, prevailed, and after a march of several miles, he took a reluctant leave of the travellers, and turned his face homeward.[7]

The expedition finally got off to its decisive start from Nadowa on April 21, 1811, in four boats propelled by 40 French *engagés*. On his way up the Missouri, Hunt gathered in an unexpected reinforcement of immeasurable value as he encountered at intervals 6 free trappers from the dispersal of Henry's party who were on their way back to the settlements after years in the mountains: Edward Rose, Benjamin Jones, Alexander Carson, and the inseparable Kentuckians, Edward Robinson, John Hoback, and Jacob Reznor. With the invariable response that had already become traditional all eagerly agreed to return with the expedition to the mountains.

[6] Boone was then 77.
[7] His self-control was imperfectly rewarded. Less than two years later he died of jaundice, under a roof and in bed.

Hunt's experienced boatmen enabled him to make an exceptionally rapid ascent of the river, but Manuel Lisa, striving to overtake him, made one that was even swifter. Lisa, en route to the relief of Henry and the salvage of the Missouri Fur Company's disastrous Big Horn-Three Forks operation, feared that if Hunt reached the upper river ahead of him he might excite Indian hostility against him as he, Lisa, had been accused of doing by Chouteau and Pryor in 1807 and by Crooks and McLellan in 1809. Lisa started from St. Louis April 2nd, 450 miles downriver from Hunt's start at Nadowa, but, with that driving energy of which only he was capable, overtook Hunt June 2nd just above the Great Bend a few miles below the mouth of the Cheyenne. The race was described with all the colorful detail lavished on a modern sporting event by those two eminent reporters, John Bradbury with Hunt and Henry Brackenridge with Lisa. The ill feeling between the two parties, further inflamed by the intransigence of McLellan, flared to the verge of battle before being relieved by Lisa's realization that Hunt, warned by his mountain men recruits of the Blackfoot menace, had decided to abandon the Lewis and Clark route and to strike directly westward from the Aricara. The Astorians thus no longer posed a competitive threat in Lisa's field of operations on the upper Missouri.

Hunt paused at the Aricara for more than a month to complete the purchase from the Aricara and Mandan of enough horses to transport the large stock of supplies which had formerly been carried by boat. His French boatmen, so expert on water, were somewhat nonplussed by this unforeseen change to land locomotion. The party leaving the Aricara July 18, 1811, numbered 65, with 80 horses. Curiously paralleling the personnel of the Lewis and Clark party, this one also included a Negro, Edward Rose, and an Indian heroine, the young Iowa woman, Aioe. Better known as Marie Dorion, she was the wife of the younger Pierre Dorion, the interpreter. Though encumbered by two small children and an advanced pregnancy, she was to prove better able than most of her male companions to endure the hardships ahead.

The departure of the overland Astorians from the Aricara represented the second great step in the American opening of the way west to the Pacific. Lewis and Clark and every later trading expedition had depended entirely on the water-borne transportation afforded by the Missouri to reach the mountains. They had viewed the endless spaces of the country through which they were traveling only when they had paused to climb on foot to the rim of the wooded river bottom. The overland Astorians were the first large and organized party to forsake boats and venture boldly westward across the unfamiliar expanse of the plains, though like all later overland expeditions they were guided by individual mountain men who already knew the way. Hunt was retracing much of the route taken a few months before by Robinson, Hoback, and Reznor on their eastward passage from the headwaters of the Snake to the Missouri.

The decision to cut loose from the Missouri was a startling reversal of all former judgments on the necessities for far western travel, a defiant acceptance of the risks presented not only by the geographical unknown but by the technical unknown. The transfer of so great a weight of goods from the cargo holds of 4 forty-foot keelboats to the packsaddles of 80 horses became at the outset a formidable problem. On the eastern American frontier traders and settlers had for more than a century relied upon packhorse transportation, but this was a venture on a broader scale committed to greater distances and supported by fewer trained horse handlers. Forage for so considerable a cavalcade was uncertain and grazing requirements for such a herd continuously exposed it to Indian horse thieves who had had generations of practice in taking advantage of such opportunities. Hunt, the St. Louis storekeeper, had in a crisis made a decision as momentous and as daring as could any military commander.

The first stages of the overland journey were accomplished with unanticipated ease by a combination of amazing adaptability and some good fortune. Aside from the interposition of the Black Hills, this first crossing of the plains from the Missouri to the mountains acquainted its participants with all those features of plains travel that were later to become so familiar to all who followed their example. There was the same progressive diminution in the availability of water and fuel, the same gradual change from long grass to short grass to bunch grass, greasewood, and juniper, the same necessary resort to buffalo chips and sagebrush for fires, the same intermittent encounters with tremendous herds of buffalo, elk, and antelope, the same perilous increase in the number of grizzlies, and, ultimately, the same dramatic first glimpse of the distant tips of the Rockies.

Their contacts with the Indians of the northern plains, into the heart of whose country they were intruding and who were of all Indians east of the mountains the least known to white men, were more agreeable than had been expected. From the Cheyenne, upon whose cleanliness and friendliness there was much approving comment, Hunt was even able to buy 40 more horses. And despite his dark suspicions that Rose might be planning to deliver them into the hands of the Crow, upon actual contact with these already notorious bandits who were customarily as bent upon stealing horses from their ostensible friends as from their declared foes, they proved equally amiable. Possibly aggrieved by his companions' distrust, Rose chose to remain here with his older friends, the Crow. Continuing to make excellent progress, the Astorians crossed the Big Horn Mountains, ascended Wind River, and scaled the Wind River Mountains, from the crest of which Robinson was able to point out, glittering in the far distance, the three snowy peaks, called by Hunt the Pilot Knobs and later known as the Tetons, beyond which lay the site of Henry's abandoned post, the last known point on their westward course until the Columbia. They were crossing the continental divide by Union Pass, one of the highest in the Rockies where the winds were so contant and fierce that trees grew horizontally, unaware that when they had turned northwestward up the Wind from the Big Horn, had they instead kept on south one more easy day's march they would have come upon the Sweetwater's open and inviting gateway to the mountains.

They paused on the upper Green River to hunt buffalo and recuperate their horses, turned northwestward again into the mountains, left Alexander Carson with three other volunteers to trap the southeastern headwaters of the Snake, crossed Teton Pass, and

reached Henry's former location October 8, 1811. Here Hunt, heed-
ing the clamor of his weary followers, yielded to the temptation to
leave the horses and resort to canoes to descend the apparently
navigable river which was known eventually to empty into the
Columbia. And here Robinson, Hoback, and Reznor were left to
trap in the remote wilderness from which they had once started
home the previous spring. Miller, though a partner, had become
so dissatisfied with mountain travel that he chose also to remain,
along with another trapper, Martin Cass.

After building canoes, the main party cheered and sang as they
began to sweep effortlessly down the Snake at a promising rate
of 30 or 40 miles a day. For nearly 300 miles their progress was
comfortable, rapid, and only impeded by occasional easily portaged
rapids. But they had challenged an unknown river upon which
their encouraging passage so far was leading them to inescapable
disaster. The steadily increasing violence of its flow culminated
October 28th at a rockbound vortex, christened Caldron Linn by
the horrified voyagers, which wrecked the lead canoe, drowned
the expedition's most expert boatman, Antoine Clappine, and unmistakably barred further progress by water. A land reconnaissance
established that river conditions below suggested no possibility of
returning to boat transport at any lower point. Ahead stretched
the totally unnavigable canyon of the Snake.

The full import of their predicament was now apparent. They
had come too far to return to their horses. The fierce rigors of
a Rocky Mountain winter were upon them. Whichever way they
moved they could take with them only such supplies as they could
carry. Starvation was a major threat for they were in the midst
of a barren region devoid of game. Days of desperate consultation
developed a determination to attempt to reach the Columbia on
foot before winter might make all travel impossible.

After burying their goods in nine carefully secreted and separated
caches, they set out in two parties, led respectively by Hunt and
Crooks, taking routes on opposite rims of the precipitous canyon
of the Snake. The winter march became a nightmare of cold, snow,
storms, illness, and starvation. The few wretched Indians encoun-

tered were themselves too hungry in the off season for salmon fishing to part with their desperately hoarded residues of food at any price. The main detachments broke up into smaller groups, each struggling on at whatever pace its enfeebled members could sustain. On December 30th Marie Dorion gave birth to her child. She continued to keep up but the infant died ten days later during the snowbound crossing of the Blue Mountains.

Hopeless as the plight of the distracted and disorganized expedition had for a time appeared, all except Michel Carrière, who wandered from his companions' view in the Blue Mountains, Jean Provost, who was drowned crossing the Snake, and Marie's baby eventually reached the Columbia. The groups led by McKenzie and McLellan had chanced to become reunited while staggering through the mountains bordering the Snake, had gained the Clearwater River on the Lewis and Clark route, and reached Astoria by canoe January 18, 1812. Hunt with the main party arrived there February 15th. Crooks and Day, after being robbed and stripped naked by Indians, were picked up on the Columbia by David Stuart's party returning from Okanogon and reached Astoria May 1st, long after they had been given up for lost. Seven more stragglers finally turned up January 15, 1813.

The arrival of the refugees from the overland expedition represented a reinforcement only in numbers. Astoria had spent a discouraging winter, short of food and fearing Indian assault. The May 6, 1812, arrival of Beaver, Astor's second ship from New York, relieved the supply shortage but there was urgent need to get dispatches to New York to acquaint Astor with his project's situation. Young Robert Stuart was selected to make the overland journey, an effort that in many respects proved more geographically enlightening than had Hunt's trail-blazing westward journey. Only four followers were assigned him, on the theory that a small party could more easily than a large find subsistence in the wilderness: John Day, Benjamin Jones, Andre Valle, and François Leclairc. Day became too ill to proceed but two partners, Ramsay Crooks and Robert McLellan, had become so dissatisfied that they resigned from the company and elected to accompany the eastbound party.

All except Stuart himself had come west with Hunt and had there-fore had much experience, mostly bitter, with Rocky Mountain travel.

Stuart's eastward journey acquired historic importance in that he consciously sought a more passable crossing of the continental divide than that found by Lewis and Clark or Hunt and in that his quest was so successful that much of his route later became that of the Oregon Trail which eventually saved the Pacific northwest for the United States. At the start he began retracing Hunt's westward course, striking from the Columbia across the Blue Mountains to the Snake and then up the west bank of the Snake. Here he met an Indian who told him that south of the mountains enclosing the head of the Snake, through which Hunt as well as Lewis and Clark had struggled, there lay a far more open way east to the plains. The Indian promised to guide them by this new and better way but that night left camp with two horses and whatever else he could steal. Two days later Stuart picked up other clues to the more open southern route. He came unexpectedly upon Robinson, Hoback, Reznor, and Miller, destitute, starving and fishing fran-tically to keep alive. They had trapped with great success the pre-vious winter but had been robbed by Indians of all they had possessed along with the furs they had accumulated.[8] They thank-fully joined the party and, having ranged widely during their trapping excursion, added their testimony to the Indian's assertion that there lay more open country to the south.

Stuart kept on up the Snake to inspect the caches above Caldron Linn. Six of the nine had been looted by Indians who, as it later developed, had been led to the spot by three of the hungry stragglers from Hunt's party willing to make any exchange for food. Among the remaining stores were enough traps, weapons, and ammunition to refurnish Robinson, Hoback, and Reznor. In spite of their long and intimate acquaintance with wilderness peril which had com-

[8] Cass was missing and was never again seen. Unsupported speculation on his disappearance ranged from his companions' assertion that he had absconded with their only horse to the suppositions that he had been adopted by Indians, been killed by Indians, or been eaten by his starving comrades.

menced with the Three Forks disasters, they immediately decided to remain in the mountains to resume trapping. Miller, however, chose to stay with the eastbound party. His "curiosity and desire of traveling thro' the Indian countries," as Stuart's journal put it, had been "fully satisfied."

Upon reaching the Portneuf River, Stuart abandoned Hunt's route and turned south into the valley of Bear River to seek the more open route east reputed to lie in that region. He had come to the very edge of the secret. Here he was but little more than a hundred miles west of South Pass which he must soon have reached had he continued in the direction he was proceeding. But here he also encountered a band of Crow which, considering the weakness of his party, represented a fearful hazard. Forgetting his concern with the way east and thinking first of the need to elude them, he abruptly turned back north again toward the Snake and into an area with which Miller professed to be familiar. The maneuver proved useless for a Crow party trailed him and succeeded in robbing him of all his horses.

To the plains and mountains venturer no threat, except the loss of his life, was so serious and so constant as the loss of his horses. This was an almost total disaster for it immediately increased by so much every distance with which he was confronted. To the Indian the theft of horses from armed and watchful owners was a lifelong preoccupation, the one most certain demonstration of his capacity as a man and a warrior. Practice and tradition had made the performance an art. Representative Indian tactics in achieving this endlessly repeated outrage were described by Stuart in illuminating detail:

> We were all up soon after the dawn and I had just reached the river bank, when I heard the Indian yell raised . . . one of the party rode past our camp and placed himself on a conspicuous knob in the direction they wanted to run them off; when the others (who were hidden behind our camp) seeing him prepared, rose the war-whoop, or Yell, which is the most horribly discordant howling imaginable, being in imitation of the different beasts of prey, at this diabolical noise the animals naturally rose their heads to see

what the matter was—at that instant he who had placed himself in advance, put spurs to his steed, and ours seeing him gallop off in apparent flight, started all in the same direction, as if a legion of infernals were in pursuit of them . . . we rushed and got almost within shot of the nearest when repeated yells in the direction from which they came, made us desist from the pursuit in order to defend ourselves and Baggage; for there being only two Indians after the Horses, we very readily imagined that the main body were in reserve to attack our rear did we follow the foremost, or to plunder the Camp if opportunity offered—At the rate the Horses were going all attempts to rejoin them was unavailing, and had we pursued them further every thing else would have been lost to a certainty, which would undoubtedly have made our situation if possible far more deplorable than it really is.

Now on foot and with winter approaching, Stuart circled erratically through the tangle of mountains clustered about the upper Snake, at one stage drifting by raft *down* that river, until he had picked up Hunt's westward route upon which he turned eastward again. Game was scarce and the party lived precariously on fish and an occasional beaver caught in their one remaining trap. Then even these intermittent resources failed and they became so weakened by hunger that they could barely drag themselves over the successive ranges they were obliged to traverse. Continuing to backtrack along Hunt's route, they circled south of the Tetons and eventually passed from the watershed of the Snake to that of the Green. The eccentric detour had cost them more than a month but, now at the foot of the Wind River Mountains, they were again at the edge of that "more open country to the south."

Despite the lost time and the grueling hardships of the mountain circuit, success was once more in sight and their strength was renewed by all the meat they could eat for from now on they were in buffalo country. Through all of his wanderings Stuart's mind had still been on the presumed southern route. Therefore, instead of keeping on northward by Hunt's trail over the continental divide through Union Pass, he struck off southward across that wide and featureless expanse of sagebrush where the continental divide subsided to an imperceptible swell on the surface of the desert.

He was within hours of attaining the undisputed fame attached to making the great discovery. But near as he was to the revelation, the stupendous significance of South Pass was not to be realized for another 12 years. Disturbed again by Indian sign, Stuart kept on southward, crossing South Pass not from west to east but from north to south, and only once more turned eastward beyond the rampart of the Sweetwater Mountains. He thus did not reach Sweetwater River, so prominent as the eastern gateway to South Pass in all the later experiences of traders' caravans and pioneers' wagon trains,

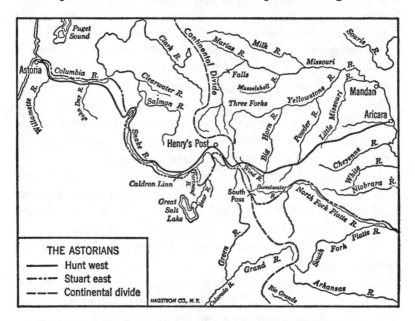

THE ASTORIANS
——— Hunt west
—·—·— Stuart east
——— Continental divide

HAGSTROM CO., N.Y.

until a point just above its junction with the North Platte.

It was only the first of November with still time to reach St. Louis before winter made plains travel too great a risk, but from its direction Stuart assumed the North Platte to be the Cheyenne and therefore that it was too late in the season to contemplate reaching the Missouri so far north. As a result of this judgment, they went into winter quarters in the river bottom just short of the North Platte's bend around the northern shoulder of the Laramie Mountains. Buffalo were plentiful and they stocked their larder with the enthusiasm of men who had recently been starving. They were scarcely settled before they were dislodged from this snug refuge by another Indian threat and they went into a second winter quarters in the North Platte bottom near the present Wyoming-Nebraska boundary. Their worst troubles at last were over. In the spring they journeyed down the Platte to the Missouri and reached St. Louis April 30, 1813.

Stuart had narrowly missed the complete success of having made the most outstanding discovery possible in Rocky Mountain exploration, but his achievement had nevertheless been notable. Though a complete solution to the mystery shrouding the great mountain gateway had been denied him, he had come much closer to one than had Lewis and Clark, Henry or Hunt. Despite his frustrating detours inspired by Indian threats he had grasped the essential significance of the southern route. The Missouri *Gazette* of May 15, 1813, reported his confident assertion that wagons could be taken to the Pacific.[9] And in any event, there can be no denying him the credit of having traced the route that was to become the Oregon Trail from the mouth of the Columbia to the north bend of the Bear and from the mouth of the Sweetwater to the Missouri.

Thirty-two months had elapsed since *Tonquin* had left New York and twenty-two since Hunt had left the Aricara, but Astor was still anxiously awaiting information on the progress of his Columbia project. He could not be certain either expedition had reached its destination.[10] The outbreak of the War of 1812 had multiplied his anxieties. He had learned that the British government was sending a fleet to the Pacific and that the North West

[9] Though there is no other evidence that John Colter's wanderings during his 1807-08 winter journey carried him as far south as South Pass, Henry Brackenridge reported that Colter had told him in 1810 that wagons could be taken across the Rockies.

[10] The Astorians made other efforts than Stuart's to get word to Astor. Hunt in the brig *Pedlar* landed an American clerk, Russell Farnham, at Kamchatka with dispatches. Farnham crossed Siberia and sailed to New York from Hamburg. When *Pedlar* was captured by a Spanish corvette and detained at the west Mexican port of San Blas, Hunt got off another messenger, Alfred Seton, overland through Mexico. After many hardships, illnesses, and delays, Seton succeeded in reaching New York by way of Cartagena and Jamaica. Stuart's journey had preceded both of these and his news was the first to reach Astor.

Company was planning a sea expedition to the Columbia. He was writing Hunt (with no idea where Hunt might be or even whether he was alive), "If my object was merely to gain money, I should say, think whether it is best to save what you can, and abandon the place; but the very idea is like a dagger to my heart." The national government was much too preoccupied with the war's accumulating disasters on nearer fronts to heed his appeals for naval aid. Left to his own devices, he dispatched another supply ship, *Lark*, March 6, 1813, in the hope it might escape the British blockade.[11] It was therefore with relief and elation that he heard from Stuart that his enterprise was not only securely established but competing successfully with the North West Company throughout the Columbia basin. "I have hit the nail on the head," he exulted.

Stuart's news was the last good news, however, Astor was ever to receive from the Columbia. Hunt had left Astoria August 4, 1812, in *Beaver* to complete trade arrangements with the Russians in Alaska. The ship's self-willed master, Captain Cornelius Sowles, asserting his ship had been made unseaworthy by storms, refused to return Hunt to Astoria and instead left him stranded in Hawaii. Sowles then sailed *Beaver* off for China, and Hunt was unable to arrange a passage back to Astoria until more than a year had passed. Thus, the only American among the senior partners was not on the scene to cope with the central effect of the war on the company's situation. The jubilant Northwester, John George Mc-Tavish, armed with the news of the declaration of war brought by express canoe from Montreal, reached the Columbia in late December of 1812 to proclaim the imminent downfall of his American rivals. The prospect of a British naval descent upon Astoria was at once as apparent to Astor's people as it had been to McTavish. An earnest regard for the company's interests might have dictated a removal of the company's property to interior posts safe from any sea-borne threat. But most of the Astorian partners, all ex-North-westers, began instead to consider their native British allegiance and their future career prospects were they to return to the North

11 *Lark* got safely around the Horn but foundered off the coast of Hawaii.

West Company's service. The presumption that British sea power rendered Astoria defenseless endowed their ignominious hesitations with a species of logic. After months of backing and filling under the pretense of discussing alternatives and examining their consciences, they sold Astor's Columbia establishment, including posts, furs, equipment, and merchandise, to the North West Company October 16, 1813, under sacrifice terms which resulted in Astor finally receiving $40,000 for property he valued at $200,000. An ironic footnote to the transaction was posted November 30th when *HMS Racoon* arrived, with officers and crew avidly anticipating the fortune in prize money about to be gained by capture of the American millionaire's fabulous fur depot, only to discover all had become the legal property of a British company.

There was a tragic aftermath to the fall of Astoria. As one of the company's interior operations, Astorian clerk John Reed had gone to the Boise River in the fall of 1813 to superintend the activities of a party of 9 trappers operating in that area. Indians, presumably Shoshone or, according to Franchère, Nez Percé who had been infuriated by an Astorian hanging of one of their number for petty theft the previous spring, made a midwinter descent on the various members of the party which had been widely dispersed by the requirements of the trapping process. Reed, Pierre Dorion, and the three indomitable Kentuckians, Robinson, Hoback, and Reznor were among those killed in the surprise attack. The only survivors of the entire party were Marie Dorion and her two children. She made her escape on horseback with the children wrapped in a buffalo robe, kept them alive during a two-month refuge in the snowbound Blue Mountains by eating the horse, and eventually crawled to the succor of an Indian town on the Columbia.[12]

Astor's empire-building enterprise had outwardly been a total failure after a loss of $400,000 of his money and 61 lives. He had, nevertheless, indirectly succeeded in his major objective, the establishment of an American foothold on the Pacific. When Captain Black of *Racoon* landed at Astoria, he changed its name to Fort

[12] Marie Dorion and her descendants later became Oregon settlers. Her son, Baptiste, was a lieutenant of Oregon militia in the Cayuse War.

George, ceremoniously raised the British flag, and formally took possession in the name of his king. This official gesture had consequences quite contrary to his intentions. The one important clause in the Treaty of Ghent ending the War of 1812 was an undertaking by each nation to return forthwith any territory taken by the other during hostilities. Captain Black had paradoxically authenticated the American claim to Oregon. Through all the next 30 years of the northwest boundary dispute, American negotiators never lost sight of that fact, and Great Britain never seriously questioned the American claim to at least the south bank of the Columbia. Under pressure from their own government British fur traders abandoned Fort George in 1824 to establish their northwestern headquarters at Fort Vancouver on the north bank.

But of greater significance than this diplomatic advantage was the new familiarity that had been gained by a few more American frontiersmen with that immense region that had so recently been totally unknown. It was due to Astor's initiative that within six years of the first great crossing by Lewis and Clark there had been two more transcontinental crossings. Trappers detached by Hunt or dispatched from Astoria had found their way in and out, through, over and around many of the most obscure recesses of that infinitely complex tangle of mountains and rivers extending from Three Forks, the headwaters of the Green, and the north bend of the Bear to the mouth of the Columbia. Every later approach had the guidance or counsel of men who already knew the country. What had seemed a heart-rending and blood-stained repulse began as a result soon to seem a remarkable advance. How certain and irreversible was to be that advance was about to be demonstrated.

IX

❦

War in the West

WESTERNERS HAD FORCED the War of 1812 upon their reluctant fellow countrymen in the impatient hope of gaining certain clearly envisaged advantages. Chief among these were, in the south, the immediate acquisition of Spanish Florida and, in the north, the immediate elimination of British influence among the Indians of the fur-bearing region between the Great Lakes and the Missouri, thus accelerating the opening of that immense area to American trade and settlement. Both of these enormous advantages were eventually gained but their realization was delayed, not expedited, by the war. Among the harsh lessons taught an instinctively aggressive people by this frustration was that war can throw wide the door to the most unforeseen and unlimited hazards and that thousands of individual riflemen, however hardy and expert, require organization, transport, supply, discipline, and leadership before they can undertake sustained campaigns. Instead of the surge of easy and certain victory prophesied by Henry Clay, the war produced a series of military disasters which for a time confronted the west with the catastrophic threats of a British seizure of New Orleans and a permanent reinstitution of the Indian barrier along the line of the 1795 Treaty of Greenville.

In the south the eagerly anticipated conquest of Florida proved disappointingly elusive. Despite such gross provocations as Wilkinson's seizure of Mobile, a Georgian investment of St. Augustine, and Andrew Jackson's burning of Pensacola, Spain obstinately and uncooperatively declined to declare war. Madison's attempt to draw from Congress a declaration of war on Spain was rebuffed by northern and Federalist votes from sections of the country already opposed to the existing war with England. Congress did grudgingly acquiesce in the retention of Mobile on the theory that this area was properly included in the Louisiana Purchase. But the acquisition of the rest of Spanish Florida was a consequence of other pressures imposed after the War of 1812 had ended.

The disappointment in the north was more distressing in that it was accompanied by wholly unexpected military reverses. Even before the formal declaration of war the west had been clamoring for an invasion of Canada in order to extinguish the British-Indian base at Fort Malden. This objective appeared within certain reach for there was no British field force in western Canada and the nearest even modest center of British military power was in the Loyalist settlements established behind the Niagara frontier during and after the Revolution. The danger that the defense of Canada might be strongly reinforced by regular troops from England was made to seem remote by the commitment of Great Britain's national energies to the life and death struggle with Napoleon in Europe. Indian capacity to resist was not more seriously regarded. There had been scattered Indian raids since the early spring of 1812 but no more evidence of a general Indian mobilization than there had been at Tippecanoe. Tecumseh had been desperately attempting to rally a united Indian effort but most Indians were waiting for some demonstration of a British intention to support the Indian cause. In June a quick American victory therefore seemed as assured as had so often been forecast by the War Hawks in Congress.

The Revolutionary veteran, William Hull, now the elderly

Governor of Michigan Territory, reluctantly accepted command of American forces north of the Ohio and even more reluctantly undertook the offensive demanded by the west. He was enough of a soldier to remonstrate against this precipitancy, pointing out that the strength of his field force, limited by congressional authorization to 300 regulars and 1200 Kentucky and Ohio militia, was inadequate for the purpose and that its supply during the circuitous march through Detroit on Fort Malden was impracticable so long as the British maintained naval control of Lake Erie. Feeling still compelled to comply with popular sentiment, he began a glum northward march through the 200 miles of swampy wilderness intervening between the Ohio frontier and Detroit. There being as yet no British force to interfere and the suspicious Indians continuing to wait for some clearer sign of British intentions, he reached Detroit safely and on July 12, 1812, tentatively crossed the river into Canada. He had been reinforced by several companies of Michigan militia but had lost nearly as many Ohio militiamen who had suddenly determined it was not their duty to participate in a "foreign invasion." Still concerned by his manpower and supply deficiencies, Hull delayed his advance on Fort Malden on various pretexts, giving the British commanders, Henry Proctor and Isaac Brock, time to arrive from the Niagara frontier with reinforcements which raised the British white force to 300 regulars and 400 militia. Fully convinced by now that his communications were threatened, Hull hastily retreated to Detroit, decided that he was hopelessly cut off and on August 16th surrendered his army of nearly 1400 men.

No blow could have struck the west with more painful impact. Through all the 20 years of border war after 1775, to the inhabitants of the frontier Detroit had loomed at its unassailable distance as at once the symbol, the citadel, and the fountainhead of British-Indian menace. From it had been launched innumerable assaults and outrages. Now, at the very outset of this renewal of that war, Detroit's original malevolence had been restored. The appalling development had, moreover, been only the principal disaster in a train of disasters. Mackinac had already fallen, July 17th, to a hastily assembled force of English fur traders and their Indian clients. Fort Dearborn, on the site that was to become Chicago, established under the Treaty of Greenville to keep the peace among neighboring tribes, had proved too weakly held to survive the stresses of actual war. During the attempted evacuation, August 15th, Indians had fallen upon the withdrawing column among the lake shore sand dunes, killing 35 soldiers and settlers, many by torment.[1] Fired by British successes and by Tecumseh's announcement that a victorious Britain would restrain American settlement behind the Greenville line, the hitherto hesitant Indians swarmed to the British standard. Within three months of the declaration of war the west's projected invasion of Canada had been transformed into an exasperated defense of its own frontiers. The major forts in the cordon of military posts guarding the northwestern border, Wayne, Harrison, and Madison, were under savage assault and all outer settlements were exposed to attack.

The third western theater of operations in the War of 1812, the Missouri frontier, appeared then less significant than the other two, but actually broader and more doubtful issues were at stake. This scattering of wilderness hamlets along the lower Missouri, the spear point of the westward movement, was the special seedbed of frontier energies upon which depended the future persistence of that movement. From it in the past five years had sprung penetrations of the farthest west to the headwaters of the Missouri and on to the mouth of the Columbia. Over this most exposed, least populated and yet most critical of frontiers hung in 1812 the threat of an Indian invasion of overwhelming proportions. Every Indian nation between the Great Lakes and the Rocky Mountains had come under British influence. Tecumseh's summons to battle, the anti-American persuasions of English traders, and the activities of Robert Dickson, the energetic British Indian agent at Prairie du Chien, had produced indications of the imminent descent of the Mississippi and Missouri by an Indian invading horde possibly numbering thousands of warriors.

[1] Among the dead was Captain William Wells, the son-in-law of Little Turtle who had commanded Wayne's scouts in 1794.

In this extreme emergency responsibility for defending the country's westernmost border was assumed by men of families whose reputations had long been established by their response to such demands in the past. The Governor of Missouri, Benjamin Howard, was a Kentuckian whose father had been a first settler of Boonesborough. The brigadier general commanding Missouri's militia was William Clark, all five of whose older brothers had been Revolutionary officers.[2] The colonel commanding the Boonslick regiment was Benjamin Cooper, a veteran of Kentucky's border wars who had fought at Blue Licks where two of his brothers-in-law had died. Among his officers were two Boones, three Callaways, two Byrds, and a Van Bibber.

The threat of a major Indian invasion by way of the Mississippi or the Missouri persisted for months but eventually failed to materialize. The difficulty of organizing any united Indian effort for a large scale operation had again been demonstrated. By maintaining a stubborn residue of trade contacts, Manuel Lisa succeeded in holding most River Indians of the lower Missouri to friendliness or neutrality even after his company had been driven from the upper river with a heavy loss in property and of 15 lives, in an attempt to maintain his Mandan post. Indian attacks on the Missouri frontier settlements failed to develop into anything more serious than sporadic hit-and-run raids. Total casualties in the most exposed Boonslick area were limited during the war to 16 killed. This was not an Indian danger calculated greatly to impress people who remembered earlier border wars in Kentucky and Tennessee and they were soon preparing to strike back. In 1813 Howard was able to lead an invasion of Illinois and in 1814 Clark, his successor as governor, to mount an offensive against Prairie du Chien. But in spite of this resolute defense and early recovery of the initiative, the war had brought mortification to this frontier also. There had been a strangling effect on the westward movement from which there was

[2] George Rogers Clark had been incapacitated in 1809 by a partial paralysis and the amputation of his right leg required by an infection resulting from his falling into his fire during a stroke. On February 20, 1812, the Virginia legislature voted him a memorial sword and a $400 pension. He died February 13, 1818.

to be no full recovery for the next ten years. American trade had been swept from the upper Missouri and unrest promoted by British traders among even more remote Indians had driven American trappers from the mountains. Men of the Missouri frontier who so recently had unhesitatingly ventured to the shores of the Pacific had for a time been forced to accept the nearer edge of the plains as a barrier.

Public opinion in the border states of Kentucky, Tennessee, and Ohio, at first stunned and then infuriated by 1812 British and Indian successes, seethed with demands that the prestige of western arms be forthwith reestablished. In coping with the exacting mechanics of getting a new and stronger army into the field, necessarily composed largely of militia, the performance did not, however, measure up to the resolve. By universal insistence, William Henry Harrison, the hero of Tippecanoe and most prominent proponent of Indian expulsion, was appointed new commander in the west. Though the lateness of the season multiplied the difficulties of wilderness supply and transport to the verge of unreason, he responded to popular impatience by undertaking an immediate offensive. Autumnal rains so much delayed his advance that it was January before his columns had reached the Sandusky and the Maumee. He remained determined upon delivering his attack, relying upon the possibility of getting at Fort Malden by crossing Lake Erie on the ice. Whatever opportunity there may have been to succeed in this maneuver was lost by a new and unnecessary disaster. The Tennessee pioneer, General James Winchester, commanding Harrison's left wing on the Maumee, made a sudden, unsupported, and unauthorized further advance to the relief of American settlers on the Raisin River, just south of Detroit. Proctor, who had succeeded to British command in the west upon Brock's death on the Niagara frontier, made a night crossing from Fort Malden to deliver a surprise attack at dawn of January 22, 1813, upon Winchester's sprawling and unguarded encampment from which only 33 were known to have escaped. Of the American army of 800, a third were killed, either in the attack or in the succeeding Indian massacre of wounded and prisoners.

His own plans disrupted by Proctor's offensive move, Harrison was forced to devote the remainder of the winter to the building and strengthening of a barrier of frontier defense forts. The position he had taken was on historic ground which had been the scene of many of the most celebrated events of earlier wilderness warfare. His left flank, Fort Wayne, was at the Miami portage, the strategic wilderness key which Pontiac had taken in 1763 and the American generals, Josiah Harmar and Arthur St. Clair, had unsuccessfully assailed in 1790 and 1791. His center, Fort Meigs, was at Maumee Rapids, where the great Indian congress had rebuffed the American peace commissioners in 1793 and Wayne had won the Battle of Fallen Timbers in 1794. His right, Fort Stephenson, was on the Sandusky at another wilderness crossroads that had been fought for in every former war from earliest French times to the death by torment of Colonel William Crawford in 1782.

As the spring of 1813 permitted the resumption of campaigning, Proctor was the first to be ready to take the field. Reinforced by nearly a thousand regulars, a strong corps of artillery, and more than two thousand Indians, he mounted an assault upon the American fortified encampment at Maumee Rapids. His artillery made little impression on the earthwork defenses, his Indians recoiled from attacking riflemen firing from the security of trenches, and, though he inflicted a loss of 650 killed and captured on one American relief column, he withdrew after a two-week siege. He returned to threaten Fort Meigs again in midsummer but only as a feint to mask an attack upon Harrison's main supply depot on the Sandusky. This move was disrupted July 31, 1813, by the unexpectedly fierce resistance of Fort Stephenson where a garrison of 150 under the command of George Rogers Clark's 21-year-old nephew, Major George Croghan, repulsed an attacking army of 3000 in a spirited defense that won wide acclaim at the time.

Though the manpower upon which he could draw in the three western states outnumbered by more than 10 to 1 the entire English-speaking population of Canada, Harrison had been held to the defense throughout the first six months of 1813 by his inability to organize an army based on the militia system. Militia had somewhat better served the needs of frontier defense in earlier years when every man's military service was compelled by the prevailing and immediate danger to his own home. In 1813 the embattled frontier lay many hundreds of miles from the centers of population of Kentucky and Tennessee and thousands who might have nevertheless been disposed to serve were dissuaded by the notorious

inadequacies of supply and discipline. It was late August before Harrison had built the roads and accumulated the stores to permit him to launch his long-delayed offensive. Even after the arrival of 3500 Kentucky militia under Governor Isaac Shelby, as redoubtable at 66 as when at 30 he had commanded at King's Mountain, had made his army of 7000 overwhelmingly superior to Proctor's British-Indian force, the way ahead was still strewn with difficulties. Any land advance upon Fort Malden, necessarily the circuitous one by way of Detroit, subjected his line of communications to the same flank attack that had ruined Hull and Winchester.[8]

In this crisis the military situation was totally reversed by a single event. Twenty-seven-year-old Oliver Hazard Perry had been diligently building a fleet at Erie of materials hauled over the mountains by wagon from the seaboard. By his sailing, Proctor and Tecumseh were as frustrated as had been Pontiac in 1763 by the sudden intrusion of sea power into the interior of the continent. Perry's brilliant victory over the British fleet September 10, 1813, decided the war in the west. Proctor abandoned Fort Malden and retreated eastward before the threat of Harrison's so much superior force. Ferried across the lake by Perry, Harrison pursued the fleeing British and Indians up the Thames with the more mobile 3000 of his army. Upon Tecumseh's insistence, Proctor selected what appeared to be a strong defensive position and attempted a stand. At the Battle of the Thames, October 5, 1813, mounted Kentucky riflemen, yelling more wildly than Indians, broke the British line by their headlong charge. Proctor's army was destroyed and scattered, its commander became a hunted fugitive. Tecumseh was killed at the head of his warriors who that day fought more resolutely than their white comrades-in-arms and inflicted most of the few losses sustained by the Americans. At the Battle of the Thames the unnatural bond between British and Indians that had first been cut at Fallen Timbers was again severed. The victory had been delayed by initial overconfidence and continuing mismanagement but had been made as inevitable by the west's overwhelming superiority in manpower, as the War Hawks had proclaimed. The decisive consequence was finally and unmistakably to prove how self-deluded from the outset of Tecumseh's agitation had been this last Indian hope that some way might yet be found to turn back the norwestward advance of American settlement.

[8] There need have been no western campaigns had the major American offensive operations of the war against Niagara and Montreal been successful. Any severance of the St. Lawrence supply route would have reduced British-Indian effectiveness in the west as abruptly as had been French-Indian effectiveness in the west by the victories of Johnson and Wolfe at Niagara and Quebec in 1759.

In the south, the last glimmer of Indian hope flickered out in 1813 as finally as in the north, but it was a more fearful extinguishment in which extraordinary heroism and infamy were inextricably mingled. In the north, Indians had fought defiantly at the side of their British ally against their American enemy whereas in the south Indians rushed to embrace their doom by fighting at the side of white invaders against fellow Indians defending their homeland. The southern Indian nations had developed well beyond their aboriginal simplicities. They had relatively organized governments, many intelligent, articulate leaders, and generations of experience with their common danger. Yet in this final crisis their prevailing inclination was to destroy each other. In all the long record of Indian inability to recognize in time the most manifest threats, of Indian failure to perceive the universality of the Indian peril, of perpetual Indian betrayal of Indian, there was no more striking example of the Indian's inherent self-destructive impulse than in the train of events leading to the downfall of the Creek nation.

Upon the death of the great Creek chieftain, McGillivray, in 1793, major responsibility for Creek leadership had descended upon Benjamin Hawkins, the humane and competent United States Agent to the Creek. Under his dedicated tutelage during the next 20 years the Creek people made long strides toward a more productive way of life with an ever-increasing number exhibiting a disposition to till the soil, to accumulate farm animals, and to keep the peace. There had begun to appear some hope that the Creek might after all succeed in that painful transition from a primitive to a civilized culture which no other Indian nation had ever been able to achieve.

The progressive process was assisted by the existence among the Creek of a large proportion of mixed bloods, a product of the Creek readiness to intermarry with whites which had persisted since their earliest Spanish, French, and English contacts. But it was violently opposed by a tradition-observing minority whose prejudices were inflamed by a swarm of conjurors, witch doctors and "prophets," by their jealousy of the generally lighter skinned propertied class, and by continuing white demands for more Creek land. The activities of this militant opposition to Creek self-improvement ranged from ravaging the flocks and fields of their progressive neighbors to occasional attacks on whites with a view to provoking an American-Creek war. The Creek majority evidenced its determination to keep the peace by the rigor with which Creek police by order of the Creek council hunted down and executed the perpetrators of outrages against whites. Further excited by Tecumseh's southern tour, by the Creek council's repressive measures, and by a supply of arms from English agents in Pensacola after the outbreak of the English-American war, the Creek revolutionaries, by now known as Red Sticks, launched attacks on the progressive faction which by the winter of 1812 had developed into a murderous civil war.

The authorities of adjoining Georgia, Tennessee, and Mississippi Territory had not been too disturbed by this spectacle of Creek self-destruction, but their complacence was dissipated by the sudden horror of the Fort Mims massacre, August 30, 1813. Settlers on the lower Alabama had taken refuge from the excesses of the Creek civil war in a hastily constructed stockade to which they had admitted a party of fleeing Creek mixed-bloods. Pursuing Red Sticks rushed the stockade's open gate and in the ensuing tumult slaughtered indiscriminately all within, white, red, or black, men, women, or children. No exact count was posible but the number of dead was estimated at the time as approaching 500. There was macabre irony in the circumstance that in this last Indian attack on a settlement east of the Mississippi many more perished than in any former such attack in all the long and troubled history of the frontier. The magnitude of the outrage incensed the national public as much as it did people on the border and there was a general demand for vengeance and punishment.

An enduring consequence of the vigor of American retaliation was the opportunity provided Andrew Jackson. His ensuing war services made him the west's hero and carried him twice to the White House. In gaining command of Tennessee's expedition, the principal effort to punish the Creek, he was preferred over his bitterest rival, the aging John Sevier,[4] and thereafter knew no rival. The difficulties associated with the management of militia, which had distracted all former commanders, particularly irritated one of his obstreperous willfulness but his campaign was saved by such support from Indian auxiliaries and allies as no other frontier commander had ever enjoyed. The collateral column invading the Creek country from Georgia was joined by some hundreds of progressive Creek, vengefully eager to assist in the punishment of their Red Stick rivals. The main column, Jackson's, invading from the north, was supported by 700 Cherokee, after long deliberation by the Cherokee council had determined it to be in the best interests of the Cherokee nation to cultivate future American favor at no greater apparent cost than an attack on their ancient Creek enemy.

In early October of 1813, while Harrison was pursuing Proctor and Tecumseh up the Thames, Jackson crossed the Tennessee with an invading army of 5000 Tennessee militia, 19 companies of Cherokee warriors, and 200 pro-American Creek auxiliaries. This was an onslaught with which the hopelessly divided Creek were helpless to cope. At the successive captures of the Creek towns of Tallassiehatchee and Talladega 500 defenders, most of them dependent upon bows and arrows by the exhaustion of ammunition during the civil war, were killed. A third town, Hillaubee, surrendered to Jackson upon his assurances of safe-conduct, but 60 of its inhabitants were dispatched by Cherokee advancing from the other side. After this demonstration that there seemed no escape in submission, Creek of all parties resisted with fatalistic valor. Jackson fought his way southward but by mid-January his militia strength had been so reduced by mutiny, desertion, and expiration of enlistments that he suffered two sharp reverses and was forced to make a hurried withdrawal to his base at Fort Strother, near the Tennessee.

---

[4] The intense animosity between the two great westerners had reached in 1803 the pitch of a near duel in which each drew his pistol but neither fired. Sevier's lifetime of public service was climaxed by two terms as governor of Tennessee and three terms in Congress. He died September 24, 1815. The other great leader of early Tennessee, James Robertson, died September 1, 1814, while serving as United States Agent to the Chickasaw.

In the spring, with a reorganized army, better disciplined by an unhesitating resort to the death penalty, he returned to complete his conquest, striking into the heartland of the Upper Creek with 2000 regulars and militia and 500 Cherokee. At Tohopeka on the Horseshoe Bend of the Tallapoosa, the remnant of the Creek had gathered for a last resistance behind log fortifications. Jackson's frontal assault supported by two cannon was checked but the defense collapsed when taken in the rear by Cherokee who had swum the river. In this last stand, March 27, 1814, the final engagement of the war, 600 more Creek died. This last of the wars between the races on the historic battleground between the Appalachians and the Mississippi had been the goriest. Not only had more settlers perished at Fort Mims than in any former assault on a stockade but in the course of the conflict many more Indians had been killed than in any former war.

The majority of the Creek, particularly of the Lower Creek most under Hawkins' influence, had all along been begging for peace on almost any terms. But in the negotiations conducted by the victor no distinction was made between hostile and pacific Creek. Jackson, the confirmed westerner, dictated at the Treaty of Fort Jackson, August 9, 1814, a peace stripping from the Creek nation two thirds of its territory and opening to white settlement a wide corridor extending from the Tennessee to the Spanish border along the Gulf. Here was at last the road to the sea sought by the Muscle Shoals speculators, by the adherents of the Lost State of Franklin, and by the formulators of the Blount and Hamilton filibustering projects.[5] Creek independence, maintained for three centuries by amazing ingenuity and spirit against every successive Spanish, French, English, and American pressure, had come to an end. The Cherokee, who had assisted so significantly in this dismemberment, were soon to discover that their own dispossession had merely been delayed.

The war with England which had never been popular in the east had lost most of its appeal also in the west. As early as March

[5] Cf. Dale Van Every, Ark of Empire, chaps. VII and XXI.

of 1813 the Czar had offered to mediate. The United States accepted but England refused. There was deep English resentment of the advantage seized by Americans in attacking during Britain's preoccupation with the Napoleonic wars. But it was likewise an unpopular war in England, and on November 4, 1813, Foreign Secretary Lord Castlereagh offered direct negotiations. Due to various misunderstandings of arrangements it was not until August 8, 1814, that the American commissioners, of whom the more prominent were John Quincy Adams and Henry Clay, met their English counterparts at Ghent.

That first meeting seemed to cast any prospect of peace out of the window. The opening statement of the British position singled out the American west, which had precipitated the war, as the victim to suffer the war's principal consequences. It was bluntly declared that there was no use even considering negotiations unless the United States initially agreed (1) to recognize the independence of England's Indian allies together with their right to permanent possession of all territory northwest of the Treaty of Fort Greenville line [6] and (2) to Great Britain's exclusive right to maintain naval forces on the Great Lakes. The unexpected implacability of the demand struck the American commissioners like a blow in the face. Yet it had to be heard and ostensibly considered. Great Britain had scaled the crest of world power. Napoleon had fallen. To the omnipotence of Britain's sea power had been added the prestige of Wellington's victorious army. The demand remained a blow that had in some fashion to be parried. There was no slightest chance that the west would accept a peace stipulating subjection to a strait jacket. With a skill reminiscent of that evidenced by Benjamin Franklin and his colleagues in the Revolution's peace negotiations, the Americans began patiently and doggedly to debate the issue.

As the weeks passed, the English commissioners held adamantly to their pose as victors who had been invested with the sole power to make decisions. There was much to support this arrogance. The

---

[6] This would have barred to future American settlement northern Ohio, most of Indiana and Illinois, and all of Michigan, Wisconsin, and Minnesota.

United States had lost the war in nearly every way a war could be lost. Every American attempt to invade the inhabited part of Canada had proved a dismal failure, including the most recent effort commanded by Wilkinson in the winter of 1813-14. Washington had been burned. Freed of European demands, new British forces were gathering to crush further American resistance. Sir George Prevost, Governor General of Canada, was poised at the head of Lake Champlain with an army of 18,000 for an invasion calculated to cut the United States in two after the fashion once attempted by Burgoyne. General Sir Edward Pakenham, brother-in-law of the Duke of Wellington, was assembling another army of 10,000 at Jamaica to seize New Orleans and throttle the west. There was dark talk at Ghent of dispatching the Duke of Wellington himself to take supreme command in North America. Still the American commissioners continued to argue.

In October the British attitude began perceptibly to soften. There had been the news of Captain Thomas McDonough's astonishing naval victory at Plattsburg which had closed the Lake Champlain invasion route. Proceedings at the Congress of Vienna had begun to suggest the possibility of new demands on England in Europe. Most of all, there had developed increasing evidence that after twenty years of war the English public was tired of war. The patience of the American commissioners was thus rewarded. The negotiators finally got down to the business of negotiating. In the processes of necessary give and take, the United States found it easiest to relinquish freedom of the seas demands which were no longer so important now that the world war seemed over. Great Britain found its most convenient field for sacrifice on its distant wilderness frontier, and the Indians for the third historic time found themselves abandoned at an international peace table. In the Treaty of Ghent, signed Christmas Eve, 1814, none of the advantages sought by the war was obtained by either side. In effect, it left the relative situation of the two nations exactly as it would have been had there been no war.

Aside from a number of brilliant naval successes, the one victory of the war which Americans could remember with satisfaction came after the war was formally over and all of its issues determined. Westerners had had the least occasion of all Americans to be satisfied with their war record. But the British threat to New Orleans was recognized as a thrust at the jugular vein, and the west responded with a militant energy not hitherto evidenced. More than 10,000 Tennessee frontiersmen rushed to join the defense army being assembled by Jackson, newly appointed major general in the United States Army. Pakenham, relying upon the disciplined valor of his Napoleonic veterans, made the supreme mistake of attempting a frontal attack on Jackson's breastworks blocking a narrow corridor between swamp and river. Under the aimed fire of thousands of the world's most expert riflemen, Pakenham lost 2000 men in twenty minutes. He himself was among the dead in that welter of blood in which any threat to New Orleans had been submerged. The overwhelming victory restored the west's self-confidence and made Jackson's military reputation forever secure.

The one significant consequence of the War of 1812 bearing upon the westward movement was in no way connected with any of the original objectives envisaged by westerners. Indian resistance to the frontier's advance had been hopeless since 1794 and without the war must have given way as rapidly as the need for new room for settlement developed. Spanish Florida had been a ripe fruit whose fall was, if anything, delayed by the war. British interference with American ocean trade had come at the close of the European war to an end which had not been by a moment hastened by the North American war. The outstanding result of the war was a sudden and immense increase in the prestige and authority of the national government.

Despite the notorious ineptitude with which the national government had waged the war and possibly even encouraged by the succession of heart-sickening disasters which this had invited, during that time a deeper sense of loyalty to the United States had developed among people who formerly had felt their first allegiance to state or section. The "Star-Spangled Banner" was written, such memorable patriotic phrases as "Don't give up the ship" and "We have met the enemy and they are ours" were endlessly savored, and a Pike, who could in 1806 lend himself insensibly to Wilkinson's Spanish schemes, could, before dying a hero's death at the taking of York in 1813, write in his last letter to his father, "still shall it be said . . . we conferred honor, even in death, on the American Name." In the period before the war factionalism had kindled fires of a bitterness not again known until 1860, but the period after the war became the Era of Good Feelings in which even politicians behaved like a band of brothers. The United States had become a truly united nation. Among the new fields of authority this unity had opened to the national government none was more significant than its assumption of responsibility henceforth to supervise, control, and, above all, to *limit* the progress of the westward movement.

X

℘

The New Line

No EMPLOYMENT THROUGH the ages has so fascinated generals in their headquarters, diplomats at their peace tables, or rulers in their council chambers as the drawing of lines on maps. These impressions of pen on paper have often failed to correspond to the realities of the related situation, but they have as often assumed nevertheless and abortive reality of their own by their having affected the thinking of all concerned with that situation. The gulf between these two realities has seldom been more strikingly illustrated than in the two historic attempts to stem the westward surge of American settlement by governmental fiat.

The first, proclaimed by the king in 1763, had undertaken to maintain border peace by defining a boundary to guard the wilderness region occupied by the Indians from settler encroachment. The Proclamation Line enjoyed the practical advantage of coinciding with two of the continent's more prominent physiographic features. In shielding the centers of Indian population in the south, it followed the crest of the Appalachians. In the north, after the readjustment of 1768, it designated the Ohio River as the boundary

between the two races. Though thousands of settlers poured through
the central gap, that first Line succeeded for 20 years in obstructing
the northward and southward spread of settlement from its original
lodgment in Kentucky and Tennessee. But the Line had in the
meantime utterly failed in its larger objective of maintaining
peace by having served instead to promote, intensify, and prolong
border warfare. Indian nations, with active British encouragement,
persisted for 10 years after the Revolution in asserting its un-
diminished legitimacy and in fighting, with British support, for
its continued recognition. The influence of the Proclamation Line
upon the course of events was not eliminated until the military
overthrow of its British and Indian wardens achieved by Wayne's
1794 campaign. It was in the light of this formidable precedent
that the United States in 1825 proclaimed a new boundary. It coincided with an even more prominent natural feature, the western
edge of the continent's woodland, and it succeeded so well in
retarding the frontier's westward advance that it escaped by the
narrowest of margins denying the last precarious opportunity to
extend American dominion to the Pacific.

Among issues left unsettled by the Treaty of Ghent ending the
War of 1812 were the disposal of eastern Indians by some more
enlightened course than extermination, the negotiation of boundaries
with Spain in the southwest and Great Britain in the northwest,
and the westward rush of population accelerated by the current
economic depression. These were urgent problems with which
states and sections could not deal and with which therefore the
national government must. Fired by the new prestige which it had
paradoxically won by its misconduct of the war, the Federal establishment undertook with great vigor and confidence to provide
sweeping solutions for all of them.

All were directly connected with the westward movement and
thus were problems with which no other government had ever
before had to wrestle. No other nation had ever experienced, as the
central factor in its development, a continuing removal of a large
proportion of its population into an ever-widening expanse of trackless wilderness. Hitherto, this unique American movement had

been conducted by random and unco-ordinated individual initiative and characterized by every sort of violence, misery, and bloodshed. Henceforth, Congress and the President were now determined it would be regulated and guided so that it might proceed in a more orderly manner and with due regard for the welfare not only of the Indians and settlers but of the nation.

To implement this assumption of frontier responsibility the United States in 1816 and 1817 established Forts Crawford, Edwards, and Armstrong on the Mississippi, Howard at Green Bay, and Smith on the Arkansas. At each were stationed detachments of the enlarged regular army to keep the peace between Indians and whites, to supervise each successive Indian withdrawal necessitated by each permitted advance of settlement, and to expel settlers who had advanced without permission. Indian land cessions were negotiated at general conferences with careful attention to compensation and a guarantee of future annuities and federal protection in the new locations to which Indians were being required to move. As a further guard to frontier peace, English traders, perennial promoters of Indian unrest, were excluded from operations on American soil.

The response to this orderly opening of new land to settlement in the area east of the Mississippi heretofore unoccupied by whites became by far the greatest shift in population since the advent of the westward movement. In the five years following the war, a half million homeseekers crossed the Ohio in the north, and another quarter of a million the Tennessee in the south. The problems of survival which had haunted earlier frontiers had eased for this new generation of migrants in but one respect. The Indian danger which once had been every family's daily concern had faded from the border scene. But every other hardship and difficulty imposed by existence in a forest clearing was as burdensome as before, while these later comers were denied the zest of adventuring into the unknown which had had so great an appeal for their predecessors. Their's was an economic adventure. They were investing years of self-denial, privation, and toil in the chance that they would gain future advantages for their children that must have remained beyond reach had the hazards of migration not been accepted. The conviction that effort and risk were certain of reward, that the range of opportunity in the west was incalculable, that no man was required to set a limit upon his expectations had begun to dominate the American outlook. Evidence to support these assumptions was overwhelming. The population of Kentucky and Tennessee had in scarcely more than half a man's lifetime increased from a harassed and starving thousand to a secure and comfortable million. There was every assurance that each additional region torn from the wilderness might progress as rapidly. The pioneer of 1815-20 proposed not only to take advance of this certain increment but to assist and expedite it. He had come to possess and improve land, to build towns, roads, mills, schools, churches, to establish commonwealths. Though no longer committed to hunting game for his food and fighting Indians for his life, he was not otherwise much to be distinguished in appearance, manners, and morals from his buckskin-clad precursor who had been first to cross the mountains into the interior valley. He was as ragged, as poor, as opinionated, as intransigent, as aggressive, and above all, as determined to govern himself. Within five years he had added four new states to the multiplying Union: Indiana, 1816; Mississippi, 1817; Illinois, 1818; Alabama, 1819.

This sudden tide of white population sweeping into territory until then preserved for Indian use demanded an immediate determination of what to do with those original occupants. In the north the Indians could be required for a while longer to move northwestward into the remaining area of wilderness occupied only by other Indians. But in the south, the major Indian nations were so situated that there was no direction in which they could be pushed. They were already encircled by territory inhabited by whites. The states concerned insisted that they be altogether removed to the still wild region beyond the Mississippi and beyond the farthest white frontier.

Such an enforced migration of an entire race was not a new idea. Jefferson, for one, had in 1803 considered a principal virtue of the Louisiana Purchase to be in its having made available a new home for the eastern Indians along the west bank of the Mississippi which he did not foresee being required for American use for generations to come. Some Indians, attracted by the prospect of more primitive hunting grounds at a more comfortable distance from white settlements, were willing to make the move demanded of them by their white neighbors. Several small bands of Shawnee, Delaware, Cherokee, and Creek had of their own volition sought new homes west of the Mississippi during and after the Revolution. Responding to the increasingly urgent demands of Georgia, Tennessee, and Mississippi, the national government began after the War of 1812 to press harder on the southern Indians to abandon their native land in favor of the new opportunities and new homes to be had in the far west. This was no greater hardship, it was urged, than hundreds of thousands of white families had eagerly accepted in their migration from the seaboard, and it offered, it was further pointed out, the one avenue to that permanent peace necessary to Indian survival. Such arguments and persuasions in the end became unanswerable. But it was not a process, even for those Indians amenable to the move, unaccompanied by many frictions. Government rationing failed, whites despoiled them en route, and the earlier colonies of transplanted Cherokee and Creek on the Arkansas promptly became embroiled in a bitter war with the resident Osage who resented this invasion of their hunting grounds by strange Indians as much as they would have one by strange white men. Most southern Indians gradually and reluctantly recognized the necessity of removal, though a considerable number particularly of the more advanced Cherokee and the Seminole branch of the Creek, objected violently and succeeded in delaying their departure for many years. It was not, however, a question dependent upon Indian consent. Indians, in both north and south, were confronted by the physical power of a white population outnumbering them 100 to 1 which they could no longer hope even momentarily to resist.

At the same time the national government was taking command of settler-Indian relations it was undertaking negotiations with

Great Britain and Spain of the previously undetermined northern and southern boundaries of the Louisiana Purchase. In 1818, the United States and Great Britain agreed upon the 49th parallel as a boundary from the Lake of the Woods to the Rocky Mountains. West of the mountains the "Oregon country" was ruled open to traders and trappers of both countries pending future resolution of the conflicting claims of Spain, Russia, Britain, and the United States to that remote region. This obscure dispute did not constitute a problem causing concern to either negotiator in 1818. Any question posed by the occupation of Oregon by white settlers was not one considered likely to arise within the next century, if then.

The boundary treaty with Spain was more momentous. Spain had not recovered from the disastrous invasions of the Napoleonic wars and its American empire was dissolving under waves of revolution, but the Spanish negotiators bargained as stubbornly as though Spain were still a world power. The halting progress toward an agreement was at first impeded and then hastened by another sensational expression of the west's determination to possess Florida. Under cover of a punitive expedition against the Seminole authorized by the War Department, Jackson in the spring of 1818 pursued irregular bands of rebellious Red Sticks and runaway slaves across the Georgia border into Spanish Florida. In the course of a whirlwind campaign, he dispersed the Indians and Negroes, seized two British citizens, Alexander Arbuthnot and Robert Ambrister, on Spanish territory, charged them with conspiring with the Indians, court-martialed and executed them, and raised the American flag over St. Marks and Pensacola, after compelling their Spanish garrisons to capitulate. This flagrant affront to two world empires was disavowed by the United States, but it had offered a renewed demonstration of frontier aggressiveness which re-impressed upon Spanish negotiators Spain's inability to defend Florida. The ensuing treaty, signed February 22, 1819, by Secretary of State John Quncy Adams and Spanish Minister to the United States Luis de Onis, amounted to an exchange of a Spanish cession of Florida, which all Americans then ardently desired, for an American relinquishment of any claim on Texas, about which few Americans then much cared.[1] There was a slight American bonus in the implied reversion to the United States of Spain's former claim to Oregon. The mutually recognized Spanish-American boundary was defined by the treaty as a line running along the eastern and northeastern borders of the present Texas, thence north to the Arkansas, thence west to the continental divide, thence north to the 42nd parallel, thence west to the Pacific. This negotiated division of the continent affirmed permanent Spanish possession of all of the present states of Texas, New Mexico, Utah, Arizona, Nevada, and California, together with portions of Oklahoma, Kansas, Colorado, and Wyoming.

By these deliberately accepted international agreements of 1818 and 1819 the national government had accepted the Rocky Mountains as a practial western limit to the territory of the United States and had renounced any future intention of expansion southwestward. Henceforth, the energies of the nation were to be concentrated upon the prosperity-producing utilization of the eastern portion of the midcontinent. The astounding westward extension of American dominion which had so distinguished the earlier years of the young republic had been pronounced a completed process.

Scant as had proved the nation's interest in the southwest, there remained a momentary concern with the northwestern area dramatized by Lewis and Clark, by the early activities of American fur traders, and by the threat of a British-induced Indian invasion from the north during the War of 1812. It was determined, in conformity with the national government's general assumption of responsibility for the maintenance of frontier peace, to tighten control over trade rivalries and Indian behavior by a display of American military power among the nations of the upper Missouri. Colonel Henry Atkinson was directed in 1819 to ascend the Missouri with an

[1] This was a view with which Henry Clay violently differed. He had declared in Congress: "He was not disposed to disparage Florida, but its intrinsic value was incomparably less than that of Texas ... It was quite evident that it was in the order of Providence . . . that the whole of their continent, including Texas, was to be peopled in process of time . . . In our hands it will be peopled by freemen, carrying with them our language, our laws, and our liberties."

expedition of 1100 soldiers, transported in 6 steamboats, to establish military posts at the Mandan and wherever else necessary to assure recognition of American sovereignty by Indians of the region and trespassing British traders. Atkinson's steamboats broke down, only one getting as far upriver as Council Bluffs, more than hundred of his men died of scurvy, and Congress became so appalled by the pyramiding costs that the project was abandoned. The empire-building enterprise degenerated into a subsidiary exploration conducted by Major Stephen Long with a party of 19. Long ascended the Platte in 1820, probed the eastern slopes of the Rockies along the South Platte, climbed Pike's Peak, became lost among the southern tributaries of the Arkansas, and returned, after many mishaps, including the theft by deserters of all of his papers, by way of Fort Smith.

The great significance of Long's exploration sprang from his earnest confirmation of Pike's judgment on the uninhabitability of the central and southern plains. Pike in 1807 had reported:

> These vast plains of the western hemisphere may become in time as celebrated as the sandy deserts of Africa; for I saw in my route, in various places, tracts of many leagues where the wind had thrown up the sand in all the fanciful forms of the ocean's rolling waves, and on which not a speck of vegetable matter existed. But from these immense prairies may arise one great advantage to the United States, viz: The restriction of our population to some certain limits, and thereby a continuation of the Union. Our citizens being so prone to rambling and extending themselves on the frontiers will, through necessity, be constrained to limit their extent on the west to the borders of the Missouri and Mississippi, while they leave the prairies incapable of cultivation to the wandering and uncivilized aborigines of the country.

Long, fully agreeing with this estimate, now reported, in the words of his scientific assistant, Dr. Edwin James:

> We have little apprehension of giving too unfavourable an account of this portion of the country. Though the soil is in some places fertile, the want of timber, of navigable streams, and of water for the necessities of life, render it an unfit residence for any but a nomade

population. The traveller who shall at any time have traversed its desolate sands, will, we think, join us in the wish that this region may for ever remain the unmolested haunt of the native hunter, the bison, and the jackall . . . In regard to this extensive section of country, I do not hesitate in giving the opinion, that it is almost wholly unfit for cultivation, and of course uninhabitable by a people depending upon agriculture for their subsistence. Although tracts of fertile land considerably extensive are occasionally to be met with, yet the scarcity of wood and water, almost uniformly prevalent, will prove an insuperable obstacle in the way of settling the country . . . This region, however, viewed as a frontier, may prove of infinite importance to the United States, inasmuch as it is calculated to serve as a barrier to prevent too great an extension of our population westward.

Thus was born the myth of the Great American Desert. School children of the next two generations saw it graphically defined upon every map in every geography. The existence of an immenese uninhabitable area between the eastern woodland and the Rocky Mountains became a conception firmly fixed in the national consciousness.[2] To a national government already committed to the restraint of expansion in the interest of political and economic coherence, Long's confirmation of Pike's judgment on the sterility of the plains offered a welcome and solid basis upon which to erect a fully formulated national policy.

Secretary of War John C. Calhoun had been making an exhaustive survey of the problem of Indian removal. The logic of his eventual determination appeared unanswerable. His proposal proceeded step by inexorable step: (1) to satisfy the states and their white inhabitants and to minister to the Indians' own good, it was imperative that Indians be removed from their homelands east of the Mississippi; (2) simple morality dictated the nation's ac-

[2] The opinion that only wooded land was fertile had been strongly held since the beginning of the westward movement. Pioneers searching for superior land invariably appraised the quality of the soil by noting the size of the native trees. When the advancing frontier eventually reached the extensive prairies of Illinois, the earlier comers preferred the islands of woodland and ignored the equally rich expanses of grassland in the development of which they would have been spared the labor of clearing.

ceptance of responsibility for finding them new homes; (3) along
the eastern edge of the plains stretched ample room supplied plenti-
fully with game; (4) the Indians could be required to make the
move were the demands of justice met by assuring them protection
in their new homes from the future encroachment of white settlement; (5) providentially, the plains country to which the Indians
could be moved had been determined by the Pike and Long
reports, and by other evidence, to be unfit for white occupation;
(6) therefore, finally, a line should be established by decree of the

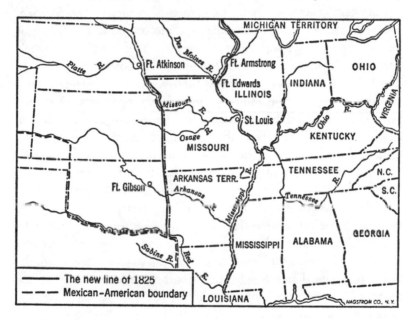

national government, corresponding to this natural climatological
line, beyond which white settlements should be forever prohibited.
The definitive line proposed by Calhoun ran north from the Red
River along the western border of Arkansas Territory, thence north
and east along the western and northern borders of Missouri to
the Mississippi, thence indefinitely northward up the Mississippi.

President James Monroe approved the Calhoun recommendation
and upon his reporting it to Congress January 27, 1825, congressional
approval gave it the final stamp of a national decision. This Monroe

frontier doctrine, prohibiting white interference in the Indian world, was considered at the time as significant as the other and more famous Monroe Doctrine, opposing European interference in the New World. The two doctrines were based on the same theory. Each sought to guard developing American democracies against outside influences until they had had time to gain stability. The primary objective of Monroe's Indian Line doctrine was not defense of Indian interests but defense of American interests. The presidents and congressmen, state governors, and legislators, who continued for the next generation almost unanimously to support the doctrine, were persuaded that renewed expansion was certain to slow national progress by dissipating national energies. The 1820's and 1830's were the era of internal improvement, of the American System, of the building of canals, turnpikes, and a National Road, of the encouragement of local industry, and of the appearance of steamboats on every navigable waterway. In what is now the eastern half of the United States there then remained untold resources still untapped and 500,000 square miles of territory still unpopulated. A tremendous effort to realize upon this enormous potential had been made, but a greater effort was recommended by every elected official or candidate for office. There was nearly universal agreement with the proposition that the country's advance toward unity and prosperity required a sustained attention to the improvement of communications, the development of industry, and the strengthening of political ties which must under no circumstances be interrupted or distracted by the divisive dangers of any further adventures in expansion.

Succeeding Presidents Adams, Jackson, and Van Buren accepted and endorsed Monroe's Indian Line doctrine. Successive congresses enacted statutes strengthening its provisions and prohibitions. By the doctrine's comprehensive charter, the Indian Intercourse Act of 1834, unlicensed whites were strictly forbidden to enter the plains region which had been formally designated the Indian Country. The enforced removal of eastern Indians had been continued until an unbroken phalanx of more than 30 Indian nations was ranged along the Indian side of a western frontier officially declared permanently immovable and impenetrable. To keep the peace along this interracial dividing line, the army had been enlarged, new frontier forts built, military roads constructed, regiments of dragoons raised. It was an army whose primary mission was not so much to guard the border against aggressors from without as from aggressors from within. Upon the extent of the United States an officially determined limit had been set with the officially declared intention that it be maintained indefinitely. The government of the United States, by the deliberate and cumulative decisions of a succession of congresses and administrations, had undertaken to place the plains, the Rockies, and the Pacific beyond the American horizon.

XI

ॐ

The Frontier People

FROM ITS INITIATION the westward movement had been propelled by the individual enterprise of a people who had evidenced as little regard for governmental edict as for common prudence. In their first crossing to the Monongahela they had exhibited no more respect for the restraints of the Proclamation Line, the evictions by the British army, the admonitions of their own provinces, or the protests of land companies than for the objections of their Indian antagonists. In moving on into Kentucky and Tennessee they had repudiated the jurisdiction of their states, and in holding their ground they had defied every effort of enemy powers to dislodge them while at the same time extorting the privilege of self-government from their own nation. In crossing the Mississippi they had demonstrated anew that their conception of their own interests admitted no more distinction between American and foreign territory than between either and Indian country. When now confronted by new and more formidable barriers to their further advance, they nevertheless continued by every attitude and action to ignore every interposition of national or multinational authority. The same decade that witnessed the federal government's considered attempt to limit expansion witnessed the resurgence of individual enterprise on an explosively widening scale. During those ten years the inhabitants of the American frontier forced their way up the Arkansas and the Red against the combined resistance of army and Indians, founded colonies in the heart of Spanish Texas, drove their wagons across the Great American Desert to Santa Fe, and roamed at will across the farthest west from Sonora to the Canadian Rockies and from San Diego Bay to the mouth of the Columbia. The response of the frontier people to the imposition of authoritarian restraint had been a longer leap forward than any yet made by the westward movement.

Immediately following the War of 1812 the frontier's spearhead on the lower Missouri resumed its westward thrust. In 1815, 50 wagons a day were reported ferrying the Mississippi to St. Louis. By 1817 the population of the Boonslick-Franklin area 230 miles up the Missouri was numbered not in hundreds but in thousands. Settlement continued to push westward along the fertile Missouri bottoms at the rate of 30 to 40 miles a year. These settlers of this outermost frontier were a hardier type than the land seekers then swarming across the Ohio and the Tennessee. They more resembled the earliest comers to the Monongahela and the Kentucky and, like them, were not only seeking land to cultivate but an isolation offering wider opportunities to hunt and wander. By 1827 their advance had reached the Great Bend of the Missouri at the mouth of the Kansas, and they were founding at Independence the most renowned of all wilderness crossroads. Here they had come up against the barrier presented by the national government's newly proclaimed Indian Line and the far more impressive barrier presented by the edge of the plains.

They had been warned that from here on all land had been officially designated Indian Country, that they could not hope to gain legal title to a foot of it, and that the Army of the United States stood ready to assist the Indians in resisting their intrusion. This might not have deterred them any more than they had been deterred when they had crossed the Appalachians and the Ohio in defiance of similar warnings. It was the sudden change in climate, the abrupt alteration in its every aspect of the face of the earth, that gave them pause. The very success which had marked their advance this far added to their frustration. The essential mechanics involved in the establishment of a new home in a wild environment had in their experience been totally dependent upon the constant availability not only of water but of wood. Wood had been considered indispensable for the construction of stockades, cabins, barns, fences, furniture, tools and implements. In this treeless and increasingly arid expanse now confronting them the maintenance of a family by dependence on the soil appeared clearly impracticable.[1]

But a desire to find a new family home had not been the only incentive that had kept the original frontier people in the forefront of the westward movement. Stronger impulses had been to escape the restraints and demands of ordinary society, to seek strange experiences and novel scenes. To men who had ventured this far the endless vista to the west which they had at length sighted offered greater satisfaction for these impulses than any they had previously envisaged. The racial stock which on the Pennsylvania-Virginia frontier had produced the Kentucky long hunters had by now bred a new generation of long hunters, the mountain men, capable of ventures even more complex and hazardous. Instead of vanishing into the unknown for 2 and 3 years, they began disappearing for 10 or 12. That they could not take families on such extraordinary excursions represented the ultimate escape from restraint. Those so burdened could ease the weight of responsibilities by earnestly forecasting an early and fortune-laden return. A species of reason could be lent these ready promises by the reports of the number of beaver in the streams of the Rockies and the prevalence of silver in Mexico. As a consequence of this insistence of individual venturers upon continuing to range westward, Independence became not the termination of a movement but the point of origin for a wider movement. From it sallied the wagon trains of the Santa Fe traders, the supply caravans of mountain men, and, within a genera-

---

[1] This plains subsistence problem was not satisfactorily solved until the construction of railroads and the introduction of the windmill and barbed wire.

tion, the covered wagons of pioneers bound for Oregon and California.

The first test of the national government's determination to contain the westward movement came on the southwestern frontier. West of the Mississippi stretched a 300-mile-wide belt of territory, extending 800 miles from the mouth of the Missouri southward into east central Texas, that displayed none of the natural threats to settlement brandished by the plains. It was as felicitously wooded and watered as any on the continent. This was also the area in which settlement must most surely be prevented were the government's containment policy to serve its purpose. The process of removing Indians from their former homes in the east had involved the progressive re-establishment of Cherokee, Creek, and Choctaw on the Arkansas and Red with protection from settler encroachment guaranteed by the federal government as an essential consideration in the removal treaties. The Red River had been accepted as the Spanish boundary with the implied assurance that law and order in Spanish territory would not be disturbed by the trespasses of American citizens. These were solid commitments to which the faith of the United States had been pledged. To redeem the pledge a considerable portion of the regular army was stationed in the area, forts were constructed, military roads built, and government agents assigned the Indians to watch over their rights.

The valleys of the Arkansas and the Red, however, offered physical advantages exceptionally attractive to a people as restless, impulsive, and acquisitive as this third generation of frontiersmen. It was a beautiful region of inviting streams, rivers, hills, forests, and meadows, made easy of access by its proximity to already settled border districts. Upon it fell a rainfall equaling that in the Carolinas or Virginia, and it abounded in game with buffalo, deer, and bear more numerous than in Kentucky and Tennessee at the first coming of the long hunters. These were irresistible temptations. At the close of the War of 1812 there was an immediate rush up both rivers of hunters and trappers, illegal squatters, and unlicensed traders. This was soon followed by a migration of more substantial settlers. They came by keelboat from Kentucky and

Tennessee or by wagon from Missouri or trudged overland, as in the earlier days of the Wilderness Road, hunting and trapping en route as they filtered southwestward. By 1820 hundreds of families had cleared corn patches and built cabins at choice sites until here, too, they had reached the edge of the plains as far west as what is now eastern Oklahoma. The recently relocated Indians, finding their new lands no safer from white trespass than had been their old, dispatched delegations to Washington to lodge indignant protests. In compliance with the government's urgent directives, the army repeatedly evicted the intruders at bayonet's point. The squatters merely moved to other locations in the forbidden area or slipped back and forth across the international boundary to return the next season to sites from which they had been driven. The ebb and flow of the contest between the police power of a government and the recalcitrance of one group of its citizens constituted in every respect a repetition of earlier efforts to repel squatters by the British army on the Monongahela in the 1760's and by the American army on the Ohio in the 1780's. Again, as had previously been the case, it was the government's resolve that was first to weaken.

The squatters' persistence had remained unshaken by other difficulties and dangers more disturbing than military evictions. They had come to a border seething with anarchy and violence in which every family's safety was its own responsibility. The transplanted Cherokee, Creek, Choctaw, and Delaware had become involved in a peculiarly vicious war with the resident Osage. Under cover of the general tumult, which kept the army preoccupied, frequent depredations were commited among the scattered settlements by roving parties of both belligerents. The widening opportunities for taking horses, loot, and scalps attracted other bands from the wilder nations of the adjacent plains. Not least among the hazards of border existence was the lawlessness associated with the proximity of an international boundary across which ruffians of every race could drift back and forth at will. Yet, in the face of such uncertainties, perils, privations, and prohibitions, the migration continued, with the population of Arkansas Territory passing 14,000 in 1820 and 30,000 in 1830. Once more the frontier people had come to stay.

Moreover, they were already contemplating the country south of the Red River, as little discouraged by the circumstance that this was a foreign country as they had been by their government's interdictions in their own. Since the first Americans had crossed the Mississippi to what was then Spanish soil, they had nursed an interest in Texas born of the frontiersman's predisposition to consider any distant land surely more attractive than any land he yet knew. As in all frontier movements there had been forerunners. American traders and horse hunters had occasionally crossed the Sabine as early as the 1780's, attracted by the enormous herds of Texas wild horses. In 1801 Philip Nolan, a Wilkinson protégé, was killed by Spanish soldiers while undertaking such an excursion devoted to the capture of wild horses for sale in the United States. Before 1812 a few Americans had gained Spanish permission to settle in the Nacogdoches area, among the earliest of whom was Daniel Boone, a nephew of the great Daniel. In 1812 Lieutenant Augustus Magee of the United States Army, whose current duty was the maintenance of order along the Louisiana-Texas boundary, resigned his commission for the purpose of organizing, with Wilkinson's approval,[2] an American invasion of Texas under pretense of assisting Mexican patriots then revolting against royalist Spain. He was joined by more than 800 Americans, some interested primarily in loot but many regarding the expedition as an opportunity to acquire grants of Texas land. Magee died early in the campaign but the invasion met with an initial success that extended to the capture of San Antonio. The filibusterers appeared for a time to have seized effective control of Texas 32 years in advance of its eventual annexation by the United States. At the Battle of Medina, August 18, 1813, however, the invaders were overwhelmed by a reinforced royalist column. Of the Americans engaged only 93 were known to have escaped back across the border.

[2] As further evidence of the continuity of expansionist intrigue on the southwestern frontier, Dr. John H. Robinson and Wilkinson's son, James, both of whom had been with Pike in 1807, were associated with this 1812-13 campaign.

For more than a century Spanish authorities had been painfully aware of the continuing menace to Mexico represented by the population vacuum in Texas. Sporadic efforts to promote any appreciable immigration of Mexican or European settlers to so remote a region had invariably failed. Its isolation, distance from markets, lack of communications, and the fierce hostility of its Indians posed difficulties from which all ordinary colonists recoiled. In 1820, the Spanish Cortés, harassed by the ten-year-long Mexican revolution, decided as a choice among many evils to permit the entry under certain circumstances and careful regulation of a limited number of American settlers in the hope that they might assist in the control of Indian belligerence while at the same time providing a counterweight to the activities of Mexican patriots and a possible bulwark to the intrusion of unauthorized Americans. Moses Austin, whose fortune gained in a Missouri lead mine operation had been lost in the post-war depression, was the first American to recognize the new opportunity. Making the 800-mile journey on horseback accompanied only by a black servant, he reached San Antonio in December 1820, to petition the Spanish governor for permission to settle 300 American families in Texas. After many rebuffs and delays he gained a hearing by making the point that he was not actually an American but a Spanish citizen and a Catholic by virtue of allegiances he had accepted when taking residence in Missouri in 1797. Overtaxed by his exertions, he died June 10, 1821, before learning his petition had been granted. Responsibility for organizing the colony devolved upon his 27-year-old son, Stephen, an obligation which was discharged with patience, sagacity, resolution, and history-making success.

The task confronting Stephen Austin upon his return to the United States to recruit colonists appeared formidable. Frontier history was again repeating itself by placing extraordinary burdens upon the first to undertake any new venture. His role was comparable to that of Richard Henderson who had dealt in 1775 with the need to persuade people to undertake the original settlement of Kentucky. His colony's site in Texas, like the first in Kentucky, was a remote and little known region, plagued by hostile Indians, and separated from the nearest American frontier by 200 miles of wilderness. It had other enormous disadvantages that had been unknown to Kentucky. The colonists must renounce their allegiance to the United States, subscribe to Catholicism, become residents of a country that had for 12 years been disrupted by bloody revolution, and accept the prospect of living henceforth under a changing government whose future policies were totally unpredictable.

The challenge provided a test of the frontier's disposition as acute as was the current test on the Arkansas of the government's resolution. The response demonstrated that there had been in this third frontier generation no diminishment in the impulse to embrace hazards. Austin was deluged with more letters applying for admission to his projected colony than he could find time to answer. He wrote the Spanish governor of Texas that he could as readily bring 1500 families as 300. The postwar depression had stimulated the response by giving many who might otherwise only have been tempted a valid excuse to make a new start. Public land in the United States was priced at $1.25 an acre while in Texas 4000 could be had for the equivalent of $200. But economic pressure did not provide an explanation accounting for the enthusiasm of the response. Men were not subjecting their families to such hazards for the sake of acres or dollars. Almost without exception the applications were from the frontier districts of Kentucky, Tennessee, Missouri and Arkansas Territory. They were from men who had been long conditioned to the esoteric satisfactions associated with being first in a new country and in whom the inclination to continue to venture had become a compulsion.

Austin's first families began arriving on the Brazos in December of 1821, some coming across the Gulf by schooner, others overland with wagons. The success of the Mexican Revolution required Austin's immediate departure for Mexico City to seek a new sanction from the new Mexican government which was not granted until April 14, 1823. Meanwhile, the settlers on the Brazos were suffering all of the vicissitudes that had been visited on the first settlers of Kentucky or Tennessee. They built the same one-room cabins, huddled in the same stockades, made the same struggle to escape starvation,[3] and dealt with community problems by resort to the same local self-government. Theirs was a re-enactment of former frontier experience with the exception of two distinctions which marked their difficulties as more harassing than any known before. They had come not to the edge of an Indian country but into the center of one. And the period in which violence threatened survival was destined to last many years longer here than had been the experience of Kentucky, Tennessee, Ohio, Missouri, or Arkansas.

In the earlier years of the colony the Indian danger posed the most demanding problem. During the century since Spain's first penetration, the Indians of Texas had gained less respect for white antagonists than had Indians farther north who had had always to deal with American frontiersmen. Spanish provincial governors had seldom been provided the military resources to punish Indian offenses. The few Mexican settlers, most of them unarmed, had courted safety by constant appeasement. A principal consideration leading to the Spanish and Mexican governments' decisions to permit American immigration had been the hope that the Americans might asume the burden of suppressing the Indian menace. This hope was justified as the newly arrived settlers promptly built stockades, invariably pursued raiders, and continued practicing the aggressive defense measures with which they had so long been familiar. When the initial Indian hostility became an acute emergency, they did not hesitate even to mount and arm their slaves. Other early problems were crop failures due to drought and the frequent horse-stealing inroads of Mexican and American outlaws from the no man's land along the international boundary. Still, in the face of so many widely reported disadvantages and perils, new American settlers continued to arrive. Each year the stream thickened. By 1830 the population of Austin's colony alone had increased to 4200. Again the frontier people had come to stay.

Since Americans had first crossed the Mississippi the lure of Texan land had been more than matched by the lure of Mexican silver.

---

[3] A major item in this emergency diet was horse meat. In parts of Texas wild horses outnumbered the buffalo.

From the days of Cortés' conquest the fabled riches of Mexico had gripped the imagination of the world. The northernmost Mexican town associated in the public mind with silver production was Santa Fe. But it was separated from the mouth of the Missouri by a 900-mile expanse of wild and desolate country which stretched across the most arid section of the plains and the hunting ground of the predatory Comanche. There was a secondary barrier even more forbidding than the distance, the terrain, and the Indians. Santa Fe had so far proved not the door to a market but the gate to a prison. The cornerstone of Spain's imperial policy was the rigid prohibition of trade between Spanish colonies and the people of other nations. In their earliest years on the lower Missouri, Arkansas, and Red in the first half of the eighteenth century, the French had made repeated efforts to open trade relations with Santa Fe. But Spanish official resistance had remained inflexible. Parties that managed to reach Santa Fe were subjected to confiscation of their goods and imprisonment.

When American hunters and trappers first began to roam widely west of the Mississippi, they were drawn in the direction of Santa Fe as by a lodestone. The very name had a pleasant ring that summoned up exotic visions of Mexican treasure and Spanish women. The Kentuckian, James Pursley,[4] whose career was reported in detail by Pike, was the first known to have reached his goal. After several adventurous years of trading and trapping during which he ranged from the Osage to the Mandan and then south again across the more distant plains, in June of 1805 he accompanied an Indian delegation to Santa Fe where he became a resident, supporting himself and prolonging his welcome by the practice of carpentry. Upon Pike's return from his congenial capitvity, his report on conditions south of the border had stirred added interest. Before 1810 Manuel Lisa had made a number of unsuccessful attempts to extend the trapping and Indian trading operations of his company to include trade with Santa Fe. In the great dispersal of free trappers during the Missouri Fur Company's 1810 withdrawal from the northwestern Missouri, Ezekiel Williams' party approached the

----

[4] Pike's spelling. More recent authorities have tended to prefer Purcell.

borders of New Mexico and several members, including the re-corded Joseph Philibert, visited New Mexican communities. It was becoming apparent that though official rejection of formal trade was still adamant the gregarious local inhabitants were privately disposed to welcome the random visits of individual American trappers.

With the outbreak of the Mexican Revolution, alert Americans in Missouri began at once to anticipate the lifting of restraints on trade with Santa Fe. Proceeding on this assumption, Robert McKnight conducted a pack train to Santa Fe in 1812. His goods were confiscated and he and his men imprisoned. Encouraged by a recurrence of reports of revolutionary successes, A. P. Chouteau and Julius De Mun made a similar attempt in 1817 to extend a trapping and trading enterprise on the Arkansas across the border into New Mexico. They lost their goods but after some weeks of imprisonment and mistreatment were permitted to return.

It was Mexico's assumption of self-government in 1821 that finally opened the door to trade with Santa Fe. Even then, the first Ameri-can efforts to exploit it proved premature. Thomas James, Colter's 1810 trapping companion on the upper Missouri, and John Mc-Knight, whose brother had been 10 years in a Spanish prison, left St. Louis May 10, 1821, with a stock of trade goods, ascended the Arkansas by keelboat, continued overland, were robbed by Comanche, and reached Santa Fe December 1st in time to assist in the local celebration of Mexican independence, but as a result of their many misadventures were staggered by an over-all loss of $7500 in the undertaking. Hugh Glenn and Jacob Fowler [5] started from Covington, Kentucky, June 14, 1821, with a trading-trapping expedition which after many difficulties with Indians reached the head of the Arkansas. Glenn went on ahead to Santa Fe to gauge the attitude of Mexican officials while Fowler, following Pike's 1807 route with his party of trappers, was hospitably received by the inhabitants of Taos.

[5] Whose personal account, *Journal of Jacob Fowler*, Elliott Coues, ed., New York, 1898, is made eminently worth reading not only by his colorful narrative but by his unique employment of the English language.

A later starter, the trapper, William Becknell, was the first to reach Santa Fe and the first to achieve a complete and profitable transaction. After an organizing meeting at the home of Ezekiel Williams, he left Franklin September 1, 1821, with four companions and a small cargo of traps and trade goods borne on pack animals. He reached Santa Fe November 16th, precisely the right moment to take the fullest advantage of Mexican realization that they were at last winning the revolution, was welcomed by local officials, was able to sell his few goods at an exhilarating profit, and finished his business with so much dispatch that he could start his return home December 11th. His arrival at Franklin January 29, 1822, with rawhide bags bulging with silver dollars stirred intense excitement. The Santa Fe Trail had at last been opened.

Becknell himself was first to take advantage of the glittering new opportunity. He set out May 22, 1822, on his second Santa Fe venture with 21 men and 3 *wagons*. The ensuing first crossing of the plains by wheeled vehicles marked one of the greater milestones in the westward movement. The astonishing demonstration that the transport of heavy cargoes such distances over so forbidding a terrain was not only possible but practicable attracted hundreds of eager emulators. This was the sort of enterprise, combining novelty, danger, distance, and an incidental chance of quick, large gain, which most appealed to frontier inclinations. By 1824, 26 wagons were employed in the annual trek by 180 men who realized a combined profit of $190,000. The merchandise shipped in 1828 in 100 wagons was valued at $150,000 upon which a net return of 40 per cent was expected. More than personal profit was involved. The annual influx of silver had a striking effect on the economy of the American frontier where specie had formerly been almost unknown. And the inhabitants of the border, who mattered most, had discovered that the Great American Desert was not a serious barrier.

Like all frontier ventures, the Santa Fe trade imposed extreme demands upon those who sought its rewards. Distance, excessive heat, long stretches without water, and danger from Indians made each journey a physical feat. The Indian peril steadily mounted

The more distant Plains Indians, enraptured by the prospect of so much loot, stalked the caravans, seizing every opportunity to stampede grazing stock or cut off stragglers or attempt hit-and-run attacks in which men could be killed and wagons pillaged. The national government's basic objection to the westward extension of settlement did not apply to this westward extension of trade and some tentative federal assistance was offered. There were desultory efforts to survey the route, the nearer Indians subject to federal control were enjoined to keep the peace, and in 1829 a detachment of regulars, at President Jackson's direction, provided an escort for that year's caravan as far as the Mexican border. Most years the traders were left to shift for themselves, a recourse in which they rapidly developed remarkable self-sufficiency. Each year's caravan was composed of many small "proprietors," each of whom had his own stock of trade goods or of equipment with which he proposed to undertake trapping upon reaching the far southwest. These smaller parties assembled at Council Grove, 150 miles southwest of Independence, the terminus for Missouri River boat traffic. Here by the town-meeting procedures of frontier self-government officers were elected, camp and march regulations adopted, guard rosters drafted, and mutual defense measures agreed upon. The Santa Fe caravan was in effect a traveling frontier settlement, a projection across the plains and into a foreign country of the frontier experience, even to the circumstance that the ringed wagons at night duplicated the stockade in the defense of which all were mutually responsible. With characteristic frontier adaptability, these processes were continually improved in the light of experience. Traders soon discovered, for example, that for plains traffic mules[6] were more serviceable than horses and that oxen were superior to either. In the management of Santa Fe wagon trains methods, skills, devices, and expedients were developed and perfected. Standards for plains travel had been established that were to prove of immeasurable advantage to the later immigrant trains upon

[6] The later prevalence of mules in Missouri was a consequence of the importation of Mexican stock by returning Santa Fe traders.

whose success depended American occupation of Oregon and California.

The arrival of Fowler's party of trappers at Taos had meanwhile led to consequences bearing on American prospects in the far west very nearly as significantly as had the opening of the Santa Fe Trail. As a further encouragement to American trade which they for a time regarded as a benefit to the Mexican community, Mexican officials were quite willing to permit American trapping in Mexican territory. The further hope that Mexicans might by observation and imitation learn to practice so profitable a profession endured over a shorter period for it soon became apparent that Mexicans were not temperamentally adapted to an enterprise requiring exposure to such excessive labor, hardship, isolation, and peril. The American response, on the other hand, as had so often before been the case when frontiersmen perceived a new opportunity, was literally explosive. Each year's train from Missouri brought more recruits, eager to trap this new field in which undepleted beaver streams were so many hundreds of miles nearer to supply bases in Taos and Santa Fe than were any to their old base in St. Louis.[7] Even William Becknell turned from his successful trading to engage in trapping ventures. Within the next three years Americans had trapped the Pecos and the Rio Grande, had crossed the continental divide to trap the San Juan, the lower Green, the Sevier, and the Provo and had pressed southwestward to trap the Salt, the Verde, and the Gila. Parties led by men bearing some of the most famous names in frontier annals, Etienne Provost, William Wolfskill, Joseph Walker, Antoine and Miguel Robidoux, Sylvester and James Pattie, Ceran St. Vrain, Bill Williams, and Ewing Young, had ranged the southwest from the shores of Great Salt Lake to the mouth of the Colorado. In so short a time they had become intimately familiar with every creek and spring, mesa

---

[7] The 16-year-old Kit Carson, whose family while intermarrying with the Boones had made the same successive moves westward from North Carolina to Kentucky to Missouri, reached Taos by the 1826 train. His next return home to the Missouri frontier was in 1842 after he had roamed the transmountain west so thoroughly that he was prepared to serve as John C. Fremont's guide.

and canyon, in 300,000 square miles of formerly unknown mountain and desert, their impetuous energy having carried them throughout New Mexico, Arizona, southern Colorado, and southeastern Utah.

American penetration of the southwest had been accomplished with the consent of foreign neighbors, first Spain and then Mexico. Advance into the northwest was confronted by the same difficulties of distance and Indian hostility and the added challenge of foreign rivalry. The competition of English traders had been active, determined, and supported by the same great fur company resources that had overmatched Astor's Columbia project. The terms of this rivalry were somewhat qualified by the Convention of 1818 in which the two nations agreed that all territory east of the Rockies and south of the 49th parallel, the present United States-Canada boundary, be reserved exclusively for American use and all north of it for British. By the same agreement title to all territory west of the continental divide was left subject to later negotiation with the right to its use by traders and trappers of both nations in the meantime conceded. In less diplomatic language, the Columbia had been put up for grabs. This grabbing process flourished for the next 28 years before a final verdict was returned in the competition to determine which nationals were the more aggressively grasping.

During the War of 1812 American traders had been driven from the upper Missouri. Almost the only American to remain active even on the lower river had been Lisa, and the remnant of the Missouri Fur Company had become commonly known as Manuel Lisa's company. English traders had taken advantage of the opportunity to promote antipathy to Americans among all Indians dependent upon English supply sources. The full advantage that might have been gained during this 10-year lapse in the American trade effort had been lost, however, through the ferocity of the internal competition between the two great English combines, the Hudson's Bay Company and the North West Company, which had wasted the energies of their employees, depleted trapping areas, debauched the Indians, and destroyed profits for all concerned.

The American government's inclination to defend American interests wherever and whenever they conflicted with British interests, a disposition stimulated by the memories of two wars and 50 years of Anglo-American controversy, had led to the 1819 dispatch of the Atkinson expedition, also called the Yellowstone expedition in reference to the fortification of that river which constituted its major objective. It had been planned that this military undertaking would be conducted in such overwhelming strength that there could be no question of so completely dominating the upper Missouri that the Indians of the region must forthwith recognize American ascendency. The government's resolution proved shortlived. After Atkinson's initial attempt even to get upriver had ended in so inglorious a fiasco, Congress, hard-pressed for money by the developing depression, declined to appropriate funds to renew the attempt at military occupation. Once more the frontier was left to its own devices. These, as always before, proved fully adequate.

The proportions of the army's 1819 preparations had hastened the reawakening of border interest in the northern fur trade. Frontiersmen whose attention had not already become fixed on prospects in Arkansas, Texas, or Sante Fe were beginning again to look toward the upper Missouri. The Missouri Fur Company was reorganized in 1819 with a number of new partners. Manuel Lisa died the next year but able Joshua Pilcher, a veteran of the Sioux trade, proved a worthy successor. In the fall of 1821 Pilcher with an advance party established Fort Benton at the mouth of the Big Horn on the same site the company had abandoned in 1810. In the spring of 1822 two of the partners, Michael Immell and Robert Jones, set out upriver with 180 men and a determination to recover the rich beaver territory in the sinister Three Forks area from which the company had been driven by the Blackfeet 12 years before.

While the old company was displaying these new energies a rival enterprise, among the most striking in frontier history, was taking shape. Andrew Henry had long been a friend and neighbor of William Ashley, a merchant-soldier-politician who had moved from Virginia to Missouri in 1809. Henry wanted to go back to the mountains and Ashley wanted money to advance his political career.

Henry's wilderness experience and Ashley's organizing ability made them a potent team. They inserted an advertisement in the Missouri *Gazette* of February 13, 1822:

TO Enterprising Young Men: The subscriber wishes to engage ONE HUNDRED MEN, to ascend the river Missouri to its source, there to be employed for one, two or three years. For particulars enquire of Major Andrew Henry, near the Lead Mines, in the County of Washington, (who will ascend with, and command the party) or to the subscriber at St. Louis. William H. Ashley.

The character of the Missouri *Gazette's* circulation was indicated by the number among its readers of young men sufficiently "enterprising" to welcome an employment committing them to years in a wild and distant region from which Blackfeet had driven every previous American who had ever ventured so far. Another list of never to be forgotten frontier names soon appeared on the rolls of the new company: Jedediah Smith, Thomas Fitzpatrick, William Sublette, James Bridger, James Clyman, John Weber, Johnson Gardner, James Beckwourth, Edward Rose, Hugh Glass. The Ashley-Henry organization's success was founded on their understanding of the frontier temperament which led them to take full advantage of individual enterprise. Their recruits were not to become paid employees of an impersonal company but to remain free trappers the returns from whose labors under company guidance and with company support would be evenly divided.

The 1821-22 resurgence of the American fur trade was matched by a comparable resurgence on the British side. The ruinous rivalry between the two great English companies was resolved in 1821 by the British government's insistence upon a merger, combining the capital and prestige of the older with the vigor and aggressiveness of the younger, that retained the name Hudson's Bay Company. Under the leadership of a dynamic new young governor, George Simpson, the reorganized and revitalized English fur trade began making rapid, forceful moves to regain the time and ground it had wasted. As a result of these several developments when Americans and Englishmen renewed their competition for the natural wealth of the far west, it was with a fairly equal start and on nearly equal if different terms.

The American race upriver for the privilege of being first to confront English and Indian opposition got under way that same spring of 1822 that witnessed Becknell's departure in the other direction for Santa Fe with the first wagons to cross the plains. Henry managed the earliest start, April 15th, followed May 8th by a second contingent, and then by the larger and slower party of Jones and Immell. Henry suffered two disasters en route by the wreck of his second keelboat with a $10,000 cargo and, after passing the Mandan, by the loss to the Assiniboin of the horse herd he had accumulated to enable him to operate beyond the head of navigation at the foot of the Rockies. He was, as a consequence, forced to build his fort at the mouth of the Yellowstone instead of the more advanced location at the Falls which he had intended. Ashley, leaving June 21st with a third expedition, joined him here in October and soon thereafter Jones and Immell passed through on their way up the Yellowstone to the Missouri Company post at the mouth of the Big Horn. These lonely rivers that had known no Americans since 1810 had been suddenly enlivened by processions of Americans. Ashley returned that fall to St. Louis to bring up more men and supplies. From the advance depots of both companies parties were dispatched to undertake trapping operations in the Blackfoot country ' on the headwaters of the Missouri.

Ashley started upriver again March 10, 1823, with his reinforcements, followed soon by Pilcher with his support party. En route Ashley encountered Jedediah Smith, who had wintered with Henry, paddling southward on the first of that incredible traveler's immortal journeys. Smith had been dispatched with word of Henry's desperate need for more horses, which could presumably be more reasonably acquired from the Sioux or Aricara than from the avaricious Crow. Continuing his ascent of the river, Ashley approached the Aricara with circumspection, keeping his boats anchored well offshore. There was need for discretion. The Aricara were notorious for deceit and violence, in their relations with other Indians as much as with whites. Their two towns with their earthen houses within palisaded walls and ditches constituted twin fortresses, and they had been well supplied with guns during the recent years of British trade. They professed friendliness, however, and a willingness to sell horses. Smith with a party of some 40 men camped on a sandspit adjoining the Aricara palisade to conduct the negotiations, procuring upwards of 20 horses the first day. That night a violent storm threatened Ashley's boats and possibly confirmed the Aricara in a design which presumably they had contemplated from the outset.

Earlier in the night one of Smith's horse tenders had entered the town in quest of feminine companionship, a phase of hospitality for which the Aricara were noted. Toward morning Ashley's interpreter, Edward Rose, ran from the town to report the visitor had been killed. The storm prevented the removal of either horses or men from the sandspit party's camp which was in point-blank range of the lower town's palisade. At dawn of June 2, 1823, the Aricara opened fire. Smith's men fought back from breastworks contrived from the carcasses of their fallen horses, but their return fire was ineffective against their fortified opponents. In the unequal contest 14 Americans were killed and 9 wounded. Ashley's terrified French boatmen refused to row his keelboats to the rescue. The sandspit survivors were with the greatest difficulty extricated by small boats and swimming. Ashley withdrew downstream to the protection of the nearest river-bottom woodland.[8]

The wounded and all who were inclined to abandon the expedition were sent by one keelboat with news of the Aricara attack to the army post at Council Bluffs, Fort Atkinson, 640 miles below. The hard core of his American free trappers stayed with Ashley. They had no more thought than he of waiting for possible help or of renouncing their design to reach the mountains. Smith volunteered to go overland to the mouth of the Yellowstone to summon Henry. By the union of the two parties it was considered that sufficient strength would have been developed to regain freedom of movement. So expeditious was Smith's daring dash that Henry,

---

[8] There is an eyewitness account by a participant in this engagement in *James Clyman American Frontiersman*, Charles L. Camp, ed., San Francisco, 1928.

descending the river by boat, joined Ashley July 2nd at his island camp off the mouth of the Cheyenne.[9] He brought with him news of other disasters as depressing as the Aricara battle. The Blackfoot onslaught, in conjunction with the dispersal of manpower required by the nature of trapping operations, had proved as catastrophic in 1823 as in 1810. Henry had lost 4 men and the Missouri Fur Company 9, including Jones and Immell, along with the major portion of that company's equipment and fur catch. It was evident that the Indians of the upper Missouri, emboldened by their many successes over Americans, represented a deterrent which made profitable trading and trapping operations on the river impossible. Instead of admitting defeat, Ashley and Henry began immediately to survey expedients by which the mountains might be reached overland.

A grandiose military effort to reopen the river was, however, already under way. The news of the Aricara attack had reached Colonel Henry Leavenworth, commander at Fort Atkinson, near the mouth of the Platte, June 18th. His record in the War of 1812 had been distinguished by gallantry and he was fully conscious that as senior military officer on the Missouri he represented not only the dignity of the United States Army but the sovereignty of the United States. It did not require the urging of Pilcher, who chanced to be at his company's nearby Fort Lisa and who realized how entirely the Missouri fur trade depended upon suppression of Indian interference with river traffic, to incline Leavenworth to consider inflicting upon the Aricara the punishment that they had so flagrantly invited. His initial reaction was illustrated by the language of a letter written by his advisor, local Indian agent Benjamin O'Fallon,[10] to his superior in the Indian service, William Clark: "The whole Arickara nation . . . owes us blood and I am in hopes that no true American will tamely stand by and . . . recognize a white flag, so long as the brow of an Arickara is decorated with the scalp of our people." Pilcher enlisted company employees in

---

[9] The Aricara, unaware that he had been informed of their recent malevolence, attempted to entice his passing flotilla ashore by waving welcoming blankets.

[10] Son of Dr. James O'Fallon, George Rogers Clark's brother-in-law and associate in Kentucky's Yazoo and French conspiracies, 1790-94.

a support detachment and undertook to rally his old friends, the Sioux, to join in the gathering assault on their old enemies, the Aricara.

Leavenworth started upriver June 22, 1823, with six companies of infantry and a small corps of artillery, employing both water and land transport in his northward march. By the time he reached Ashley's camp July 30th, Pilcher's Sioux had continued streaming to join him until their total number had aggregated nearly 800. Leavenworth's army had increased to over 1100, including his 223 soldiers, Ashley's 80 trappers and boatmen, and Pilcher's 40 Missouri Fur Company followers. Its earnest commander christened his combined force the Missouri Legion and invested his principal supporters with appropriate temporary rank.

As the avenging force neared the Aricara towns, the Sioux galloped ahead. The equally belligerent Aricara came out to meet them and a spirited cavalry action developed. Most of the Aricara were equipped with trade muskets, commonly known as London fusils, while less than a third of the Sioux possessed guns. From the count of the known dead, 2 Sioux and 13 Aricara, the fire of the Sioux archers had been more effective than that of the Aricara musketeers. When the head of the white column was sighted, the Aricara retired behind their palisades and the Sioux drew aside, interested in observing the combat conduct of the Americans.

Leavenworth invested the two towns but delayed his contemplated attack until his artillery could be brought up. The next morning, August 10, 1823, the army's 2 six-pounders, several swivels, and a 5½-inch howitzer commenced the bombardment while the attack formations of soldiers, traders, trappers, and boatmen awaited the momentarily expected order to deliver the assault. The cannon fire made less impression on the palisade and earthen Aricara houses than had been anticipated, and the ammunition dwindled before what Leavenworth considered a sufficient preparation for an assault had been achieved. To the diversion of the Sioux and the disgust of the traders and most of his officers, Leavenworth seized upon various pretexts to continue to delay ordering an attack. Losing interest in the war, the Sioux began stealing his horses and mules. With the fear that he might be taken in the rear by his Sioux allies added to his former apprehensions, Leavenworth eagerly accepted an Aricara offer to negotiate. The upshot of the parley was Leavenworth's undertaking to forgive Aricara misdeeds in return for an Aricara promise to restore Ashley's losses and to keep the peace henceforth. After another day of aimless discussion of terms during which one of Ashley's horses was replaced, the Aricara slipped away to the plains in the night, leaving Leavenworth with possession of their empty towns as the only reward of his ambitiously conceived campaign.

This third effort of the regular army to impress the Indians of the upper Missouri with the military power of the United States had been as sad a failure as the first by Pryor in 1807 and the second by Atkinson in 1819. The infuriated Pilcher, addressing Leavenworth, set forth his view of the realities involved with terrible clarity:

> You came to restore peace and tranquillity to the country . . . your operations have been such as to produce the contrary effect, and to impress the different Indian tribes with the greatest possible contempt for the American character. You . . . have by the imbecility of your conduct and operations, created and left impossible barriers.

Upon Leavenworth's beginning his withdrawal downriver, somebody set fire to the deserted Aricara towns. He considered this a breach of the truce he had negotiated and announced the "dishonorable discharge" of Pilcher and his followers. The ensuing feud between Leavenworth's critics and defenders blazed on for years, but at the moment the traders were left to the bleak contemplation of their immediate problem. Failure to punish the Aricara had ensured the multiplication of other Indian attacks. Continued upper river operations had been made clearly impracticable by the constant threat to so long and indefensible a line of communications. This imposed a particularly crippling handicap on Pilcher's Missouri Fur Company which had been tied to the river, dependent upon hired employees, and forced to the verge of bankruptcy by its tremendous losses. But for Ashley, with his corps of free trappers, there was still room for maneuver. Dropping down to Fort Kiowa, the Berthold, Pratte and Chouteau firm's trading outpost in the Sioux country near the mouth of White River, he began to buy horses to enable him to reactivate his enterprise by a strike overland across the plains to the mountains.

Ashley's command decision placed the Aricara episode in its true perspective as a major turning point in far western history. So far American penetration had been directed southwestward toward Texas and Santa Fe or northwestward up the Missouri, except in the one instance of the disastrous venture of the overland Astorians, 14 years earlier. The renewed demonstration of the national government's inability to furnish protection had left the American traders no alternatives other than to relinquish hope of gaining mountain beaver or to accept the fearful and unfamiliar hazards of plains transport and distances. In unhesitatingly accepting these hazards, Ashley and his associates moved with vigor and dispatch. Enough horses were accumulated to permit Henry to get off for the Yellowstone by September 1st. As soon as more horses could be purchased or borrowed, Smith set out toward the end of September with the understanding that he was to keep on beyond the Yellowstone region until he had crossed the mountains to trap the Columbia country. Irked by this spectacle of Ashley's initiative, Pilcher changed his mind on the feasibility of plains travel and hastily got off a party in Smith's wake. Under the leadership of Charles Keemlee and William Gordon, both survivors of the Jones and Immell massacre, it reached the Big Horn where it was despoiled by the Crow, committing this final spasm of effort by the Missouri Company to total failure.

Smith's overland party was limited to less than 20 but among them were men each of whom could be counted a host: William Sublette,[11] Thomas Fitzpatrick, James Clyman, Edward Rose.

[11] Whose grandfather, Colonel William Whitley, early in the Revolution founded the famous station that guarded the Kentucky end of the Wildnerness Road.

Smith was launched on the most significant journey in the history of far western exploration since Lewis and Clark and one which for distance, duration, and danger has had no rival in the world history of exploration. His many thousands of miles of unceasing travel during the next seven years, much of it through regions never before traversed by white men, were achieved in the face of an unparalleled series of disasters. These began at once. Due to an exceptionally dry fall, he had scarcely lost sight of the Missouri before encountering a waterless expanse in crossing which his party escaped death by thirst by the narrowest of margins. He saved two of his weaker followers by burying them to their necks to conserve body moisture until he could return to their succor from an eventually discovered water hole. He continued to strike directly west, crossing the South Dakota Bad Lands and then the Black Hills. On the western slopes of the Hills Smith was mangled by a wounded grizzly which at one stage in the struggle seized his head in its jaws. Clyman stitched eyebrow, ear, and scalp back in place and after ten days' rest to recuperate from the loss of blood Smith was able to ride on. He had procured some badly needed extra horses from a Sioux hunting camp and now bought more from the Cheyenne. Threading a way among the immense herds of game in the valley of Powder River, he crossed the Big Horn Mountains and, guided and sponsored by Rose, reached a winter camp of tolerant Crow on Wind River. Here, as planned, he met the John Weber party, dispatched up the Big Horn by Henry after Henry had abandoned his post at the mouth of the Yellowstone to establish a new one at the mouth of the Big Horn where he had once been situated in 1810. The parties achieving the Wind River tryst had between them covered 1300 miles by widely circuitous routes. The resort to overland travel was already beginning to function in accordance with schedules which were soon to prescribe future meetings in distant mountain areas at the end of journeys measured in years and thousands of miles.

Smith paused at the Crow camp only to breathe his exhausted men and horses. He was on his way to the Columbia, and a successful spring hunt required a prompt arrival in any projected trapping area. Still following the general route taken by Hunt's westbound Astorians, he attempted in February 1824 to get over the divide by Union Pass which Hunt had crossed in late summer. In midwinter the depth of the snow made passage impossible. Taking more careful counsel with the Crow, Smith heard of the "more open country to the south" of which Stuart had heard on the Snake 10 years earlier and which the Crow explained could be gained by rounding the southeast shoulder of the Wind River Mountains. He took the easy turn up the Popo Agie which Hunt had missed, crossed southeastward over the low watershed to the Sweetwater, and ascended it to South Pass. It was a frigidly wintry journey with March winds so cold and violent that campfires were often blown out or blown entirely away.

He and his 11 half-frozen companions were taking historic steps. They were the first to find the eastern approaches to the great mountain gateway. Others had reduced the scope of the unknown without coming upon this heart of the mystery. Lewis and Clark had reached the lower Snake from the Missouri's headwaters and descended the Columbia to the Pacific. Hunt and Stuart had between them traced the upper Snake, the connection between the Snake and the upper Bear, and the Platte from the mouth of the Sweetwater to the Missouri. When Smith had reached the Bear, he had filled in the last link in the route that was to become the Overland Trail. White men had then traversed every foot of the entire way west from the mouth of the Platte to the mouth of the Columbia over which empire-building wagon trains would pass into possession of Oregon. It was this ascent of the Sweetwater that in covered-wagon days was always regarded as the most memorable stage of that momentous road. Fitzpatrick was one of that little company making it for the first time now. When the first settlers' wagon train made it, 17 years later, Fitzpatrick was its guide.

During this first crossing of South Pass from east to west, Smith had no immediate idea, however, of the significance of his achievement. He realized that, while passing through this 20-mile-wide gap in the Rockies, he had unwittingly crossed the continental divide only after he came upon streams running westward. What interested him more was the quantity of beaver on the Green and its tributaries.[12] After a successful spring hunt, he sent Fitzpatrick with two men down the Platte with the catch. Clyman had been lost and given up for dead. Smith with the other 7 men turned westward and northwestward. There was still his Columbia mission to discharge.

He had come upon disturbing signs that British trappers had been in this rich beaver country before him. How early, vigorous, and wide ranging had been that penetration, launched from posts on the Columbia, no American yet realized. In its closing years the North West Company had taken active advantage of the opportunity presented by the dispossession of the Astorians. In the winter of 1818-19 Donald McKenzie had established a camp on the Boise River from which he had extended operations as far south as the upper Bear and as far east as the upper Green. This feverish exploitation of the southern reaches of the Snake country continued through the next four seasons with the express intention of skimming off the cream of the region's natural wealth before the Americans put in their expected appearance. Drawn by the new activity in an area which had formerly harbored only a few wandering bands of Shoshone, the Blackfeet began ranging as widely through the region, traveling many hundreds of miles from their distant homeland to pounce with impartial gusto on strange Indians or white trappers. Finan McDonald, commander of the 1823 Snake country brigade who had crossed the Rockies with Thompson in 1807, returned with 4000 skins after repeated bloody encounters with Blackfeet to report, "when that Cuntre will see me agane the Beaver will have Gould Skin." It was this Blackfoot menace that gave Smith the entering wedge of his opportunity.

That spring of 1824 while Smith was struggling through blizzards up the Sweetwater, Alexander Ross, the onetime Astorian, was struggling southward over snowbound passes with that year's Hudson's Bay Company Snake country brigade. Since the merger the Company had accepted the collaboration of an increasing number

[12] Etienne Provost, working out of Taos, was trapping that spring a few miles away on the other side of the Uintah Mountains.

of free trappers, though they were paid for the skins that they collected less than 10 per cent of the price their American counterparts received from American companies. Most of these independent trappers, termed freemen by the British, were former employees of the North West Company or the half-breed descendants of earlier traders. They were not highly esteemed by their employers. Alexander Ross described his auxiliaries as "a more discordant headstrong, ill designing set of rascals than form this camp, God never permitted together in the fur trade." Simpson characterized free-

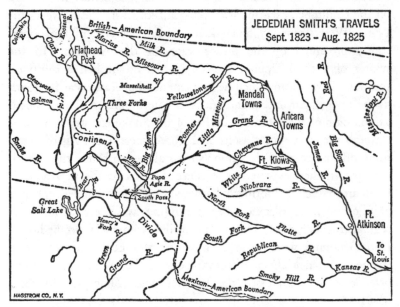

men as "the very scum of the country and generally outcasts from the service for misconduct . . . the most unruly and troublesome gang to deal with in this or perhaps any other part of the world." A number of these freemen, including four American ex-Astorians, had deserted the British trade to range independently to such distances that by 1823 some of them were beginning to appear at Taos and St. Louis. Among these freemen attached to the Company's service was a group of Iroquois, many with their families, who some years earlier had ventured west in the hope of improving their fortunes.

Smith, trapping his way westward and northwestward from the Green, came upon the isolated camp of Ross's Iroquois. So accidental a meeting could hardly have resulted from the crossing of stranger and more distant paths. Smith had been born on the New York frontier almost within sight of Unadilla, the Revolutionary stronghold of the Iroquois. From that common point of origin the parties to this meeting on the Snake had had to make tremendous journeys, Smith by the Ohio, the Missouri, and the American plains, the Iroquois by the Great Lakes, the Saskatchewan, and the Canadian plains, and both by endless traverses of the Rockies, to have come to this ultimate chance encounter. The Iroquois were short of food and ammunition and in intense fear of the Blackfeet. They were glad to sell him their furs, which they owed to their own company, in return for his protection.

Smith buried his fur catch which had been much augmented by this fortunate acquisition and escorted the Iroquois to Ross's main camp. He had instantly recognized his opportunity. His principal mission was to acquire as rapidly as possible a working knowledge of the Columbia country, and there could be no quicker way to accomplish this than to require the British, who were already familiar with it, to provide him with a conducted tour of it. Ross could not object for by the Convention of 1818 Americans had an equal legal right to move as they chose in the area while the Company had sternly instructed its representatives to avoid physical conflict with Americans. Smith brazenly followed Ross's homeward march north to Flathead Post in northwestern Montana where the Americans wintered as the most unwelcome guests of the Hudson's Bay Company.

Ashley in St. Louis in 1823-24, as had Astor in New York in 1812-13, was committed to months of anxious waiting upon news of the fate of his company's far-ranging parties. He occupied some of the interim in running unsuccessfully for governor of Missouri, a result, however disappointing to his personal ambitions, which greatly benefited his country by continuing to focus his restless energies on the mountain enterprise. Until late summer of 1824 all the news was bad. Indian hostility had persisted on the upper

Missouri until Fort Kiowa had become the northernmost American trading post on the river. The formerly more moderate Mandan, Sioux, Minnataree, and Crow had joined in the harassment. Henry had had 6 more killed. In September, however, the news turned suddenly better. Henry, having dispatched his Yellowstone brigade west through South Pass in the wake of Smith, came downriver with the Big Horn fur catch. Henry was through with the fur business, having for the second time been convinced that the maintenance of mountain posts required too great an effort to permit a a profit, but his 1824 return of furs was of sufficient dimensions to keep Ashley's company alive. That September also brought encouraging word from Fitzpatrick who with his two companions had struggled, weaponless and destitute, into Fort Atkinson. On his way east down the Sweetwater with the Smith party's Green River catch he had been shipwrecked at Devil's Gate, had retrieved and cached the furs at Independence Rock, and was already on his way back up the Platte with pack horses to get them.[13]

Ashley was a leader capable of precedent-shattering decisions. He agreed with Henry's judgment on the inefficacies of the trading-post system but he was beginning to envisage another trading pattern, never before attempted, by which advantage might yet be taken of the unanticipated penetration west of South Pass by his company's advance brigades. With a hastily organized support party of 80 men he met Fitzpatrick at Fort Atkinson, sent the Green River furs to St. Louis further to bolster his company's credit, and on November 3, 1824, guided by Fitzpatrick, struck westward up the Platte. He was erecting another outstanding milestone in the westward movement. With him he was taking a sufficient store of supplies to enable his corps of free trappers to remain in the mountains as long as they chose.

That same week his opposite number in the British trade, George Simpson, governor of the Hudson's Bay Company Northern De-

---

[13] That summer Hugh Glass and James Clyman, each alone, without weapons and subject to Indian indignities, were suffering the same privations as Fitzpatrick while likewise making their way from the mountains to the mouth of the Platte.

partment, was arriving on the Columbia to make comparable decisions bearing upon the momentous convergence of rival forces about to develop. He had come west prepared to abandon the southern Columbia basin as an area in which Indian hostility, added to the distance over which supplies must be transported, made operations unprofitable. But after consultation with local commanders he came to another conclusion more in accord with his government's preference that British territorial claims be maintained by continued activity in the region. Simpson ordered Fort George moved to the north bank of the Columbia where it became Fort Vancouver and directed his field brigades to trap the area south of the river so improvidently and exhaustively that American trappers might be discouraged from entering it. This was regarded as a sufficient deterrent to keep all Americans at a distance for an indefinite period. No thought was entertained by anybody concerned, including either government, that any effort by American settlers to cross the stupendous barrier of plains and mountains might ever develop.

To undertake this pre-emptive harvest of furs south of the Columbia, Simpson selected the most capable and aggressive of his brigade commanders, Peter Skene Ogden. The mission was considered so urgent that the expedition set out from Flathead Post December 12, 1824, accepting the supreme hazard of mountain travel in midwinter in order to gain the advantage of a spring hunt as far as possible to the south. Smith promptly packed up and trailed along. On his laborious way south Ogden crossed back and forth over the continental divide by passes first used by Lewis and Clark, trapping as he progressed whenever ice conditions made this feasible. His exasperating shadow, Smith, kept within close range, occasionally selling a few furs to Ogden at the low British price to provide for his essential needs.

While Ogden and Smith were pushing southward through mountain snowfields, Ashley was pressing westward up the Platte. His objective was likewise so urgent that he had felt obliged to risk the incredible hardships of midwinter travel on the high plains. At the forks of the Platte he was compelled to forgo taking the direct route to South Pass over which Fitzpatrick had traveled three times in recent months. He kept instead to the better wooded South Platte for the sake of the more available fuel and shelter for which he had so much need at this rigorous season. Occasionally pausing to rest men and horses or to take cover from recurrent blizzards, he kept stubbornly westward over the Laramie and Medicine Bow ranges, somewhat approximating the later route of the Union Pacific Railroad, and at one stretch below South Pass retracing a short segment of Stuart's eastbound route. Reaching the Green River April 19, 1825, he dispatched three detachments, north, west, and south, to search for the Weber and Smith parties of whose location he had no clearer idea than that they must be somewhere west of South Pass. When found they were to be directed to assemble for the delivery of their furs and the procurement of new supplies at a designated meeting place on Henry's Fork of the Green at the foot of the Uintah Mountains. He himself built boats and attempted an exploration of the lower course of the Green with the hope that if he did not come across trace of his men he might, in the meantime, ascertain whether it was the Colorado or the fabled Buenaventura believed to flow westward into the Pacific.

As the advance of spring made traveling easier, Ogden, headed upon what must in time prove a collision course with Ashley, pushed southward. After crossing the Snake, Smith, his unwanted companion, disappeared. There is no record that Smith had known that Weber had wintered on the Bear but, with his amazing instinct for deciphering the geographical unknown, he shortly found Weber's party. Ogden had started with 61 men and 268 horses but had been plagued by the desertion of a number of his freemen. He was also plagued by a growing apprehension that many more Americans than Smith could have made their way this far west in the last few months. On May 4th he learned from Shoshone "that a party of 25 Americans wintered near this & are going in the same direction we had intended going." He nevertheless kept on down the Bear but, before reaching Great Salt Lake, crossed southeastward from the Bear watershed into the valley of the Weber where he camped in Ogden Hole, site of the present city of Ogden.

On his way he encountered two freemen who had deserted Michel Bourdon's 1822 Snake country brigade from whom he gathered even more disagreeable news. The deserters had since 1822 visited New Mexico and returned with an American party led by Etienne Provost which had suffered an attack in which 6 fellow deserters had been killed by Indians. Before Ogden opened the alarming vista of Americans swarming into the mountains not only from distant St. Louis but from this nearer and hitherto unsuspected base at Taos. The next morning Provost himself rode in to complain of British incitement of the Indian massacre of his trappers the previous autumn. Ogden stiffly denied the allegation while voicing his own indignation over the American practice of instigating desertions. There was evidence of the disconcerting rapidity with which events were moving in the revelation that Provost was not yet aware of the presence of other Americans in the vicinity. Ogden morosely observed in his diary, "the whole country (is) overrun with Americans." But much worse was coming.

That afternoon of May 23, 1825, Weber's party, of whose movements and adventures since leaving the Big Horn in 1824 no record has been found, reappeared on the stage of history. A procession of 25 Americans, accompanied by 14 of Ogden's deserters, approached the British camp bearing an American flag. Their spokesman was not Weber or Smith but a free trapper, Johnson Gardner, whose aggressiveness made him a natural leader of his like-minded companions. Ogden served the Hudson's Bay Company which was sponsored by the British government while Gardner could speak with no other authority than that stemming from the concensus of a frontier town meeting. Nevertheless, he demanded to know by what right a British party flaunting the flag of Great Britain was trespassing on "American territory." Neither Ogden nor Gardner was aware that Ogden Hole was below the 42nd parallel and therefore within the borders of Mexico. In any event, Ogden could not be convinced that the country west of the Rockies had been formally conferred upon the United States. It had been his custom, in order to impress Indians, to fly his country's flag over his encampments but, perhaps happily, the standard Gardner had come to tear down had chanced not to be raised that day. The argument, at times violent and obscene, extended into the next day. Ogden, though outnumbered and increasingly uncertain of the loyalty of his remaining followers, clung to his affirmation that he had no intention of abstaining from trapping the region unless and until ordered to withdraw by his own government.[14]

The furious dispute did not quite reach the pitch of overt conflict. But under cover of the altercation the Americans were bringing into play a weapon more effective than gunfire. Attracted by the American offer of $3.00 per skin, in contrast to the 30 cents Ogden was authorized to pay, more of Ogden's freeman were deserting, taking their season's fur catch with them. As the only hope of escaping this steady attrition, he was obliged to begin a precipitate retreat May 27, 1825, and to keep on northward until he could feel certain he had outdistanced American subversion. He found some consolation summer trapping in American territory on the headwaters of the Missouri, then moved westward to Fort Walla Walla to report the disastrous outcome of his southern venture.

This first clash in the farther mountains between American free trappers and the Hudson's Bay Company had seemed an overwhelming victory. Individual enterprise had successfully challenged a rival reinforced by all the organized resources of a long-established and government-sanctioned monopoly. It was unquestionably an initial victory and, moreover, one that was soon consolidated. Ashley's hope to explore the lower Green was grounded on the rocks of impassable canyons but his major purposes were accomplished. He encountered several of Provost's Taos trappers who presently produced their leader. At Ashley's June 7, 1825, meeting with Provost on Duchesne River he got the answer to both questions he most wanted answered. Provost was able to assure him that the Green was the Colorado and that Ashley's wandering brigades had learned of the appointed meeting place on Henry's Fork. Guided

[14] Definitive detail bearing on this historic confrontation and its significance may be found in *Peter Skene Ogden's Snake Country Journals, 1824-25 and 1825-26*, E. E. Rich, ed., London, 1950; Frederick Merk, *Fur Trade and Empire*, Cambridge, 1931; and Dale Morgan, *Jedediah Smith and the Opening of the West*, Indianapolis, 1953.

by Provost, Ashley crossed the Wasatch Mountains to the Weber in search of his people, learned they had already left for the meeting place, and arrived himself at the rendezvous June 30th.

This first general ingathering of mountain men was attended by 120 venturers who had in the past year ranged from Canada to New Mexico and from the Missouri to Great Salt Lake. Months of lonely wandering tormented by constant privation and peril had suddenly been succeeded by convivial days of ease, feasting, and celebration. There were jubilant encounters with old friends thought long since dead, as when Jedediah Smith met James Clyman. Every campfire was livened by eagerly exchanged accounts of pranks, achievements, and horrors, as when James Beckwourth revealed his storytelling talents. Days were devoted to contests to demonstrate who was the best shot, whose horse was fastest, and whose capacity was most nearly bottomless, all competitions never susceptible to final settlement. But there was also earnest attention to business which had formerly required the long journey back to Taos or St. Louis. Furs could now be sold, new supplies and equipment purchased, and profits calculated without leaving the mountains. With typical frontier adaptability all had instantly recognized the miraculous efficacy of this novel fur-trade device Ashley had invented. The consequences were to mount. The American fur trade had been given a sudden driving impetus which would enable it to cope with its organized, depot-based British rival. The institution of the rendezvous had enabled mountain men to flourish. Upon that flourishing depended the nation's advance to the Pacific.

The year 1825 witnessed the establishment by the national government of a western limit to the expansion of the United States. National administrators and lawmakers had deliberately determined that the nation's future prosperity, stability, and general well-being would be better served were its extent restrained within certain compact and more managable bounds. The governmental purposes sought by the establishment of the Line of 1825 and its predecessor, the Line of 1763, were identical. The results were likewise identical. Both imposed immense added burdens on the people engaged in the westward movement without, however, appreciably slowing their advance. As when the direct course of a stream is dammed, the movement found alternate outlets. While Monroe and Calhoun were formulating their 1825 doctrine of rational limitation, the real frontier had already irrationally vaulted far beyond those limits. During the 1825 congressional debate on the proposition, Austin's Texas colony was taking firmer root, many more wagons were rolling to Santa Fe, and an unruly band of American trappers were carrying the flag into distant regions as unknown to mapmakers as to statesmen. The frontier people had once more far outdistanced the most established conceptions of their contemporaries. Again it was they, not the overwhelming majority of their orthodox fellow citizens, who were shaping the nation's destiny.

XII

༂

Jedediah Smith

AMERICANS HAVE TENDED to cherish more lasting regard for many of their folk heroes than for other more historic figures. Jedediah Strong Smith was a genuine hero whose actual exploits were more astonishing than any that could be conjured up by legend or fable. During the few active years of his deplorably short life, he dominated the far western scene in an era when it was afflicted by greater dangers than any to which it was ever later to be subjected. Wherever he appeared he became the immediately acknowledged leader of companions whose turbulent individualism ordinarily rejected other men's direction. They continued to follow him as readily even after many of his former ventures had proved so desperately hazardous that he had once lost half his party and on another occasion four fifths. In all three of the most sanguinary Indian battles of his period he was the white commander. He lost two score of his followers to overwhelming Indian attacks but, though he was forever striking out across unknown expanses devoid of food or water, he never once lost a man to thirst or starvation or any threat that could be parried by a commander's foresight or sense of responsibility. He was the original pathfinder who found a way across vast regions for the exploration of which other men who came years later received public acclaim. The range of his achievements was prodigious. He was first to discover and make westbound use of the Sweetwater-South Pass mountain gateway, first to cross from the Missouri to the Pacific shores of California, first to identify and cross the Sierra Nevada, first to identify and cross the Great Basin, and first to travel overland from San Diego Bay to the Columbia. As a consequence of his incessant roamings, the last great blank space on the map of North America was filled in. Yet, despite these extraordinary services, even his name faded from the nation's memory for a hundred years, and only in this century has the significance of his contribution to his country and to general knowledge begun to be realized.

Though he rivaled George Rogers Clark as the greatest of all frontiersmen in the long succession of extraordinary personalities who had proved natural leaders in moments of wilderness crisis, in many respects he was the least representative of all. He conformed to type by being a remarkable hunter, an aggressive Indian fighter, a confirmed wanderer, and by coming from a family that had moved progressively westward with the frontier from New Hampshire to the New York headwaters of the Susquehanna, to the northwestern corner of Pennsylvania, to the Western Reserve in Ohio, while he, as a youth, had kept on westward to Illinois and Missouri. But he totally departed from the frontier norm in his personal habits and convictions. He neither smoked nor chewed, drank seldom and little, never swore, was deeply religious and carried his Bible with him wherever he went. As a final dissonance, he applied so much forethought to his affairs that his frontier adventures made him a rich man.

In a truer sense, however, he fully represented the frontier. Whenever confronted by the unknown, he was relentlessly driven by the impulse to know what lay beyond. He could never rest until he knew, and no difficulty or danger was ever sufficient to repel him. Since freedom of movement over distances so extensive required accumulations of supplies and equipment, he trapped diligently wherever he went to provide means to keep on going. No attributes of the American frontier contributed more to its success than this widely shared impulse to keep moving onward, coupled with an equally developed instinct for contriving practical means to make this continued venturing possible. And none more distinguished it from other frontier cultures. In Smith's time Englishmen and Frenchmen from the St. Lawrence and Hudson Bay were ranging widely across what is now western Canada and northwestern United States, but their initiative was dependent upon their role as agents of a fur monopoly to whose prudent dictates they were subject and whose commercial program left no scope for individual enterprise which might lead to progressive consequences. The Spanish inhabitants beyond the other American frontier, occupying New Mexico settlements established under the sponsorship of church and state, had had during the two centuries since their arrival so little interest in the region northwest of their border that prior to the appearance of American trappers in Taos the continental divide had been crossed in the single significant instance of the 1776 expedition chronicled by the friar, Escalante.[1] When Smith visited Monterey and San Francisco in 1828, he was astonished to learn that the Spanish residents after a 58-year occupation of California had been moved by so little curiosity about the country stretching inland from the seacoast that they professed uncertainty whether the distantly glimpsed whiteness of the Sierra range was due to chalk or snow.[2] By contrast, within four years of Smith's arrival on the Missouri he had, without governmental assistance or encouragement or any other support than that based upon his expectations as

[1] Visits to the Indian country northwest of the divide were prohibited by law. There is some evidence that New Mexican traders occasionally and surreptitiously violated the injunction. In 1813, for example, seven were charged in court with having ventured as far as Utah Lake on a slave-hunting foray.

[2] The Spaniards with whom Smith talked were either remarkably uninformed of their own recent past or were attempting to mislead him. An earlier generation had been far more enterprising than they indicated. During the more energetic occupation period Spanish military commanders had repeatedly penetrated the central valley in pursuit of Indian deserters or marauders. Gabriel Moraga, for example, had reported 46 such punitive expeditions in the course of which he had ranged from the upper Sacramento to the Tehachapi and, in one instance, east across the Mojave Desert to the Colorado.

a trapper, made his way across the intervening 1500 miles of plains, mountains, and deserts to the Pacific, while having meanwhile found any number of men eager to accompany him.

Notable as were his achievements as leader, hunter, fighter, organizer, negotiator, explorer, and discoverer, his greater reputation rests upon his being unquestionably the most indefatigable traveler of all time. The sheer distance covered by horse, foot, or paddle, all of it through trackless country and much of it country never before entered by civilized man, established a record never approached by any other voyager. Measured only by straight lines from point to point on the map, taking no account of the winding of rivers and game trails to which he was often committed or of frequent detours to seek more passable terrain or of continual excursions en route to hunt or trap, in the nine years of his compulsive challenging of the unknown he traveled more than 16,000 miles.

A recapitulation of his earlier journeys, mentioned in the previous chapter, may serve better to set the stage for the even more extensive travels upon which he was about to embark. In 1822 he had started up the Missouri with Henry's second party, been shipwrecked, reached the mouth of the Yellowstone with Ashley, hunted up the Yellowstone, and wintered on the Musselshell. In 1823 he had descended the Missouri to meet Ashley with Henry's horse message, made his way overland with Ashley's dispatch to Henry after the Aricara battle, returned down the Missouri with Henry to rejoin Ashley, and then had journeyed westward overland to winter on Wind River. In 1824 he had found the Sweetwater, crossed and twice recrossed South Pass, trapped south down the Green and northwest across the Snake, and followed Ross through the mountains to Flathead Post. In 1825 he had shadowed Ogden southward again across the Snake, located Weber near Great Salt Lake, and joined Ashley at the Henry's Fork rendezvous. In these first three years of his fantastic career, he had traveled more than 5000 map-point to map-point miles. But he was only warming up. In the ensuing 12 months alone he would cover another 5600.

As a consequence of the number of pelts procured from Smith's

Iroquois and from Hudson's Bay Company deserters added to all those taken by his own adherents, Ashley found waiting for him at the 1825 rendezvous some 9000 pounds of beaver with a St. Louis value of upwards of $50,000. There was the added profit of selling to free trappers and friendly Indians the store of goods, equipment, and supplies he had brought overland with him. His institution of the rendezvous was proving an enormous success with every promise that it might continue to flourish. The collected fortune in fur would gain realizable value, however, only by its safe delivery in St. Louis. A sufficient escort would force the withdrawal from the mountains of a great many men and horses who might better be permitted to get back to trapping. Ashley decided to move north with his precious cargo to the Big Horn where downriver transport by bullboat[3] would require fewer men and no horses. A further advantage of the water route was the possibility that he might contact General Atkinson's current upper Missouri expedition which he had learned before leaving St. Louis was projected for the summer of 1825. With Smith as guide and second in command, he took the South Pass, Sweetwater, Popo Agie route northward, fought off Blackfoot and Crow attacks to which he lost most of his horses, gained the Big Horn, built boats, and on August 19th achieved the hoped-for junction with Atkinson at the mouth of the Yellowstone.

The success of the United States Army's Yellowstone expedition of 1825 had been as striking as had been the failures of the three former official attempts to impress the Indians of the upper Missouri. Disturbed by the earlier debacles, Congress had finally voted sufficient funds to undertake a more significant showing of the flag. Atkinson left Council Bluffs May 14, 1825, with Benjamin O'Fallon as Indian Commissioner, in 8 keelboats transporting 476 soldiers. All the way up the river Indians were astonished by the thunder

---

[3] The fur trade bullboat was constructed of several buffalo hides stitched together, caulked with elk tallow and stretched over a willow or cottonwood frame. It ranged from 15 to 30 feet in length, from 6 to 12 in width, drew 18 to 20 inches of water, was usually pointed at both ends, and represented an adaptation of the circular Indian bullboat, often pictured, which was nearly unnavigable.

of artillery salutes, exhibitions of fireworks, the roll of martial music, and the glitter of troop parades. The display of military magnificence successfully paved the way to negotiation of treaties of peace and allegiance with Sioux, Cheyenne, Aricara, Mandan, Minnataree, and Crow. There was not time to proceed as far as the Blackfoot country, and as a result those fiercest scourges of the fur trade remained unimpressed. It became Atkinson's turn to be astonished when two days after his arrival at the mouth of the Yellowstone, Ashley's bullboats swept suddenly into view. Ashley gladly accepted the guarantee of safety for his furs represented by so formidable an escort and returned downriver with Atkinson. His arrival with the great fortune from the mountains which had been so often sought and never before won stirred intense excitement in fur-minded St. Louis.

The mountain veteran, Andrew Henry, had renounced the fur trade the year before, on the very eve of its first triumph. To succeed him as field commander Ashley's choice fell upon the 27-year-old Smith, a decision he had undoubtedly had in mind since directing his lieutenant to accompany him downriver. Smith lingered in St. Louis only 26 days before setting out October 30, 1825, with a reinforcement of 70 men and 160 horses and mules to rejoin his mountain comrades. His late start exposed him to the full fury of a winter which that year was of unprecedented severity throughout the plains and Rocky Mountains region. He lost so many of his horses that he was obliged to take refuge with the Pawnee and there to await the arrival of Ashley the next spring with the 1826 supply caravan. Ashley had brought with him a cannon which became the first wheeled vehicle to cross South Pass. The combined parties reached the rendezvous in Cache Valley and a reunion with the mountain section of the organization which had been trapping during the interval since the last rendezvous.

Ashley had come to another important decision. Satisfied with the fortune he had gained and more interested in his political career, he was planning to withdraw from the mountain enterprise. As an astute businessman, he may also have sensed that competition was about to become much more rigorous. Astor's American Fur

Company was moving in on the Missouri, and the Hudson's Bay Company, stung by the Ogden Hole humiliation, was reorganizing its far western operation along more aggressive lines. At any rate, Ashley sold his mountain interests July 18, 1826, to the partnership of Jedediah Smith, David Jackson, and William Sublette, with the proviso that he would continue to forward the annual supply shipments and so enable them to concentrate on their trapping activities.

In the new partners' agreement apportioning territory to be worked the coming season, Jackson and Sublette undertook to gather the certain returns to be gained by trapping the familiar Snake country to the north while Smith selected the area south and southwest of Great Salt Lake. This was a region still totally unknown, somewhere in the depths of which must lie answers to the two most vexing questions still precluding a comprehension of North American geography. Ashley's company, the Hudson's Bay Company, and the governments of the United States and Great Britain were almost as interested in solutions of the twin mystery as was he. The geographical puzzle, as was usually the case, had to do with the courses of rivers. The mouths of the Willamette (then known as the Multnomah) and the Sacramento (then known as the Buenaventura) had long been known. The volume of water at their outlets had led to the assumption that both rose many hundreds of miles inland as did their companions, the Snake and the Colorado. The recent discovery of Great Salt Lake in the area where the great freshwater rivers were presumed to rise had been disconcerting but not considered necessarily conclusive.[4] Sometime

---

[4] Credit for the discovery has long been debated. Etienne Provost's party was trapping the valley of Great Salt Lake in the fall of 1824 when scattered by the Shoshone massacre, but no evidence has come to light that he or any of his men saw the lake. John Weber's party wintered on the Bear that year, and the story gained currency among those present that some time between late fall of 1824 and early spring of 1825 James Bridger rode downstream to the river's mouth where he determined the lake's saltiness by tasting its water. He is reputed to have decided that he must have reached the Pacific. The earliest documented reference to discovery of the lake was in Peter Skene Ogden's letter of July 1, 1826, in which he referred to "the same lake I saw last year." His claim to discovery is discounted, however, by the entries in his daily journal during the period he was in the general area. On May 5, 1825, he wrote in reference to the sighting of thousands of gulls: "I presume some large body of Water near at hand at present

during the previous months four trappers from the Ashley company's encampment in Cache Valley, generally supposed to have been James Clyman, Louis Vasquez, Moses Harris, and Henry Fraeb, had circumnavigated the lake by canoe, discovering it had no apparent outlet, as might have been presupposed by reflection on its saltiness, and noting en route that the country beyond its western and southwestern shores appeared the most forbidding desert yet encountered by Americans. Nevertheless, the preconceived notion that one or the other or both of the great far western rivers must rise somewhere in the area could not yet be ruled out. The well-watered slopes east and southeast of the lake continued to leave room for the more hopeful assumption. Discovery of either would, in addition to the competitive advantage of a prior acquaintance with so important a water route, endow the firstcomer with the treasure in fur to be gained by trapping virgin beaver country the many hundreds of miles down it to the Pacific.

It was with these immense rewards in mind that Smith eagerly struck out into the unknown southwest. If he came across the upper Buenaventura, he proposed trapping down it to the sea and then turning north to return to the next year's rendezvous by way of the Columbia. In any event, there awaited him the exhilaration of heading again into country in which he had no idea what to expect beyond the next ridge. He set out August 16, 1826, in the extreme heat of a desert midsummer, off on a journey, interrupted only by occasional pauses measured in days, during which he would cover a map distance equivalent to traveling from New York to New Orleans to Los Angeles to Seattle to Atlanta and back to New York. The composition of the 17-man party with which he started was in keeping with the frontier tradition established by the first two great transcontinental ventures. His clerk, Harrison Rogers, was from

---

unknown to us all." His May 22, 1825, entry mentioned: "two of our trappers who Came in inform me they had seen a large lake equal in size Winipeg." It was that day that the Americans invaded his Ogden Hole camp from their camp downriver in the direction of the lake. He was preoccupied with defense the following four days and on the 27th began his precipitate retreat northward. Bridger would seem to remain the most likely candidate.

Boonslick and one of his trappers, Peter Ranne, was a Negro.[5] He passed Utah Lake which Escalante had reached in 1776 and Provost in 1824 and continued southwestward into country whose few Indian inhabitants had never before seen white men. He found a bewildering pattern of cliffs and deserts veined by dwindling streams, clouds of dust, blazing heat, remarkably colored mountains, the only corn-growing Indians he had seen west of the Mandan, but few beaver and no Buenaventura. The first great river he struck was not that hoped-for waterway to San Francisco Bay but the Colorado continuation of the Green, churning through monstrous canyons toward the Gulf of California. In descending the Virgin and clambering down the Colorado through Black and Boulder canyons, past the site of present Hoover Dam, to the town of the statuesque and marvelously tatooed Mojave Indians, near present Needles, he had filled in another missing link which would lead 5 years later to the opening of another great transcontinental route, the Old Spanish Trail. He had marched from the farthest west reached by Escalante to the northernmost point reached by Father Francisco Garcés' Colorado River journey in 1775. His progress so far had been a fearfully exhausting effort in which he had lost more than half of his horses but he felt no impulse to turn back.

From the Mojave he was able to buy fresh horses, stolen by Indian runaways from still-distant Southern California ranches, and to engage two of the thieves as guides across the new desert that now stretched to the westward. His attention was still fixed on the Buenaventura and an eventual return by way of the Columbia. He kept on west, crossing the repellent Mojave Desert as had Garcés, climbed the pine-crested San Bernardino Mountains and descended with his starving followers into the comparative plenty of Southern California. Upon his arrival November 27, 1826, at San Gabriel

[5] Detail on Jedediah Smith's movements and adventures may be found in Maurice Sullivan's *The Travels of Jedediah Smith*, Santa Ana, 1934, which includes all known fragments of the Smith journal; Harrison Clifford Dale's *The Ashley-Smith Explorations*, revised edition, Glendale, 1941, which includes known portions of Rogers' journal; and Dale Morgan's *Jedediah Smith*, Indianapolis, 1953, a masterly examination of available evidence which includes references to an hitherto undiscovered Ashley diary.

Mission, he was welcomed by the excited fathers who were astounded by the sudden emergence of this pack of gaunt and leathery Americans out of a region considered impassable.

California Governor José Echeandia took a necessarily sterner view of the startling American intrusion. Mexico's defense policy, as Spain's had been, was based on the presumption that distance and forbidding terrain could be depended upon as a sufficient barrier indefinitely to delay further American advance westward. It was a most disagreeable disillusionment to have Americans unexpectedly turning up 1500 miles west of their nearest known settlements on the Missouri. He summoned Smith to San Diego with the intention of sending him to Mexico City for trial on charges of illegal entry. With the aid of a newly found friend, Captain William Cunningham of the Boston trading ship *Courier,* Smith persuaded the governor that his people were not invaders or the forerunners of invaders but only a party of hunters and trappers who had wandered farther than they had intended. Having won Echeandia's reluctant permission to "return by the way he had come," he experienced a change from years of overland travel by sailing to San Pedro Bay in Cunningham's ship.[6]

He left San Gabriel January 18, 1827, with fresh horses and supplies purchased from Mexican ranchers, but he had no slightest intention of returning as ordered by the way he had come. He was still obsessed with the mystery of the elusive Buenaventura and he had the season's beaver hunt yet to conduct. Regaining the Mojave Desert he turned northwestward into the southern end of the great central valley of California. He proposed to find the Buenaventura on its unmistakable lower reaches and then to ascend it in the direction of Great Salt Lake until he had made sure of its headwaters. During his progress northward, he began to find some beaver in the streams entering the valley from the mountains, but was meanwhile making a more momentous discovery. Always on his right there reared skyward the tremendous, unbroken rampart of the Sierra Nevada. What was instead becoming unmistakable was that

[6] The great traveler proved sadly subject to seasickness.

neither the fabled Buenaventura nor any other California river pierced this barrier to afford a gateway for east-west travel. He had solved the last great mystery shrouding North American geography, but it was a solution that added enormously to his immediate problems, for the time was approaching when he must consider getting back to the summer rendezvous with his partners.

Reaching the American, clearly not the Buenaventura but appearing the most likely river issuing from the mountains he had so far encountered, he attempted in early May to work his way up it over the Sierra. It was a hopeless effort. He was assailing mountains upon which collects a deeper seasonal snowfall than does any other region on earth. Withdrawing after the loss of many horses, he left his main party encamped on the Stanislaus with assurances that he would return with supplies by September 20th at "the latest." Accompanied by only two men, he renewed his assault on the mountains May 20th. This time with the smaller and more manueverable group he got across after a struggle but was then confronted by a fiercer struggle in getting on eastward across the burning deserts and rugged mountains of central Nevada and northeastern Utah. The three made it, eating 7 of their 9 horses and mules and frequently going days without water, by the narrowest of margins. Passages from Smith's journal offer vivid glimpses of the ordeal:

June 24th N E 40 Miles. I started verry early in hopes of soon finding water. But ascending a high point of a hill I could discover nothing but sandy plains or dry Rocky hills . . . When I came down I durst not tell my men of the desolate prospect ahead, but framed my story so as to discourage them as little as possible . . . With our best exertion we pushed forward, walking as we had been for a longtime, over the soft sand. That kind of traveling is verry tiresome to men in good health who can eat when and what they choose, and drink as often as they desire . . . We dug holes in the sand and laid down in them for the purpose of cooling our heated bodies . . . Our sleep was not repose, for tormented nature made us dream of things we had not and for the want of which it then seemed possible, and even probable, that we might perish in the

desert unheard of and unpitied . . . June 25th. When morning
came it saw us in the same unhappy situation, pursuing our journey
over the desolate waste, now gleming in the sun and more insuport-
ably tormenting than it had been during the night . . . June 27th
North 10 Miles along a valley in which were many salt springs.
Coming to the point of the ridge which formed the eastern boundary
of the valley I saw an expanse of water Extending far to the North
and East. The Salt Lake, a joyful sight, was spread before us . . .
Those who may chance to read this at a distance from the scene may
perhaps be surprised that the sight of this lake surrounded by a
wilderness of More than 2000 Miles diameter excited in me those
feelings known to the traveler, who, after long and perilous journeying, comes again in view of his home.

The next day they staggered on to the flooding Jordan River
which was so high with the spring runoff from Wasatch snowfields
that, after having been for weeks in daily danger of death for lack
of water, they found great difficulty in getting across it on rafts
of rushes. On July 3, 1827, Smith, going on ahead, reached the Bear
Lake rendezvous where his appearance was fittingly welcomed by
a salute fired from the cannon brought overland by Ashley the year
before, the first wheeled vehicle to pass over the Overland Trail
route through South Pass.

His partners had not been idle during his absence. They had
trapped the headwaters of the Yellowstone in the face of continual
Blackfoot attacks, had discovered the eventually famous geysers,
had made a very large fur catch, and William Sublette, accompanied
by Moses (Black) Harris, had made a winter journey, much of it
on snowshoes, to and from St. Louis to arrange with Ashley for
supplies.

Smith rested in the comfort and companionship of the annual
encampment for only 10 days before starting out again. In planning
their respective future operations, the three partners strikingly
demonstrated the insignificance which men of their mountain experience had become accustomed to attach to common conceptions
of time and distance. It appeared perfectly natural to all of them
that in making his necessary return with supplies to his California

party Smith proposed, after circling south to the Mojave Desert to avoid the worse Nevada deserts and reaching the Stanislaus, to trap north along the Pacific coast and only to turn eastward again after reaching the mouth of the Columbia. Since it was unlikely that soextensive a journey might permit him to make the next summer's rendezvous, it was understood that in that event he would rejoin his partners on the headwaters of the Columbia the *second summer following*. This extraordinary itinerary, specifying a time and place for the reunion of men who would remain for 20 months without word of each other, was nevertheless followed to the letter. The intervening months proved to involve, in addition to all the familiar hazards and exigencies of mountain and desert travel, a dozen Indian attacks, a foreign imprisonment, and the violent death of 41 of their followers.

Smith set out July 13, 1827, with a party of 18 men which this time was even more representative than the last, including a mulatto, a Spaniard, 2 French-Canadians, and 2 Indian women. The mainspring animating his incredible and apparently inexhaustible energies was revealed by his journey entry:

> My object was to relieve my party on the Appelamminy (Stanislaus) and then proceed further in examination of the country beyond Mt. St. Joseph (Sierra Nevada) and along the sea coast. I of course expected to find beaver, which with us hunters is a primary object, but I was also led on by the love of novelty common to all, which is much increased by the pursuit of its gratification.

En route to the Colorado the strange behavior of the Indian inhabitants, alternately more approachable and more wild than they had been the year before, together with other signs, indicated that in the interim American trappers from Taos had pushed this far west. The Mojave, however, appeared as outwardly inoffensive as before. Smith had no way of knowing that they had a few months before suffered a number of killed in a quarrel with a segment of the Young-Pattie-Yount party and were grimly watching for an opportunity to take their revenge. The opportunity came when the American force was divided while ferrying their goods across the river on cane grass rafts. The 10 men on the east bank were clubbed to death in the sudden surprise attack and the two women made captive. Among the fallen was Silas Gobel who had so recently withstood with Smith the rigors of the Nevada desert crossing. With the 8 survivors, one wounded and all of them armed with only 5 guns, Smith gained the west bank. His journal succinctly describes his reaction to the situation:

> We took our position in a cluster of small Cotton Wood trees, which were generally 2 or 3 inches in diameter and standing verry close. With our knives we lopped down the small trees in such a manner as to clear a place in which to stand, while the fallen poles formed a slight breastwork. We then fastened our Butcher knives with cords to the end of light poles so as to form a tolerable lance . . . Some of the men asked me if I thought we would be able to defend ourselves. I told them I thought we would. But that was not my opinion . . . Gradually the enemy was drawing near, but kept themselves covered from our fire. Seeing a few indians . . . within long shot I directed two good marksmen to fire they did so and two indians fell and another was wounded. Uppon this the indians ran off like frightened sheep and we were released from the apprehension of immediate death.

On foot, with almost no food, guided only by their leader's memory of his former crossing, the little party plodded from one scanty waterhole to the distant next across the sun-baked Mojave Desert. In the San Bernardino Valley Smith paused only to obtain beef and horses from an outlying ranch and resumed his march northward. He reached the Stanislaus camp September 18, 1827, two days within the margin he had promised, but had been able to bring with him none of the supplies upon which his further operations depended. It was therefore necesary that he submit to the risk of establishing contacts with Mexican authorities on the coast.

Governor Echeandia, now seated in Monterey, was incensed by Smith's impudent return to California after his so recent expulsion and resolved to discourage, once and for all, American trespasses on Mexican territory. Smith was imprisoned, threatened with transportation to Mexico City, and only saved by the friendly intercession of American and British captains whose trading vessels chanced to be calling at Monterey and San Francisco. During months of patient negotiation Echeandia gradually weakened. Smith was permitted to sell his 1500 pounds of fur to Captain John Bradshaw of the Boston ship, *Franklin,* and to withdraw from California with his partially re-equipped expedition.

When he resumed his journey, leaving San Jose December 30, 1827, with 19 men, including 9 who had been with his first California expedition and 7 with his second, he was burdened by an extraordinary added encumbrance. Having left only 47 serviceable traps there could be no hope of any substantial beaver catch and he had, therefore, undertaken to bridge this prospective profit gap by dealing in livestock. He was taking with him more than 300 horses and mules which would take on many times their California value when delivered in the central Rockies. Driving this semiwild herd hundreds of miles through the forested defiles of the coastal mountains was shortly to prove an infinitely complicated task.

Circling San Francisco Bay, he turned northward, still headed, as he had been since his original departure from Great Salt Lake nearly two years before, for the mouth of the Columbia. He kept on up his Buenaventura (the Sacramento) which he now realized rose not many hundreds of convenient miles to the east but in the north well to the west of the Sierra barrier. Streams were trapped in passing, but he kept on steadily northward, except for one delay of two weeks while waiting for Rogers to recuperate after he had been mauled by a grizzly. Finally approaching the Sacramento's unhelpful head, he turned northwestward into the tangle of mountains embracing the Trinity and the Klamath. The management of his fractious horse herd was made more irksome by occasional showers of arrows from lurking Indians who could dog each day's march, kept safe from retaliation by the impenetrable cover of surrounding thickets and crags. He had invaded a precipitous, thickly wooded, fog-bound, rain-drenched region as embarrassing to traverse as any on the continent. The expedition toiled on, reaching the ocean June 8th and crossing what is now the Oregon border June 24th. Progress was often limited to a mile or two each day.

The extreme difficulty of driving the horse herd made it necessary that he continually scout ahead to find the most feasible route.

On July 14, 1828, accompanied by John Turner, a survivor of the Mojave massacre, and Richard Leland, an Englishman hired at San Jose, he undertook another such reconnaissance. Rogers, left in command of camp on the Umpqua River in southwest Oregon, had been instructed under no circumstances to allow Indians of the neighborhood, with whom there had been a dispute over a stolen ax, to enter the camp. Little attention was paid, nevertheless, when several groups of Indians wandered in and the danger was compounded by the preoccuption of the Americans with drying their weapons after a recent downpour. Taken off guard by the sudden, premeditated assault of their visitors, all in camp were butchered except Arthur Black, a veteran of the first California expedition, who escaped into the forest and miraculously made his way after many misadventures[7] to Fort Vancouver, the Hudson's Bay Company post on the Columbia.

Upon returning to camp, Smith was attacked by its triumphant despoilers but escaped across the river with his two companions and also reached the sanctuary of Fort Vancouver, August 10, 1828, having in the course of this final depressing lap of his quest at last found and descended the Multnomah (the Willamette).

Dr. John McLoughlin, the Company's already noted far western chief factor, received the fugitives sympathetically and provided Smith with a strong armed party commanded by Alexander McLeod to return to the Umpqua with him to make an attempt to recover as much of his property as could be located. McLoughlin could afford to be generous. The Company had recovered swiftly from the reverse suffered at Ogden Hole. Under a new policy approved by the directors, profit-seeking was subordinated in the northwest to a determination to resort to any expedient to discourage American penetration. Freemen and Indians were paid prices matching

---

[7] The Indians of Oregon were distributed among many tribes, some small and nameless, whose behavior varied widely. Among the Indians encountered by Black in his flight, for example, some robbed and mistreated him, others befriended and guided him.

those offered by Americans and operations pressed so aggressively that for the next ten years the more loosely organized American fur industry labored under many disadvantages. The Company's representatives were instructed to treat intruding Americans with personal friendliness but strictly admonished never to furnish them with supplies or other assistance that might encourage commercial competition.

With McLeod's protection and assistance and after a Company offer of immunity to the guilty Indians, Smith was able to recover 38 horses, 635 skins, a residue of equipment, and, fortunately for history, remnants of the Rogers and Smith journals. Upon his return to Fort Vancouver he met the autocratic Governor of the Company, George Simpson, back on the Columbia that spring on one of his periodic inspection tours. There ensued a somewhat stiff and guarded negotiation but Smith had no practicable alternative to accepting Simpson's rather fair offer of $2369 for his fur and horses.

The tragic Umpqua interruption to his journey finally terminated, Smith still had the rendezvous with his partners to anticipate. He set off up the Columbia March 12, 1829, accompanied by Arthur Black,[8] crossed from Fort Colville to Clark Fork and located David Jackson on the Kootenai in the maze of mountains of extreme northwestern Montana. It was an incredible tryst to be kept by men who in the two years since they had made the appointment had wandered so widely and been subjected to so many misadventures. Together they joined the third partner, William Sublette, August 5, 1829, on Henry's Fork of the Snake near the Tetons. Along with the personal gratifications of the reunion there were many grim stories to be exchanged at that rendezvous. Smith had not been the only partner to encounter hazards. During his two-year absence the other two had lost 12 men to the Blackfeet and 4 to the Shoshone.

The past two years had not enabled Smith to contribute much to the firm's profit-and-loss account, and he was as loyal a partner and as diligent a businessman as he was a compulsive adventurer. To make up for lost time, that winter and spring he trapped the head-

---

[8] John Turner, the only survivor other than Smith of both the Mojave and Umpqua massacres, elected to remain in Oregon.

waters of the Missouri in the heart of the Blackfoot country. As a result of this final defiant effort, the partnership's St. Louis sale for the year's catch totaled $84,499.14 The general sharpening of competition and the increasing weight laid on independent operations by the corporate giants, the Hudson's Bay Company and

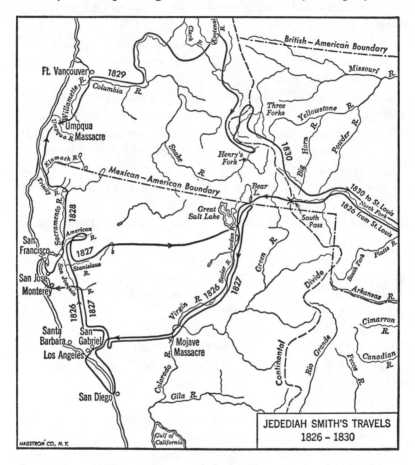

the American Fur Company, led the partners to decide this a sensible moment to close their books. They sold their mountain interests August 4, 1830, to Thomas Fitzpatrick, Milton Sublette, James Bridger, Henry Fraeb, and Jean Gervais who thereafter operated as the Rocky Mountain Fur Company.

Meanwhile the last achievement of Smith, Jackson, and Sublette had been almost as significant as the great traveler's explorations. When William Sublette left St. Louis that spring of 1830 with the firm's annual supply caravan bound for that year's rendezvous on Wind River, he transported his goods not on pack horses but in 10 wagons. His was the first wagon train to cross the central plains, the first ruts in the Overland Trail. Wagon wheels had now rolled to Santa Fe and to the foot of the Rockies. Soon they would be rolling all the way to the Pacific.

Smith returned across the plains with the wagon train and its rich cargo, reaching St. Louis October 11, 1830, where he remained for nearly six months, a far longer period than he had remained in one place since as a youth he had left his home in Ohio. He sought to give others the impression that he had determined to press his amazing luck no further and to settle down to enjoy the comfort he had earned. His one portrait, a sketch drawn from memory by a friend after his death, shows him at this period as a thin, ascetic-looking young man, fashionably dressed in high rolled collar, stock, and silk waistcoat, with none of the scars left by the grizzly nor any other indication of his wilderness experience on his diffidently smiling face. He bought a house, installed two domestic slaves in it, and invited his brothers, Ralph, Austin, Peter, and Ira to live with him. Through all his distant adventuring he had maintained a strong feeling for family ties. His Christmas Eve 1829 letter from Wind River to his parents from whom he had not heard since he left home had opened with, "Your unworthy Son once more undertakes to address his Mutch Slighted Parents," and closed with "May God of his infinite mercy allow me soon to join My Parents, is the Prayer of your undutiful Son."

However, instead of journeying eastward to see his aging parents in Ohio, he first turned westward once more. He had seen all of the transmountain west except the southwestern route to the Pacific by way of Santa Fe and he was moved by a need to see that, too, in order to complete his map of that vast expanse of so recently discovered country so much of which he was the only man to know first-hand.[9] For yielding to this temptation there was a certain practical excuse. He had money to invest and the Santa Fe trade appeared a particularly appropriate enterprise, considering his inclination and experience. There was an added advantage in the opportunity to supervise the apprenticeship of his brothers while they gained acquaintance with far western venturing.

He was joined in the Santa Fe project by his two mountain partners, Jackson and Sublette. They started from Independence with an exceptionally strong caravan of 24 wagons and 87 men that for good measure included the extra insurance of a six-pounder cannon. The day that they were starting out they received an unexpected reinforcement in the person of their old associate and friend, Thomas Fitzpatrick. He was on his way from the mountains to St. Louis to buy supplies for his company but upon sighting them instantly decided to accompany them with the off-the-cuff understanding that he could get his supplies from them after the train's arrival in Santa Fe. Thus the caravan as it rolled southwestward enjoyed the matchless guarantee of its security provided by the presence riding at its head of four of the most seasoned and wilderness-wise leaders the far west has ever produced.

For Jedediah Smith, however, there awaited a danger from which there could be no escape even though it was one with which he had more experience than any man alive. On the Cimarron stretch of the trail, always dreaded for its heat and aridity, the train began to suffer intensely from thirst. Smith, as he had so often done on other deserts, rode ahead May 19, 1831, to look for water. He found a water hole but it was one around which crouched in ambush a band of Comanche hunters lying in wait for the approach of buffalo. The approach instead of a lone white man had been unexpected but was welcomed as offering a substitute prey. Dis-

[9] Smith's map has not been found but his major discoveries of the interior drainage of the Great Basin, the Sierra Nevada rampart, and the courses of the Sacramento and Willamette Rivers were incorporated in Albert Gallatin's famous 1836 map, based on information furnished by Smith. Much more detail on Smith's routes was included in the 1839 map prepared by David H. Burr, geographer to the House of Representatives. Most popular maps generally circulated in school books and atlases, however, continued to ignore the Sierra Nevada watershed until after John Fremont's 1842-45 expeditions.

covering their presence only after it was too late to withdraw, he killed two and wounded another before succumbing to their numbers. He who had seen so many fall around him while achieving fame as the pre-eminent leader of his kind came to his death in an obscure and accidental misadventure witnessed only by his brutish assailants. A vast section of the continent had been made known by him but the spot where his life ended was to remain forever unknown.

Finally abandoning their anguished search for him, his companions only learned of his fate through Indian stories relayed by Mexican traders after they had reached Santa Fe. Friends composed an eloquent eulogy, carried by the *Illinois Magazine* of June 1832. Among its many moving allusions were:

> If there is any merit in untiring perseverance and terrible suffering in the prosecution of trade, in searching out new channels of commerce, in tracing out the courses of unknown rivers, in discovering the resources of unknown regions, in delineating the characters, situation, numbers and habits of unknown nations . . . let us not cast into oblivion the memory of one so deserving . . . where shall we find another, who has braved and overcome more dangers and perils? . . . Where one who has suffered so much, and still with unbroken spirit? . . . All who were intimately acquainted with (him) must look upon his death as a public calamity . . . though he fell under the spears of savages, and his body has glutted the prairie wolf, and none can tell where his bones are bleaching, he must not be forgotten.

But the memorial he might most have appreciated was furnished by the closest comrades of his last journey. His partner, Jackson, and his 21-year-old brother, Peter, kept on that same year from Santa Fe to San Diego and San Francisco. The way west that Jedediah Smith had opened was already being taken by scores and would soon be by thousands.

XIII

༄

Mountain Men

THE WESTWARD MOVEMENT which paced and shaped the development of the young United States has customarily been accepted as a perfectly natural occurrence, an inevitable consequence of the existence of unoccupied land into which people tended to gravitate. It was, on the contrary, a phenomenon without parallel in the history of any other nation and sprang from a spontaneous impulse never manifested in any other race. Its consequences were more obvious than its origins. It was initiated in the period of popular excitability that culminated in the Revolution and thereby invested independence with unforeseen resources that guaranteed its permanence. Without it the seafaring republic must have clung to the Atlantic with a future limited to that of a maritime community of the stature of another Holland or Portugal. The fortuitous crossing into the central valley that coincided with the Revolution instead expanded the infant nation's boundaries at a totally unexpected rate which immediately imposed upon it all the opportunities and responsibilities of a continental power. The rapidity of this expansion was the most astounding of the westward move-

ment's many remarkable attributes. A man born in a cabin on the
Monongahela while it was still subject to assault by Indians was not
yet 50 when the first covered wagon rolled into Oregon. In so
brief an interval had the United States risen from insignificance to
greatness.

The key to the extraordinary achievement and to its even more
extraordinary speed was the personal initiative of the individual
frontiersman. It was this that set the American experience apart
from the world's every other experience with colonization or migration. Former population movements of comparable geographical
extent, the mass migrations of Asian steppe peoples, Scythian,
Germanic, Mongol, or Tartar, were the organized and cohesive
wanderings of whole nations bent on loot or conquest or better
pasture for their herds. The westward extension of American settlement was, on the other hand, a self-centered and self-propelled
surge of individual men and individual families, each manifesting
an eccentric and personal volition pattern, that became a diffuse
general movement unsupported by any form of social or governmental coherence that was not self-generated during the movement's earliest stages. It was a progression that throughout ran
far in advance of the intentions of a laggard government or an
unsympathetic public, both of which perpetually considered it a
foolhardy threat to the country's long-term welfare. The frontiersman as perpetually chose his own course, deaf to all admonitions
and without regard for any inclinations other than his own. The
frontier's accentuation of the individual's independence reached its
apogee of vitality in the instance of the mountain man of the 1820's.
He represented what had become a unique type at the moment of
its most complete development but he was still only the follower
of a special way of life adopted long before. He had inherited
capacities that were the product of a long and unbroken succession
of frontier adaptations to wilderness experience.

The first frontiersman occupied a cabin on the Susquehanna, the
Potomac, or the James beyond whose doorway loomed the margin
of the primeval forest. He was a transplanted European farmer who
had made one great break with every former experience by crossing

an ocean to exchange the familiar burdens of an old country for the unknown hazards of a new. But he was no more of a woodsman and had no more inclination to become one than when he had boarded ship. The necessity of supplementing his family's food supply obliged him, however, to resort to forest produce, the collection of wild fruits and nuts, the snaring of birds and rabbits, eventually the more productive hunting of deer, elk, and bear. If through caution or ineptitude he was slow to adapt to his wilderness environment, the recurrence of Indian attacks made the development of his acquaintance with it imperative. Those more apt responded to this acquaintance with increasing zest. Such a man soon learned the simple lesson that hunting can be more fun than working. If troubled by concern that he might be neglecting the needs of his family, there was always the reassurance of remembering that in a primitive agricultural society the returns from a fur catch could prove more remunerative than from the surplus of a corn patch.

He was meanwhile making the greater discovery that in the forest there awaited a freedom he had never before imagined. There he was free of all the restraints, anxieties, and forfeits imposed by society, from rents, debts, and taxes to his neighbors' opinions. During his ever-lengthening sojourns in the wilderness he could sleep when he chose, wake when he chose, eat when he chose, wander where he chose, and enjoy all the incidental excitements and pleasures of hunting, fishing, and trapping while his masculine ego was regularly nourished by his realization that he was subjecting himself to exceptional hardships and dangers. He had returned to the natural state of primitive man. He had found it an existence offering an atavistic appeal, an appeal still dimly and briefly felt by the most sedate banker or merchant in his vacation hunting camp. The call of the wilderness continued to draw him on until he had crossed the mountains from the Atlantic world into an entirely different world. He had become a long hunter, finding new satisfactions in viewing scenes no other man had viewed and venturing farther than any other man had ventured. He had changed as much as his surroundings had changed. His wilderness wandering had become an existence that was identical in most of its aspects with that of his Stone Age contemporary, his great enemy, the Indian. He recognized this resemblance and found further satisfaction in the identification. He decorated his buckskin shirt and leggings with beads and fringes, wore a breechclout, sometimes painted his face, and always allowed his hair to grow to a length that flaunted a defiant invitation to any Indian bold enough to attempt to take his scalp. He had become in essence a barbarian. This was a productive transition. Men who shrank from barbarity could not have driven the frontier westward at the rate that was imperative were American dominion to cross the Mississippi and reach the Pacific before it was too late.

In responding to the appeal of wilderness freedom the wandering hunter had not, however, escaped the natural man's equally basic urge to mate. This it developed he could achieve without forfeiting his new-found freedom, for, amidst the waves of violence beating upon the border's thin line of cabins and corn patches, there was growing to womanhood a new generation of frontier girls as hardy and self-reliant as frontier boys. The fortitude of such a wife made it feasible to establish a new home in the wild country beyond the mountains to which formerly he had been able only to make intermittent visits. This became a more convenient center from which even wider wanderings were possible but it never became more than a temporary dwelling place, often little more than a camp, which could be readily moved as often as he wished to another site made to seem more attractive by being even more isolated. Acceptance of family ties had paradoxically bestowed upon the freedom-seeking wanderer a more complete freedom. Division of labor among father, mother, and children dealt more efficiently than could a single man with the primary needs of food, clothing, and shelter. The frontier family became a miraculously self-sufficient subsistence unit. Wherever it lodged, whether for a day, a season, or a year, it was able to extract from a wild environment the essential requirements for its maintenance. Meanwhile children born in the wilderness responded even more readily than had their parents to the demands and rewards of a wilderness way of life. Girls were lyeing corn and weaving nettle cloth at 6 or 7 and marrying at 13 or 14 to rear a new brood. Boys were learning to hunt and trap before they learned to hoe or reap and long before, if ever, they learned to read. Meanwhile, also, the ever-threatening Indian danger had dictated the most intense application to gaining increased .proficiency in every wilderness craft and skill. In a single generation the original frontier people had evolved into a distinct and fully developed hunter-nomad culture.

It was this nomadic tendency, born of the impulse to pursue the freedom offered by the wilderness, that directed the main course of American history. The firstcomers had crossed the mountains just in time to save the Ohio Valley from the rival aspirations of England, Spain, and France. They had, without consciously seeking to achieve this, established in their little stockades on the Kentucky and the Cumberland the tremendous reality of American sovereignty. But they did not stop with this momentous achievement. Moved by the same restless urge that had brought them this far, they continued to carry that sovereignty on westward. They had become true nomads, so completely adapted to their environment that they could roam in it as they pleased. Their roaming produced few changes in that environment. Their great service to the nation's development was the precipitancy with which they were opening paths for the swarms of their less imprudent followers who were for their part bent upon totally transforming the wilderness. Behind the earliest invaders of the forest, excited by their strange example, waves of land-seeking, property-developing, permanent settlers were crossing the mountains to erect houses, mills, roads, towns, and states. The earlier comers had already moved on. It was this impulse of the original frontier people to keep moving on from normally populated areas in order to continue to enjoy the freedom permitted by isolation that continued to sweep the American frontier westward at a pace that confounded foreign powers, their own government, and all observers.

They kept on across the Mississippi into Missouri, Arkansas, and Texas. Their continuously aggressive penetration of the wilderness had become a way of life. But they were brought to a stand at the edge of the plains. They had had many former experiences with barriers—the eastern mountains, the Proclamation Line, international boundaries, unending Indian war. These they had scorned and surmounted. But the plains appeared a more unassailable barrier. The frontier family, the essential dynamo that had energized the advance this far, could go on no farther. The treeless and desiccated expanse ahead afforded no opportunity for those intermediate lodgments upon which had most depended the frontier's earlier sweep over mountains, through forests, down rivers, and across boundaries. Yet the frontier people's great mission had been only partially accomplished. They had come hardly more than a third of the way across the continent. This abrupt and dismaying frustration was not destined, however, to prove the premature end to their story.

To the young man of the frontier this sudden barrier represented merely a new and more interesting challenge. The distance stretching away to the fabled western mountains beckoned to him as irresistibly as the freedom of the forest had appealed to his Holston grandfather or his Boonslick father. He was even better equipped than his long-hunting and stockade-building forebears to cope with the challenge. He had been fitted by the accumulated experience of three frontier generations to make himself as completely at home in any wilderness, whether it was forest, plain, mountain, or desert, as might the Indian who had been native to it through a hundred generations. Having been a hunter and wanderer since childhood, preparation for this longer hunt involved little more than oiling his rifle. The most that he required was some initial assistance in transport and some assurance of the future replenishment of his ammunition. Both were furnished by the fur company which would also provide a market for the returns from his hunting. That it was impossible to take a family with him on so extensive an excursion afforded another escape from restraint. Having reached the mountains, the institution of the rendezvous permitted him to remain as long as he chose. He remained for years. In that immense and infinitely varied region there was each successive season unlimited opportunity to indulge his every inbred craving to view new country, realize new experiences, essay new ventures. He had become a mountain man.

Of all the memorable figures that have enlivened the American frontier scene the mountain man was unquestionably the most colorful, the most striking, the widest departure from the behavior of his fellow countrymen. He had been able to achieve a personal fulfillment to which ordinary men must remain lifelong strangers. Never elsewhere in recorded history has the human male been afforded comparable scope to indulge his deepest, most instinctive, and most commonly frustrated yearnings. The mountain man's world was a kaleidoscope of horses, guns, and campfires, of startling and impromptu travels, of the closest comradeship with like-spirited companions, of perpetually novel scenes and situations, of a never-ceasing succession of amazing demands and adventures. His constant preoccupations were hunting, trapping, fishing, and fighting. The extraordinary hardships and dangers to which he was daily subjected reinforced his self-esteem with the comforting assurance that he was an equally extraordinary man. He could even feel that he was a material success for each year he amassed a fortune in furs even though almost as invariably he as soon lost or squandered it. Meanwhile his long isolation in the wilderness had not deprived him of the enjoyment of sex. His comparative wealth enabled him to select the Indian maiden who most suited his fancy upon whom to confer the privilege of becoming his devoted consort.

Washington Irving, who in his 1837 history of the period was enabled to draw upon personal acquaintance with contemporaries who had spent years in the mountains, captured the essence of the mountain man's temperament in his famous description of the free trapper's outward appearance:

> It is a matter of vanity and ambition with them to discard everything that may bear the stamp of civilized life, and to adopt the manners, habits, dress, gesture and even walk of the Indian . . . His hair, suffered to attain to a great length, is carefully combed out, and either left to fall carelessly over his shoulders, or plaited neatly and tied up in otter skins, or parti-colored ribands. A hunting-shirt of ruffled calico of bright dyes, or of ornamented leather, falls to his

knee; below which curiously fashioned leggins, ornamented with strings, fringes, and a profusion of hawks' bells, reach to a costly pair of moccasons of the finest Indian fabric, richly embroided with beads. A blanket of scarlet, or some other bright color, hangs from his shoulders, and is girt around his waist with a red sash, in which he bestows his pistols, knife, and the stem of his Indian pipe; preparations either for peace or war. His gun is lavishly decorated with brass tacks and vermilion, and provided with a fringed cover, occasionally of buckskin, ornamented here and there with a feather. His horse . . . is selected for his speed and spirit, and prancing gait, and holds a place in his estimation second only to himself . . . He is caparisoned in the most dashing and fantastic style; the bridles and crupper are weightily embossed with beads and cockades; and head, mane and tail, are interwoven with abundance of eagles' plumes, which flutter in the wind. To complete his grotesque equipment, the proud animal is bestreaked and bespotted with vermilion, or with white clay, whichever presents the most glaring contrast to his real color. Such is the account given by Captain Bonneville of these rangers of the wilderness, and their appearance at the camp was strikingly characteristic. They came dashing forward at full speed, firing their fusees, and yelling in Indian style. Their dark sunburned faces, and long flowing hair, their leggins, flaps, moccasons, and richly-dyed blankets, and their painted horses gaudily caparisoned, gave them so much the air and appearance of Indians, that it was difficult to persuade one's self that they were white men, and had been brought up in civilized life.

The great event of the mountain man's year was the annual rendezvous when the long months of hardship and loneliness were rewarded by weeks of roistering festivity. Irving's account caught the bizarre quality of the occasion:

The hunting season was over, all past tricks and manoeuvres forgotten, all feuds and bickerings buried in oblivion. From the middle of June to the middle of September, all trapping is suspended; for the beavers are then shedding their furs and their skins are of little value. This, then, is the trapper's holiday, when he is all for fun and frolic, and ready for a saturnalia among the mountains . . . The leaders of the different companies . . . mingled on terms of perfect good fellowship; interchanging visits, and regaling each other in the best style their respective camps afforded . . . the "chivalry" of the various encampments engaged in contests of skill at running, jumping, wrestling, shooting with the rifle, and running horses . . . They drank together, they sang, they laughed, they whooped; they tried to out-brag and out-lie each other in stories of their adventures and achievements . . . The presence of the Shoshonie tribe contributed occasionally to cause temporary jealousy and feuds. The Shoshonie beauties became objects of rivalry among the more amorous mountaineers . . . The caravans of supplies arrived at the valley just at this period of gallantry and good fellowship. Now commenced a scene of eager competition and wild prodigality at the different encampments. Bales were hastily ripped open, and their motley contents poured forth. A mania for purchasing spread itself throughout the several bands—munitions for war, for hunting, for gallantry, were seized upon with equal avidity—rifles, hunting knives, traps, scarlet cloth, red blankets, garish beads, and glittering trinkets, were bought at any price, and scores run up without any thought how they were ever to be rubbed off . . . For a free mountaineer to pause at a paltry consideration of dollars and cents, in the attainment of any object that might strike his fancy, would stamp him with the mark of the beast in the estimation of his comrades . . . Now succeeded another outbreak of revelry and extravagance. The trappers were newly fitted out and arrayed, and dashed about with the horses caparisoned in Indian style. The Shoshonie beauties also flaunted about in all the colors of the rainbow. Every freak of prodigality was indulged to its fullest extent, and in a little while most of the trappers, having squandered away all their wages . . . were ready for another hard campaign in the wilderness.

Finally, there was the unforgettable Indian maid, pictorialized by Irving with equal zest:

The free trapper, while a bachelor, has no greater pet than his horse; but the moment he takes a wife, (a sort of brevet rank in matrimony occasionally bestowed upon some Indian fair one, like the heroes of ancient chivalry, in the open field,) he discovers that he has a still more fanciful and capricious animal on which to lavish his expenses. No sooner does an Indian belle experience this promotion, than all her notions at once rise and expand to the dignity of her situation; and the purse of her lover, and his credit into the bargain, are taxed to the utmost to fit her out in becoming style . . . In the first place, she must have a horse for her own riding; but no jaded, sorry, earth-spirited hack; such as is sometimes assigned by an Indian husband for the transportation of his squaw and pappooses: the wife of a free trapper must have the most beautiful animal she can lay her eyes on. And then, as to his decoration: headstall, breast-bands, saddle and crupper, are lavishly embroided with beads, and hung with thimbles, hawks' bells, and bunches of ribands . . . As to her own person, she is even still more extravagant. Her hair, esteemed beautiful in proportion to its length, is carefully plaited, and made to fall with seeming negligence over either breast. Her riding hat is stuck full of parti-colored feathers; her robe, fashioned somewhat after that of the whites, is of red, green and sometimes grey cloth, but always of the finest texture that can be procured. Her leggins and moccasons are of the most beautiful and expensive work-manship . . . Then as to jewelry: in the way of finger-rings, ear-rings, necklaces, and other female glories, nothing within reach of the trapper's means is omitted, that can tend to impress the beholder with an idea of the lady's high estate.

Mountain men vanished from the far western scene as suddenly as they had appeared upon it. The period of their flourishing had lasted a short ten years before the profusion of beaver dwindled and a change in the style of men's hats produced an even more dis-couraging diminishment in the price. In none of those years did mountain men aggregate more than 500. The total number during the whole period who spent sufficient time in the mountains to consider themselves mountain men probably did not exceed 2000. This compares roughly with the number of men who held the Kentucky and Cumberland perimeters during the Revolution. These two groups were in their separate fashions the heroes of the fron-tier's two greatest crises. Geography and climate imposed upon these later frontiersmen added hazards and demands from which even their hardy predecessors might well have recoiled. Behind the showy trappings of the midsummer festival loomed a year-round existence requiring incredible endurance. The environment which the moun-tain man had elected to make his own could scarcely have been more rigorous. His continual movements alternated between the

forbidding vastnesses of glacial heights and the repellent expanses
of burning deserts. He was constantly beset by blizzards and sandstorms, heat and cold, hunger and thirst. He never knew shelter
and seldom knew rest. His chances of obtaining food could range
within days from as many buffalo as he felt like shooting to such
ants and crickets as he could manage to catch. However favorable
his momentary luck with weather and game, he was under all
circumstances condemned through two thirds of the year to unrelieved physical misery by the very nature of his principal occupation—trapping beaver. Hiram Chittenden, the great chronicler of
the fur trade, thus describes the basic process:

> The universal mode of taking beaver was with the steel trap, in
> the use of which long experience had taught the hunters great skill.
> The trap is a strong one of about five pounds' weight, and was
> valued in the fur trade period at twelve to sixteen dollars. The
> chain attached to the trap is about five feet long, with a swivel near
> the end to keep it from kinking. The trapper, in setting the trap,
> wades into the stream so that his tracks may not be apparent; plants
> his trap in three or four inches of water a little way from the bank,
> and fastens the chain to a strong stick, which he drives into the bed
> of the stream at the full chain length from the trap. Immediately
> over the trap a little twig is set so that one end shall be about four
> inches above the surface of the water. On this is put a peculiar bait,
> supplied by the animal itself, castor, castorum or musk, the odor
> of which has a great attraction for the beaver. To reach the bait
> he raises his mouth toward it and in this act brings his feet directly
> under it. He thus treads on the trap, springs it and is caught. In his
> fright he seeks concealment by his usual method of diving into deep
> water, but finds himself held by the chain which he cannot gnaw in
> two, and after an ineffectual struggle, he sinks to the bottom and
> is drowned.

Beaver skins were only valuable when they had thickened during
the colder months, and the trapper was as a result committed to
spending every day of fall, winter, and spring floundering waist-
deep in ice water, except for intervals when solid freezing made
trapping totally impossible. Along with the bodily torment the
necessary solitude of his trap-tending exposed him to more frequent

attack by his two deadliest enemies, grizzlies and Blackfeet. The great bear, always quarrelsome and aggressive, was a monster of destruction when ineffectually wounded. The trapper's unavoidable relations with the Indians of the plains, mountains, and deserts represented a perpetual problem that ranged from exasperating to mortal. Friendlier Indians were insistent beggars who remained constantly alert to steal his horses or property, while throughout the mountain man's heyday hostile Indians, notably the far-ranging, implacable Blackfeet, sought every opportunity to kill him. Contemporary official reports list the deaths at the hands of Indians of some 500 trappers. Many others must have fallen, unrecorded. Considering the numbers involved this reflects a casualty rate comparable to that during the earlier Ohio Valley Indian wars.

Nothing so sharply distinguished the mountain man as his astounding capacity to withstand, and even to relish, hardships and dangers so extravagant. His stamina was literally inexhaustible. This inbred trait was most enlighteningly illustrated by the career of Hugh Glass. He was the mountain man's mountain man, the single figure who most completely represented his kind. Stories of his exploits and misadventures became the favorite saga most often dwelt upon around mountain campfires or in St. Louis and Taos barrooms. The tales varied in minor details but remained in agreement on all essentials and have been supported by a sufficient accumulation of contemporary evidence to permit an acceptable recapitulation of his remarkable experiences. Just about everything that could happen to a mountain man happened to Hugh Glass.

He first came to notice on the Missouri when he joined Ashley's 1823 expedition. All that was afterward recalled about his background was that he had come "from Pennsylvania." [1] He may have been past his first youth inasmuch as in all stories circulated by his companions he was invariably referred to as "old Glass," though

---

[1] The Glass family was prominent on the early Virginia-Pennsylvania-Kentucky frontier. Samuel and William Glass fought at the Battle of Point Pleasant in 1774. Andrew and Anthony Glass served in Pennsylvania's border militia during the Revolution. A "Lieutenant Glass" commanded Fort Armstrong in 1779. Robert Glass was with the 1781 Coshocton expedition. Michael Glass served in George Rogers Clark's Vincennes campaign.

this is not conclusive since "old" was a frontier term commonly indicating exceptional respect or affection. His misadventures began promptly when he was wounded at Ashley's sandspit battle with the Aricara. He recuperated soon enough to start from Fort Kiowa with Andrew Henry's party making its September 1823 overland march to the mouth of the Yellowstone. This led to the most celebrated of all his exploits.

On the fifth day out he suffered the disaster most dreaded by mountain men. He was mangled by a wounded grizzly bear. His injuries were so frightful by the time rallying companions had completed the execution of the bear that it was obvious he could not be moved. It remained imperative, however, that the 80-man expedition proceed without delay if it was to accomplish its purpose of re-establishing the upper Missouri operation before winter had set in. In response to a reward offered by Henry, to which many members of the party contributed, two men volunteered to remain to attend the helpless and presumably expiring Glass. Most accounts agree that the two were John S. Fitzgerald and the 19-year-old James Bridger. The horribly injured invalid evidenced no signs of improvement, and after 5 days' waiting his attendants concluded their vigil was useless. They took his rifle, knife, and other effects and upon rejoining Henry reported that Glass had died, as all had expected he would, and that they had buried him.

However, after they had departed, perhaps stimulated by the angry realization that he had been abandoned, Glass summoned the strength to crawl to a spring and to pick some wild cherries. On this meager fare he had sufficiently recovered after 10 days to contemplate the enormous effort of making his way the 100 miles back to Fort Kiowa. Before his stumbling progress had proceeded far, he sighted a pack of wolves dragging down a half-grown buffalo calf. Accounts differ on his response to this development. Some say that after he had waited until the wolves had satisfied their first hunger he was privileged to inherit the remains. Others say that his despoilers had overlooked his razor which he was able to use to strike sparks from a stone to ignite a grass fire which routed the wolves. In either event he lived off what was left of the calf while his wounds partially healed. He then resumed his struggle toward Fort Kiowa, depending on roots, berries, and decayed buffalo carcasses for food en route. At the end of 6 weeks he reached the post.

All accounts agree that he was possessed by a burning determination to rejoin Henry in order that he might confront his faithless nurses. Joseph Bazeau, in charge of the fur post, was sending a party of 6 upriver under Antoine Langevin to make the first attempt since the midsummer campaign to run the Aricara blockade. Toussaint Charbonneau, the aging Lewis and Clark interpreter, was a member of the crew of the dugout canoe. Glass, though still weak, stiff, and sore, eagerly joined them upon realizing that this represented the earliest possible opportunity to get back to Henry. During the journey upriver 3 men in a canoe bound downriver passed unobserved, the failure of either party to sight the other no doubt due to the care with which each was attempting to avoid being sighted by the Aricara. One of the men in the other canoe was Fitzgerald, the man Glass most desired to encounter.

The Langevin party found the charred Aricara towns still deserted. What they had no reason to surmise was that after their withdrawal to the plains the Aricara had elected to resettle on the southern outskirts of the Mandan towns. As the little party unsuspectingly approached the Mandan, Charbonneau, with the innate discretion that had kept him alive so long and was to enable him to live to past 80, disembarked to make his own cautious way overland. Glass went ashore to hunt. The vengeful Aricara cut off the party still afloat, killing all five. Glass, too, was perceived and attacked but saved at the last moment by the chance intervention of several mounted Mandan.

Though still lame from his recent wounds, he did not linger at the Mandan. He set off alone, on foot, in midwinter, for Fort Henry, 260 miles away at the mouth of the Yellowstone. When he found it abandoned, he kept on, trudging another 220 miles through the snow up the Yellowstone to the new Fort Henry at the mouth of the Big Horn. Here he received the astounded and tumultuous welcome due one returned from the dead, but along with it the most unwelcome news that Fitzgerald was no longer there. Glass was reported to have become soon reconciled with the abashed Bridger whom he forgave in view of his youth.

Only 6 months had passed since his so nearly fatal encounter with the grizzly and most of those months had been devoted to desperate and lonely travels. Nevertheless, when Henry proposed sending a dispatch to Ashley, Glass promptly volunteered for the mission, still intent on his pursuit of Fitzgerald whom he considered primarily responsible for his abandonment. On February 28, 1824, in the fearful cold of a plains winter, he set out with 4 companions on the 750-mile overland journey to Fort Atkinson at the mouth of the Platte. They crossed the Tongue to the Powder and from its headwaters to the still ice-encumbered North Platte. Here they built a bullboat and began their descent of the intractable river, the first and one of the few attempts to navigate a waterway soon to become upon better acquaintance generally execrated as "a mile wide and a foot deep." After reaching the open plains they sighted an Indian encampment which they heedlessly assumed to be friendly Pawnee, all Indians in their winter robes tending to look alike. Only after they had landed and been encompassed by their exultant hosts did they realize that the outstretched arms into which they had walked were Aricara. Glass managed to tear loose from his assailants, though without his rifle, and contrived to elude their pursuit among river bottom rocks and willows. Two of his companions were killed. The other two, with one rifle between them, also succeeded in escaping and made their way down the Platte to arrive eventually at Fort Atkinson in May.

Glass headed northeastward toward the somewhat nearer Fort Kiowa. Once more he was stranded on the plains alone and without firearms but, though this time he had more than 300 miles of precarious travel before him, he nevertheless felt easy and confident for he was possessed of the luxurious advantages of restored health plus a knife. The meat he required to sustain his 20 miles a day progress was everywhere available. It was the buffalo calving season. Recently born buffalo calves were so ill-advisedly curious and trusting that whenever they had strayed or been otherwise separated from their mothers they were disposed to run to any moving creature, even a hungry man. As a consequence of these several advantages, Glass felt "right peart," according to his account of the episode published in the *Missouri Intelligencer,* and without special incident other than an encounter with friendly Sioux reached Fort Kiowa in 15 days. Joining a traders' party bound downriver, he resumed his search for Fitzgerald.

He ran his quarry to earth at Fort Atkinson but was again and finally denied whatever revenge he may have anticipated. Fitzgerald had in the meantime enlisted in the 6th Regiment and was safe in the sanctuary represented by the uniform of the United States Army. Glass did, however, recover his rifle and gain the entire garrison as an absorbed audience for the recital of his adventures. These, as always with a mountain man, were only beginning.

Reaching Franklin, he promptly joined the 1824 Santa Fe trading caravan and upon reaching Taos became one of that year's famous assembly of trappers fanning westward and northwestward across the southern Rockies. The one incident associated with his next three years that has come to light was reported in George C. Yount's account of Glass once having been obliged to travel 700 miles to have an arrowhead cut out of his back. He was at the 1828 Bear Lake rendezvous and thereafter became a figure of increasing standing and influence among his fellow mountain men during a period that competition was becoming so much sharper not only with the British but between American companies. In 1832 his luck, as had Jedediah Smith's, at last faltered. With two companions,[2] he was killed while crossing the frozen Yellowstone by his old enemies, the Aricara.

Retribution came swiftly and was marked by mountain pungency. The wandering band of Aricara next encountered a trapping party led by Johnson Gardner, redoubtable challenger of the British at

[2] George Yount asserted that one of these was Edward Rose, who had first come to the mountains 25 years before, though Zenas Leonard described Rose's participation in a Blackfoot-Crow battle two years later in 1834. Both Negro mountain men, Edward Rose and James Beckwourth, lived intermittently among the Crow and their identification was often confused then as it has been since. Beckwourth maintained that he was the hero of the engagement described by Leonard.

Ogden Hole, and stole some of his horses while professing friend-liness. Gardner seized three to hold as hostages for the restoration of his horses and when they were not returned he executed them, by burning according to Beckwourth. There was for Gardner, in his grim administration of mountain justice, the added satisfaction of realizing that he had punished the murderers of his old friend, Glass, for from them he had recovered the by now celebrated Glass rifle.

The mountain man, whose eccentric and perpetually dangerous way of life was so well represented by the experiences of Hugh Glass, had little appreciation of the service that he was rendering his country. He was an utter hedonist, engrossed in his own self-indulgent and often fantastic impulses. But that service had been immense. His extemporaneous yet vigorous competition with the powerful Hudson's Bay Company denied at a critical last moment Great Britain's opportunity to establish what must otherwise have become an unassailable and permanent claim to the entire trans-mountain area. The sudden currency of stories of his adventures stirred in the American people a dawning interest in a distant and mysterious region that had until then seemed to most as far beyond the bounds of sensible American concern as were the Andes or the Mountains of the Moon. Above all, his restless and insatiable curi-osity had made him within half a dozen years familiar with every most remote and inaccessible corner and recess of more than a million square miles of hitherto unknown plains, mountains, and deserts so that he was ready, when the time shortly came, to serve as sure and experienced guide not only to the wagon trains of the pioneers but to every government explorer. He had taken the next to the last stride, a prodigiously long and arduous stride, in the remarkable advance of the frontier people from the crest of the Appalachians to the Western Ocean.

XIV

℘

Artists, Writers, and Scientists

THE 1820-40 FRONTIER PERIOD, the two decades during which wandering parties of incredibly venturesome hunters, trappers, and traders ranged with wilful abandon across far western plains, mountains, and deserts, was the most colorful and dramatic era in the annals of the westward movement. It had another distinction. It was also as colorfully and dramatically recorded by the men who were engaged in the enterprise. There exist any number of accounts written by men who were describing in vigorous detail what they themselves had experienced and hundreds of pictures painted by men who were depicting what they themselves were at that moment viewing.

The earlier and starker frontier established by the first crossing of the eastern mountains had bequeathed posterity no such advantages. Contemporary records of the occupation of the Ohio Valley were limited almost entirely to occasional personal letters, sparse official reports, fragmentary diaries, and delayed collections of reminiscences gathered long afterward when the events recollected had all but faded from old men's memories. Least of all did any artist leave the crudest sketch to assist a later generation in visualizing what life may have been like on the Monongahela, the Kentucky, or the Cumberland. There has survived no contemporary representation even of frontier contrivances so transcendentally important to the westward movement as the stockade or the flatboat.

But with the frontier's crossing of the Mississippi there came a sudden burst of evocative reporting by participants and eyewitnesses more revealing than any with which the world of strange and far adventure has ever been blessed. Beginning with the great Lewis and Clark Journals, very many men were so impressed by the extraordinary novelty of their experiences that they felt compelled to give an accounting of them for the benefit of others less privileged. They have made it possible for a reader in an armchair today, more than a century later, to recapture some sense of identification with that distant scene animated by mountain men and Blackfeet, traders and Mandan, dragoons and Comanche, bullboats and trail wagons, buffalo and beaver, Indian belles and grizzly bears, a scene wreathed in the smoke from campfires and gun barrels, shimmering in the gleam of deserts and snowfields, decorated by the night glow of tepees and the glitter of barbaric trappings.

Of authentic mountain men who spent years amidst such scenes in the late 1820's and early 1830's, ten produced enlightening personal accounts of their experiences which eventually gained publication. Several told their stories to friends or literary advisers who did the actual writing, in some instances at a much later date which may have somewhat impaired the detailed reliability of the recollections involved. But three wrote their own stories immediately after returning to civilization and four others kept journals. In every instance there is the special interest and impact invested in any story told by a man who is telling something that had happened to him.

The most noted and most sharply disparaged of all the mountain men's personal narratives was the autobiography of the flamboyant James Beckwourth. He was a member of Ashley's 1823 party and thereafter roamed the far west until at the age of 68 in California he encountered T. D. Bonner, a writer of whose career nothing else is known, who listened to the Beckwourth saga, transcribed it ostensibly at Beckwourth's "own dictation," and arranged for its New York publication by Harper and Brothers. It had developed into a story crammed with the wildest exaggerations expatiating upon its hero's incredible prowess as warrior and wooer, yet interspersed with these splurges of self-glorification were many revealing statements of ascertainable fact that have added materially to the store of contemporary evidence upon which any understanding of the period must be based.[1]

The first mountain man's story to reach publication, as well as the most enlightening and the most entertaining in many ways, was that of James Ohio Pattie. After seven years as a Taos trapper during which he had ranged as far as California where he had suffered Mexican imprisonment, and Mexico City, where he had sought redress, he returned, penniless and in failing health, to his native Kentucky in 1830. With some assistance from Timothy Flint, the eminent frontier clergyman and frontier chronicler, he wrote his account while his memory of his experiences was still fresh. Many of his adventures were so extraordinary that his narrative was long discounted, but more recent evidence has tended to establish his basic veracity.[2]

The next firsthand account to appear in print was the only one in its time to command wide public attention which rendered it as a result by far the most important. Captain Benjamin Bonneville took leave from the army in order to spend the years 1832-36 in the mountains as head of his own small fur company during which he experienced all the hardships, adventures, and perils to which wandering trappers could be subject. Upon his return to Washington he undertook to write a book based upon his journals, notes, and recollections but, upon meeting Washington Irving, delegated

---

[1] Bonner, T. D. *The Life and Adventures of James P. Beckworth,* New York, 1857. Reprint. Bernard DeVoto, ed. New York, 1931.
[2] Pattie, James Ohio. *Personal Narrative.* Timothy Flint, ed. Cincinnati, 1831. Reprint, Reuben Gold Thwaites, ed. Cleveland, 1905.

the unfamiliar task to the capable hands of the author who had just completed his fascinating history of the Astorians.[3]

While Zenas Leonard was in the mountains from 1831 to 1836 he was intimately associated with such pre-eminent mountain men as Thomas Fitzpatrick, William Sublette, Joseph Walker, and George Nidever. His wanderings carried him as far west as California and he was on the scene of many of the most dramatic occurrences during his years in the mountains. Upon his return to his home in Clearfield, Pennsylvania, he wrote a clear, factual, reportorial story of his experiences which was forthwith printed as a book in the plant of the local newspaper. Parts of his journal had been stolen by Indians but the events he described were so recent that his memory must be considered generally reliable. His is the most circumstantial of any of the firsthand accounts left by mountain men.[4]

Joseph Meek, who had enlisted with William Sublette at 18, told his story 40 years later to Frances Fuller Victor in Oregon. Mrs. Victor was not then an experienced chronicler but she was intensely interested in her subject and Meek was a superlative teller of tales. The resulting book, in spite of various discrepancies, recaptured more of the primitive color, flavor, and feeling of the mountain period than has any other, including Irving's.[5]

Five other mountain men, Richens Wooten, Osborne Russell, James Clyman, George Nidever, and Warren Ferris, either kept journals or dictated recollections which, fortunately preserved over the long interval, finally became books many years later to add eventually to the precious store of what can be known firsthand about their times. The contributions of Clyman and Russell were of particular value.[6]

[3] Washington, Irving. *The Rocky Mountains*. 2 vols. Philadelphia, 1837. Reprint, Edgeley W. Todd, ed. Norman, 1961.

[4] Leonard, Zenas. *Narrative*. Clearfield, 1839. Reprint, W. F. Wagner, ed. Cleveland, 1904. Reprint, John C. Ewers, ed. Norman, 1959.

[5] Victor, Frances Fuller. *The River of the West*. Hartford, 1870.

[6] Conard, Howard Louis. *"Uncle Dick" Wooten*. Chicago, 1890. Russell, Osborne. *Journal of a Trapper*. Boise, 1921. Reprint, Aubrey L. Haines, ed. Portland, 1955. Camp, Charles L., ed. *James Clyman, American Frontiersman, 1792-1881*. Revised edition, Portland, 1960. San Francisco, 1928. Ellison, Wil-

There was other eyewitness testimony than that of the mountain men themselves to shed light on the period. The point of view of their British competitors was given in the journals kept by the Hudson's Bay Company brigade leaders, Peter Skene Ogden and John Work. Two observant travelers, John K. Townsend in 1834 and Thomas J. Farnham in 1839, crossed the plains and mountains to the mouth of the Columbia and another, John B. Wyeth, journeyed as far as the 1832 rendezvous at Pierre's Hole. All three wrote books describing in detail what they had seen and experienced. Perhaps the most original of all contemporary observers was Sir William Drummond Stewart, a wealthy English sportsman who developed a passion for hunting and traveling in the closest association with mountain men. He reported his impressions by means of two novels devoted largely to mountain background and atmosphere.[7]

The initiation of trade with Santa Fe was reported by contemporary chroniclers who had themselves contributed to the achievement, Thomas James and Jacob Fowler. All aspects of life on the Santa Fe Trail were described in detail by the veteran trader, Josiah Gregg, whose work became almost at once a western classic.[8]

The United States Army's military influence played an insignificant role in the frontier's early advance across the plains and none

liam H., ed. The Life and Adventures of George Nidever, 1802-1883. Berkeley, 1937. Ferris, W. A. Life in the Rocky Mountains, 1830-1835. Salt Lake City, 1940. Paul Chrisler Phillips, ed. Denver, 1940.

[7] Rich, E. E. (ed.). Peter Skene Ogden's Snake Country Journals, 1824-25 and 1825-26. London, 1950. Lewis, William S., and Phillips, Paul C. (eds.). The Journal of John Work. Cleveland, 1923. Townsend, John Kirk. Narrative of a Journey Across the Rocky Mountains. Philadelphia, 1839. Reprint. Reuben Gold Thwaites, ed. Cleveland, 1905. Farnham, Thomas J. Travels in the Great Western Prairies. 2 vols. London, 1843. Reprint. Reuben Gold Thwaites, ed. Cleveland, 1906. Wyeth, John B. Oregon: or a Short History of a Long Journey. Cambridge, 1833. Reprint. Reuben Gold Thwaites, ed. Cleveland, 1905. Stewart, William Drummond. Altowan. New York, 1846. Stewart, William Drummond. Edward Warren. London, 1854.

[8] James, Thomas. Three Years among the Indians and Mexicans. Waterloo, 1846. Reprint. W. S. Douglas, ed. St. Louis, 1916. Reprint with Introduction by A. P. Nasatir, Philadelphia, 1962. Fowler, Jacob. Journal. Elliott Coues, ed. New York, 1898. Gregg, Josiah. Commerce of the Prairies. 2 vols. New York, 1844. Reprint. Reuben Gold Thwaites, ed. Cleveland, 1905.

at all in its early penetration of the mountains. Nevertheless, the army's first ventures in undertaking to regulate the behavior of Plains Indians were of interest as the prelude to that later period when the mounted regulars became a dominating factor in the far west. Those first essays at showing the flag on the plains were described by participants, James Hildreth and Philip St. George Cooke.[9]

In the advance of the French frontier across the Great Lakes and the Mississippi, and of the Spanish Frontier north from Mexico, missionaries had been invariably in the forefront. There had, on the other hand, been no appreciable religious effort associated with the advance of the American frontier into the Mississippi Valley. But in the frontier's penetration of the far west, missionaries came again into prominence. Daniel Lee, Joseph Frost, Samuel Parker, and Pierre-Jean De Smet, who crossed the mountains between 1834 and 1840 to preach to the Indians of the Pacific northwest, wrote notable accounts of their experiences.[10]

The world's concern with the determination of truth by means of the scientific method of experimentation and observation had been mounting for a century and it was inevitable that sooner or later the so little known American far west must tempt an investigation by inquiring scientists. Their response to the opportunity was slow, however. Edwin James, a physician who had studied botany and geology, accompanied Major Stephen Long's 1820 exploring expedition to the foot of the Rockies, and upon his return wrote the semiofficial report on its findings. His 1000-page account is made interesting by the detail with which he recorded what he saw, but its value was diminished by the ineptitude with which the expedition's operations were conducted and some doubt was cast on his

[9] Hildreth, James. *Dragoon Campaign to the Rocky Mountains.* New York, 1836. Cooke, Philip St. George. *Scenes and Adventures in the Army.* Philadelphia, 1857.

[10] Lee, D., and Frost, J. H. *Ten Years in Oregon.* New York, 1844. Parker, Samuel. *Journal of an Exploring Tour Beyond the Rocky Mountains.* Ithaca, 1838. De Smet, Father P. J. *Letters and Sketches.* Philadelphia, 1843. Reprint. Reuben Gold Thwaites, ed. Cleveland, 1906.

scientific judgment by his conclusion that the southern plains, though teeming with game, must remain forever uninhabitable. The naturalist, Thomas Nuttall, crossed the plains and mountains to the Columbia in 1834, but his recording of the journey was confined to reports on his botanical observations and his one account of general interest was of his 1819 tour of the lower Arkansas.[11]

Meager as had been the scientist's response to the far western opportunity, the eventual initiative of a German savant more than restored the balance. Alexander Philip Maximilian, Prince of Wied-Neuwied, had served with distinction as a major general in the Napoleonic Wars but upon the return of peace all of his interest and energy became centered upon natural history. An amateur's enthusiasm, a singular application, and the means to indulge his avocation soon lifted his efforts to a professional level. After spending two years in the wilds of South America investigating that continent's plants, animals, and natives, his attention turned to the wilds of North America. In 1833 he ascended the Missouri as far as the Blackfoot country, hunted, camped, collected, witnessed Indian battles, interviewed trappers, and wintered with the Mandan, the most interesting of western Indians. His curiosity was insatiable, his investigations scrupulous and all-encompassing. All that he saw or heard or learned he set down in meticulous detail. His methodical account of the natural history of the northern plains become a unique contribution to any later attempt to comprehend the period.[12]

Words, however well chosen, can never prove as illuminating as pictures. Of these we have been endowed with hundreds to enable us to see as well as to imagine the mountain man's panoramic background. Three dedicated artists who became vitally interested

[11] James, Edwin. *Account of an Expedition from Pittsburgh to the Rocky Mountains.* 2 vols. with atlas. Philadelphia, 1823. 3 vols. London, 1823. Reprint. Reuben Gold Thwaites, ed. 4 vols. Cleveland, 1905. Nuttall, Thomas. *A Journal of Travels into the Arkansas Territory.* Philadelphia, 1821. Reprint. Reuben Gold Thwaites, ed. Cleveland, 1905.

[12] Maximilian, Prince of Wied. *Travels in the Interior of North America.* London, 1843. Reprint. Reuben Gold Thwaites, ed. 3 vols. and atlas. Cleveland, 1906.

in their task devoted years to the preservation of scenes which were so soon to pass forever from view.

The first to embrace the great responsibility was George Catlin.[13] Catlin had developed a general interest in Indians during a childhood spent in Wyoming, the Pennsylvania valley which had suffered so excruciatingly in the Indian wars before and during the Revolution. After becoming dissatisfied with the practice of law he turned to a somewhat dilettante study of painting. The whole course of his career was determined by a chance encounter in Philadelphia with a delegation of far western Indians en route to Washington. He thereupon resolved to devote his life to the faithful portrayal of the still wild western Indians before they had been altered as dismally by white contacts as had already been the eastern Indians. During the years 1832-40 he visited more than 40 Indian nations from the Great Lakes to the foot of the Rockies, painting everything he saw. His talent as an artist was limited but he was a sharp observer with a special interest in detail. As a result of his tireless devotion to his objective, he was able to bring back with him more than 500 oil paintings illustrating every phase of contemporary Indian life. His collections were so widely exhibited in the United States and Europe that the world's visual conception of the North American Indian became an image shaped by Catlin's presentation of the western Indians he had visited and painted.[14]

The year following Catlin's 1832 ascent of the Missouri, Charles Bodmer, a young Swiss painter, visited many of the same scenes as a member of Maximilian's party. His function was to serve as camera for his scientific employer, and many of his efforts were more successful in capturing and perpetuating what he was seeing than could be any camera study. He was a far more talented artist than Catlin. Bodmer's Indians are real and endowed with all the

[13] Samuel Seymour, an English-born Philadelphia engraver and painter, had accompanied Stephen Long's 1820 expedition, but his work was ineffective, commanded little attention, and survives in only 9 uninteresting reproductions in the London and Philadelphia 1823 editions of Edwin James' account of the expedition, several of which were again reproduced in the Cleveland 1905 reprint.

[14] Catlin, George. *Letters and Notes on the Manners, Customs and Condition of the North American Indians*. London, 1841. Among many later editions: London, 1866 and London, 1876, each in 2 volumes with 360 colored plates.

individual personality of which a skilled portraitist is capable. His landscapes are instinct with the haunting beauty and loneliness of the plains. Under Maximilian's scholarly influence, he devoted the most observant attention to every detail of native costume, weaponry, gear, house furnishing, achieving the sharply defined precision of the best photography without losing the interpretive impact of an artist's selectivity. Through Bodmer's perceptive eyes, we can see the west of 1833.[15]

Catlin's and Bodmer's travels in search of subjects were confined to the river transportation facilities of the American Fur Company and neither got beyond the foot of the Rockies. This was a distinction reserved, among contemporary artists, to Alfred Jacob Miller, a Baltimore painter who had studied abroad. He owed his opportunity to that extraordinary mountain enthusiast, Sir William Stewart, who recruited him for his 1837 hunting party with a commission to paint mountain scenes to embellish Stewart's ancestral castle in Scotland. The joint effort became an immensely productive enterprise. Stewart showed Miller the mountains and all of its denizens and with equal interest and gusto Miller painted all that he was shown. His sketching caught mountain men and Indians, horses and buffalo, at moments filled with action and meaning. His were the first pictorial representations of such natural monuments as Chimney Rock, Devil's Gate, Independence Rock, the Wind River Mountains, and the Tetons. He was deeply impressed by his experience and his work is suffused with an emotional quality missing in Catlin and Bodmer.[16]

Three years after Maximilian wintered with the Mandan and Bodmer produced his magnificent paintings of their Buffalo Dance, the Mandan were exterminated by a smallpox plague which raged until it had reduced by half the numbers of every other north plains nation. By then steamboats were regularly coursing waters that had so recently known only the lonely canoes of Lewis and Clark,

---

[15] Volume 25 of *Early Western Travels*, Reuben Gold Thwaites, ed. Cleveland, 1906, reproduces 81 Bodmer plates.

[16] DeVoto, Bernard. *Across the Wide Missouri*. Cambridge, 1947, reproduces 64 of Miller's paintings, 13 of them in color.

Manuel Lisa, Alexander Henry. The once lordly beaver trade was degenerating into a dreary marketing of buffalo hides. The irrepressible free trapper was drifting to more mundane occupations as storekeeper, guide, or Oregon farmer. The world of the mountain man was swiftly fading from view. Nevertheless, thanks to Pattie and Leonard and Beckwourth, to Clyman and Meek and Nidever, to Maximilian and Irving and Farnham, and most of all to Catlin and Bodmer and Miller, it can never altogether fade.

XV

ॐ

1832

THE FRONTIER FORCES that had been accumulating during the mountain men's penetration of the Rockies produced in 1832 a series of widely separated yet closely related effects. The entire scene was as suddenly transformed as when one slide is replaced by another in a magic lantern. The remote wild region that had known only roving hunters and trappers was invaded by emulators and rivals who had been drawn by the opportunity that had been revealed by their adventuring. These second comers ranged from minor eastern businessmen with a dawning interest in far western commercial possibilities to a corporate giant bent on establishing a total monopoly of the fur trade. No transition in the advance of the American frontier had from the beginning been more familiar or more inevitable than the prompt intrusion of investment capital into every newly penetrated area. The alert readiness of American entrepreneurs to risk strange and unproven ventures had as clearly exemplified the basic American temperament and as directly promoted the country's astounding growth as had the original frontiersmen's audacity. Never had this characteristic transition proceeded more rapidly than on the mountain frontier of the 1830's. The revolutionizing developments of 1832 were in themselves significant but assumed a larger significance by serving as certain harbingers of the far greater revolution to come eight short years later.

The drumbeat of premonitory events commenced its roll early in the spring. On March 26th the river steamboat *Yellowstone* steamed from St. Louis on a voyage to Fort Union at the mouth of the Yellowstone, 1800 miles northwestward across the plains. Built in Louisville on the order and according to the specifications of the American Fur Company, she had the year before engaged in a shakedown cruise as far as Fort Tecumseh. This time she made it all the way to the Yellowstone and by returning to St. Louis July 7th firmly established the feasibility of mechanical transportation on the longest river in the world. Her primary mission had been to contribute an overwhelming advantage to the company's design to monopolize the far western fur trade. The identity of some of her passengers produced consequences of more enduring meaning. One was George Catlin, making his memorable ascent of the Missouri to paint Indians while they still looked like Indians. The traveling exhibition of his paintings and collections was to arouse in the American public a mounting interest in the mysterious far west. Two other passengers were Rabbit's Skin Leggins and No Horns on His Head, survivors of the Nez Percé-Flathead delegation which had come to St. Louis to learn what they could of white men's magic and other white accomplishments which might prove of benefit to their people. Misconstruction of their quest as an appeal for orthodox religious instruction precipitated a nationwide surge of evangelical concern which resulted in the earnest dispatch of American missionaries to the northwestern Indians which, in turn, accelerated the early settlement of Oregon. Meanwhile, the appearance of *Yellowstone,* amidst clouds of smoke and the clank of machinery, astonished the Indians of the upper Missouri as much as had the first steamboat the inhabitants of Kentucky in 1811. They termed the craft *The Fireboat,* assumed its progress due to sorcery, and resignedly accepted it as conclusive evidence of the white man's inherent superiority. The new speed and capacity given river transportation increased the flow of white men's goods and cultivated the Indian market for them, but also expedited the spread of white men's diseases, including a terrible scourge of smallpox from which the nations of the northern plains never recovered. Most of all, *Yellowstone's* successful voyage forecast with glaring clarity the shape of things to come. Among its many other startling indications of what the future held in store was the inclusion in the vessel's return cargo of 5 tons of buffalo tongues.

While the first steamboat to reach the land of the Aricara, the Mandan, and the Assinaboin was churning upriver to bring an end to an era, a land expedition of scarcely less moment was getting under way. On May 1st, Captain Benjamin Bonneville, West Point graduate and close friend of Lafayette, left Fort Osage on the Missouri with an unstintedly equipped caravan of 110 men and 28 wagons prepared for a two-year "exploring tour" of the Rocky Mountains which continued through four years. His principal financial backer was Alfred Seton, a New York insurance executive who as a young Astorian had witnessed with never to be forgotten pain the lowering of the American flag on the Columbia in 1813. Bonneville had been granted leave from the army on the assumption that he would report his determinations with regard to geography, Indian behavior, and British activities to the war department. He was also collecting information useful to Astor's American Fur Company. Though ostensibly in pursuit of personal profit, he roamed more vigorously than he trapped and his four very active years in the mountains remained in every commercial respect a cumulative failure. Whatever his outward failures and secret successes, he was responsible for three historic achievements. The book describing his adventures, written by Washington Irving, stirred the imagination of the American people with the first full, widely circulated account of mountain men and the amazing country in which they circulated. His dispatch of a subsidiary expedition under Joseph Walker found the central route along the Humboldt to California. And, in his initial westward march in 1832, he was the first to take a wagon train over the great divide by way of South Pass. The least of his achievements was his attempt to attach his name to Great Salt Lake, a body of water which in all his wanderings he had not once sighted.

Bonneville had been in many ways prepared to cope with the difficulties with which he was confronted in the mountains. He was a professional soldier, accustomed to commanding men, and he had had some plains experience. But almost at his heels, that spring of 1832, there set out another land expedition composed of total amateurs, all of whom had for the first time crossed the Mississippi less than a month before and none of whom had ever before ventured west of the Appalachians. Nathaniel J. Wyeth was a young Boston ice merchant whose imagination had been fired by the picturesque vehemence of the Boston schoolmaster, Hall J. Kelley, who since he had learned of the fall of Astoria had been conducting an eccentric and fanatic one-man campaign to persuade an oblivious American government and public of the urgent need to reestablish an American foothold in Oregon. Having been convinced by Kelley's tireless propaganda that Oregon offered fishing, farming, and trading opportunities certain to prove profitable, Wyeth's project became a minor key reproduction of Astor's historic 1811 design. He got off a small supply vessel around the Horn and then with 20 devoted followers he set out from Boston for the mouth of the Columbia. Upon reaching the edge of the plains at Independence, it became apparent that his elaborate but theoretical preparations were not fully adapted to the demands of transmountain travel. His enterprise was saved from initial frustration by the generosity of William Sublette who was on the verge of leaving with that season's supply caravan and permitted Wyeth and his remaining 18 followers to accompany him. By the time they had reached the rendezvous at Pierre's Hole 7 of Wyeth's men, including his brother Jacob, and his cousin, John Wyeth, had been sufficiently disillusioned by the rigors of western travel to decide to turn back with William Sublette's returning eastbound party.

Wyeth and his 11 still loyal followers resumed their westward course under the guidance and protection of Milton Sublette's band of trappers and promptly became involved in the Battle of Pierre's Hole, the most noted engagement ever waged between mountain men and Indians and one which was reported as variously and confusingly by participants as have been some Civil War battles. So far Wyeth had been shepherded by two most proficient mentors, first William and then Milton, Sublette, but late in August he was obliged, if he wished to continue westward, to press on alone. He had some difficulty finding his way and finding enough to eat but he did not lose sight of his objective. He kept on down the Snake and down the Columbia, arriving at Fort Vancouver October 29, 1832, only to learn that his supply ship, *Sultana,* had been lost at sea and that his remarkable effort was doomed to commercial failure. His venture had not, however, been without striking significance. His party represented the first appearance on the far western scene of intruders who were not explorers, hunters, trappers, or fur traders. They were not wandering frontiersmen but commercially enterprising easterners who were seeking to get to Oregon in order to engage in farming and salmon fishing. They were the forerunners of a totally new order. The persistence, stamina, and adaptability of these complete amateurs were astonishing and the sheer physical aspects of their feat as notable. Wyeth's greenhorn New Englanders were the first to make a continuous continental crossing from the shores of the Atlantic to the shores of the Pacific and the first to travel westward from the lower bend of the Missouri by way of South Pass, the Snake, the Blue Mountains, and the lower Columbia all the way to the valley of the Willamette, almost the entire distance by the route that was to become the Oregon Trail.

At the most widely separated points many other occurrences in 1832 indicated a frontier ferment that was evidencing the course soon to be taken by greater events. In Washington, the national government took another halting step toward recognizing the responsibilities of sovereignty by congressional authorization of a corps of dragoons to cope with the plains' vast distances. In Wisconsin, Black Hawk's Sauk and Fox were annihilated at the Battle of Bad Axe, bringing to an end the last flicker of Indian resistance to the advance of settlement east of the Mississippi. In Texas, American settlers, having temporarily expelled Mexican government garrisons, met in convention ostensibly to declare their sympathy with the revolution of Santa Anna's liberal party but actually to lay the groundwork for their independence. In California, David Jackson and Peter Smith were demonstrating the narrowing of far western distances by starting east with their purchase of 600 mules and 100 horses, and Ewing Young, in his second excursion from Taos to the Pacific, was hunting sea otter off the coast while several of his followers, including notably Isaac Williams and Isaac Sparks, were deciding to become permanent residents of California. In Oregon, one of Wyeth's men, John Ball, was becoming the first American to undertake farming on the Willamette. The frontier's main settlement line had still nowhere emerged from the continent's central belt of woodland, but flying spores of the westward movement were carrying over immense distances to lodge and fruit.

These unmistakable presages of what the future held in store escaped attention at the time. What most concerned frontier leaders and observers was the immediate effect of the American Fur Company's resolve to monopolize the fur trade. John Jacob Astor had been saddened but not at all discouraged by the collapse of his Astoria venture. Upon the conclusion of the War of 1812, he had expanded the activities of his American Fur Company on the Great Lakes and under the vigorous leadership of the veteran Astorians, Ramsay Crooks and Robert Stuart, extended its operations to and across the Mississippi. By 1822 Crooks was opening a regional headquarters in St. Louis, called at first the Western Department, in the face of the opposition of long established local traders fiercely jealous of outsiders. Much of this opposition was overcome by a series of purchases and mergers which included drawing into the company's orbit the important Pratte and Chouteau interests. These mergers culminated in 1827 in one with the Columbia Fur Company which had become active on the upper Missouri, and in the recruitment of Columbia's energetic head, Kenneth McKenzie, as manager of the American's developing upriver operation, at first called merely the Upper Missouri Outfit. McKenzie, another ex-Northwester and a relative of the great explorer, Alexander Mackenzie, became the dominating figure on the Missouri for the ensuing many years.

William Ashley's current success in employing the transplains convoy, the rendezvous, and free trappers to tap the fur riches of the Rockies was absorbing St. Louis attention. Astor was resolved to exploit those same mountain sources, but on the advice of his Canadian-trained western managers decided to abide by his plan to make his drive to the mountains by way of the river, continuing to organize supply by means of water transport instead of pack trains or wagon trains and to rely on permanent posts instead of rendezvous. It was a fateful decision. Had he elected in 1828 to strike directly westward across the plains, the complex of posts he was presently to establish in the strategic isolation of the upper Missouri would have been situated instead along the main route west that was to become the Overland Trail. What effect this might have had on the westward migration of the 1840's remains a subject for speculation.

Under McKenzie's forceful management the post building got under way at once. In 1828 Fort Floyd was built at the mouth of the Yellowstone on the site Andrew Henry had abandoned in 1823. It was soon enlarged and renamed Fort Union, becoming the company's principal center on the upper river. The proposed penetration of the rich beaver country at the head of the Missouri was contingent upon the contrivance of some counter to the Blackfeet's traditional anti-Americanism. By a stroke of unexpected good fortune, Jacob Berger, a onetime Hudson's Bay Company trapper who had during his later wanderings been one of the few white men ever to establish tolerable personal relations with the Blackfeet, negotiated a temporary and uneasy truce with them. Thereafter, a portion of the Blackfeet depended, at least sporadically, upon the company for a portion of their trade needs, and its operations could be extended into that dread area to which access had been denied Manuel Lisa, John Colter, George Drouillard, Andrew Henry, and all who had since ventured into it.

Astor's second great western design seemed on the verge of a success as complete as had been the failure of his first. In 1832 Fort

McKenzie, replacing temporary Fort Piegan, was established near the mouth of the Marias to serve the Blackfeet, Fort Cass at the mouth of the Big Horn to serve the Crow, and the voyage of *Yellowstone* was proving the practicability of relying on mechanical transport. The moment had come to extend operations into the mountains to compete with the Rocky Mountain Fur Company and the roving bands of free trappers associated with it. To conduct this carefully planned aggression the company had engaged as field

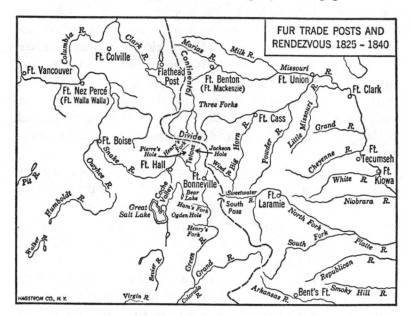

agents a number of frontier figures long distingiushed in the fur trade. The veteran mountain men, Hugh Glass and Etienne Provost, had been recruited to persuade free trappers to bring their furs to company posts instead of to the annual rendezvous. American Fur Company parties had already been dispatched into the mountains to trap and to attempt to open preliminary trade relations with other trappers and with Indians. As principal leaders of these brigades the company had enlisted the services of Henry Vanderburgh, a West Pointer, born in Vincennes, who had been active in the old Missouri Fur Company, and Andrew Drips, a Pennsylvania frontiersman who had also been long associated with the river trade. Both lacked mountain experience which they were about to gain with a vengeance.

The 1832 rendezvous in Pierre's Hole was the most memorable of all ingatherings of mountain men. Among stalwarts of the breed recorded as having attended were Thomas Fitzpatrick, William and Milton Sublette, James Bridger, Joseph Meek, Henry Fraeb, Zenas Leonard, George Nidever, Robert Campbell, John Gervais, Antoine Godin, Alexander Sinclair, Alfred Stephens, and two unidentified nephews of Daniel Boone. Many hundreds of friendly Flathead, Nez Percé, and Shoshone had assembled to enjoy the festivities and to profit by the competitive demand for their furs, horses, and women. Also present was a less welcome party of 90 American Fur Company men led by Vanderburgh and Drips. Amid all the outwardly heedless merriment there were a number of most serious questions demanding the most sober consideration. During the past few months Indian hostility, despite the Berger truce on the Missouri, had been more rather than less troublesome than usual. Milton Sublette had been wounded so severely that all hope for his recovery had been abandoned for days. Fitzpatrick had arrived, a white-haired, walking skeleton, more dead than alive, after having survived an attack on the Green and having made it on foot, alone and weaponless over the hundred miles of intervening mountains. The new American Fur Company competition was certain to compound the Indian hazard as well as to accentuate every other difficulty.

The center of interest at Pierre's Hole, at any rate before the battle, was therefore the American Fur Company invasion and the threatening new light it cast on the future of free trapping. This first test of strength between the two combines resulted in a complete triumph for the Rocky Mountain Fur Company, headed by Thomas Fitzpatrick, Milton Sublette, Henry Fraeb, Jean Gervais, and James Bridger who had a collateral supply agreement with William Sublette. Bonneville's expedition, an American Fur Company supply party commanded by Lucien Fontenelle, and William Sublette's annual Rocky Mountain Fur Company caravan had been engaged in a race across the plains. Sublette was first to arrive at Pierre's Hole and the prior display of goods gained the bulk of the free trappers' furs as well as attracting many desertions from the ranks of the American Fur Company. Realizing the inevitable consequences of unlimited competition, Fitzpatrick proposed a reasonable division of the mountain beaver country. Vanderburgh, bound by his instructions, refused with the warning that his company was determined to take all of it.

When the rendezvous broke up and the various brigades moved off to resume their winter trapping, Vanderburgh and Drips resumed their practice of following their more experienced rivals in order to profit by their superior knowledge of routes and trapping areas, in the same fashion and for the same purpose as Jedediah Smith had trailed the Hudson's Bay Company parties of Alexander Ross and Peter Skene Ogden in 1823-24. To shake off their unwanted shadows Fitzpatrick and Bridger resorted to the savage expedient of crossing the mountains into the Blackfoot country, still made as dangerous as ever by the large proportion of Blackfeet who were still as hostile as ever. The American Fur Company partisans stubbornly hung on and the desperate game of follow the leader culminated in tragedy October 15, 1832. On the branch of the Jefferson called Philanthrophy by Lewis and Clark and currently known as Stinkingwater, Vanderburgh was killed by Blackfeet who dismembered his body and on a later visit to Fort McKenzie brazenly exhibited his arms as trophies of their exploit. The Rocky Mountain Fur Company did not entirely escape. In another brush with Blackfeet, Bridger had a three-inch arrowhead imbedded in his back which could not be removed until three years later when he encountered the medical missionary, Marcus Whitman, at the Green River rendezvous of 1835.

In its attempt to invade the mountains, Astor's company had lost the first round and was never to gain a semblance of the monopoly it had sought. In 1832 Fitzpatrick's association of free trappers were able to ship furs worth $85,000 while the American Fur Company mountain brigades had not begun to meet expenses. The company persisted in the struggle, taking full advantage of its great resources in steam transportation and permanent supply depots. On the river and the plains this was an advantage that sufficed. Competition could be discouraged by local offers of three or four times what furs were worth until it had ceased to exist. In the mountains no device sufficed. There operations demanded a degree of personal initiative, endurance, and risk which could not be hired for wages. During the next five years the free trappers were under greater pressures from the corporate competition of the Hudson's Bay Company, striking south from the Columbia, than from the American Fur Company, striking west from the Missouri.

Meanwhile, more sinister shadows than the evils of unrestrained competition were threatening all concerned. Trapping so persistent had all but exterminated the mountain beaver and at the same time the price of beaver was steadily declining. Astor, sensitive to the trend of the world market, saw what was coming and sold his western enterprise to his subordinates in 1834. Fitzpatrick, judging in his own way the situation as surely, announced his retirement from the fur trade at the 1836 rendezvous.

The noon of the mountain man was fading into twilight as swiftly as his day had dawned, but the brief service he had rendered his nation had been of incalculable value. He had been confronted by the tremendous distances of a region about which nothing was known other than that its perils were countless. In no longer time than might mark a child's passing from cradle to schoolroom he had made himself familiar with its every water hole, gulch, and game track, with its unpredictable weather and unpredictable savages, with the infinite range of hazards with which it shrouded its mysteries. His knowledge had fitted him for his indispensable contribution. He had become fully prepared to guide, guard, and counsel his all-important successor, the pioneer, already waiting in the wings to take the center of the far western stage and there to play his climactic role.

XVI

༇

Texas

THE AMERICAN FRONTIER had been thrust westward by men prepared to accept difficulties judged unreasonable and unjustifiable
by the majority of their fellow countrymen. These difficulties which
had been terrifying from the outset were multiplied and augmented
when the frontier reached Texas. People who had come to the
Monongahela, the Holston, the Kentucky, the Cumberland, or the
Arkansas had shared a common realization that they were flouting
the will of every existing government, that they were claiming land
to which they knew they might never be able to prove title, that
they were inviting the certain dangers of Indian war and the probable dangers of foreign war, and that whatever their troubles they
could expect little or no support from their disapproving country.
So, in every respect, had the Texans. On the Missouri frontier there
had been the added disadvantage that by crossing an international
boundary the firstcomers had been obliged to swear allegiance to a
foreign power. So had the Texans. In addition to facing all of these
principal perils with which former frontiers had been afflicted,
Texans were subjected to others never hitherto encountered. Earlier

frontiers had been forced to consider secession and independence but had never been driven over the brink. Texas had been born in the abyss. Texans were compelled to endure the rule of Spain and Mexico, to embrace the ultimate hazards of revolution, and to assume the unlimited burdens and responsibilities of independent nationhood. It was in Texas that the frontier experiment withstood the test of every conceivable contingency and only in Texas that the frontier dream of total self-sufficiency was fully realized.

The means by which American settlers occupied Texas had been an uninterrupted continuation of the process by which the existing American frontier had been occupied. The vast majority of early Texans were direct migrants from the so recently established American frontier south and west of the Ohio. The same pattern of individual initiative which had distinguished the westward movement in its crossing of the Appalachians and the Mississippi to the edge of the plains distinguished its southwestward swirl across the Mexican border to occupy the watered and wooded portion of eastern Texas. The frontier people had, in the meantime, developed adaptation capacities so well demonstrated that they needed to feel no hesitation about keeping on into the distant interior of a foreign country. They had been moving on for generations and there was in them as yet no inclination to come to rest. Their reach for Texas had depended upon measures and methods experience had long since proved practical and sufficient. Those who proceeded overland, driving pack horses or wagons or trudging on foot, camping and hunting en route, were conforming to a travel pattern familiar since the earliest days of the Wilderness Road. Those who resorted to water-borne transport by taking flatboats down the Mississippi and up the Red or coastal schooners across the Gulf to the shores of Texas were repeating the experiences of the Ohio flatboat migration to Kentucky. Once arrived, their behavior continued to conform to every tradition of their frontier forefathers. Their immediate political organization by communities, their assumption of self-government, and their defiance of all interference or opposition fostered as successfully as it had in every previous instance the maintenance of their occupation.

Every attitude of the Texas frontier of the 1830's was shaped by what had been learned on the early Kentucky and Tennessee frontiers. There were the same earthen-floored cabins, the same stick and clay chimneys, the same communal stockades, the same dependence upon the first corn crop, the same uncertainties regarding land titles, the same local government by town meeting and the same Indian danger. Indian hostility threatened the firstcomers, remained a problem over a period as long as it had in the Mississippi Valley, and was resisted by the same reliance upon neighborhood militia, neighborhood forts, and neighborhood counterstrokes. Though Indian assaults were not promoted and supplied by foreign powers and never mounted to the proportions of an organized invasion that threatened the settlers' expulsion, the immense expanses of the adjacent plains offered mounted Indians even more favorable opportunities for surprise attack than had ever been enjoyed by Wyandot or Shawnee on the forested Ohio. The more populated interior communities had by the 1830's become relatively safe, but on the expanding outer perimeter of settlement the danger remained constant. During 1836, the climactic year of the Texas Revolution, for example, there erupted a series of peculiarly vicious raids that would have aroused the widest public concern had not people's attention been so entirely concentrated on the nearer war with Mexico.[1]

Most early Texas settlers were one-wagon families with a great many children, a few tools and utensils, possibly a cow, and occasionally a black slave or two. They had come from a harsh environment to one even more forbidding. They were to become the heroic founders of a great commonwealth, but this was not uppermost in their minds at the time. The average head of a family was looking for land but with perhaps more interest looking for better hunting and with the most interest of all looking for an opportunity to win at one happy stroke an unlimited fortune. Early Kentuckians and Tennesseans had been entranced by the fancied ad-

---

[1] James T. De Shields in his *Border Wars of Texas*, Tioga, 1912, gives detailed accounts of 1836 border raids in which 51 settlers were killed. Cynthia Ann Parker, the most noted of all Indian captives, was taken by Comanche in this year.

vantages inherent in a conquest of New Orleans. Early Texans were
dazzled by the more extravagant loot awaiting them in the Halls
of Montezuma. All through the 1830's and early 1840's Texans
volunteered even more eagerly for the successively projected invasions of Mexico than they rallied to the defense of their homes.
Texas was universally regarded as a very big country. Most early
Texans saw no reason it should not eventually extend at least
to the Isthmus of Tehuantepec with princely shares of the vast
domain available to each of the invaders.

While realizing that they had become a distinct and important
element in the structure of the nation, the frontier people on both
sides of the border were in the 1830's becoming more reflective and
more articulate. They had always been quick to characterize their
enemies but now they were becoming as prone to characterize themselves. They had developed a special language in which to express
their common point of view and a growing appreciation of their
own special culture. Some had even taken to writing books. Their
press was opinionated and fiercely regional. Their orators were
more than able to hold their own in Congress. Their political power
had waxed until they had been able to seize control of the national
government. Though most frontier people still lived at a bare subsistence level in cabins to which at most a room or two had been
added, many of their leaders were becoming more sophisticated
and more cosmopolitan. The developing diversity of frontier types
was illustrated by the contrasting characteristics of the five immigrants who became the outstanding heroes of the Texas Revolution.

Erastus (Deaf) Smith had developed a proficiency in every back-
wood skill and craft that made him the idol of his fellow rebels.
He could hardly have been called the eyes and ears of the Texas
army for he could not hear. But lack of hearing had sharpened his
other senses. As chief of scouts in the 1836 campaign, he was able
to keep Texas commanders constantly informed of the enemy's
every movement and disposition. Smith was an old-fashioned frontiersman of the original primitive school, as much at home in the
wilderness among the pine hills and tidal marshes of Texas as had
been Simon Kenton or Michael Stoner in the forests and glades of

Kentucky. Like them, the range of his ability to interpret the meaning of every sign that might indicate what was occurring about him extended from the flight of birds in the sky to the position of a leaf in the dust.

James Bowie was a Tennessean whose family had prospered after migrating to a Louisiana plantation. He was socially cultured, spoke English, French, and Spanish with equal facility and had a special capacity for making and holding friends, but gained greater fame as an alligator wrestler, a lassoer of wild cattle, an associate of Jean Lafitte, the pirate, and for his skill in hand-to-hand fighting which attached his name to his favorite weapon. He visited Texas at first in pursuit of adventure and land speculation but presently accepted Mexican citizenship and married Ursula de Veramendi, daughter of the Mexican vice governor. His theatrical reputation and his no less theatrical personality made him a popular and natural leader of the Texas revolt.

William Travis was a hot-headed young Alabama lawyer whose family had moved to that frontier when he was 9. Outraged by the breakup of his marriage, which was reported to have been signalized by his shooting the suspected corespondent, he cut loose from his former associations and came to Texas at the age of 23 to make a new start. His resumption there of frontier law practice was colorfully unorthodox and, when mixed with land speculation, political agitation, and assorted gallantries, soon attracted wide public attention. His picturesque temperament and his early and aggressive sponsorship of the Texas revolt gained him that post in the Alamo from which he was able to pen the dispatch Texans were never to forget: "I shall never surrender or retreat."

David Crockett so successfully personified the frontier that he was able to make as successful a profession of the role. He was the first backwoodsman to win fame in the east simply and entirely because he was a backwoodsman. During the previous half century thousands of his exact stamp had enlivened the region west of the mountains but he was the first westerner able to project the type's personality in a fashion to capture the nation's fascinated attention. As a member of Congress from Tennessee, he appeared in Wash-

ington some weeks before the arrival of another Tennessean,
Andrew Jackson, to assume the presidency, and thus gave the east
an anticipatory look at the kind of people who were gaining
control of the nation's destiny. Crockett's coonskin cap, his rifle,
his jokes, his total independence which ranged to an unhesitating
defiance of Jackson himself, startled and captivated all observers.
His widely read book, *A Narrative of the Life of David Crockett,
Written by Himself,* may have required some ghost-writing assistance but it presented his image, and that of his kind, as he
had intended it to be presented. In him the Tennessee frontier, at
the moment it was ceasing to be a frontier, had contrived self-
expression. He had been able to record much of the flavor of a time
that was passing forever. If the accent was on humor, this was an
accent the frontier had preferred even in its darkest hours. Though
he had been only 8 when Wayne's Treaty of Greenville had controlled the Indian menace, he was an authentic frontiersman who
had sprung from an authentic frontier family. His grandfather had
been killed by Cherokee in the Year of the Three Sevens and his
father had been at King's Mountain. He himself had spent the first
40 years of his life in Tennessee's backwoods, rearing children in
a cabin, spending more time in the forest than in his corn patch,
mustering sociably with the militia, participating as sociably in local
politics. He was said to have won the votes of his constituents by
his exceptional ability as a marksman and by his even more exceptional ability as a storyteller. Upon being defeated for a fourth term
in Congress, largely by the influence of an exasperated Andrew
Jackson, he yielded at 49 to the frontiersman's recurring impulse to
wander. Texas, recently launched upon its struggle for independence, appeared an interesting destination. Many other recruits from
the southwestern frontier were hastening to the defense of Texas
but his national reputation gained him a special reception. Two
months after he arrived he died in the Alamo.

The achievements of the fifth of the Texas heroes of 1836, Samuel
Houston, towered over those of the other four and as well over
those of most Americans of his time. He was the George Washington of the Texas Revolution. It was his unique distinction to

preserve his adopted people in a war for survival and thereafter to deliver an empire ino the keeping of his native land. The story of his life offers conclusive proof of the old saw that truth is stranger than fiction. It was also the story of the frontier which in that period of expansion was the nation's story. As indelibly as had George Rogers Clark, John Sevier, or James Robertson, he imprinted the stamp of his individuality upon it. His life encompassed a complete fulfillment of the frontier experience. His relations with Indians were as intimate and as enduring as his white associations. If the frontiersman's governing impulses were to gain greater freedom, to wander at will, to seek strange adventures and, incidentally, to court an opportunity to achieve an unlimited improvement in his condition, Sam Houston satisfied all of these yearnings in the fullest possible measure. He was the total frontiersman.

He was born March 2, 1793, in the Valley of Virginia, that traditional cradle of frontier energies, of which his grandfather had been one of the earliest settlers. In 1807 his widowed, 50-year-old mother moved with her nine children to uncleared land in eastern Tennessee, on the border of the Cherokee country and near he blockhouse maintained during the Revolution by a cousin, James Houston. Sam Houston grew rapidly to a handsome six feet but along with the striking presence and stature had come no inclination to take gracefully to he farming or storekeeping chores proposed by his older brothers. He disappeared and it was only discovered after some months that he was living in a Cherokee town on an island at the mouth of the Hiwassee River. It had been 15 years since the Cherokee had last attacked the settlements and during he peaceful interval their many similarities in outlook, habits, and interests had led to many friendships among the inhabitants of opposite sides of the border. His preference for the Cherokee was considered at the time no more dubious than might be any teenage boy's running away with a gypsy caravan or a circus. Though occasionally and temporarily retrieved by his disapproving family, he kept returning to his sylvan sanctuary and spen the beter part of three years with his Indian friends. To any frontier youth the Indian way of life with its indulgence of indolence and personal caprice and its emphasis on hunting and sports constituted an ideal existence. The Cherokee were delighted with him, listened raptly to his oratorical quotations from the *Iliad*, and bestowed upon him the Cherokee name, The Raven. His foster father was the Cherokee chief, Oolooteeskee, whose white name was John Jolly. This boyhood escapade which loomed so large at the time continued in after years to loom as large. It was to have a profound effect on Houston's later life and on the history of Texas and the United States.

He pleased his mother by remaining in the settlements to teach school the summer months of 1812, and the outbreak of war gave him a new perspective. Soldiering appealed to an imagination ordinary occupations had failed to stir. As an ensign in the regular 39th Infantry he participated in Andrew Jackson's invasion of the Creek country, winning his commander's lifelong favor as well as popular recognition as the outstanding individual hero of the Battle of Horseshoe Bend. In the storming of the rampart he was first over the barrier, suffering three wounds from which he barely recovered and which were to cause him recurring pain throughout the ensuing 50 years of his life.

After his discharge he served as Indian Agent to the Cherokee long enough to become instrumental in persuading John Jolly's band to migrate to the Arkansas in compliance with the national government's Indian removal policy. His career had by now passed through the first three stages common among aspiring young men on the frontier. He had served his forest apprenticeship, had proved himself in battle, and had gained governmental preferment. The next two stages were so predictable as to seem predetermined. After studying law for six months he was admitted to the bar. His intelligence, his personality, his instinctive eloquence, and his military record made him a professional success. To the stalwart, wavy-haired, blue-eyed hero of Horseshoe Bend who enjoyed the personal regard of Andrew Jackson the door to political advancement stood open. In 1823 he was elected to Congress and in 1828 Governor of Tennessee. His meteoric rise appeared certain to continue. Many were already beginning to speculate on his becoming

Tennessee's likeliest candidate to succeed Jackson in the White House.

Then, without the slightest warning, there came the stunning occurrence, shrouded in the darkest mystery, which became the turning point in Houston's life and set off a train of consequences that made it a major event in American history. The young governor had married 18-year-old Eliza Allen in January of 1829. It was hailed as an ideal match. He was, after Jackson, Tennessee's most distinguished citizen. She was the beautiful daughter of a proud and aristocratic family. He was ardently in love and his bride appeared even to her closest friends pleased with her choice. But three months later she fled in tears to the refuge of her father's home. The sensation was magnified when it became apparent that the cause of the separation was to remain a secret. Houston refused to offer any explanation whatever and the Allens revealed only their fury. Public opinion assumed that he had questioned his wife's chastity and then, too late, repented. Dr. William Hume, the clergyman who had married them, after consulting with both families was unable to shed light on the question that was agitating everybody in Tennessee and soon, as the astonishing story spread, in the country. "I know nothing that can be relied on as true," he reported. "Which of the two is to blame I know not." Houston's stubborn refusal to give any accounting of what had occurred swung the public's verdict toward his condemnation.

Four days later, April 16, 1829, he resigned as governor of Tennessee and in another eight days he left the state for the west. In his letter of resignation he had referred only to "private afflictions . . . deep . . . incurable" which had been precipitated "by my own misfortunes rather than by the fault or connivance of anyone." There was a more revealing, but still mystifying, glimpse of the drama in the letter from Houston to his wife's father, written at the time of the separation but first made public a year later, in which he said:

> Whatever had been my feelings or opinions in relation to Eliza at one period, I have been satisfied . . . and believe her virtuous . . . if mortal man had dared to charge my wife or say ought against

her virtue, I would have slain him. That I have and do love Eliza none can doubt and that I have ever treated her with affection she will admit; that she is the only earthly object dear to me God will bear witness . . . Eliza stands acquitted by me . . . She was cold to me, and I thought did not love me . . . You can think how unhappy I was to think I was united to a woman who did not love me.

When this letter was published as part of a political maneuver to discourage any possible consideration of a return to Tennessee, he still refused to defend or explain his position, remarking simply, "I courted the sympathy of no one . . . I have acquiesced to my destiny."

The mature Houston had fled from despair, just as had the boy from discipline, to the sanctuary of life with his Indian friends. John Jolly's band of Cherokee had found an uneasy new home on the Arkansas, 700 miles from their native land, and Houston took up his abode with them. He dressed and behaved like an Indian, in all outward respects became an Indian. He took another young and beautiful bride, Tiana Rogers of the distinguished Cherokee family which had furnished so many chiefs and was eventually to produce Will Rogers. Houston's affection for Indians was genuine. Many thousands of Cherokee, Creek, and Choctaw had been by now forced to migrate from their ancestral homes to the edge of the plains. Most were unhappy with the transition and all complained of their mistreatment by the federal agents charged under the removal treaties with their protection. Houston became their champion and made repeated trips to Washington to represent their interests, once appearing at the White House in full Indian regalia.

Jackson's regard for Houston had not diminished. He stood ready to back the effort were Houston to consent to return to Tennessee to seek rehabilitation by running for re-election as governor. Meanwhile, however, he was alarmed lest Houston's primary intention in heading west was to take a hand in the troubled affairs of Texas. He exacted Houston's promise that he would abstain from any such venture. Jackson was angling for the purchase of Texas from Mexico and feared with some cause that the intrusion on the scene of so noted an American would produce new frictions. Not completely trusting Houston's promise, he ordered him kept under surveillance. Many others among Houston's friends were ceasing to trust him. In adopting the Indian way of life he had embraced the supreme Indian vice of drunkenness along with other more innocent practices. The man who had known the excitement of adulation and power could not become resigned to the monotony of existence in a tepee. For a time he played with the prospect of Rocky Mountain adventure and spent nights of discussion with Benjamin Bonneville, then planning his expedition. The drinking bouts were becoming more frequent and more prolonged. In the opinion of his friends and his country his once brilliant career was ending in sodden oblivion.

Suddenly he emerged from the gathering shadows at one sensational bound. In April of 1832, while on another trip to Washington to further the interest of his Indian protégés, he encountered in the street the Ohio congressman, William Stanbery, who had recently in a speech in the House accused him of attempting to profit by fraudulent Indian contracts. Houston caned his detractor. The House cited him for contempt. Exercising his privilege as a former member, Houston appeared on the floor in his own defense. Before a packed chamber he delivered an address with taste and dignity that nevertheless rang with emotional force and patriotic fervor. Among the professionally appreciative spectators of his extraordinary performance were his defense attorney Francis Scott Key, author of the "Star-Spangled Banner," and Junius Brutus Booth, the greatest actor of his time. The House voted that he be reprimanded and the Speaker did so, very gently, but the occasion had provided Houston with a great personal triumph. The country had been made to realize that he had not lost his onetime powers. Before the widest possible audience he had shed the blanket and resumed the toga.

Jackson's hopes to purchase Texas had been disappointed. The succession of Mexican revolutionary governments had clung to one doctrine common to all. Each regarded any American proposal to buy Mexican territory as an insult. Jackson had been a vigorous supporter of Aaron Burr's 1806 reach for Texas and he had not changed his views. In his estimation the acquisition of Texas was more than ever an imperative necessity. He concluded that the time had come to reactivate the Burr undertaking under the present more propitious conditions. Houston's restored prestige appeared to render him the most effective available instrument. Jackson released him from his promise, furnished him with a personal loan, and dispatched him as his secret emissary to Texas.

On December 2, 1832, Houston, traveling alone, crossed his Rubicon, the Red River, into Texas. The appearance of an American of such renown was hailed by Texans, then beginning to grope, with much division in their councils, toward independence. On February 13, 1832, Houston was reporting to Jackson:

> I am in possession of some information that . . . may be calculated to forward your views, if you should entertain any, touching the acquisition of Texas by the United States . . . My opinion is that Texas, by her members in Convention, will, by 1st of April . . . form a State Constitution. I expect to be present at that Convention . . . *I will never forget the country of my birth.*

The American colonization of Texas was entering its second decade when Houston arrived. Many other American promoters, called *empresarios* at the time, had followed Austin's example in negotiating land grants with the Mexican government, though Austin's original project remained the most considerable and he the most influential Texan. The accelerating influx of Americans, which had by 1830 passed 4000 in Austin's colony alone, increasingly alarmed Mexican authorities. In 1830, the further immigration of Americans was prohibited. They continued to come. The recurrence of revolution in Mexico kept the succession of Mexican governments too occupied with internal conflicts to interfere forcibly in distant Texas. It had been the policy of Austin and his fellow *empresarios* to cultivate amicable relations with Mexico and to deprecate talk of independence or annexation. Most colonists, whose land titles depended on Mexican sufferance, shared this practical point of view. But there remained irreconcilable difficulties which precluded any workable understanding between the American settlers and their Mexican overlords. Foremost among American grievances were: (1) Title to land could be taken only after avowing membership in the Catholic Church. (2) The seats of government, both federal and state, were at a great distance, leading to the same neglect of regional needs that had exercised early Kentucky and Tennessee. (3) Slavery had been prohibited and, though the edict had not been enforced in Texas, there was no assurance that it might not be in the near future.[2] (4) The corrupt and authoritarian Mexican judicial system was supremely irritating to Americans who had been accustomed to convenient, honest courts and trial by jury. These grievances were serious but had been kept endurable by Mexican preoccupation with revolutions which had left Texas able to practice de facto self-government. In 1835, however, the revolutionary general, Antonio de Santa Anna, had made himself master of Mexico and was re-establishing Mexican garrisons in Texas. The crisis was at hand.

During most of Houston's first three years in Texas, Stephen Austin had been in Mexico, much of the time in prison, attempting to negotiate an accommodation of Mexican-American differences. Houston had undertaken the practice of law in Nacogdoches, the Texas gateway town nearest the American border which, as a result of that proximity, had from its founding been a hotbed of lawlessness and intrigue. He became a Catholic so that he might own land and became also the on-the-ground representative of the gigantic land schemes of the Galveston Bay and Texas Land Company, controlled by Samuel Swartwout, Collector of the port of New York, who had been one of Burr's principal backers. Houston's mission in Texas was developing according to plan. The majority of landowning Americans in Texas were still reluctant to take up arms and he agreed with their restraint. In his judgment a declaration of independence, as a preliminary to annexation, was eventually inevitable, but at the same time he believed that the longer the mo-

---

[2] Immigration to Texas had been predominantly from slave-holding regions. Contemporary estimates placing the 1835 American population in Texas at from 25,000 to 30,000 included 3000 to 4000 slaves.

ment was postponed the greater would prove the development of American strength by continued immigration. It was Santa Anna's dispatch of troops that broght the possibility of further delay to an end.

Austin, finally freed from prison, returned to Texas in September 1835. He had been the spokesman for that large majority of Texas settlers who, confronted by the specter of Mexican military superiority, saw more hope of protecting their families and property through continued negotiation than by armed defiance. But he had recently had ample opportunity to study Mexico's new ruler. "War," Austin announced, "is our only recourse." The pacifist party ceased to exist and all Americans in Texas accepted the prospect of imminent conflict. Houston, commissioned military commander for the Department of Nacogdoches by the local Committee of Vigilance and Safety, issued a call to arms addressed primarily to United States public opinion that reverberated with such phrases as "All that is sacred is menaced by a arbitrary power," "The morning of glory is dawning," "Volunteers from the United States will . . . receive liberal bounties of land," "Come with a good rifle, and come soon," "Liberty or Death."

A wave of excited sympathy swept the United States. The recent revolts of Poles and Greeks against the Czar and the Sultan had stirred the deepest interest among the democracy-revering inhabitants of the world's most successful republic, and a parallel was at once recognized in this near revolt against autocracy which had moreover been undertaken by fellow Americans. The deepening national division over the slavery issue made official intervention impossible but spontaneous popular mass meetings were held in countless cities and towns from Boston to New Orleans. Funds were subscribed. Hundreds of eager volunteers streamed toward Texas. Most came from the southwestern frontier but a few from as far as Ohio or New England, among them one contingent subsidized by Swartwout's New York land company.

The Texas convention, termed for the moment the Consultation, on November 3, 1835, adopted a constitution, largely written by Houston, which declared Texas an autonomous state under the authority of the Mexican Constitution of 1824, and proceeded to dispatch Austin to the United States to raise funds and to elect Houston Commander in Chief of the Armies of Texas. Houston had continued to oppose an outright declaration of independence. In his judgment the great test of Texas survival would come the following year when Santa Anna launched the major invasion he was known to be preparing. Houston proposed to devote the interim to a similarly professional organization of Texas defenses.

But before he could assume personal command of the Texas forces already in the field, they had undertaken impetuous offensives against the Mexican garrisons in south Texas and were achieving a series of wildly acclaimed triumphs, culminating in the capitulation of the army of 1400 Mexicans occupying San Antonio. By early December of 1835 there once more was no Mexican soldier north of the Rio Grande. Texas was ecstatic. It was assumed that the war had been won. Most settlers who had taken arms returned to their homes. The volunteers from the United States, left with no further apparent function, began immediately to contemplate new exploits. Under the heedless leadership of James Fannin, Francis Johnson, and Dr. James Grant, schemes were enthusiastically hatched for an invasion of Mexico. Houston's provident directives were scorned. He was forced to realize that as commander in chief he had lost effective control of his so-called armies.

Texas was providing another and more than usually incisive example of the intermingled elements of strength and weakness in a frontier society. Even when confronted by the direst threat any man considered his judgment at least the equal of any other's. Frontiersmen invariably rose with striking vigor and competency to meet an emergency, but once the emergency was deemed past were as prone as Indians to return irresponsibly to their personal concerns. This anarchic disposition was as evident in the political as in the military sphere. Every frontier was notably efficient in achieving the democratic co-operation of individuals responsive to the practical demands of local self-government, but this political genius was seldom so successful in coping with the wider and more complex demands involved in the co-operation of groups of communities. After the capture of San Antonio had led to the presumption the war had ended victoriously, the provisional government of Texas, created by representatives of the several settlements, was rendered impotent by factional quarrels and conflicts of local interests. The need for Houston's leadership was conceived to have passed and there were proposals that he be replaced by a more enterprising commander. Houston accepted a "furlough" which he devoted to a visit to the Texas Cherokee upon whom he used his great personal influence to forestall an Indian uprising which could fatally compromise Texas resistance to Santa Anna.

The convention reassembled at Washington-on-the-Brazos March 1, 1836, voted unanimously for a declaration of independence March 2nd, and on March 4th re-elected Houston commander in chief. It had met under circumstances so threatening that the imperative need of Houston's leadership had become obvious to all. The new-born republic was being swept toward immediate extinction by an avalanche of military disasters. January's dreams of booty-seeking excursions into Mexico had been dispersed almost overnight by the dreadful realization that Texas was in mortal peril. Santa Anna's invasion had developed months earlier than even the prudent Houston had foreseen. The scattered revolutionary forces in south Texas, engaged in leisurely and optimistic preparations for their contemplated dash across the Rio Grande, were destroyed piece-meal by Santa Anna's swift-moving dragoon columns. Santa Anna himself descended upon San Antonio. The defenders, under the dedicated leadership of Travis, Bowie, and Crockett, barricaded themselves in the walled compound of the Alamo, the rambling old mission on the outskirts of the town. There, after a defiant 12-day stand, they died to a man, furnishing Texas history with an honor roll usually considered to number 183. The Alamo fell March 6, 1836. On March 20th the last remaining organized Texas military force, Fannin's 450 men making a fatally delayed withdrawal from Goliad, surrendered to an overwhelming Mexican encirclement. A week later 371 of the prisoners were shot by order of Santa Anna, who had determined to solve Mexico's Texas problem once and for all by the extermination of its American inhabitants.

By the time Houston had undertaken the assembly of a new defense force at Gonzales, the deluge of military catastrophes appeared to have removed any remaining hope of the republic's survival. The convention's interim government was fleeing northward in a frantic search for safety that continued to the refuge of Galveston Island. Santa Anna's army of 7000 was sweeping across Texas in several columns, burning, destroying, killing, committed to a basic directive that envisaged the obliteration of every evidence of American occupation. Houston conducted a masterly retreat, much impeded by the need en route to arrange for the safety and transport of a horde of woman and children refugees. A great proportion of the Texas forces destroyed in the south had been volunteers and adventurers from the United States, but for his new army he was obliged to depend on settlers, most of whom, though unrivaled as fighting men, were constrained to think first of the safety of their families. His force swelled to 1500 and then as his necessary retreat persisted contracted to 800.

Intoxicated by his many victories, Santa Anna made a reckless dash between Houston and the coast with a column of 1400 cavalry in the hope of capturing the fleeing Texas government. Houston followed, having become the pursuer in place of the pursued. He overtook his quarry near the mouth of the San Jacinto River where the present Houston ship canal enters Galveston Bay. After some hours of apparent indecision during which, however, he consulted none of his officers, he determined to put all to the issue by launching an immediate assault upon Santa Anna's camp.

The overconfident Mexicans were enjoying a midafternoon siesta when the storm broke. The Texas attack was delivered by what had become a genuine frontier army composed of men long accustomed to every extreme of violence who fully realized that they were fighting for homes and families and everything that they most valued. The charge of the single long thin line was irresistible. So impetuous was the onslaught that it swept to the center of the Mexican camp in its first fierce rush and within moments the engagement had ceased to resemble a battle. The furious Texas war cry, "Remember the Alamo," was echoed by their victims' despairing pleas of "Me no Alamo." More than 600 Mexicans were struck down before Texas vengeance had been sated. The Mexican assumption that they need fear no attack from an enemy so much weaker in numbers had laid them open to a surprise from which they had been unable even momentarily to recover. Texan losses were limited to 6 killed and 24 wounded. Among these miraculously few casualties one was of particular moment. Houston's shattered right leg brought him as near death as had his former wounds at Horseshoe Bend. As the pursuit and capture of fugitives continued the next day, it was belatedly discovered that among the prisoners was the disguised Santa Anna. In the one action an invading army had been destroyed and the ruler of Mexico made a captive. There could have been no more complete victory.

Custody of Santa Anna gave the Texan cause a breathing spell for which there was need. The leaderless Mexican forces evacuated Texas, though the new Mexican government refused to recognize the independence Santa Anna had promised as the price of his freedom. A famous battle had been won but the war was not over. Mexico was far from resigned and contemplated new invasions. Houston returned from his New Orleans hospital in time to be elected first nonprovisional president of Texas in September 1836. The little republic was bankrupt and the prospect of its continued survival still faint. Much seemed to hinge on prompt recognition by the great powers, particularly the United States. Texans looked eagerly and confidently to Jackson, their champion, not only for recognition but annexation. But Jackson hesitated while the delay became agonizing. Jackson had been a leading proponent of American southwestward expansion since as a 21-year-old lawyer he had crossed the mountains to the Tennessee frontier in 1788. He was now President of the United States, however, and as faithfully committed as had been Washington, Adams, or Jefferson to guarding the integrity of the union. As a passionate southerner he had no sympathy with northern antislavery sentiment, yet reflection had roused a fear that annexation of Texas must so enlarge slaveholding territory as to make secession inevitable. Finally, on the last day of his last term, he reluctantly agreed to a technical recognition of Texan independence by consenting to the accreditation of an American minister to Texas.

That segment of the American frontier which had survived by its own efforts for the past 14 years was thereafter compelled to continue to shift for itself during the next 10 years through all the trials of a prolonged commercial depression, of perpetual Indian troubles, and of recurrent Mexican invasions. Before they were at last acknowledged as fellow Americans, the lodgment of the frontier people in Texas had been held over a span of years almost exactly matching the 1769-1794 period in which the first transmountain frontier had fought most of its own battles. It was only then, as had been the happy former experience, that the nation inherited what its forerunners had won.

XVII

༄

California

THE WESTWARD MOVEMENT of the American frontier was an overland process, with auxiliary resort to water-borne transport on occasionally available lakes and rivers. Its goal was the shores of the Pacific, a goal that had been always in mind since the first Europeans to land on the shores of the Atlantic had launched at once their quest for the Northwest Passage to the Western Ocean. Sea-borne explorers, ranging so much more swiftly and widely, soon discovered those far' shores. California's situation on them had made it a region known to mariners two centuries before the first long hunters had crossed the Alleghenies. But the eventual American occupation of California stemmed from persistence in the same movement across the continent's land mass that had achieved the penetration of the Mississippi Valley, the plains, and the Rockies.

All of California's early history was maritime. Cortés landed on the tip of Lower California only 14 years after his conquest of Mexico, attaching the name to a region presumed to be the haunt of mermaids and Amazons. In 1542, as a companion effort to collateral Spanish explorations of the continent's interior by Coronado and De Soto, Juan Cabrillo, sailing north from Mexico, discovered the bays of San Diego and Monterey and his lieutenant, Bartolomé Ferrelo, kept on northward as far as what is now the Oregon border. After 1565 the Manila galleon, on its annual voyage to and from Mexico, customarily picked up its eastbound landfall at Cape Mendocino and skirted the California coast to its destination at Acapulco. In 1579, the English sea rover, Sir Francis Drake, after his looting of Spain's Peruvian and Mexican treasure houses, lingered along the coast of California which he named New Albion. In 1602 Sebastián Vizcaíno gave names to and landed in the bays of San Diego and Monterey, inspected the Channel Islands, and coasted northward until storms and scurvy turned him back at Cape Mendocino. California had become a household word generations before the founding of Jamestown, Quebec, or Plymouth. At the same time, so little was known of California beyond the view from the sea of its fog-shrouded, rock-bound shore line that the time-honored legend that it was an island was not altogether discounted until well into the eighteenth century.

The explosion of Spanish energy which had achieved the conquest of the West Indies, Mexico, Peru, and the Philippines had long since abated. Spanish imperial policy had degenerated into a lethargic resolve to hold what had been gained in the New World by keeping prospective intruders at a safe distance. Outposts were established in Texas only after Spain had been disturbed by the appearance of the French on the Mississippi. The comparable threat posed by the southward extension of the Russian grasp on Alaska precipitated an equally belated Spanish colonization of California.

After fearful initial hardships, miseries, and misadventures, the Spanish occupation of California developed from the original San Diego settlement in 1769 into the establishment of presidios at San Diego, Santa Barbara, Monterey, and San Francisco; the pueblos of Los Angeles and San Jose, and 21 missions stretching at intervals approximately a day's journey from San Diego to Sonoma. The mission system, to an even more decisive extent than on the earlier northern frontiers of Mexico, became the central, driving force accomplishing the colonization of California. The Indians of California, aside from a few in the Colorado River bottom, had never practiced agriculture. Under the stern tutelege of their Franciscan mentors, thousands were compelled to perform their tasks as farm laborers along with their duties as converts. California began soon to reveal that prosperity potential for which it has ever since been noted. The mission communities flourished. The San Gabriel Mission, for example, grazed 150,000 cattle, 20,000 horses, and 40,000 sheep, and cultivated corn, wheat, garden vegetables, oranges, lemons, limes, figs, and grapes. The indefatigable fathers' table was laden with a variety of meat, fruit, wine, whiskey, and liqueurs judged by the rare traveler, usually received with bountiful hospitality, to excel the fare enjoyed by the wealthiest inhabitant of parent Mexico or Spain.

Separated from Mexico by a great distance made to seem greater by the intervening deserts, early California's few contacts with the outer world were by way of the sea. The great English navigator, Captain James Cook, did not approach the California coast on his memorable third voyage to the north Pacific, but one consequence of his discoveries suddenly widened California's narrow window on the world. His report on the number and value of sea otter attracted an ever-increasing number of seagoing traders and hunters to waters which until then had scarcely known a sail from one year to the next. Otter hunting spread southward along the coast. Trading ships which had formerly touched only Hawaii and China began to drop into California ports. Several itinerant visitors from the sea were distinguished. In 1785, Jean François de Galaup, comte de La Pérouse, engaged in his circumnavigational exploration that was to end in mysterious disaster, put in at Monterey long enough to report to his government his conclusion that California was so defenseless that it might be possessed by any power that so elected. In the early 1790's, the English explorer-navigator-surveyor, Captain George Vancouver, was repeatedly entertained in California ports. In 1805, the romantic attachment between the visiting Russian nobleman, Nikolai Rezanov, and a California maiden attracted more attention than another Russian project, soon accomplished, of establishing a fort on California territory. There had been in the meantime a most undistinguished visitor who had attracted almost no attention but whose advent furnished a far clearer presage of California's future than had that of any of the others. The first American ship of the many that were to follow had appeared in a California port. In 1796, the trader-hunter, Ebenezer Dorr, commanding *Otter,* had put in at Monterey for supplies.

Spain had responded to the increase in maritime activity by making in 1790 one spasmodic effort to reassert exclusive Spanish sovereignty in north Pacific waters but had bowed to Great Britain's Nootka Sound ultimatum. After 1810 the revolution in Mexico reduced the power of either the Spanish or Mexican government to take a strong position. But the threat to California from the sea did not, after all, appear too serious. There was, besides, a modest profit, by which local officials particularly benefited, in supply transactions with trading vessels which represented California's sole commercial intercourse. An occasional seafarer left his ship to reside in California, usually marrying a señorita and merging into the population. Life in California flowed on as placidly as before the ships had multiplied. Even the revolutions convulsing Mexico produced few repercussions to disturb the calm of California's isolation.

Then, November 27, 1826, came the portentous event from which California's peace was never to recover. Jedediah Smith and 18 fellow mountain men emerged from the desert to camp before the San Gabriel Mission. The bearded, long-haired, skin-clad, weather-beaten, heavily armed intruders were as sinisterly alien in appearance and deportment as the first band of Goths glimpsed by a Roman outpost. Their arrival had forever dispelled the illusion that the 1500 miles of mysterious wilderness stretching eastward to the Mississippi constituted a barrier protecting California's security. This was, moreover, a direct and flagrant intrusion. Lewis and Clark and the Astorians had made their way to the Pacific nearly a thousand miles farther north through country to which no nation had clear title, but this third display of American aggressiveness had been flaunted by men who had on their way west unhesitatingly violated the acknowledged Mexican border even before they had reached Great Salt Lake. The significance of the threat was soon compounded. Smith had not yet had time to get across the northern California border on his way to the Columbia before another band of American trespassers, led by James and Sylvester Pattie, had turned up in the extreme south.[1] Echeandia's patience had reached the vanishing point. He threw the intruders into his San Diego jail.

James Ohio Pattie deserved recognition as one of the more notable figures of American frontier history and, instead, drifted into an obscurity in which his career was forgotten for generations. His experiences and achievements were more varied and colorful than those of any other mountain man and he himself described them in a book which gives more detail on what could and did happen to a mountain man than has any other firsthand account. He and his deeds were the natural projections of the way of life of long established frontier stock. His family had moved westward with the frontier from the Potomac. His grandafther had served on the Kentucky frontier under George Rogers Clark and Benjamin Logan during the Revolution and his father had commanded the most exposed fort on the Missouri frontier during the War of 1812. In 1824, at the age of 20, he embarked with his father, Sylvester, upon a wilderness venture which developed into an odyssey prolonged through seven years, ranging from the Missouri to the Rio Grande, from the Yellowstone to the Gulf of California, and from San Francisco to Vera Cruz. His activities ranged as widely, from hunting and trapping to mining and the practice of medicine, while he experienced successive disasters and triumphs, made and lost fortunes, and survived innumerable encounters with hunger, thirst,

[1] There is some evidence that another American, Richard Campbell, who had taken the precaution to become a naturalized Mexican citizen and provide himself with a passport, reached San Diego from Santa Fe with a party of New Mexican traders in 1827.

accident, exposure, imprisonment, grizzlies, and Indians. His climactic adventure was precipitated by his California visit.

In the fall of 1827, after having been engaged in that year's series of bloody battles between American trappers from Taos and Indians of the Colorado and Mojave deserts, Pattie, with his father and 6 companions, undertook to trap the lower Colorado. When their horses were stolen by Indians they resorted to rafts which became useless when they were caught between the tidebore at the river's mouth and the river's flooding. They buried their furs in the sand and attempted to cross the desert to Spanish settlements they had heard existed nearer the coast. They were perishing from heat, hunger, and thirst when succored by Christian Indians from Santa Catalina Mission in Baja California. Their lives had been saved but their freedom lost. Taken to San Diego under guard, they were consigned to solitary confinement which the governor indicated would continue indefinitely as a warning to other trespassers. The elder Pattie died in prison but the younger's lot was somewhat alleviated by the sympathetic attentions of the jailer's sister.

Months of protest and appeals supported by the intercession of Captain John Bradshaw of the New England trading ship, *Franklin*, failed to gain the Americans' release. One momentary hope was dispelled when a search party dispatched to recover the buried furs as ransom discovered that in the interim they had been ruined by floods. Their liberty was finally regained as a consequence of a community catastrophe. A smallpox epidemic was alarming California, particularly threatening the Indian population clustered about each mission. Pattie chanced to have in his possession a small quantity of vaccine originally accumulated to protect the health of workers in his New Mexican silver mining enterprise. After long and stubborn disputation, a grim bargain was struck between the governor and his prisoners. In exchange for the parole of himself and his companions, Pattie undertook to save California from the smallpox plague. He embarked in early 1829 on a tour of the settlements and missions that carried him from San Diego beyond San Francisco to the Russian station on Bodega Bay, vaccinating, according to his count, more than 20,000 persons.[2] His account of this singular excursion, together with his description of the places visited, is filled with detail, much of which has continued to appear authentic in the light of later scrutiny.

As an official reward for his services, he was offered a grant of land and 1000 head of cattle, horses and mules, provided he accepted Mexican citizenship and became a Catholic. He considered the award grossly insufficient and his conscience was offended by the political and religious conditions imposed. Enraged, he participated for a time in a local insurrection against Echeandia, then journeyed to Mexico City to present his case to the Mexican government, maintaining that official persecution had cost him the loss of his furs, that an unjust imprisonment had caused the death of his father, and that the enormous service he had rendered the people of California had been repudiated. He gained a sympathetic hearing but no compensation. Broken in health and fortune, he returned to Kentucky to write his book. After its publication he was lost to sight, though he must have resumed his wanderings, for William Waldo, an early California associate of Ewing Young and William Wolfskill, reported his death in the snows of the Sierra Nevada in the winter of 1849.

The California incursions of Smith and Pattie had been incidental to other designs. Smith had set out to find the Buenaventura and had kept on to San Gabriel for supplies when his failure to find it had prolonged his travel time. Pattie had been driven by the Indian theft of his horses and the wreck of his rafts to seek a similarly unpremeditated contact with California settlements. But Pattie had hardly taken ship for Mexico before there came another influx of Americans whose immediate and intended destination was California and who fully realized that the deliberate action

---

[2] His store of vaccine must have been successively replenished, according to the practice of the time, by extracting replacement serum from patients previously treated. The first recorded vaccinations in California were of 54 persons in Monterey by a Russian ship's doctor in 1821. Pattie's vaccination census may have been exaggerated. Hubert Howe Bancroft found no reference to an epidemic in 1829 while noting an extraordinary increase in the mission Indian death rate that year.

was in flagrant violation of Mexican law. Their leaders were the Tennessean, Ewing Young, and the Kentuckian, William Wolfskill. Both were veteran mountain men of the specially hardened Taos stamp. Young had come to Santa Fe with Becknell's first expedition and Wolfskill with his second. Thereafter, they had engaged in annual trapping enterprises, usually in partnership, that had ranged across the mountains and deserts of the southwest from the headwaters of the Green to the mouth of the Gila. They had participated in the succession of desperate encounters with southwestern Indians with which Pattie and Smith had become involved. They had learned every peak, canyon, and pass of that infinitely harsh region. As a consequence of perpetual passport and license difficulties with New Mexican authorities, both had applied for Mexican citizenship, regarding it as a gesture no more significant than any practical adaptation required by any strange environment of any frontiersman. Having trapped every stream east of the Colorado, they determined to extend their operations to California. Young was the first to make the move. In the winter of 1829-30, with a party of 21 that included the boy, Kit Carson, he crossed the Colorado and followed the Smith-Garcés route up the Mojave to San Gabriel. Again a band of brazen, rifle-brandishing Americans had materialized out of the vast eastern desert to disturb the peace and quiet of California. From now on such appearances would become so frequent as to cease to create sensations.

This third party of American intruders was more numerous than Pattie's and more obstreperous than Smith's. They had been accustomed for years to circumventing the government of New Mexico and were endowed with even less respect for the far weaker government of California. To the inhabitants' relief they soon moved on to undertake trapping the mountain streams of the central valley. Here they encountered another party of interlopers, Ogden's Hudson's Bay Company brigade, which had just made an even longer journey, a tremendous circuit from the distant Columbia by way of the Nevada, Utah, Colorado, and Mojave deserts. The two remained commercial rivals but, if threatened by official interference, could become allies constituting a stronger military force than any at the disposal of California's government. The last prospect that Mexican officials could prevent the alien trapping of California waters was fading. The Americans' physical prowess was emphasized when they assisted a Mexican column in subduing a band of Indian deserters, and again when they pursued and punished another band of Indians who had stolen their horses. Local California authorities became so resigned to the inevitable that Young was able to establish trade relations at San Jose that had been denied Smith. The hopelessness of discouraging the trespass of American trappers was again demonstrated when Young paused at Los Angeles on his way back to Taos with his fur catch. Local officials conceived that they might attempt a mass arrest if their dangerous visitors were first made sufficiently drunk. The liquor-plying phase of the strategem was a predictable success. No approach could have been more welcomed by mountain men. But they proved as dangerous drunk as sober. In an obscurely excited altercation among themselves one of them, James Higgins, killed another, James Lawrence, without attracting the condemnation or even, apparently, the attention of their companions. This facile resort to violence by men who had for years been inured to every form of violence made a profound impression on the pueblo's inhabitants. No further attempt was made to detain the barbarous visitors.

The next year, 1831, the American tide swelled to three parties: William Wolfskill's, David Jackson's and Ewing Young's second.[3] Each successive venture to California had experimented with new routes and trails until the way from Santa Fe and Taos to Los Angeles and San Diego was becoming as familiar as a highroad. There was an added significance in the Jackson and Wolfskill enterprises. Jackson, with his associate, Peter Smith, Jedediah Smith's younger brother, returned to Santa Fe with a herd of horses and mules purchased in California, thus adding returns connected with commercial intercourse to those sought by trapping.

[3] There was further indication of the mountain men's acceptance of perpetual exposure to danger as a natural way of life in the presence in Young's party of Isaac Galbraith, a survivor of the Mojave massacre of Jedediah Smith's relief expedition, and John Turner, a survivor of both that and the Umpqua massacre of his Oregon expedition.

Wolfskill's party broke up in Los Angeles and many, including most notably Wolfskill himself, became permanent residents. California's isolation was fast disappearing.

The American threat was still premonitory. But accompanying its devolopment there came an internal upheaval which radically altered the structure of California society. By the central Mexican government's Secularization Act of 1833 mission lands were thrown open to settlement by Mexican lay citizens. More than 700 grants, many of them of immense size, were made to private owners in the course of the next few years. It had been a reform intended to encourage the settlement of California and at the same time to improve the lot of the Indian inhabitants. It succeeded in neither purpose. It failed to stimulate immigration from Mexico, the grants were claimed by Mexicans already residents of California, the Indians were demoralized and so sudden and fundamental a change in the order of society produced outbursts of violence. The new landowners developed a new recalcitrance that extended to repeated revolts against the authority of their Mexican governors. Some of the communities of mission Indians, when unexpectedly relieved of restraint, pillaged missions, slaughtered cattle, burned storehouses, and uprooted vineyards as they sought to obliterate every evidence of their former condition. Under the central government's edict, immense land holdings of the missions, formerly comprising all the more valuable land in the coastal and frequented areas of California, were eventually parceled out to private grantees. The rancho succeeded the mission as the focus of California life. For the proprietary families, each possessing endless leagues of land and countless head of cattle and horses, the new regime provided a wonderfully gratifying existence, guarded from economic anxieties, distinguished by social amenities, and graced by the personal privileges of an idyllic caste system. The rancho period was the glamour age of California though it was not an age destined to endure beyond the lifetime of the men who first began to enjoy its rewards.

For that same year of 1833 witnessed another event that warned of a greater change than that succeeding the downfall of the mis-

sions. So far American intrusions had been by way of the southwestern deserts through territory over which Mexico exercised
sovereignty and subject to some degree of control by Mexican authorities of New Mexico and Sonora. The new American intruders
of 1833 reached California by striking straight west from the
American main gateway to the mountains, the South Pass-Bear
River axis, thereby opening the route that was about to become
the California fork of the Overland Trail, the path of the pioneers
and the 49ers.

Their leader was one of the most noted of all mountain men,
Joseph Reddeford Walker, a Tennessean who had, like Ewing
Young, been one of the Becknell's four companions on his first
Santa Fe expedition. He was at the time Bonneville's lieutenant.
Bonneville, possibly as a cover to his secret services to the War
Department, maintained in the contemporary account he furnished
Washington Irving that Walker had been detached with orders
merely to explore the Great Salt Lake area and that his epochal
California journey had been a breach of discipline. There appears
little doubt, however, that before they had departed from Bonneville's main camp Walker's men were well aware that their destination was California. A similar conflict of testimony obscures the
total number of Walker's company. Bonneville said he assigned
40 of his employees to the expedition. Three men who were members of the Walker party, Joseph Meek, Zenas Leonard, and George
Nidever, differed widely in their later reports on its roster, making
the total, respectively, 118, 58, and 35 to 40. Meek's was unquestionably another of the obvious exaggerations of which he was so
often guilty, and the discrepancy between Leonard and Nidever
may be at least in part accounted for by the impulsive volunteering
of a group of free trappers who elected to join the party after its
initial organization when they realized that it was headed for
California.

Walker marched westward from Great Salt Lake into the desert
until he had picked up the westward flowing river discovered
and trapped by Peter Skene Ogden in 1829. This was the soon to
become world famous watercourse which, after having been called

Unknown River (by Ogden), Mary's River (in honor of an Indian woman in Ogden's party), and Barren River (by Leonard), was subsequently given by John Charles Fremont the name of Alexander von Humboldt, the eminent German scientist whose extensive travels had never brought him within thousands of miles of the stream. Upon reaching the desert "sink" in which the Humboldt finds its end, Walker kept on westward and southwestward into country no white man had ever penetrated. His progress had been at the steady and rapid rate of which travelers so seasoned as his mountain followers were uniquely capable and had been uneventful except for an often-criticised encounter with the benighted root-digging, insect-eating natives of the region. Swarms of hungry and naked desert Indians had hung about his camps and marches, watching with desperate eagerness for an opportunity to steal a horse or a mule or even the least item of property from the incredible store of wealth possessed by these strange wanderers into this land of utter poverty. Exasperated, Walker unleashed his followers and they, with the frontiersman's age-old aversion to Indians, shot, rode down, and otherwise dispatched more than thirty of their miserable and overmatched tormentors. After what appeared to him so inconsequential a pause, Walker pressed on toward his goal. The snow-crested California mountains finally loomed ahead. He crossed the Sierra in the neighborhood of Tioga Pass, enjoyed a breath-taking view of Yosemite, marveled at the size of the Big Trees, and advanced thankfully from the cold of the heights and the heat of the desert into the lush central valley.

He had reached California by striking directly westward across the midcontinent. His had been in every respect a remarkable feat. He had started from the Missouri frontier with the first wagon train to make the South Pass crossing over the great divide. He had been first to cross the Great Basin from east to west. He had been first to sight, to approach, and then to scale the great Sierra barrier from the east. His tremendous journey ranks with those of Lewis and Clark, the Astorians, and Jedediah Smith. In some of its aspects his achievement was even more significant. He had found the direct central route over which the westward movement would presently advance at a single bound all the way to California.

The explorers descended the San Joaquin, were delighted by the extraordinary prevalence of deer, bear, elk, and antelope while being disappointed by the absence of buffalo, were terrified by the memorable display of falling stars November 12, 1833, which was similarly terrifying people everywhere in the United States, sighted and skirted San Francisco Bay, crossed the Coast Range, and attained their ultimate goal when on November 20, 1833, 68 days after losing sight of Great Salt Lake, they stood on the shores of the Pacific. That the first other white men they encountered after leaving the Green River rendezvous should be fellow trappers eloquently signified the utter loneliness of the immense expanse they had traversed. The New England sea otter-hunter, *Lagoda*, appeared offshore. Her commander, John Bradshaw, who had befriended Smith and Pattie, responded to their signals, entertained them aboard, and presided over their later contacts with Mexican authorities at Monterery.

Walker's followers were mountain men most of whom regarded the California journey as an entertaining personal adventure, an intriguing experience that capped the many less exotic adventures they had hitherto experienced in the far west. But the company's clerk, Zenas Leonard, prophetically perceived the tremendous issues involved. In his book, published in 1839, he wrote of "this vast waste of territory" in which he and his companions had for years been wandering:

What a theme to contemplate its settlement and civilization. Will the jurisdiction of the federal government ever succeed in civilizing the thousands of savages now roaming over these plains, and her hardy freeborn population here plant their homes, build their towns and cities, and say here shall the arts and sciences of civilization take root and flourish? yes, here, even in this remote part of the great west before many years, will these hills and valleys be greeted with the enlivening sound, of the workman's hammer, and the merry whistle of the plough-boy. But this is left undone by the government, and will only be seen when too late to apply the remedy. The Spaniards are making inroads on the South—the Russians are encroaching with impunity along the sea shore to the North, and further North-east the British are pushing their stations into the very heart of our territory, which, even at this day, more resemble military forts to resist invasion, then trading stations. Our government should be vigilant. She should assert her claim by taking possession of the whole territory as soon as possible—for we have good reason to suppose that the territory *west* of the mountains will some day be equally as important to the nation as that on the *east.*

After two months of California hospitality, enjoyed somewhat boisterously by many of his men, Walker started his return journey February 14, 1834, adding to his notable exploration the discovery and passage of Walker Pass in the southern Sierras and, by turning northward, the length of Owens Valley along the eastern face of the range. He attempted to cross the Nevada desert in the approximate area Smith had crossed in 1827 but soon concluded the extreme heat and aridity made this route impracticable and veered north to the Humboldt.

Meanwhile six of his followers had elected to remain in California. The inclination of mountain men to become California residents was developing into a trend with a bearing on California's future as significant as had had their original coming. Among the more noted members of the Smith, Pattie, Young, Wolkskill, and Walker expeditions who had exchanged their role as alien intruders for that of scarcely less welcome alien inhabitants were Lewis Burton, Nathan Daily, Job Dye, George Frazier, Isaac Galbraith, Richard Laughlin, George Nidever, John Price, Daniel Sill, Isaac Slover, Isaac Sparks, J. J. Warner, Isaac Williams, William Wolfskill, Ewing Young, and George Yount. The total number who remained in California tended to fluctuate as some returned to their wanderings but was generally considered at the time to run to more than a hundred. Hubert Howe Bancroft's Pioneer Register and Index in his *History of California* listed 117 former trappers as residents during the period before 1840. Desultory official efforts to punish or expel the intruders recurred, but the most serious such attempt in 1840 was thwarted by the threatening dispatch of American and British warships to California waters. Some of the intruders had invited toleration by providing themselves with Santa Fe or Chihuahua passports, others had accepted Mexican citizenship, and still others possessed sufficient means to obtain residence permits from local authorities.

The influx of American trappers into California in the 1830's was a continuation of the process by which they had in the 1820's swarmed into New Mexico. As certainly as water seeks its level were they men whom nothing could deter from rushing wherever there appeared new opportunity for adventure or gain. Their arrival in New Mexico had kept that province's governors in a constant state of alarm and anger. Their advent among the so much less numerous and more widely scattered inhabitants of California struck Los Angeles and Santa Barbara and Monterey with an even sharper impart that it had Taos and Santa Fe. Their aggressiveness disturbed and disconcerted the less energetic Californians. They were perpetually restless, perpetually moving about, perpetually hitting upon new plans for new activities, new schemes, and devices for making quicker and larger profits. Most tended at first to persist in the occupation with which they were familiar, but soon tended to turn from trapping beaver on California's streams to seek the greater rewards of hunting sea otter off California's coast. Wolfskill and Yount, for example, in 1831, built a schooner of timber from the San Bernardino Mountains with which to undertake the hunting of sea otter. Nidever, Sill, and Burton were among those who made Santa Barbara their otter-hunting base. This was an enterprise requiring men as hardy as they. The trapping rivalries of the Rockies had carried over to the Pacific. British and Russian otter-hunting ships made a practice of employing bands of seagoing northwest Indians to attack their American competitors. At the same time, as had always been the case with American frontiersmen, there was a stronger impulse than the initial quest for adventure and gain. Just beneath the surface was the governing instinct to make full use of a novel environment, to take possession. Soon—Wolfskill was among the first—some were turning to land culture as farmers, vineyardists, cattle raisers. Others became merchants or traders in California's principal product, hides and tallow, and still others, as some had in New Mexico, adapted their superior skills to gainful employment as carpenters, blacksmiths, coopers. One even became a baker.

These first Americans to reach California across the plains and mountains were not true settlers. They were as yet unable to bring families with them so that they might establish American communities. Many had instead married Mexican women and accepted ostensible Mexican citizenship. But as representatives of their parent stock, the frontier people, they had made another solid lodgment. As in the instance of every former lodgment, it would never be relinquished. Mexicans' hope of retaining California was already as certainly doomed as had been the Indians' hope.

XVIII

&

Oregon

IN ITS PROGRESSIVE OCCUPATION of new regions, the westward movement may be considered to have fulfilled its primary function
wherever it had achieved the establishment of permanent communities of American families. In Texas, proximity and climatic
similarities had invited occupation by a resolute persistence in the
step-by-step process which had been everywhere carrying the frontier
across the wooded and watered eastern half of the continent. This
self-perpetuating advance to clear new sites in the next belt of woodland to the west was not a process adaptable to the western half.
The plains, mountains, and deserts posed problems of aridity and
isolation for which experience had not prepared the frontier family.
California, the next unmistakably arable region, appeared too distant and beyond an intervening terrain too harsh to permit its
occupation in accord with a family migration pattern which offered
as its longest former leap the 200-mile crossing of the Appalachians.
In California, as a substitute, an initial American penetration had
nevertheless been achieved by mountain men whose tremendous
journeys could be maintained by the returns from trapping en route.

Oregon, though so familiarly wooded and watered as to seem by report as inviting to settlement as had once been Kentucky and Tennessee, appeared also too remote to permit family migration, and there even the access of American trappers was made impracticable by the growing power of the Hudson's Bay Company's regional fur-trade monopoly. The immense physical difficulties awaiting any attempt to settle Oregon were compounded by the circumstance that the northwest was a no man's land. The United States had since 1818 consented to regard title to the country west of the continental divide and north of the Mexican border (the northern boundary of the present states of Utah, Nevada, and California) as subject to negotiation with Great Britain at some indeterminate future date. This apparently insuperable barrier of American governmental disinterest, British de facto occupation, and an isolation presumably precluding settlement was surmounted by way of a train of events set off by the personal fervor of Hall J. Kelley, a Yankee schoolmaster, and William Walker, a Christian Wyandot church worker. Between them these two obscure private individuals altered the course of history and offered the United States another empire.

The British citadel in the northwest about to be assailed by two such unlikely champions was Fort Vancouver, the Hudson's Bay Company's western headquarters, across the river from the present Portland. Its castellan was Chief Factor John McLoughlin, the white-maned, six-foot-four giant whose rule was as autocratically humane and judgment as sagaciously generous as his mien was impressive. His domain, fortified by a system of interior posts controlling every most strategic location, extended over the entire valley of the Columbia and most of what is now British Columbia. To make his province more self-sufficient he had encouraged agriculture and industry in the area about Fort Vancouver where an army of retainers, numbering 700 with their families, cultivated farms and orchards, tended herds of cattle, horses, and hogs, and operated sawmills, gristmills, fisheries and boatyards. The Indians of the northwest, largely dependent upon the company for trade goods, had been firmly attached to company and British interests.

The company establishment on the Columbia, with regular and swift communications by express canoe with Hudson Bay and the Great Lakes and by annual supply ships with England, had become a closely knit segment of the world-wide British Empire of which it was a significant outer bastion.

McLoughlin's official conduct in holding this bastion had been a prescribed phase of a fully developed policy calculated to coordinate company and imperial interests. After the 1825 Ogden Hole confrontation between American and British trappers, it had been determined at the highest British levels that the United States could probably not be indefinitely denied access to the Pacific. By the same formulation of long-range policy, it was determined that British occupation of the area north of the east-west stretch of the lower Columbia be maintained and that meanwhile American penetration of the area south of it be deterred by an accelerated exhaustion of its fur resources. It was taken for granted that any advance by American settlers into so remote and inhospitable a region was unlikely to develop in the foreseeable future and, therefore, that by discouraging American trappers any American move toward the Pacific could at the very worst be kept at an appropriate distance from the area of permanent British occupation in the northwest. In pursuance of this policy, Hudson's Bay Company brigades during the late 1820's and early 1830's engaged in furious competition, without regard for profits, wherever the less well organized and disciplined American trappers were operating in or west of the mountains. At the same time, equally forehanded efforts were made to carry out this exhaustion program in more distant areas in the hope of anticipating American competition. Brigades under Alexander McLeod in 1829 and Michel Lafromboise and John Work in 1932 trapped intensively and extensively in California which company parties continued to frequent for the next 10 years. One of the more striking of all far western journeys was made in the furtherance of this campaign by Peter Skene Ogden in 1829-30. His journal and papers were lost in a canoe wreck but there is evidence to suggest that, after returning to the Humboldt he had discovered the year before, he turned southeastward across the Great Basin to the Colorado, descended the Colorado to the Gulf, and then crossed the Mojave Desert to undertake trapping in the central valley of California. By whatever route he reached California, it was only to be mortified by the discovery that even such stupendous traveling had failed to outdistance American competition when he encountered on the San Joaquin Ewing Young's party of American trappers from Taos. In spite of such occasional surprises, the over-all effect of the company's wide-ranging and shrewdly directed activities was to consolidate its fur-trade monopoly in the northwest and thereby Great Britain's grasp on the region.

The immediate response to this challenge did not come from the frontier people, who had reacted so promptly and vigorously to all former challenges, or even from their forerunning representatives, traders and trappers, whose zest was diminishing with the decline in the beaver market. It came from a citizen of Boston who knew nothing about Oregon other than what he could find to read which was largely limited to the published accounts of Lewis and Clark and the several English sea-borne explorers. Nevertheless, Hall Kelley had become obsessed by a conviction that Oregon was an earthly paradise of such commercial and strategic importance that it must be forthwith claimed and possessed by the United States. He considered his cause so imperative that he embarked on a private crusade dedicated to the enlightenment of his fellow countrymen and his government.[1] He memorialized Congress, appealed to congressmen by open letters in newspapers, issued pamphlets and broadsides, composed manuals for emigrants, and staged weekly meetings to interest and inform prospective settlers. His frenetic efforts to stir public concern for Oregon served little more than to gain him a passing reputation as a crackpot, though his constant reiteration of the word Oregon may have made

---

[1] Congressman John Floyd of Virginia, son of the noted Kentucky pioneer, had in the 1820's been a similarly fervent advocate of the immediate acquisition of Oregon. Even with the advantage of his forum as a member he found Congress almost as indifferent to his appeals as it remained to Kelley's, though in 1824 the House, without Senate concurrence, had authorized the president to effect a military occupation of Oregon.

the term vaguely familiar to many who might not otherwise ever
have heard of it. Congress and the public remained apathetic while
he became more and more agitated. He was actually meeting with a
success which he did not realize. His one important convert had
been Nathaniel Wyeth who, on his second westward journey in
1834, took with him the two missionaries who founded the first
American colony in Oregon.

This development had been the upshot of a series of unrelated
events in which the accidental interplay of forces had been of incredible unpredictability. As Washington had so often said during
the darkest hours of the republic's infancy, Providence appeared in
every crisis disposed to assure the future of the United States. The
story of the founding of Oregon's first American settlement had
begun more than 20 years before with the earliest British fur traders'
crossing of the Rockies to the Columbia. Iroquois employees, who
had become Catholic converts in Canada, acquainted the Flatheads
and Nez Percé of the upper Columbia basin with a semblance of
Catholicism and planted in them the idea that its priests, the "black
robes," were the special custodians of white wisdom. Primitive
Indians, with their own religious regard for the supreme power
of all forms of supernaturalism, were disposed to ascribe the obvious
superiority of white tools and weapons to white command of magic.
After brooding over this for some years, in 1831 the Nez Percé and
Flathead dispatched a delegation to visit the borders of the United
States in order to inspect white institutions in an attempt to discover
if there might not truly be occult secrets by an understanding of
which their people might profit. They were directed to ask specifically that "black robes," of whose wisdom they had heard, be sent
to instruct them in white accomplishments. After many misadventures while making so long a journey, much of it through the
territory of enemy nations, four of the delegates reached St. Louis
and were kindly received by William Clark, United States Superintendent of Indian Affairs. Inadequate interpretation left their
mission somewhat unclear but their mention of "black robes" led
Clark to refer them to local Catholic authorities who were, however,
without the resources to respond to their appeal. Two of the older

Nez Percé sickened, were baptized before death, and interred in the Catholic cemetery. The other Nez Percé and the Flathead started homeward aboard the steamboat *Yellowstone,* an example of white metaphysical powers with which they were much impressed. One died on the Missouri and the other was killed in the mountains by Blackfeet before he had regained his homeland. The mission had proved an apparent failure. The visit of the inarticulate Indians had attracted little attention and their misunderstood purpose had been dismissed as another illustration of Indian irrationality.

But the series of accidents that was to lead to an American Oregon was still in sequence. Shortly after the discouraged departure of the surviving visitors, William Walker, a well educated Wyandot convert to Methodism, came west to investigate the suitability of Iowa as a site to which the Wyandot might be transplanted from their homes on Lake Erie in conformity with the national government's Indian removal policy. He reported that Iowa was totally unsuitable for Wyandot occupation but while in St. Louis learned from Clark of the recent Nez Percé-Flathead visit. Walker's evangelical enthusiasms were excited. He wrote a letter to his church superiors in Ohio, untruthfully stating that he had himself interviewed the pilgrims, carefully omitting any mention that their request had been for Catholic teachers, and phrasing their appeal for spiritual instruction in eloquent words of his own invention. When the letter was published in the *Christian Advocate and Journal* of March 1, 1833, the reaction to it became a sensational stirring of the entire Protestant community in America. The hearts and consciences of countless devout congregations were touched by contemplation of the distance and danger braved by these remote savages to deliver a prayer for salvation. Walker's passing reference to their deformed heads struck a final sympathy-arousing chord.[2] Funds were subscribed, mass meetings held, mission societies organized. The emotions and energies of a religious generation were dedicated to

---

[2] Not having seen them, Walker presumably drew his mistaken conclusion from the tribal name. White names for Indian nations were often adopted accidentally or attached to other nations than those identified by earlier observers. The Nez Percé, for example, did not make a practice of piercing their noses nor did the Flathead flatten their heads.

dispatching Christianity to the Flathead. The Methodists were first to reach the stage of action. In the spring of 1834 two ordained ministers, Jason Lee and his nephew, Daniel Lee, with three lay assistants, started west with Wyeth's second expedition.

It was a journey providing the pious tourists with a quick and thorough education in mountain manners, affairs, conditions, and personalities. Aside from experiencing all the ardors, alarms, and anomalies of plains and mountain travel, they were with or encountered many of the most notable figures associated with that eventful year: Thomas Nuttall and J. K. Townsend, the naturalists, William Drummond Stewart, the English adventure-seeker, Benjamin Bonneville, still mysteriously occupied after the expiration of his leave, Thomas McKay, stepson of John McLoughlin and son of the Astorian who had died aboard *Tonquin,* together with a host of outstanding mountain men, including Thomas Fitzpatrick, William and Milton Sublette, James Bridger, Joseph Meek, and Kit Carson. It could have been these headlong contacts with the realities of the mountain world that prepared Jason Lee for the momentous deviation that he never attempted to explain. It was a decision that could not have been evaded for at the 1834 rendezvous on Ham's Fork he also encountered some hundreds of Nez Percé and Flathead. The establishment of a mission among them had been the objective for which funds had been subscribed and his expedition organized. But, instead of acceding to their eager solicitations that he accompany them to their homeland, he elected to continue in Wyeth's company to Fort Vancouver. Whether or not he at the moment fully understood the significance of what he was doing he had on that July 4th of 1834 exchanged the role of missionary for that of colony-builder.

Upon reaching the lower Columbia, where Lee was 500 miles west of his intended field of operations, Wyeth established a trading post on Wappato Island at the mouth of the Willamette while Lee sought McLoughlin's counsel on his religious commitments. McLoughlin was disturbed by both intrusions but his opposition was urbane, diplomatic, and, he thought, far-sighted. He could not in any event arbitrarily forbid either invasion of the Hudson's Bay

Company's territory for under the Convention of 1818, and its renewals, it had been stipulated that citizens of both nations had equal freedom of movement in the region west of the Rockies. He had little fear that Wyeth's commercial competition would develop into any threat to the company's entrenched monopoly, but felt some anxiety lest the establishment of American missions among the Indians of the interior might interfere with the company's control over them. Choosing what seemed the lesser of two evils, he earnestly advised Lee to locate his mission on the Williamette. The Indians of western Oregon, having been exposed to white trading contacts from the sea for more than two generations, had been so reduced in numbers by disease that they had become of little commercial concern to the company. Lee was open to persuasion. He had observed the behavior of mountain Indians amidst the excesses of the summer rendezvous, and upon inspection he had realized by how much the lush Willamette Valley excelled in climate and fertility the arid region east of the Cascades. Wyeth's confidence in the future prosperity of western Oregon may also have influenced him. At any rate, in reporting his decision to his church sponsors he argued that he conceived his mission to be not only to the Flathead and Nez Percé but to all the Indians of the northwest and that this supreme purpose could be more sensibly served by establishing its headquarters in a situation nearer the seacoast where subsistence and supply were more available than in the isolated interior.

In the late summer of 1834, Lee, supplied by McLoughlin with tools and other assistance, began the erection near the present Salem of an establishment he continued to term a mission but which more resembled a communal farm. The structure of hewn logs with clapboard roof and stick-and-clay chimney, the subsistence problems, and many other aspects of the effort were familiar duplications of the experiences of first settlers on the earlier frontiers of Kentucky or Tennessee, Missouri, Arkansas, or Texas. But there were greater contrasts. Here there was no Indian danger and there were neighbors. In adjoining French Prairie there already existed a farming settlement of retired Hudson's Bay Company servants, French-Canadians with Indian wives and litters of half-breed children. And Lee's colony was distinctly not yet a true settlement for it was a monastic community without women members or family life.

He was necessarily more concerned at first with mundane than with spiritual labors. His principal preoccupation was with planting and cultivating the virgin soil in order to hasten the day his establishment might become self-sustaining. He preached on Sundays to congregations that were none too responsive. His French neighbors were friendly and co-operative but either irreligious or theoretically Catholic. Of the few Indians whose attention he had been able to attract, most had come to the mission with diseases which they hoped might be treated.

In encouraging and subsidizing the struggling American mission at French Prairie, McLoughlin had committed as momentous a mistake as had Captain Black when he had raised the British flag over Astoria in 1813, but there were no immediate indications that this might be so. The project appeared an infinitely doubtful experiment predetermined to collapse under the weight of its own inherent incongruities, an accident born of a sequence of accidents marked by the sole certainty that its early termination was inevitable. It was therefore no more than natural that McLoughlin should take it for granted that the threat posed by this second American lodgment in Oregon would pass as swiftly as had the first at Astoria, leaving British domination of the northwest as unaffected. What he did not perceive was that there were undercurrents in motion which were the reverse of accidental or experimental. Gathering about Lee's rude shelter for invalid Indians were threadlike tentacles of force, extending toward it from the limitless reservoirs of energy accumulating not only on the American land frontier but on the Pacific sea frontier. Among Lee's gradually growing circle of neighbors, assistants, recruits, and adherents were ex-sailors from trading and otter-hunting ships, ex-Northwesters, ex-Astorians, men who had traveled with Smith, Young, Walker, Bonneville, and Wyeth, Russians, Hawaiians, Iroquois, Delaware, and even three shipwrecked Japanese.[3] Most had become self-reliant and self-willed during wanderings subjecting them to every sort of hardship and danger, and having once elected to take root were not to be easily dislodged.

William Walker who had unwittingly served as the original agency to get Lee off to Oregon had no further part to play in the Oregon story. But his companion agitator, Hall Kelley, who had indirectly provided the means to get Lee to Oregon, now came full circle and appeared in person on the Oregon scene. Exasperated by his failure to win popular support for his crusade, Kelley determined to go see his promised land for himself. Traveling alone over a rambling but stubbornly persistent circuit by way of New Orleans, Vera Cruz, and Acapulco, suffering assorted misadventures, including robbery and illness, pausing once to give the Mexicans unsolicited advice on a railroad project, he kept on until in San Diego he met Ewing Young. Kelley's first great contribution to his Oregon cause had been the conversion of Nathaniel Wyeth. He now made his second with the conversion of Ewing Young. Excited by Kelley's enthusiastic and apparently informed accounts of Oregon, Young assembled 16 fellow mountain men then foot-loose in California, gathered upwards of a hundred horses and mules for sale to the supposedly flourishing American colony, and accompanied Kelley to the Columbia. This impromptu project was attended by the same array of unexpected confusions that had attended every Oregon enterprise since Astor's first. The governor of California had written McLoughlin, warning him of their coming and unjustly alleging that Young's stock had been stolen. As a consequence the usually hospitable McLoughlin, to Kelley's final exasperation, treated them with the coldest disdain. Young quarreled not only with McLoughlin but with the American colonists, carrying the dispute to the point of threatening to open a distillery. But he and his turbulent followers, even if initially unwelcome, had introduced

---

[3] Among Oregon residents at the time were Marie Dorion and her son, Baptiste, survivors of the Snake River massacre of Astorians in 1813, and John Turner, a follower of Jedediah Smith, who had survived both the Mojave and Umpqua massacres in 1827 and 1828.

an infusion of frontier vigor of which the infant colony had pressing need, had opened the road to American migration from California, and had become a nucleus attracting other mountain men to a consideration of their prospects were they to turn settler. No recruits could have proved more useful to a community in so precarious a situation.

Kelley, embittered by his Oregon visit which had proved as frustrating as had all of his former endeavors, returned home by sea to make his third great contribution when the attention of President Jackson was caught by his furious charges that the Hudson's Bay Company was serving British interests and opposing American interests by engaging in a wicked conspiracy to prevent American occupation of Oregon. Jackson, always the rampant expansionist, dispatched Lieutenant William Slacum of the United States Navy as his personal emissary to report on conditions confronting American residents of California and Oregon, much as he had sent Houston to Texas in 1832. Slacum, sailing by way of Hawaii, reached Fort Vancouver January 2, 1837, where he was hospitably received by McLoughlin and furnished company assistance in making an inspection tour of the Willamette colony. Slacum reminded both McLoughlin and the colonists that the American claim to Oregon had not been forgotten, that it would in time be pressed, and that the United States had continued to consider the Columbia American territory since the discovery by Gray, the exploration by Lewis and Clark, and the regime of the Astorians. At French Prairie he was able to compose some of the differences, jealousies, and suspicions that had arisen between missionaries, mountain men, and French settlers and to promote a cattle company to supply the colony's great need for farm animals. McLoughlin, still laboring under the misapprehension that the Williamette colony posed a lesser threat to British domination than might commercial competition, willingly invested in the project. Later that year Ewing Young, making the last of his great journeys, succeeded in driving 630 head of California cattle through mountains and Indian country to the Willamette, thereby enormously improving the colony's prospects. Slacum's report upon his return assured that Congress could no longer remain indifferent to the Oregon question which began rapidly to assume proportions as a national political issue.

The year 1837 which brought the acquisition of cattle was distinguished by another even more important acquisition. The first Methodist reinforcement of its Oregon mission, headed by Dr. Elijah White, arrived by sea May 18th. With the party were three young women, Anna Pitman, Susan Downing, and Elvira Johnson, who became the brides, respectively, of colonists Jason Lee, Cyrus Shepherd, and H. K. W. Perkins. With this establishment of family life the grotesque little colony had become, by every frontier definition, a settlement.

The certainty of its permanence and growth depended upon but one other factor. Development of this remote American lodgment into an assured extension of the dominion of the United States required its steady augmentation by a renewal of the overland advance of the frontier people, even though this must now traverse the immense intervening expanse of plains, mountains, and deserts. This altogether improbable feat was to be accomplished much sooner than McLoughlin, Congress, the governments of Great Britain, France, and Mexico, or anybody else, could then have dreamed.

XIX

༽

The Frontier of 1840

THE CENTRAL, westward-thrusting spear of the frontier people's occupation of the continent's interior had crossed the Mississippi long before the advance of settlement had at the base of the great salient passed either in the north or the south beyond the headwaters of rivers flowing into the Atlantic. But upon reaching the edge of the plains the thrust had come to a full stop. During the 60 years before 1830 its drive had carried westward 800 miles. During the 10 years after 1830 its westward progress had advanced not an additional foot. Meanwhile, the salient had expanded beyond recognition. Between 1820 and 1840, the northwestward tide of emigration had contributed to an increase of 2,132,009 in the population of the states of Ohio, Indiana, Illinois, and Michigan and the territory of Wisconsin, while in the southwest the states of Alabama, Mississippi, and Louisiana had increased by 963,756. These northwestward and southwestward advances of the settlement line, however, had been the unresisted occupation of territory long since recognized as belonging to the United States. The historic mission of the frontier people, the deliverance into the keeping of their country of vast regions which it might never otherwise have gained, appeared to have lapsed into inertia. Since confrontation by the plains barrier, penetrations of the country beyond had been confined to the personal ventures of traders, trappers, and missionaries.

The national government's determination to halt the westward movement had proved a successful policy wherever the Line it had drawn had coincided with the natural barrier of the edge of the plains. Independence, founded in 1827, was still in 1840 the westernmost settlement on the main American frontier. Detachments of the regular army, operating from a strategically located cordon of forts, enforced the national government's dictate and guarded from white trespass the country beyond the Line reserved to Indian occupation. Americans might legally cross the Line only when issued licenses to trade or hunt by federal authorities, and there was a blanket restriction upon the ownership of land west of it. The accumulation along it of Indians, aware of their rights and quick to appeal to the army or Washington, was an added deterrent. The western side of the Line was occupied by a phalanx of Indian nations, both eastern Indians who had been moved there from their former homes and nearer western Indians who had been pushed westward to the edge of the plains by the earlier advance of white settlement. Along the Line from the headwaters of the Mississippi to the Texas border were ranged, from north to south, Chippewa, Sioux, Winnebago, Sauk, Fox, Oto, Missouri, Iowa, Kickapoo, Delaware Shawnee, Ottawa, Kaskaskia, Peoria, Miami, Iroquois, Osage, Quapaw, Cherokee, Creek, Choctaw, and Chickasaw.

The national government's removal of eastern Indians had during the past 10 years been continued with a degree of insistence that partially satisfied their former white neighbors and the state governments concerned, but not without the infliction of sufferings that had excited much public sympathy and political controversy. Most eastern Indians were reluctant to move to a strange clime which in no way resembled their familiar homeland and had in fact been judged unfit for white occupancy. But nations which had terrified the frontier only a generation before were now too weak, compared to the overwhelming power and population of the United States, even to gain a hearing for their protests. A considerable section of the Cherokee, passionately attached to their ancestral mountains, resisted until their removal from the rain-drenched watershed of the Tennessee to the dusty flats of the Arkansas was compelled by a column of 7000 federal troops under Major General Winfield Scott. Hundreds sickened en route in the heat of 1838's summer and the cold of the following winter. More than 4000 Cherokee men, women, and children died along the harrowing road to the alien plains which became known as the Trail of Tears. Many Creek for a time evaded removal by fleeing to Florida's Everglades to join other Creek who had earlier taken refuge there, where, united with runaway slaves, they had become known as Seminole. The final expulsion of all but a minority of these intransigents was only achieved after an exceptionally painful eight-year war costing 1500 American lives. The Indian removal program, though possibly made inevitable by racial, social, economic, and political factors, was not furnishing one of the brighter pages of American history.[1]

During the decade preceding 1840 there had been one indication that the impulses and energies of the frontier people might have lost little of their former vitality. After the Black Hawk War, thousands of illegal settlers crossed the Mississippi into that portion of the designated Indian country now known as Iowa. They ignored their government's presumed proprietorship of all public lands as arbitrarily as had their forefathers on the Monongahela and assumed the right to govern themselves with as little hesitation as had the first Kentuckians or Tennesseans. They organized associations to oppose the government's denial of their land titles, set up their own courts, refused to admit the jurisdiction of Michigan Territory and Wisconsin Territory to which successively they were presumed to be subject, engaged in an armed boundary dispute with Missouri, and clamored so insistently for recognition of their

---

[1] The removal period was distinguished by the career of the Cherokee scholar, Sequoyah, son of the Revolutionary trader, Nathaniel Gist, and Wurteh, sister of Old Tassel and Doublehead, who had invented the Cherokee alphabet in 1821 in furtherance of his continued, earnest efforts to prepare his people for the demands of the transition from a primitive to a civilized culture.

autonomy that they were admitted as a territory in 1838. There was further evidence in the early occupation of Iowa that the pause in the westward movement had been due to climate more than to government fiat. Firstcomers to Iowa tended to settle along the wooded rivers, remaining suspicious of the equally good or better land in the intervening prairies. Like all their predecessors in the Mississippi Valley, they based their appraisal of any new land's fertility upon the number and size of the trees.[2]

While the westward thrust of the settlement line had appeared to have come to a full stop during the decade preceding 1840, the winds of change had been sweeping over the vast region beyond it. William Clark, who as Brigadier General, Territorial Governor, and United States Superintendent of Indian Affairs had been the national government's principal administrator on the plains frontier since 1807, had died September 1, 1838. Given a new mobility by the organization of a regiment of dragoons in 1833, the regular army had become able to range more widely across the plains in the course of assuming its responsibilities as keeper of the peace among both white and red plainsmen. On the southern plains the annual wagon train of Santa Fe traders was still setting out early every summer though the trade was beginning to decline under the pressure of falling prices and the exactions of Mexican authorities who had been made progressively more anti-American by Mexico's unabating conflict with Texas. On the northern plains the American Fur Company still maintained its complex of forts and steamboats which enabled it to control the commerce of the river which the decline in the beaver market had left largely devoted to buffalo hides. The northern Indians had been ravaged in 1837 by a smallpox plague so virulent that most nations had been reduced by thousands and the Mandan altogether wiped out. On the central plains the great buffalo herds had retreated until buffalo were seldom sighted east of the forks of the Platte. The withdrawal was

[2] There was another suggestion that the frontier temperament had not yet been devitalized in the presidential election of 1840. William Henry Harrison, as dedicated a dispossessor of Indians in the northwest as Andrew Jackson had been in the southwest, in a campaign of which the symbol was the log cabin and the slogan "Tippecanoe," won in a landslide by an electoral vote of 238 to 60.

sharpening competition among plains nations whose survival was largely dependent upon buffalo hunting. The Sioux smallpox losses had been somewhat less than their rivals', a relative resistance to the disease which may have been due to earlier exposures in their former eastern range, and their already superior numbers were gaining them a military superiority over other Plains Indians which they were never to lose.

In the mountains the changes had been even more striking. The mountain man's sun had set. The last rendezvous was held in 1840. The price and number of beaver had dwindled until trapping had become less an occupation than an avocation. Mountain men were drifting to California or Oregon or back to Missouri or settling down in semipermanent hunting camps, sometimes dubbed forts. Two of the more important posts which had been established were shortly to become famous. At the junction of the North Platte and the Laramie, the Rocky Mountain Fur Company had in 1834 established a post called Fort William, after William Sublette, a name changed to Fort John, after its sale to the American Fur Company, and finally, and enduringly, to Fort Laramie, in commemoration of an early trapper of whose exploits nothing was known other than the report that he had been killed by Indians there in 1821. On the left bank of the Snake above the Portneuf, also in 1834, Nathaniel Wyeth had built Fort Hall which he had in 1837, as a blow at the Rocky Mountain Fur Company in retaliation for what he regarded as a breach of contract with him, sold to the Hudson's Bay Company.

Among all these epoch-ending changes the most significant mountain development bearing on the coming resumption of the westward movement was the 1835-40 travels of missionaries. The Presbyterians and Congregationalists had joined forces to answer the Macedonian cry from the Nez Percé and Flathead to which the Methodists through their representative, Jason Lee, had failed directly to respond. In 1835 Samuel Parker, the 56-year-old pastor of a girls' school in Ithaca, N.Y., and 35-year-old Dr. Marcus Whitman, a medical missionary though not an ordained minister, set out across the plains with that year's American Fur Company overland supply column commanded by Lucien Fontenelle. Among the swarms of Indians visiting the Green River rendezvous were many hundreds of Nez Percé and Flathead, still professing apparent eagerness to receive religious instruction. Appreciating the magnitude of the task as well as of the opportunity, the missionaries decided that Whitman would return east to organize a larger effort while Parker would keep on westward in the company of the Indians to make a personal inspection of the field. Parker's ensuing journey included a tour of the Columbia basin so thorough that he was able to put together the clearest map of the area so far produced. Upon his return to Ithaca he published *Journal of an Exploring Tour Beyond the Rocky Mountains* in 1838.

The public's attention had recently been attracted to the so little known far west by Washington Irving's publication of *Astoria* in 1836 and his *Rocky Mountains* in 1837. He had revealed a strange, distant scene of adventure, hardship, and danger across which moved predatory Indian occupants and no less predatory white intruders. His skill as a writer had invested his work with a feeling of realism, but, aside from one short excursion to the nearer plains, he had drawn all his material from the testimony of others. Parker's book had a different and perhaps more effective impact. It was the first dealing with the route west that was about to become the history-making Oregon Trail which had been written by an author who had himself made the whole of that extraordinary journey. Moreover, he was a plain, ordinary eastern greenhorn, an elderly minister of the gospel, presumably in no way prepared by experience or physique for so fearful a trial. The book inadvertently created the impression that if he could make it to Oregon, then almost anybody could. Many aspects of his account added to its effectiveness. He saw all with the clear, unprejudiced eye of the neophyte, yet reserved the right to independent and very personal judgment. His descriptions were matter of fact, his remarks pithy, his conclusions pungent. His readers then, along with his readers now, could gain a remarkably complete sense of what it might be like to journey across the plains and through the mountains to Oregon in 1835.

With his first view of the plains, he demonstrated the independence of his judgment by denouncing the time-honored theory of the uninhabitability of the region then depicted in all atlases and school books as the Great American Desert:

> No country could be more inviting to the farmer, with only one exception, the want of woodland. The latitude is sufficiently high to be healthy; and as the climate grows warmer as we travel west, until we approach the snow-capped mountains, there is a degree of mildness, not experienced east of the Alleghany mountains. The time will come, and probably is not far distant, when this country will be covered with a dense population.

As he kept on westward, he responded to each of the dramatic experiences every westbound traveler was bound to encounter, on an almost certain schedule. There were the frightful storms which periodically swept across the immense expanse of the plains:

> Towards the night of the 10th, we had an uncommon storm of thunder, hail, rain, and wind. The horses and mules could not be controlled, and they turned and fled in all directions before the storm. The whole caravan was scattered; but when the storm abated, they were again collected without much difficulty, and nothing was lost. If any hostile band of Indians had been about us, it would have been easy for them to make us a prey. But the Lord not only rode the storm, but was also near for our defence. The scene was alarming, and yet grand and truly sublime.

When they reached buffalo country he became as excited as had every man who had ever encountered a first opportunity to participate in that supreme sporting spectacle:

> The buffaloes present, with their shaggy shoulders, necks and heads, a very majestic appearance, and if their natures were unknown, their appearance would be terrific. But they are timid and inoffensive, showing no disposition to injure any person, except in self-defence, when wounded or closely pursued. Their strength is great; and although they look clumsy, they run very swiftly. It requires a horse of more than ordinary speed, to outrun them for any considerable time . . . I do not feel authorized to sport with animal life,

but I thought it not improper to try my horse in the chase. He ran very swiftly, was not at all afraid, and would have run into the midst of them, had I not held him in check. He appeared to enjoy the sport. I shot one through the shoulders, which had received a wound, which must have been fatal. Not at that time being sufficiently acquainted with such an undertaking, as our guide afterwards said, I put myself in considerable danger; for I dismounted my horse, to have the opportunity of taking a more steady aim, than I could have done upon his back. The danger was, that, if the wounded buffalo had turned upon me, I should not have been able to have regained my seat upon the saddle, and with the speed of my horse have fled from his pursuit. But fortunately he did not rise upon me, and I returned to the caravan unhurt and unconscious of danger.

Then there came his first Indian alarm:

While we were encamped at noon of the 24th, and our horses and mules were turned out under guard, and we were preparing our breakfast, or what should be dinner, we were alarmed with the call, "secure your animals! secure your animals!" I looked around to see what was the cause of the alarm, and saw about a mile and a half distance, a considerable number of Indians coming on horse back at full speed. We had not more than half secured our animals and prepared for defence, when the Indians were close upon us; whether friends or foes, we could not tell, until they were nearly within rifle shot, when they, according to custom, as an expression of friendship, fired their guns into the air, and then rushed into our camp, and exchanged salutations of peace. They were Ogallallahs, headed by eight of their chiefs. They were clad in their war habiliments, and made somewhat of a terrific appearance. The chiefs dined with us, were very talkative among themselves . . . Every thing, however, went on pleasantly.

The next day he had an exceptional opportunity to observe wild Indians when his party bivouacked near an encampment of more than 2000 Sioux:

These are the finest looking Indians I have ever seen. The men are generally tall and well proportioned; the women are trim and less pendulous than what is common among Indian women, and all were dressed, and for heathen, cleanly . . . These Indians appear not only friendly to white men, but also toward each other. I saw no quarreling among them. Their minds are above the ordinary stamp, and the forms of their persons are fine. Many of them are "nature's grenadiers." The women are also well formed, their voices are soft and expressive, and their movements graceful. I was agreeably surprised to see tall young chiefs, well dressed in their mode, leading by the arms their ladies. This was not what I expected to see among "savages." It is true they are heathen in all the guilt of sin, and without God in the world, and without hope; but in decency and politeness, as well as in many other particulars, they differ from those Indians on our frontiers, who have had more intercourse with bad white men, and who have had access to whiskey.

He saw more of the Sioux during his party's pause at Fort Laramie and was increasingly troubled by the language barrier to religious instruction:

Some of the Ogallallahs came to my tent while I was reading the bible, and observed me so attentively, that I was led to believe that they were desirous to know what I was doing, and why I was spending my time in retirement. I endeavored to make them understand by the language of signs, that I was reading the book of God, which teaches us how to worship him, and I read to them aloud, and showed them how they must read, and they pronounced letters and words after me . . . After spending some time in these exercises, I sang a hymn, which greatly interested them . . . On the 29th . . . one of the men, whom I tried to instruct last sabbath, came to me again, and wished me to instruct him once more. Which I did, and endeavored to point him to God; and sang the hymn, "Watchman, tell us of the night." He, and some others with him, shook hands with me, as a token of their satisfaction. He went away and brought others with him, and I went through the same exercise again; and they again shook hands with me.

He had had his first encounters with storms, buffalo, and Indians, and now came to the traveler's next traditional sensation, grizzlies:

We saw today tracks of grizzly bears, which were perfectly fresh. One with a large cub passed out of some gooseberry and currant bushes near the river, as we proceeded around to an open spot of ground for an encamping place. I did not have an opportunity to see them, but their tracks manifest them to be frightful. Their strength is astonishingly great. Lieut. Stien of the dragoons, a man of undoubted veracity, told me he saw some buffaloes passing near some bushes, where a grizzly bear lay concealed; the bear with one stroke tore three ribs from a buffalo and laid it dead. It has been said, if you meet one of these bears, you must either kill or be killed.

His account of South Pass, the great mountain gateway, was explicit and accompanied by a prophecy:

The passage through these mountains is in a valley, so gradual in the ascent and descent, that I should not have known that we were pasing them, had it not been that as we advanced the atmosphere gradually became cooler, and at length we found the perpetual snows upon our right and upon our left, elevated many thousand feet above us . . . It varies in width from five to twenty miles; and following its course, the distance through the mountains is about eighty miles, or four days' journey. Though there are some elevations and depressions in this valley, yet comparatively speaking, it is level. There would be no difficulty in the way of constructing a rail road from the Atlantic to the Pacific ocean; and probably the time may not be very far distant, when trips will be made across the continent, as they have been made to the Niagara falls, to see nature's wonders.

At the rendezvous he observed the riotous exuberances of the annual festival with close attention. His detailed report on a duel waged on horseback between rival champions launched the fame of Kit Carson. His considered estimate of the character of mountain men became a classic appraisal:

They appear to have sought for a place where, as they would say, human nature is not oppressed by the tyranny of religion, and pleasure is not awed by the frown of virtue. The fruits are visible in all the varied forms to which human nature, without the restraints of civil government, and cultivated and polished society, may be supposed to yield. In the absence of all those motives, which they would feel in moral and religious society, refinement, pride, a sense of the worth of character, and even conscience, give place to un-restrained dissoluteness. Their toils and privations are so great, that they are not disposed to take upon themselves the labor of climbing up to the temple of science. And yet they are proficients in one study, the study of the profuseness of language in their oaths and blasphemy. They disdain common-place phrases which prevail among the impious vulgar in civilized countries, and have many set phrases, which they appear to have manufactured among themselves, which they have committed to memory, and which, in their imprecations, they bring into almost every sentence and on all occasions. By varying the tones of their voices, they make them expressive of joy, hope, grief and anger. In their broils among themselves, which do not happen every day, they would not be ungenerous. They would see "fair play," and "spare the last eye;" and would not tolerate murder, unless drunk-eness or great provocation could be pleaded in extenuation of guilt. Their demoralizing influence with the Indians has been lamentable, and they have imposed upon them, in all the ways that sinful pro-pensities dictate.

The great gathering of men who had been so perpetually exposed to hazards offered ample scope for Whitman's professional skills. Parker reported with sober relish how the young doctor rose to the occasion:

While we continued in this place, Doct. Whitman was called to perform some very important surgical operations. He extracted an iron arrow, three inches long, from the back of Capt. Bridger, which he had received in a skirmish three years before, with the Blackfeet Indians. It was a difficult operation in consequence of the arrow being hooked at the point by striking a large bone, and a cartilaginous substance had grown around it. The doctor pursued the operation with great self-possession and perseverance; and Capt. Bridger manifested equal firmness. The Indians looked on while the operation was proceeding with countenance indicating wonder, and when they saw the arrow, expressed their astonishment in a manner peculiar to themselves. The skill of Doct. Whitman un-doubtedly made upon them a favorable impression. He also took another arrow from under the shoulder of one of the hunters, which had been there two years and a half. After these operations, calls for surgical and medical aid were constant every hour of the day.

Engrossing as had been the many novel experiences of their journey, the two missionaries were most absorbed at the rendezvous by their encounter with the horde of visiting Nez Percé and Flathead. It was to save these particular heathen that they had been dispatched:

We . . . enquired whether they wished to have teachers come among them and instruct them in the knowledge of God, his worship, and the way to be saved; and what they would do to aid them in their labors. The oldest chief of the Flatheads arose, and said, he was old, and did not expect to know much more; he was deaf and could not hear, but his heart was made glad, very glad, to see what he had never seen before, a man near to God.

Parker and Whitman were faced by the same situation under the same circumstances as had been Jason Lee in the same place the year before. They had a different response:

Taking the various circumstances under deliberate and prayerful consideration, in regard to the Indians, we came to the conclusion, that, though many other important stations might be found, this would be one. So desirable did this object appear, that Doct. Whitman proposed to return with the caravan and to obtain associates to come out with him the next year, with the then returning caravan, and establish a mission among these people, and by so doing, save at least a year, in bringing the gospel among them. In view of the importance of the object, I readily consented to the proposal, and to go alone with the Indians the remainder of my exploring tour. Dr. Whitman on further consideration felt some misgivings about leaving me to go alone with the Indians, lest, if any calamity should befall me, he should be blamed by the christian public. I told him to give himself no uneasiness upon this subject; for we could not go safely together without divine protection, and with it, I could go alone.

Placing himself under Indian guardianship, Parker accompanied them on their return to the Columbia. Among his many revealing observations on Indian customs, manners, behavior, and character, nearly all of them commendatory, was included a strikingly acute account of an Indian buffalo hunt:

Today we unexpectedly saw before us a large band of buffalo. All halted to make preparation for the chase. The young men and all the good hunters prepared themselves, selected the swiftest horses, examined the few guns they had, and also took a supply of arrows with their bows . . . They advanced toward the herd of buffalo with great caution, lest they should frighten them before they should make a near approach; and also to reserve the power of their horses for the chase, when it should be necessary to bring it into full requisition. When the buffalo took the alarm and fled, the rush was made, each Indian selecting for himself a cow with which he happened to come into nearest contact. All were in swift motion scouring the valley—a cloud of dust began to arise—firing of guns and shooting of arrows followed in close succession—soon here and there buffalo were seen prostrated; and the women, who followed close in the rear, began the work of securing the valuable acquisition; and the men were away again in pursuit of the fleeing herd. Those in the chase, when as near as two rods, shoot and wheel, expecting the wounded animal to turn upon them. The horses appeared to understand the way to avoid danger. As soon as the wounded animal flies again, the chase is renewed, and such is the alternate wheeling and chasing until the buffalo sinks beneath its wounds . . . It was interesting to see how expertly the Indians use bow and arrow, and how well the women followed up the chase, and performed their part in dressing those buffalo which were slain.

Having entered territory controlled by the Hudson's Bay Company, he was much impressed by the contrast in atmosphere between the American and British mountain frontiers:

The gentlemen belonging to the Hudson Bay Company are worthy of commendation for their good treatment of the Indians, by which they have obtained their friendship and confidence . . . This company of long standing, have become rich in the fur trade, and they intend to perpetuate the business; therefore they consult the prosperity of the Indians as intimately connected with their own.

I have not heard as yet of a single instance of any Indian being wantonly killed by any of the men belonging to this company. Nor have I heard any boasting among them of the satisfaction taken in killing or abusing Indians, as I have elsewhere heard.

The Nez Percé delivered him to other Indians who with equal consideration conducted him down the Columbia. On the river he met Nathaniel Wyeth. Anyone traveling anywhere west of St. Louis in the years 1832-36 was certain sooner or later to meet Wyeth. At Fort Vancouver, Parker received the traveler's welcome that had become proverbial:

At two in the afternoon, arrived at Fort Vancouver, and never did I feel more joyful to set my feet on shore, where I expected to find a hospitable people and the comforts of life. Doct. J. McLaughlin, a chief factor and superintendent of the business of the Company west of the Rocky Mountains, received me with many expressions of kindess, and invited me to make his residence my home for the winter, and as long as it might suit my convenience.

Parker refused to rest, however, and instead pressed on until he had sighted the Pacific so that he might regard his transcontinental journey as complete. The next spring he toured the interior as far as Fort Colville with Indian guides and camp attendants until he had:

explored the most important parts of this territory, and gained all the information within my reach, as to the several objects proposed in my instructions from the Board of Foreign Missions; and especially having ascertained to my entire satisfaction the two most prominent facts, namely, the entire practicability of penetrating with safety to any and every portion of the vast interior, and the disposition of the natives in regard to my mission among them.

He then returned homeward by sea, visiting Hawaii and Tahiti en route, surviving tremendous gales rounding the Horn, and reaching Ithaca May 23rd after, as he put it, "an absence of two years and two months, and having journeyed twenty-eight thousand miles." He reported not only to the Mission Board but to the

American public. Readers of his book could in 1838, three years before the departure of the first emigrant train, realize in all practical detail what it might be like to travel overland to Oregon. His great journey had been made possible by the guidance and protection of mountain men and Indians, but it was he who kept so attentive a journal, he who wrote the book, he who made available to the American public a factual up-to-the-minute report on the way west.

Meanwhile, Whitman had not waited to learn what Parker might have learned by his exploration. Having brought back with him from the 1835 rendezvous two Indian boys to exhibit to church groups, Whitman had been able to stir additional enthusiasm for the project. He started westward again in the spring of 1836 with a companion missionary, Henry Spalding. The expedition had some of the aspects of a honeymoon for each took with him a bride. It was, nevertheless, none too congenial an excursion. The two men differed sharply in temperament, Eliza Spalding was a near invalid, and Henry Spalding had been an earlier suitor rejected by the statuesque, tawny-haired Narcissa Whitman. But Whitman's physical and moral vigor, proved in this instance as well as on many later occasions, sufficed to surmount all difficulties.

The journey proceeded with all the usual labors and hardships but without unusual threats or mishaps. As far as the Green River rendezvous, the missionaries were shepherded by Thomas Fitzpatrick in command of that year's supply caravan. The rest of the way to the Columbia they were in the keeping of a Hudson's Bay Company party headed by John McLeod and Thomas McKay. Two achievements made the venture an outstanding event in the westward movement. Whitman had persisted in taking his wagons with him beyond Fort Laramie and then across the Green and had succeeded in getting the last one, though by then reduced to a two-wheeled cart, as far as Fort Boise. His was the first wheeled vehicle to get so far west, deep into the Columbia basin. Even more significant, Narcissa Whitman and Eliza Spalding were the first white women to make the transcontinental crossing, thus joining the immortal company of the trail-breaking Indian heroines, Sacajawea and Marie Dorion.

With the arrival of the Whitman and Spalding families at Fort Vancouver, McLoughlin recognized the inevitable. Whatever the consequences, the penetration of the interior by American missionaries could no longer be avoided. He assisted them in the establishment of their stations, the Whitmans on the Walla Walla at Waiilatpu and the Spaldings on the Clearwater at Lapwai. Henceforth, hundreds of American congregations in the Ohio Valley and along the seaboard, composed of ordinary, stay-at-home citizens, were vested with an emotional identification with the fortunes of their representatives on the Willamette, the Walla Walla, and the Clearwater, along with a most articulate interest in the Oregon question. Statesmen in Washington could not continue much longer to sidestep the issue.

Protestants had produced a well-intentioned response to the original Nez Percé-Flathead appeal for "black robes," but even the enterprising Parker-Whitman-Spalding mission had neglected the remote Flathead who had from the first been the most earnest supplicants. Their appeals persisted. A fourth Flathead deputation in 1839 finally elicited a Catholic response which, if long delayed, soon developed into the most energetic and best organized of all missions to the mountain Indians. The young Belgian Jesuit, Jean Pierre De Smet, who had come to America with a burning desire to emulate the services of his famous predecessors, the French Jesuit missionaries of the seventeenth century, was commissioned to investigate the field. He set out, on the first of his many amazing journeys, with the fur-trade caravan in the spring of 1840 and was welcomed so enthusiastically by 1600 Flathead who had come to greet him at Pierre's Hole that he realized there was no need for preliminary studies of the project. To save precious time he recrossed the mountains through the dangerous Blackfoot country and returned to St. Louis by the Missouri to organize the Catholic effort which soon led to the establishment of 6 assiduous missions. De Smet's labors were in an area too remote from the main transcontinental routes to have significant effect on the westward movement, but his travels and writings have shed invaluable light on conditions in the northern Rockies during the 1840's.[8]

The frontier of 1840 thus presented seven interrelated manifestations of energy bearing on the possibility that the westward movement might resume. There was (1) the westernmost range of the settlement line along the lower bend of the Missouri which had been occupied by Kentuckians and Tennesseans whose innate restlessness was being perpetually stimulated by the constant departure from their midst of upriver steamboats, traders' wagon trains, trappers' supply caravans and plains-ranging dragoon columns. There were (2 and 3) the great trade routes stretching off across the southwest plains to Santa Fe and up the Missouri as far as the Blackfoot country at the foot of the Rockies, both declining in importance but both still active. There was (4) the central route west across the plains and over the mountains, opened and used by American trappers, to which in the very years marked by the collapse of the beaver market new attention had been called by the ventures of American missionaries. And finally there were the three outlying colonies of Americans, all beyond the acknowledged borders of the United States: (5) Texas, a self-declared independent republic still adamantly claimed by Mexico; (6) California, at an immense distance from the American settlement line and unquestionably a part of Mexico; and (7) Oregon, at as great a distance and in territory which though theoretically claimed by the United States was physically controlled by Great Britain.

Of these centers of frontier energy, Texas was the most active and its place in the westward movement the most certain. The Texas branch of the frontier people had performed their principal mission when they had settled the region and fought successfully for independence. The constant threat of renewed invasion from Mexico and a deluge of fiscal and economic embarrassments had not diminished the determination of Texans to hold their ground. Undeterred by the widely advertised difficulties in the new country, immigration,

---

[8] Another Catholic effort, launched from Canada with the crossing of the Canadian Rockies by an expedition under Abbé François Blanchet, commenced in 1838 the establishment of Catholic missions, schools, and churches in Oregon.

...gely from the American southwest, had increased the population to 70,000 by 1840. Texans flaunted their confidence in their destiny by establishing their capital, Austin, on the westernmost fringe of their frontier. Under the aggressive leadership of their second president, Mirabeau Lamar, they launched punitive expeditions against the marauding Indians of the plains and expelled Houston's old friends, the Cherokee. The reality of Texan independence was emphasized by the recognition of France in 1839 and Great Britain in 1840. Texas had in 1837 made another formal appeal for annexation by the United States, but President Van Buren had been as concerned as had been Jackson by the dangers of disunion inherent in the slavery controversy. But both Texas and the United States could afford to wait. Texas was a fruit, guarded by Texans, that was ripe for the plucking whenever the moment seemed appropriate.

Americans in California, unlike those in Texas who had almost from the outset outnumbered their Mexican neighbors, were few. In 1840 there were less than 400 American residents in a California population of 6000 whites. There had been no later surge of immigration after the mountain man influx of the early 1830's. Some of the Americans had made substantial contributions to the region's economy, as for example, Thomas Larkin, who had come by sea to become Monterey's leading merchant, or John Wolfskill, the mountain man turned vineyardist, or the frontier physician, John Marsh, who had come by way of Santa Fe to establish a notable ranch on the San Joaquin. At the other extreme among American intruders was a fringe of wandering adventurers addicted to the theft of horses and cattle, often in association with native outlaws or Indians. Small as was the American colony, the intransigence, initiative, and energy of its members caused Mexican authorities continued and justified alarm. In 1840 Governor Juan Alvarado got wind of what he conceived to be an incipient revolt, under the reputed leadership of an ex-mountain man, Isaac Graham, and ordered the surprise arrest of upwards of a hundred foreigners, many of whom were not so much residents as vagrants or deserters from ships. After a trial, 47 were transported to San Blas, then released when Great Britain, France, and the United States registered indignant protests backed by displays of naval force. Alvarado's action may have been inept but he was indisputably far-sighted in his assumption that Americans in California were as little disposed as had been Americans in Texas to live long under alien rule.

Meanwhile, among the foreigners who had established California residence, one, the Swiss, John Sutter, took on a special significance. He had reached that long-fabled shore in 1839 at the end of a journey that was in itself fabulous. After service in the Swiss army and a career as a merchant that had terminated in bankruptcy, Sutter had left his young family and his creditors to seek a new fortune in the New World. Arriving in New York in 1834, he had kept on, as instinctively as once had William Johnson or John Stuart, to the farthest frontier. There he had engaged in Santa Fe and Indian trade, though with indifferent success. Impelled to make another new start, he had set off for the Pacific with the 1838 supply caravan. Among his companions was the last official contingent of Oregon-bound missionaries, including Elkanah Walker and William Gray and their brides. Furthering his rapid education in far western conditions, he encountered at various stages of his transcontinental crossing such outstanding mountain figures as James Bridger, Andrew Drips, Joseph Meek, and Sir William Drummond Stewart. At Fort Vancouver Sutter's attention was drawn to California while his plausible and confident personality so impressed his hosts that he was advanced a substantial line of credit. He sailed first to Hawaii and then to Alaska before disembarking at Monterey where his address and the scope of his plans made as favorable an impression on Mexican authorities as had already been made on Hudson's Bay Company factors, Honolulu merchants, and Russian officials. Still operating on credit, he established Fort Sutter, at the site of Sacramento, which he soon furnished with artillery and supplies acquired from the Russians at their abandonment of Fort Ross while developing around it a flourishing complex of stock-raising, farming, trapping, fishing, and colonizing enterprises. The history of his personal empire in California was brief but dramatic. His domain was shortly to become the western terminus of the overland emigration to California and the scene of the gold discovery.

In Oregon the little mission colony, conforming to the invariable practice of American settlers whenever they had found themselves in a wilderness beyond the jurisdiction of established government, had set up a species of self-government with a constable and magistrate. In March of 1838 the colonists took the next step by drawing up a memorial to Congress petitioning for the protection of the laws of the United States. Jason Lee took the petition with him that spring when he set out for the east on horseback with two adult white companions and two Chinook boy converts to seek to promote support for his struggling colony.[4] In response to the petition, bills were introduced in both houses but Congress took no action. He had more success with his religious sponsors among whom he kindled a renewed interest in Oregon. He was able to take back with him by sea a support party, known as the Great Reinforcement to distinguish it from the First Reinforcement in 1837 which had brought the first American women to Oregon. This 1840 accretion included 6 ministers, 4 young women teachers, a physician, and a number of artisans. With accompanying families it totaled 51 persons. Oregon's American population had risen to near the one hundred mark, roughly the number that had held the stockades of Kentucky in 1775 or those of Cumberland the last winter of the Revolution. The new lodgment was to prove as firm.

The event of 1840 bearing most significantly on the westward movement attracted little attention then and has escaped wide notice since. The first settler to take his family with him made his way overland to Oregon. Joel Walker, brother of the famous Joseph Reddeford Walker, was also a mountain man. He had engaged in the Santa Fe trade as early as 1822 and thereafter in many trapping expeditions to the Rockies. But unlike most of his kind he had also maintained a home in the settlements in which he had reared a white family. It was, however, a home on the extreme frontier where he was perpetually exposed to the excitements of comings and goings to far places he himself knew well. It was not, there-

---

[4] His young wife died three months after he left. He brought back with him a second wife who died two years later after the birth of a daughter.

fore, too surprising that he should decide to move to Oregon, though that was farther than he had previously ranged. Having come to the decision, he loaded his wife and 5 children in a wagon and set out in the spring of 1840. Unexpected accompaniments en route were two other Oregon-bound wagons driven by the independent missionary, Harvey Clark, and his associates, Alvin T. Smith and P. B. Littlejohn. The Green River stage of the journey was made with the American Fur Company supply train, commanded that season by Andrew Drips. It was fitting that this first overland emigrant family should travel with the last trappers' caravan on its way to supply the last rendezvous.

Walker was not making a unique decision in determining to undertake the transport of his family to Oregon by wagon. People of the western Missouri frontier, long informed of plains and mountains conditions by their trader and trapper neighbors, had for 20 years presumed the feasibility of wagon travel westward. John Colter, the first American to range south of the fearfully difficult Lewis and Clark transcontinental route, had told Henry Brackenridge in 1810 that wagons could be taken over the Rockies. The *Missouri Gazette* had reported in 1813 the opinion of Robert Stuart, the returning Astorian, that wagons could be taken to the Pacific. In 1826 the *St. Louis Inquirer* had quoted William Ashley on the practicability of "communicating between this point and the Pacific Ocean" with the explicit statement "so broad and easy is the way that thousands may travel it in safety, without meeting with any obstruction deserving the name of mountain." In 1830 Charles Keemlee mountain man turned newspaperman, had written in the *St. Louis Beacon* that the recent operations of Jedediah Smith, William Sublette, and Thomas Fitzpatrick had demonstrated the "folly and nonsense of those 'scientific' characters who talk of the Rocky Mountains as the barrier which is to stop the westward march of the American people." [5]

[5] This frontier confidence was not shared elsewhere. Congress was deeply perturbed by the concept of a future state so distant that the attendance of its senators and representatives would require a year's travel. As the Oregon question gained prominence the English public was advised by the *Edinburgh Review* that, "The world must assume a new face before the American wagons may

Frontier theory had been repeatedly proven in practice. Through the years wheeled traffic had rolled deeper and deeper into the enormous distance stretching west of the settlement line. Since William Becknell's first venture, traders' wagon trains had every year crossed the southwest plains to Santa Fe. In 1826, William Ashley had taken a wheeled cannon to Bear Lake. In 1830, William Sublette had supplied the Wind River rendezvous deep in the Rockies by wagon train. In 1832, Benjamin Bonneville had taken 20 wagons through South Pass to the Green River. In 1836, Marcus Whitman had got his residual two-wheeled cart as far as Fort Boise.

There were therefore existing wheel tracks when Joel Walker set out. His distinction lies not in his having taken a wagon but in his having taken a family with the sole and premeditated purpose of settling with wife and children in a new home at the end of his journey. He had no great difficulty getting as far as Fort Hall. There he was convinced by the protestations regarding the ruggedness of the route beyond advanced by the Hudson's Bay Company, always on the alert to discourage anything that resembled emigration. Walker sold his wagon and went on to Oregon by pack train. His arrival there with his sturdy family appears to have aroused little comment, while he was so unimpressed with Oregon that a few months later he moved on south to California. His westward pilgrimage had, however, attracted the rapt attention of two of his old mountain comrades, Joseph Meek and Robert (Doc) Newell. Trapping was petering out as a tolerable occupation. The life of a settler in so slightly inhabited a country appeared an interesting alternative. They bought the wagons abandoned at Fort Hall by Walker and Clark, bundled their Indian families into them, and struck off for Oregon in Walker's wake. Their familiarity with the country

---

trace a road to the Columbia as they have done to the Ohio." John Dunn, after 8 years service with the Hudson's Bay Company in Oregon, assured the readers of his book detailing his professional experiences "there is no secure, expeditious, or continuous track, which can ever be used as a highway, so as to afford facilities for an influx of emigrants overland." Most American opinion agreed that overland emigration was impossible. Horace Greeley termed it "an aspect of insanity."

perhaps exceeded their familiarity with wagons but they got through to Columbia with at least the wheeled under carriages. They were inclined to feel sheepish over their excessive and apparently impractical exertion in making a journey so much more easily made by pack train, but Marcus Whitman, devoted, like Jason Lee, to his station not only as a mission but as a colony, greeted them exultantly:

> You have broken the ice, and when others see that wagons have passed, they, too, will pass, and in a few years the valley will be full of our people.

The three veteran mountain men had drawn the curtain revealing the stage upon which the sensational last act of the tremendous drama of the westward movement was about to be played.

XX

⁊

The Final Crossing

FAMILIES REPRESENTING the most venturesome and aggressive strain of the frontier people, recent Kentuckians and Tennesseans, had in 1841 been occupying the area around Independence for 14 years. This was longer than many of them ever before had remained in one place. For the past 70 years they had been accustomed to moving on two or three times a generation. The same urge still possessed them. Hundreds of their unattached men had since 1810 ranged on westward so widely and persistently that the whole vast region stretching before them to the Pacific was as well known, by word of mouth, to the inhabitants of Missouri's Jackson, Clay, and Platte counties, the westernmost apex of the settlement line, as was the other half of the continent stretching behind them to the Atlantic. Every fireside had heard countless and endless stories of plains, mountains, and deserts; of Blackfeet, Shoshone, and Utah; of buffalo, antelope, and grizzlies; of rivers, lakes, and springs; of trails, passes, and fords; of hailstorms, sandstorms, and snowstorms. The far west had been invariably pictured as a forbidding and dangerous country, extending to incalculable distances, yet every

332

man who had ever roamed it had been invariably drawn back to it. The head of any Missouri frontier family, accustomed since boyhood to the excitements of periodic testings of new locations, tantalized by the perpetual temptation to see all this for himself, was filled with an incurable restlessness. But he remained frustrated by the baffling prospect. Nowhere in the immense westward expanse did there appear to exist a site inviting the establishment of a farm to take the place of the one he would be abandoning and upon which the subsistence of his family depended. Wherever a favored spot, such as one of the grassy valleys in which trappers staged their rendezvous, suggested a chance to raise a crop, it was too remote from any conceivable market to make one worth raising. The conclusion seemed inescapable that there could be no way to combine an acquaintance with the country and his devotion to his family. Then word had begun to trickle back of its two most distant regions, California and Oregon. Both were reported to be blessed with climates as suitable for farming as Missouri and both bordered on the sea, suggesting an availability of markets as serviceable as that offered by the Mississippi's familiar waterways. To strike out for either would meanwhile give a man a chance to see the whole of the extraordinary country of which he had heard so much. Restlessness on the frontier had mounted until, like the accumulation of powder in a magazine, it needed but a spark to set off an explosion. The fuse was lighted, pinched, and relighted by the totally unrelated impulses of four men as separate in background, nature, and situation as could be any four individuals: Antoine Robidoux, John Bidwell, Thomas Farnham, and John Marsh.

The ventures of the famous trading and trapping Robidoux family had for two generations ranged across a vast crescent extending from the upper Missouri to Santa Fe and on over the southern Rockies to the Pacific. In the fall of 1840, one of the more roving of the current brothers, Antoine, was visiting another brother, Joseph, who had since 1826 maintained a trading post on the bluffs above the river at the site that was in his lifetime to become St. Joseph, Missouri. Antoine had been in California and to whoever would listen he eagerly described it as "a land of perennial spring and boundless fertility" in which ranged "countless thousands of wild horses and cattle." Along the raw new frontier just below Joseph's post he found an avid audience for his tales. Platte County was in that last corner of Missouri to be purchased from the Indians and thereby opened by federal treaty to legal settlement. None of its landholders had been located there more than a year. Having just moved they were the more ready to move again, even to far off California. Among the most excited of the voluble trapper's listeners was the young schoolteacher, John Bidwell.

Bidwell, soon to become celebrated as the chronicler of the first overland emigrant train, was in no sense an experienced frontiersman but he had sprung from generations of frontier stock. Bidwells had moved from Massachusetts to the Connecticut frontier in the seventeenth century. John's father, Abram, had been born on the northern New York frontier before the Revolution and, after the interlude of an unfortunate settlement in Canada which had embroiled him with English authorities during the War of 1812, had moved progressively westward across western New York and western Ohio. At 19 John had yielded to the impulse so nearly universal in a pioneer society and struck out for the farther west to seek his fortune, winding up on the extreme frontier in Platte County where in that fall of 1840 he was making an interim living by teaching school. To keep on all the way westward to California struck him as a remarkably appropriate idea. He took a literate and articulate part in the organization, partly by correspondence, of the Western Emigration Society that winter. An agreement to assemble at Sapling Grove on the first lap of the Santa Fe Trail with the intention of setting off together for the California "paradise" described by Robidoux was signed by 500 names. As word spread a number of Arkansans and Iowans joined the majority of Missourians on the list. The initial enthusiasm was presently subdued, however, by the dissemination of a totally contrary report by another American also able to describe California from firsthand observation.

Thomas Farnham was a young Illinois lawyer whose taste for adventure had been stimulated by the lecture delivered at Peoria by

Jason Lee, during his 1838 promotion tour in the interests of his Oregon colony. Farnham's patriotic sentiments had been stirred as well. He had felt called upon to claim Oregon for his country and had enlisted 19 like-minded companions as inexperienced as he in far western travel. They called themselves the "Oregon Dragoons," though they were more commonly known as the "Peoria party." Farnham's wife had stitched them a flag embroidered with the motto "Oregon or the Grave." At Independence in the spring of 1839 they ignored the direct South Pass route and elected instead to accompany the Santa Fe caravan southwestward. Under the impact of hardships and disagreements the company split into fragments, leaving Farnham with four companions and finally with only two. From Bent's Fort, guided at times by trappers and thereafter by Indians, he struck out over the Rockies via Brown's Hole, crossing the divide by a route almost as difficult as that taken by the original Lewis and Clark assault on the mountains. Nevertheless he got to Oregon, gave the colonists advice on memorializing Congress, and sailed on the California in time to be disagreeably impressed by Mexican harassment of Americans during the Graham affair. Returning to the United States by way of Mexico, he wrote a lengthy letter describing his experiences and observations that was widely published in the nation's press and particularly noted by the frontier newspaper at Liberty, Missouri. His picture of California was as dark as Robidoux's had been glowing. Frontier storekeepers, anxious to discourage emigration from their communities, took care that this more pessimistic account was thoroughly circulated. There developed a general inclination to attach more credibility to the sober and unprejudiced appraisal of the American attorney than to that of the excitable French trapper who could be assumed to be as addicted as all mountain men to the telling of tall stories. The frontier well remembered how many premature venturers to Santa Fe had spent years in Spanish jails. Uncertainty chilled the California fever so rapidly that in the spring Bidwell, the 21-year-old schoolteacher, was the only one from his neighborhood to set out for the appointed assembly point at Sapling Grove. En route he encountered several strangers with the same destination, one of whom, Michael Nye, was armed with encouraging information. Nye had had a recent letter from John Marsh, a former resident of Jackson County who had become a resident of California, describing California in terms fully agreeing with Robidoux's account.

Marsh's route to his new home in California had been almost as erratic as had been that of his fellow resident, John Sutter. He was a New Englander, a graduate of Harvard, who in his youth had accepted employment at Prairie du Chien on the upper Mississippi frontier in the hope of making enough money to complete his medical education. During his sojourn there, which had been prolonged through 10 years, he had worked as schoolteacher, Indian agent, and trader while becoming collaterally involved in a romance with a Sioux maiden, commanding a Sioux contingent in the Black Hawk War, and eventually being charged with the illegal sale of firearms to Indians. To escape arrest he had fled in 1832 to Jackson County, Missouri, where he engaged in trade expeditions up the Missouri and to the Rockies and in storekeeping at Independence. Business reverses added to renewed fear of arrest on the old arms-selling charge had impelled him in 1835 to resume his flight. Captured by Comanche while en route to Santa Fe, he had preserved his life by demonstrations of his skills as a physician until he had found an opportunity to escape. From Santa Fe he had made his way through Mexico to California where by his fees as a physician he accumulated capital to establish a ranch on the lower San Joaquin. It had soon become apparent to him that the prosperity of Americans in California depended on such an increase in their numbers as to enable them, like the Texans, to cast off the rule of Mexico. He began writing letters to his old friends in Independence, describing life in California in the most attractive terms, urging them to make haste to join him in sharing its opportunities, advising them on the route, even sending them a map to guide them on their way. Marsh had had no personal acquaintance with the central route but had gained some knowledge of it from American mountain men and Hudson's Bay Company partisans whom he had encountered during his travels.

Marsh's letters stirred new excitement among Jackson County's inhabitants already tempted to undertake the California migration. At a meeting in Independence, February 1, 1841, 58 men pledged their intention to make the attempt. Accounts of the meeting were widely published in the United States and reached Mexico City in time for a dispatch of instructions to General Mariano Vallejo in California which reached him well before the advent of the intruders he had been directed to repel.

When Bidwell reached Sapling Grove he found but one wagon there. But soon others began to arrive. The larger, concerted effort of the Western Emigrant Society had faltered, but individual families had come to their own individual decisions much as had individual families of their forebears come to individual decisions to cross the Appalachians. As the assembly of added arrivals continued, the first necessity was organization. This being the first emigrant train, there were no precedents to guide the organizers other than by reference to practices developed by Santa Fe traders' trains. But a long inheritance of frontier experience had taught them to value the demands and responsibilities of self-government.

John Bartleson was elected captain. He was to prove unfitted by character or temperament for command, but it was an eminently natural selection. Bartleson, though not a mountain man, was an experienced frontiersman, a resident of Independence since the year of that westernmost settlement's establishment, who had had opportunity through all the years since to listen at that principal hub of western traffic to the travel accounts of hundreds. He was a personal friend of Marsh, to whose California ranch the emigrants were bound, and of Joseph Walker, the commander of the earlier expedition which had traveled the route to California that this one proposed to take. Bidwell, the high-spirited amateur, was elected secretary and began at once to keep his journal, which has fortunately survived as the famous first of scores to follow which have combined to chronicle so magnificently the era of the covered wagon.

The company assembling at Sapling Grove had gradually increased to 69, nearly a third of them women and children. It included three families, to one of which was attached a widowed sister and child. One of the disadvantages of Bartleson's exercise of command was that he and his personal followers were single, mounted men with a greater mobility than the slower moving majority encumbered by cattle and wagons. At the last moment departure was delayed to await the arrival of an unexpected and immeasurably helpful reinforcement. Father De Smet was setting out with his first mission party for which he had hired Thomas Fitzpatrick as guide. The combined train made its start May 19, 1841, with Fitzpatrick as pilot. This historic first emigrant train consisted of De Smet's 4 carts and 1 small wagon, followed by the emigrants' 8 wagons drawn by mules and 5 drawn by oxen. One more wagon was added when the delayed John Chiles overtook the column on the fourth day.

The tenuous single file of lurching wagons, alternately wallowing through mud and enveloped in clouds of dust, laden with a precious freight of women, children, and household effects, of hope and resolution and the nation's future, crept steadily northwestward across the Kansas to the Platte. It and its company were alike dwarfed by the expanse of the plains, as soon they were to be made to seem even tinier figures by the magnitude of the Rockies, to be further shrunk by the blaze of the desert, to be finally diminished by the yawning chasms of the Sierra. Behind them stretched other trails by which such families as they had pushed through the gorges of the Allegheny, down and across wooded rivers and on to the plains barrier which these inheritors of a tradition were the first to make an organized effort to breach. Ahead of them stretched the vast region infested with perils of which they had been amply warned. These, as they were about to realize, were of a magnitude no account of the experience of others could in any way prepare them. But they kept on.

Like all their predecessors on the route that by their passing had become the Overland Trail, they encountered in succession each of the inevitable, awaiting adventures: the first storm, the first Indian scare, the first buffalo, and the first sight of tens of thousands of buffalo. They began to pass in review that stately procession of great natural monuments which henceforth was to occupy so im-

pressive a place in the nation's memories: Courthouse Rock, Chimney Rock, Scott's Bluff, Independence Rock, each marking the
completion of another memorable stage of the way west.

No circumstance could have been more appropriate than that
the first emigrant train should have been piloted up the Sweetwater
and through South Pass by Thomas Fitzpatrick. He had been longer
and more continuously associated with the opening of the west than
had any other living man. He had been with Jedediah Smith in
1824 when South Pass was first approached and crossed from the
east. The next year he had not only been the first man to travel
both ways from the Sweetwater to the Missouri but for good
measure had twice made the round trip. After the wreck of his
bullboat at Devil's Gate, he had made his way to Fort Atkinson
to report to Ashley, had returned for his furs, and had delivered
them in time to turn back to the mountains with Ashley's 1825
expedition. For the next 11 years he had continuously ranged the
plains and mountains beyond any contact with the settlements.
Once, in the spring of 1831, when en route to the Missouri frontier
for supplies, upon encountering the Smith-Sublette-Jackson caravan
two days out of Independence he had without hesitation swung
around to accompany it to Sante Fe. The sustained duration of his
experiences as trader-trapper made him the most notable of all
mountain men. Into his career had been crowded uncounted exploits, engagements, disasters, and every variety of extraordinary
hazard. The Indians called him alternately Broken Hand and White
Hair, referring to the effects of two of his more striking misadventures. No man, therefore, was better fitted to become the forerunning guide and guardian of the westward migration of a people.
He knew the plains and mountains as he did the palm of his hand.
In 1835 he had guided Samuel Parker and in 1836 the Whitman
and Spalding families. Now in shepherding the first emigrant train
he was showing them a route which he had been traveling for 17
years.

The journey to and beyond Green River had been taken so often
by so many over so long a stretch of years that it did not seem too
strange even to the emigrants embarking upon it for the first time.

Most of what they were seeing and experiencing were what so often they had been told they might expect. The day-to-day itinerary and the selection of camping and grazing sites could be left to Fitzpatrick. The entries in Bidwell's journal covering this stage of their progress tended to be matter of fact, even laconic. He was more interested in occasional personal episodes. One was the first marriage:

> June, T. 1st. This morning we hastened to leave our miserable encampment and proceeding directly north, we reached Big Platte river about 12 o'clock.—The heat was uncommonly oppressive . . . This afternoon we had a soaking shower, which was succeeded by a heavy hail storm. Wonderful! this evening a new family was created! Isaac Helsey was married to Miss Williams daughter of R. Williams, The marriage ceremony was performed by the Rev. Pr. Williams, so we now have five families if we include a widow and child.

Another was the first death:

> A mournful accident occurred in the Camp this morning—a young man by the name of Shotwell while in the act of taking a gun out of the wagon, drew it, with the muzzle toward him in such a manner that it went off and shot him near the heart—he lived about an hour and died in the full possession of his senses. His good behavior had secured him the respect and good will of all the company, he had resided some 8 or 9 months on or near the Nodaway River, Platte purchase Missouri prior to starting on this expedition; but he said his mother lived in Laurel County, Kentucky, and was much opposed to his coming into the West—he was buried in the most decent manner our circumstances would admit of after which a funeral sermon was preached by Mr. Williams.

Bidwell took the crossing of the continent's backbone in stride:

> S. 18th. Left Sweet Water this morning, course S.W. crossed the divide which separates the water of the Atlantic and the Pacific oceans, and after a travel of 20 miles reached Little Sandy, a branch of Green river—1 Buffalo was killed.

A second marriage was distinguished by several piquant details:

> F. 30th. Traveled about 5 miles and encamped. Guess what took

place; another family was created! Widow Gray, who was a sister to Mrs. Kelsey, was married to a man who joined our Company at Fort Larimie, his right name I forget; but his every where name, in the Mountains, was Cocrum. He had but one eye—marriage ceremony performed by Father De Smet.

Upon reaching the northern bend of the Bear River the train divided. Fitzpatrick and the missionary party kept on northwestward to Fort Hall en route to the projected scene of Father De Smet's labors in the Flathead country. More than half of the emigrant company, including all the families except that of Benjamin Kelsey, renounced their California destination and determined instead to take the so much better known road to Oregon. They sold their wagons at Fort Hall, packed to the Columbia and reached the Willamette safely, becoming the first organized party of overland emigrants to reach Oregon. The California segment of the train, numbering 32 persons, including Bidwell, turned southwestward while Bartleson circled through Fort Hall to buy supplies and attempt to hire a guide to pilot them to the head of the Humboldt.

Now that they were entirely dependent upon their own devices and decisions, they were soon made aware of the grim difficulties springing from their inexperience. They had scheduled a junction with Bartleson at Cache Valley, a spot of which they knew the name and the general location. But they passed it without identifying it with the described aspects of the place and the slip cost them three wasted days. Upon rejoining them Bartleson reported failure to find a guide familiar with this least known of all areas in North America. They were not dismayed. Without the slightest hesitation they struck out the next day into the Utah-Nevada desert through a region across which there had been no previous passages recorded other than those of Ogden in 1829 and Walker in 1833.

In his later reminiscences Bidwell expatiated on their total ignorance, giving the impression that when they left Sapling Grove they knew little more about the way to California than that it lay somewhere to the west. This was at some variance with the facts nor was it borne out by the daily entries in Bidwell's journal set down at the time as each day they determined their next day's move. Bidwell had not been a frontiersman when he started but most of his companions had been born on the frontier. They were pragmatically practical men who would not have embarked on so unprecedented a venture without a fairly definite conception of where they were going and how they were to get there. They had been informed in some detail of the route taken by Walker on his California expedition. Bartleson had been Walker's neighbor in Jackson County in the years when Walker had served as the county's first sheriff. Many of Walker's men had been able to tell their stories of their California journey during later visits to Independence. During the recent months of association with Fitzpatrick, who had long known Walker and most of his men and had had the experience expertly to evaluate their accounts, he had been in a position to advise the emigrants on Walker's route. As it developed, they were so well acquainted, at least in theory, with Walker's route that from the day they left Cache Valley until they reached the San Joaquin there were few deviations between the way they took and the way Walker had taken.

Their great pathfinding problem lay in the difficulty of recognizing landmarks for which they had been instructed to keep watch. The sere mountains and salt flats of Nevada tended to look more alike than to exhibit the differentiated characteristics that had been described. Their foremost task was to find the head of the Humboldt (which they called Mary's River, as it was commonly known in the years before Fremont) which they were aware they could then follow westward for some hundreds of miles. Bartleson rode ahead of the slow-moving train and returned 11 days later with the report that he had found it at a distance of 5 days' travel. Meanwhile, they were realizing that the rapid diminution of their food supply had become a major threat, made infinitely more serious by the slow progress to which they were condemned by their cumbersome wagons in this trackless region. In the vicinity of Pilot Peak they, therefore, came to the hard decision to abandon their wagons, along necessarily with most of their effects. Thereafter, at intervals they ate their oxen and eventually their mules.

Following the Humboldt to its Sink, they veered southwestward, as had Walker, and, with intermittent guidance from local Indians, found and followed Walker River until the tremendous rampart of the Sierra reared before them. They had suffered excruciatingly for weeks from hunger, heat, and fatigue, but their most fearful trials were still before them. They were 14 days struggling over the mountains, staggering through canyons, scaling ridges, edging along the rims of precipices, climbing breath-taking heights, in a desperate game of blind man's buff in which each step seemed only to lead to some new and greater difficulty. Bidwell recorded that their prospect was made to seem the more hopeless by their knowing "that Winter was at hand, and that Captain Walker (the Mountaineer) had been lost in these very mountains 22 days before he could extricate himself." Actually they were crossing the mountains some miles north of Walker's westbound crossing and in the area of Jedediah Smith's eastbound crossing in 1827. Weakened by starvation and exposure, they had begun to despair of ever clawing their way out of the labyrinth of peaks and chasms when:

We had gone about 3 miles this morning, when lo! to our great delight, we beheld a wide valley . . . Rivers evidently meandered through it, for timber was seen in long extended lines as far as the eye could reach . . . Wild fowls, Geese, etc., were flying in multitudes . . . finally, the river which we had left in the Mts., joyful sight to us poor famished wretches!!! hundreds of antelope in view! Elk tracks thousands! killed two antelopes and some wild fowls, the valley of the river, was very fertile and the young tender grass covered it, like a field of wheat in May . . . The Company tarried to kill game; and abundance of wild fowl and 13 deer and antelopes were bro't in. My breakfast, this morning, formed a striking contrast with that of yesterday which was the lights of a wolf.

They reached John Marsh's ranch, their determined destination since the earliest stages of their preparations, November 4, 1841, 5 months, 3 weeks, and 4 days from the day they had set out from

Sapling Grove. He welcomed them, though he charged them exorbitantly for food and for his presumed influence in gaining them passports from Mexican authorities. Vallejo had understood better than could his Mexico City superiors that it was as unrealistic to undertake the punishment of this small band of men, women, and children as it was impossible to drive them back over the mountains.

The Bartleson-Bidwell party had won the distinction of proving the first overland emigrants to set out for California and to reach California, but they had won it by the narrowest of margins. That same month Joel Walker, after spending a season in Oregon, brought his family on to California. Also in that month another overland party whose destination had been California did reach California. One group of 1841 emigrants, having reached Sapling Grove too late to start with the Bartleson-Bidwell train, as they had expected to do, had resorted instead to the traders' trail to Santa Fe where they joined forces with another group composed of American residents of Taos, led by William Workman and John Rowland, and proceeded by the southern route to California. That single month of November, 1841, had witnessed the almost simultaneous yet completely independent entry of American settlers through the northern, eastern, and southern gates to California. These were more than coincidental. They were demonstrations that the same set of circumstances had generated the same impulse in the same kind of people. As Whitman had said, the ice was breaking. Within another twelvemonth hundreds would be yielding to the astounding impulse to attempt the distance-defying vault to the Pacific. The frontier people had been committed to another reach, this one the climacteric, as irrepressible as had been their former reaches for the Holston, the Monongahela, the Kentucky, the Cumberland, the Missouri, and the Brazos. They had solved the problem posed by their continued advance by applying to it the same key upon which they had always relied before, a total disregard of consequences.

Bidwell completed his journal, added to it an appraisal of conditions in California and, from the Russian settlement at Bodega Bay, dispatched it, as he had promised he would, back to Missouri for the information of his former neighbors. It was published at Liberty, Missouri, in 1842, to become the first of the noted guidebooks upon which later emigrants depended. But the example set by the 1841 venturers in daring to embark upon journeys so rash had in itself been sufficient to inspire emulation. Before the fate of the 1841 parties was known, another was being organized in the spring of 1842 in which the more noteworthy figures were Elijah White, Lansford Hastings, Amos Lovejoy, and Stephen Meek. White had been a Willamette missionary and was now returning with an anomalous federal appointment as subagent to the Indians of the Oregon region. Hastings was to write a much-consulted guidebook and, declaring himself an authority on overland travel, to give the advice which led the Donner Party to its macabre doom. Lovejoy was to earn his niche in western history by becoming the first emigrant to be maltreated by Indians and the companion of Whitman's memorable ride. Stephen Meek, the mountain man brother of Joseph Meek, was a veteran representative of the class upon which the emigrants were learning more and more to depend. The 1842 train, numbering 18 to 20 wagons and 107 to 114 persons, according to varying contemporary accounts, became embroiled in many internal dissensions, gained at Fort Laramie the advantage of Fitzpatrick's services as guide, suffered a much publicized Indian scare at Independence Rock,[1] left their wagons at Fort Hall, and straggled in several groups on to Oregon where their arrival doubled the American population.

The migrations of 1841 and 1842 had sprung from special circumstances. Associations centering around Independence between the emigrants and former residents of the area, Marsh, who had moved to California, Walker, who had found the central way to California, and various traders who had established commercial relations with

---

[1] Trains made a practice of surrounding their camps by the ramparts of their encircled wagons as a precaution against the possibility of Indian assault. Indians occasionally stole emigrants' stock or molested stragglers but, contrary to the illusion cultivated by countless romances and pictures, there was in the whole covered-wagon period no single instance of an overt Indian attack on an emigrant train or camp. The only emigrant lives ever lost to direct Indian action were at Mountain Meadows after emigrants had been traveling overland for 17 years. There the attack was instigated, commanded, and assisted by other white men.

California by way of Sante Fe and Taos, had set off the 1841 emigration and governed the selection of the two routes by which it was
undertaken. The 1842 emigration, in which the leading part was
taken by Elijah White, a missionary who had served in Oregon, was
in essence a repetitive continuation of the earlier missionary journeys
of the Lees, Whitman, Spalding, and De Smet. But the emigration
of 1843 was a dramatic and momentous new surge in the westward
advance of the frontier across the continent. The state of mind
that produced it may have been partially prepared by the former
experiences of explorers, trappers, traders, and missionaries but
basically it was the product of the inherited impulse of the frontier
people to keep on into new country. Suppressed by the climatic
frustration of recent years, the impulse, upon the delayed recognition
of a new opportunity to afford it satisfaction, had gathered an
urgency like that of a torrent issuing from the breaking of a dam.

In the spring of 1843 there gathered on the Missouri frontier
an assembly of 200 families. When they set out across the plains
it was with 120 wagons and 2000 head of cattle. This was a genuine
migration, fully comparable to the Ohio flatboat and Wilderness
Road migrations which had taken possession of the continent's
central valley. This one was taking possession of the entire western
half of the continent. The frontier people were again on the march.
And it was the same frontier people. The 1850 census was to show
that four fifths of Oregon's children had been born in states bordering on the Mississippi in areas which had been settled within the
lifetime of many who had made this final crossing. People who
had moved often before had been moving again; people who had
inherited a craving to see new country had taken to viewing new
country in swathes 1500 miles long.

The great 1843 wagon train, the first of a long line of greater
successors which were to continue to roll westward every year until
the completion of the transcontinental railroad, was a traveling
segment of the frontier, carrying with it every essential process
that frontier society had proven so successful through generations
of terrifying stress. The emigrants called themselves the Oregon
Company, though they were better known as the Great Emigration.

Their first and continuing preoccupation was with the organization and conduct of a functioning self-government which alone made their enterprise possible. Only self-government could cope with a range of demands that were identical with those that had always confronted every newly established settlement. On the march and in the camp they provided for the same division and assignment of duties and responsibilities connected with defense, stock tending, guard rosters, sanitation, and the recognition of special skills, with due attention to the added difficulties imposed by the circumstance that their community was in perpetual movement. They even pre-

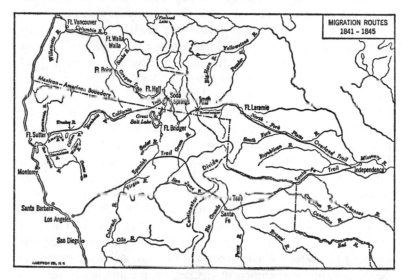

served the semblance of the stockade upon which the survival of all previous settlements had depended by arranging their wagons in a protective circle at each night's pause. They selected their leaders and came to decisions by democratic processes. Their first captain was Peter Burnett, later the first governor of California. Their orderly sergeant was James Nesmith, later a United States senator from Oregon. Their most valued counselor was Marcus Whitman, who had just completed a remarkable midwinter journey from the Walla Walla, via Taos, to Washington and New York in an effort to revive his church's interest in his mission and his country's in

Oregon. Their pilot was the veteran mountain man, John Gantt, who in beaver-trapping years had conducted his own independent fur company.

Jesse Applegate, commanding one of the sections into which it was soon discovered necessary to divide so long a column, has left us a priceless chronicle reflecting daily life with a wagon train. Among many unforgettable glimpses:

> It is four o'clock A. M.; the sentinels on duty have discharged their rifles—the signal that the hours of sleep are over—and every wagon and tent is pouring forth its night tenants, and slow-kindling smokes begin largely to rise and float away. Sixty men start from the corral, spreading as they make through the vast herd of cattle and horses that make a semi-circle around the encampment, the most distant perhaps two miles away . . . In about an hour five thousand [sic] animals are close up to encampment, and the teamsters are busy selecting their teams and driving them inside the corral to be yoked. The corral is a circle one hundred yards deep, formed with wagons connected strongly with each other; the wagon in the rear being connected with the wagon in front by its tongue and ox chains . . . From 6 to 7 is a busy time; breakfast is to be eaten, the tents struck, the wagons loaded and the teams yoked and brought up in readiness to be attached to their respective wagons. All know when, at 7 o'clock, the signal to march sounds, that those not ready to take their proper places in the line of march must fall into the dusty rear for the day . . . It is on the stroke of seven; the rush to and fro, the cracking of whips, the loud command to oxen, and what seemed to be the inextricable confusion of the last ten minutes has ceased . . . The clear notes of a trumpet sound in the front; the pilot and his guards mount their horses; the leading divisions of the wagons move out of the encampment, and take up the line of march; the rest fall into their places with the precision of clock work, until the spot so lately full of life sinks back into that solitude that seems to reign over the broad plain and the rushing river as the caravan draws its lazy length toward the distant El Dorado . . . To those who have not been on the Platte my powers of description are wholly inadequate to convey an idea of the vast extent and grandeur of the picture, and the rare beauty and distinctness of its detail. No haze or fog obscures objects in the pure transparent atmosphere of this

lofty region. To those accustomed only to the murky air of the sea-board, no correct judgment of distance can be formed by sight, and objects which they think they can reach in a two hours' walk may be a day's travel away . . . the broad river glowing under the morning sun like a sheet of silver, and the broader emerald valley that borders it stretch away into the distance until they narrow at almost two points in the horizon, and when first seen, the vast pile of the Wind River mountain, though hundreds of miles away, looks clear and distinct as a white cottage on the plain . . . But the picture, in its grandeur, its wonderful mingling of colors and distinctness of detail, is forgotten in contemplation of the singular people who give it life and animation. No other race of men with means at their command would undertake so great a journey—none save those could successfully perform it with no previous preparation, relying only on the fertility of their invention to devise the means to overcome each danger and difficulty as it arose. They have undertaken to perform, with slow moving oxen, a journey of two thousand miles. The way lies over trackless wastes, wide and deep rivers, rugged and lofty mountains, and is beset with hostile savages . . . May we not call them men of destiny? They are people changed in no essential particulars from their anscestors who have followed closely on the footsteps of the receding savage, from the Atlantic sea-board to the valley of the Missisippi . . . the sun is now getting low in the west, and at length the painstaking pilot is standing ready to conduct the train in the circle which he has previously measured and marked out which is to form the invariable fortification for the night. The leading wagons follow him so nearly around the circle, that but a wagon's length separates them . . . Within ten minutes from the time the leading wagon halted, the barricade is formed, the teams unyoked and driven out to pasture. Everyone is busy preparing fires of buffalo chips to cook the evening meal . . . It is not yet 8 o'clock when the first watch is to be set; the evening meal is just over, and the corral now free from the intrusion of cattle or horses, groups of children are scattered over it. . . Before a tent near the river a violin makes lively music, and some youths and maidens have improvised a dance upon the green; in another quarter a flute gives its mellow and melancholy notes to the still night air, which, as they float away over the quiet river, seem a lament for the past rather than a hope for the future . . . the watch is set for the night;

the council of old men has been broken up . . . the flute has whispered its last lament . . . the violin is silent, and the dancers have dispersed . . . all is hushed and repose from the fatigues of the day, save for the vigilant guard and the wakeful leader, who still has cares on his mind that forbid sleep.[2]

Beyond South Pass the train adopted a route veering south to the newly established Fort Bridger which was found to consist of no more than a huddle of untenanted hunters' huts, though it was presently to become an important station on the Overland Trail. At Fort Hall they were given the usual Hudson's Bay Company advice that the way beyond was impassable for wagons, but at Whitman's impassioned insistence the emigrants kept their wagons. They succeeded in getting them not only to the Columbia but all the way to the Dalles in the heart of Oregon. As a consequence of their resolute persistence, an empire-knitting path for wheels had been extended from the lower Missouri to the lower Columbia, and the long quest for a practical transportation route to the Pacific which had been initiated by Lewis and Clark had ended in success. Its commercial value, associated with the fur trade and the China trade, which had been envisaged then had been superseded by its unforeseen greater function as the channel for such a shift in population as could not then have been imagined. By the arrival of the Great Emigration the population of Oregon was increased fivefold and American possession of Oregon assured.

Decisive as had been the effect of the Great Emigration of 1843, collateral events contributed almost as significantly to the year's culminating success of the westward movement. There had been salient developments in opening the road to California as well as the road to Oregon. In 1842 John Chiles, a member of the Bartleson-Bidwell company, had returned overland from California to the Missouri frontier where, in association with Joseph Walker, he had organized another company of California emigrants. Several aspects of his 1843 enterprise were remarkable. He was the first settler who had been enabled to make a preliminary investigation of the route

[2] Jesse Applegate, "A Day with the Cow Column," *Oregon Historical Quarterly*, I (1900).

and the country at the end of it. After his overland passage on successive years had given him what to most men must have seemed a devastating acquaintance with the undertaking's inescapable hardships and vicissitudes, he nevertheless had elected the third year not only to attempt it again but to take his family with him. There have been few more striking demonstrations of the resolution that was a primary trait of the frontier people. His California party accompanied the Oregon train to Fort Hall where it was divided to take advantage of routes to California known to trappers since the early 1830's. Chiles took the mounted segment of the company into California by the route along the Malheur and Pitt rivers formerly traveled by Hudson's Bay Company brigades from Fort Nez Percé, while Walker took the wagons by his own former route down the Humboldt and along the eastern face of the Sierra to Walker Pass, though he was obliged to abandon the wagons in Owens Valley. The arrival of the Chiles party added strong new links to the ties of emigration that were beginning so rapidly to attach the coast of the Pacific to the United States. The men conducting it had not been striking off into the unknown in enthusiastic ignorance. Both Walker and Chiles had been in California and were familiar with all the difficulties involved in getting there. There was one other even more personal link in the new ties. With Chiles were the two daughters of George Yount, the mountain man who had reached California in 1831 and who had not seen his family since he had left the Missouri frontier for Santa Fe in 1825.

While the Great Emigration was rolling westward, the 200 American settlers in Oregon were filling the colony's jurisdictional vacuum by completing the organization of their own democratic government. After a winter of political debate, conducted under the guise of intellectual, literary, and self-improvement discussions, in the spring they had assembled in a series of "Wolf Meetings," ostensibly to deal with the control of predatory animals in an effort to disarm the opposition of the settlement's near majority of Hudson's Bay Company sympathizers. At Champoeg, July 5, 1843, a drafting committee's report on a constitution establishing a provisional government was adopted. It opened with the declaration:

We, the people of Oregon Territory, for purposes of mutual protection, and to secure peace and prosperity among ourselves, agree to adopt the following laws and regulations until such time as the United States of America extend their jurisdiction over us.

The American settlers of Oregon, separated from the seat of their government by 3000 miles and from their nearest American neighbors by 1500 miles, had maintained the great self-determination traditions of the Watauga Association, the Boonesborough Convention, the Cumberland Compact, and the Texas Declaration of Independence. In startling contrast to all other experiences in the history of colonization, it had in the American case been invariably the colonists who had succored their parent government.

That government, however, in belated response to religious and patriotic appeals from so many of its citizens, was in 1843 beginning at last to manifest a nascent concern for the westward movement and the nation's long dormant claim to Oregon. Lieutenant John Fremont of the army engineers, who had recently married the daughter of the ardent expansionist, Thomas Benton, United States Senator from Missouri, had been directed to map the emigration route to the Columbia. After a preliminary excursion to Green River in 1842, which was in itself the first official expedition to cross the continental divide since Lewis and Clark, in 1843 he followed in the wake of the Oregon train, examining wide areas on either side of the direct route, until he had reached Fort Vancouver. Beginning thereafter to exceed his instructions, he then penetrated southern and southeastern Oregon, thereby crossing the recent path of the Chiles party, skirted the western flank of the Great Basin, thereby intersecting the earlier paths of the Walker and Bartleson-Bidwell parties, made a midwinter crossing of the Sierra south of Lake Tahoe to Fort Sutter, thereby instituting a de facto invasion of Mexican territory by an armed official force of the United States, and in the spring of 1844 emerged from California by the original Jedediah Smith route of 1826 and 1827. Fremont's expeditions excited intense public interest and gained him an acclaim as the Great

Pathfinder that led to his election as United States Senator from California in 1849 and to the Republican nomination for President in 1856. His pathfinding, however, had largely consisted of the identification of routes long since found and traveled by mountain men, and he had had the practical sagacity to rely in all his movements upon the guidance and advice of such proven pathfinders as Thomas Fitzpatrick, Kit Carson, and Joseph Walker. The tremendous service Fremont rendered his country lay rather in the scientific accuracy of his reports and maps, in the colorful vigor with which he described his experiences, and in the impression made by the immediate and wide dissemination given the accounts of his expeditions. He had materially prepared the American public for the sudden great imperialist expansion of 1846.

The tide of overland immigration continued to swell, reaching a peak of 3000 in 1845 which raised the population of Oregon to 6000. The lesser 1844 California emigration was made noteworthy when the Stevens-Murphy party, guided by the old mountain man, Elisha Stevens, and including the extensive Murphy family, succeeded in getting their wagons to the snowbound crest of the Sierra and on to Fort Sutter the following spring. With the arrival of the Stevens-Murphy wagons by the Truckee River-Donner Lake route, later to be followed by most emigrant and gold-rush trains, by the first transcontinental railroad, and by modern Route 40, a functional road to California had been opened, equivalent to that opened to Oregon in 1843 by the arrival of wagons on a navigable reach of the Columbia. From now on all later emigrants and travelers of all descriptions needed only to follow existing wheel tracks.

The frontier people had risen to the final challenge. Their mission had been to open the width of a continent to the nation's dominion. Their progressive occupation of 3000 miles of wilderness had invariably been in advance of, often in defiance of, their government's intentions. They had had still less regard for the opposition of foreign governments or of the Indian nations they had been dispossessing. They had pressed on obstinately, recklessly, wilfully, until by now not only in adjacent Texas but in far off Oregon and

California they had established lodgments that had rendered those outlying regions certainly and permanently American. As a consequence of their initiative, the United States would the following year undertake a military and diplomatic occupation of vast regions of which they had already taken actual possession. For the war with Mexico and the "54-40 or fight" pressures on Great Britain, there could have been no occasion had the territory involved not already passed into the control of American settlers.

The frontier people had fulfilled their mission by occupying the last of the many regions to pass into the possession of their country as a direct consequence of their urgency. In every case there had been the strongest evidence that the opportunity must have passed forever had they been less urgent. The whole expanse of the continent from the Appalachians to the Pacific had been delivered into American keeping by their efforts. They had now occupied the entire perimeter of what was to become the entire area of continental United States.

Though their major mission had been accomplished, there was still to remain a frontier, a border of a different sort but nevertheless a frontier, for the next half century. It was no longer a frontier pushing onward but rather one squeezing inward. The plains and the Rockies remained a wilderness long after the initial crossing of the continent by wagon trains and even after the crossing by telegraph and railroad. Though the extent and stature of the United States was no longer at issue, there remained need on this residual frontier for much of the courage and resolution that had characterized the first full sweep of the westward movement. There were the same blizzards and sandstorms, the same violent alternations of heat and cold, of drought and flood, that the firstcomers had known. The same isolation, loneliness, and distance lingered long. The Indians of the plains, mountains, and deserts became more belligerent before they became less. The circle of the ingrowing frontier under developing pressures from west as well as east continued its inexorable contraction.[3] The buffalo were crowded into

---

[3] The process is illustrated by the comparative admission dates: Texas 1845, California 1850, Oregon 1850, Kansas 1861, Nevada 1872, Colorado 1876, Wyom-

a single, central herd and then this most distinctive of all features of the western scene disappeared altogether from view. Meanwhile, new unconventionally romantic figures had appeared on the frontier stage to capture the imagination of countless millions of readers of fiction and viewers of motion pictures and television. The miner, the pony-express rider, the cowboy, the sheriff, the homesteader, the sheepman, the bad man, the gunfighter, the dance-hall girl, the stagecoach driver, the cattle rustler, the vigilante had passed from a sweaty reality into a rose-tinted dust haze of immortality. The dramatic images evoked had engrossed the world and had made what was conceived to be the American west equally familiar to Indonesians, Bedouins, Brazilians, and Hottentots. In the years of its final passing, the frontier had taken on a color never before perceived.

The full proportions of the original frontier people's shaping of the nation's destiny can better be brought into focus by a retrospective glance at the long record of their successive ventures and achievements. It is a record marked at every stage by a disregard for any authority other than their own inclinations, only exceeded by their disregard of the most appalling hazards. In their first crossing of the Appalachians they defied the dictates of their own provinces, the edicts of the empire, and the combined military opposition of Indians and the British army. They held their grasp on the Kentucky and the Cumberland through 20 years of a peculiarly atrocious war until the permanence of their occupation was acknowledged by England, Spain, and France and inherited by the United States. They began at once to press on westward across international boundaries with a vigor that forced Napoleon hastily to relinquish the portion of his envisioned world empire that they had invaded. They then pushed on across another international boundary into Texas which they held in trust for the nation's eventual inheritance. And now, finally, they had made the astounding leap, at a single incredible bound, all the way to the Pacific.

This ultimate feat was in many ways more astounding than any of their previous achievements. They were not tormented by the afflictions of unending Indian war which had assailed all their former advances, but they were committed to other hazards as fearful. Family groups of men, women and children, grandmothers, babies, cattle, chickens, dogs were embarking upon a journey of many months through a totally uninhabited region in which they would be totally dependent upon their own resources and oppressed by heat, cold, storms, starvation, and unremitting toil. Some of the way was across country so featureless that their progress was inappreciable. At other stages awaited rushing rivers to sweep away their wagons, precipices up which their wagons must be lifted by ropes, burning deserts in which their oxen sickened. Always there was the need for desperate hurry since delay meant the threat of death to all in the winter snows of the last mountain barrier.

Yet their astounding decision to make the venture did not appear to them so strange and certainly not nearly so demented as it appeared to easterners then and may to us now. They confidently expected to survive by resort to the same practices by which they and their forefathers had so far survived. They were a hunting people who had long proved their ability to live off the country no matter where they wandered. Their transport procedures were not new or untried. They had for generations been accustomed not only to wandering but to wandering by wagon. Daniel Boone's family had in 1752 moved by wagon from Pennsylvania to the Yadkin. The flatboat emigrants had crossed the Alleghenies by wagons and then taken their wagons on to Kentucky aboard their rafts. Wagons had rolled down the Holston and after 1796 on over the Wilderness Road. The nearer plains had been constantly crossed by wagons since 1822. Joel Walker, the first settler to take his family all the way to Oregon, had in his youth traveled by wagon with his father's family from eastern Tennessee to western Missouri. The one novelty confronting the transcontinental emigrants of the 1840's was the circumstance that this was a longer haul than any they had formerly attempted. Otherwise they were taking with them the familiar frontier way of life they had always known—the same stockade, the same community democracy, the same total self-reliance. What they were most of all taking with them was the same compulsive determination never to rest long in one place while there still remained new country which they had not yet seen.

They were truly an extraordinary people. While the American world as we know it was built so largely on what they represented and what they accomplished, it has also lost much by their passing.

Bibliography

Among published material available in most larger libraries to the reader disposed to pursue the subject, the following have been found useful in the preparation of this work:

Abernethy, T. P. *The Burr Conspiracy*. New York, 1954.
Allen, Joseph Asaph. *History of the American Bison*. Washington, 1877.
Alter, J. C. *James Bridger*. Salt Lake City, 1925. Repr. Columbus, 1951.
Applegate, Jesse. *Day with the Cow Column*. Chicago, 1934.
Bancroft, Hubert Howe. *History of California*. 5 vols. San Francisco, 1884-86.
Barker, Eugene C. *Mexico and Texas, 1821-1835*. Dallas, 1928.
Bidwell, John. *Journal*. Liberty, 1842. Repr. Herbert Ingram Priestley, ed. San Francisco, 1937.
Bidwell, John. *Echoes of the Past*. Chico, 1906.
Billington, Ray Allen. *Westward Expansion*. New York, 1949.
Billington, Ray Allen. *The Far Western Frontier*. New York, 1956. Repr. New York, 1962.
Billon, Frederic L. *Annals of St. Louis*. 2 vols. St. Louis, 1886-88.
Bolton, Herbert Eugene. *Anza's California Expeditions*. 5 vols. Berkeley, 1930.
Bonner, T. D. *The Life and Adventures of James P. Beckwourth*. New York, 1857. Repr. Bernard De Voto, ed. New York, 1931.
Brackenridge, H. M. *Journal of a Voyage up the River Missouri*. Baltimore, 1816. Repr. Reuben Gold Thwaites, ed. Cleveland, 1904.
Bradbury, John. *Travels in the Interior of America in the Years 1809, 1810, and 1811*. London, 1819. Repr. Reuben Gold Thwaites, ed. Cleveland, 1904.
Brebner, John Bartlet. *The Explorers of North America*. New York, 1933.
Brosnan, Cornelius J. *Jason Lee, Prophet of Oregon*. New York, 1932.
Brown, John P. *Old Frontiers*. Kingsport, 1938.
Buley, R. Carlyle. *The Old Northwest*. 2 vols. Indianapolis, 1950.

Burpee, Lawrence J. *The Search for the Western Sea.* New York, 1908. Rev. ed. New York, 1936.

Camp, Charles L. (ed.). *James Clyman, American Frontiersman, 1792-1881.* San Francisco, 1928. Rev. ed. Portland, 1960.

Camp, Charles L. *Essays for Henry R. Wagner.* San Francisco, 1947.

Canoe, William Addleman. *The History of the United States Army.* New York, 1924.

Catlin, George. *Letters and Notes on the Manners, Customs and Condition of the North American Indians.* London, 1841. Among many later editions: London, 1866 and London, 1876, each in 2 vols. with 360 colored plates.

Chittenden, Hiram Martin. *The American Fur Trade of the Far West.* 3 vols. New York, 1902. Repr. Stanford, 1954.

Chittenden, Hiram Martin. *History of Steamboat Navigation on the Missouri River.* 2 vols. New York, 1903.

Clark, William. *Journal on his Expedition to Establish Fort Osage, 1808.* Kate L. Gregg, ed. Fulton, 1937.

Cleland, Robert Glass. *Pathfinders.* Los Angeles, 1929.

Cleland, Robert G. *This Reckless Breed of Men.* New York, 1950.

Conard, Howard Louis. *"Uncle Dick" Wooten.* Chicago, 1890.

Cooke, Philip St. George. *Scenes and Adventures in the Army.* Philadelphia, 1857.

Cotterill, R. S. *The Southern Indians.* Norman, 1954.

Coues, Elliott. *History of the Expedition under the Command of Lewis and Clark.* 4 vols. New York, 1893.

Coues, Elliott. *The Expeditions of Zebulon Montgomery Pike.* 3 vols. New York, 1895.

Coues, Elliott. *New Light on the Early History of the Greater Northwest.* 3 vols. New York, 1897.

Coues, Elliott. *The Journal of Jacob Fowler.* New York, 1898.

Coues, Elliott. *Forty Years a Fur Trader on the Upper Missouri.* 2 vols. New York, 1898.

Coues, Elliott. *On the Trail of a Spanish Pioneer.* 2 vols. New York, 1900.

Cox, Ross. *Adventures on the Columbia River.* London, 1831. Repr. Edgar I. and Jane R. Stewart, eds. Norman, 1957.

Crockett, David. *A Narrative of the Life of David Crockett, Written by Himself.* Philadelphia, 1834.

Cuming, F. *Sketches of a Tour to the Western Country.* Pittsburgh, 1810. Repr. Reuben Gold Thwaites, ed. Cleveland, 1904.

Currey, J. Seymour. *The Story of Old Fort Dearborn.* Chicago, 1912.

Dale, Harrison Clifford. *The Ashley-Smith Explorations and the Discovery of a Central Route to the Pacific 1822-1829.* Cleveland, 1918. Rev. ed. Glendale, 1941.

Dana, Richard Henry, Jr. *Two Years Before the Mast.* New York, 1840. Repr. Cambridge, 1911.

Debo, Angie. *The Rise and Fall of the Choctaw Republic.* Norman, 1934.

De Shields, James T. *Border Wars of Texas.* Tioga, 1912.

De Smet, Father P. J. *Letters and Sketches.* Philadelphia, 1843. Repr. Reuben Gold Thwaites, ed. Cleveland, 1906.

De Smet, Father P. J. *Oregon Missions and Travels over the Rocky Mountains in 1845-46*. New York, 1847. Repr. Reuben Gold Thwaites, ed. Cleveland, 1906.

De Voto, Bernard. *Across the Wide Missouri*. Cambridge, 1947.

De Voto, Bernard. *The Course of Empire*. Cambridge, 1952.

Duffus, R. L. *The Santa Fe Trail*. New York, 1930.

Dunbar, Seymour. *A History of Travel in America*. 4 vols. Indianapolis, 1915.

Dunn, John. *The Oregon Territory*. Philadelphia, 1845.

Ellison, William H. (ed.). *The Life and Adventures of George Nidever, 1802-1883*. Berkeley, 1937.

Farnham, Thomas J. *Travels in the Great Western Prairies*. 2 vols. London, 1843. Repr. Reuben Gold Thwaites, ed. 2 vols. Cleveland, 1906.

Ferris, W. A. *Life in the Rocky Mountains, 1830-1835*. Salt Lake City, 1940. Paul Chrisler Phillips, ed. Denver, 1940.

Flint, James. *Recollections of the Last Ten Years*. Boston, 1826.

Forbes, Alexander. *California*. London, 1839. Repr. Herbert Ingram Priestley, ed. San Francisco, 1937.

Foreman, Grant. *Indians and Pioneers*. Norman, 1930.

Foreman, Grant. *Indian Removal*. Norman, 1932.

Fowler, Jacob. *Journal*. Elliott Coues, ed. New York, 1898.

Franchère, Gabriel. *Narrative of a Voyage to the Northwest Coast of America*. New York, 1854. Repr. Reuben Gold Thwaites, ed. Cleveland, 1904.

Fremont, John Charles. *Report of an Exploration*. Washington, 1843.

Fremont, John Charles. *Report of the Exploring Expedition to the Rocky Mountains*. Washington, 1845.

Fuller, George W. *History of the Pacific Northwest*. New York, 1931.

Fuller, Myron L. *The New Madrid Earthquake*. (U. S. Geological Survey, Bulletin 494.) Washington, 1912.

Fulton, Maurice Garland. *Diary and Letters of Josiah Gregg*. Norman, 1941.

Ghent, W. J. *Road to Oregon*. New York, 1929.

Ghent, W. J. *The Early Far West, 1540-1850*. New York, 1936.

Gilbert, E. W. *The Exploration of Western America, 1800-1850*. Cambridge, 1833.

Goodwin, Cardinal. *The Trans-Mississippi West*. New York, 1922.

Gregg, Josiah. *Commerce of the Prairies*. 2 vols. New York, 1844. Repr. Reuben Gold Thwaites, ed. 2 vols. Cleveland, 1905.

Grinnell, George Bird. *The Cheyenne Indians*. 2 vols. New Haven, 1924.

Hafen, L. R., and Ghent, W. J. *Broken Hand, the Life Story of Thomas Fitzpatrick*. Denver, 1931.

Hafen, L. R. and A. W. (eds.). *To the Rockies and Oregon*. Glendale, 1955.

Hafen, LeRoy R. and Ann W. (eds.). *Old Spanish Trail*. Glendale, 1954.

Hallenbeck, Cleve. *Cabeza de Vaca*. Glendale, 1940.

Hammond, George P., and Rey, Agapito. *Narratives of the Coronado Expedition*. Albuquerque, 1940.

Harmon, Daniel Williams. *A Journal of Voyages and Travels*. Andover, 1820. Repr. Robert Waite, ed. New York, 1903.

Harris, Burton. *John Colter*. New York, 1952.

Hastings, Lansford Warren. *Emigrants' Guide to Oregon and California.* Cincinnati, 1845. Repr. Princeton, 1932.

Hebard, Grace Raymond. *Sacajawea.* Glendale, 1933.

Hildreth, James. *Dragoon Campaign to the Rocky Mountains.* New York, 1836.

Hill, Joseph J. *The History of Warner's Ranch.* Los Angeles, 1927.

Hodge, Frederick Webb. *Handbook of the American Indians.* 2 vols. Washington, 1907-10.

Hogan, William Ranson. *The Texas Republic.* Norman, 1946.

Hornaday, William T. *The Extermination of the American Bison.* Washington, 1889.

Houck, Louis. *A History of Missouri.* 3 vols. Chicago, 1908.

Hulbert, Archer B. and D. P. (eds.). *The Oregon Crusade.* Denver, 1935.

Hunt, Rockwell D. *John Bidwell, a Prince of California Pioneers.* Caldwell, 1942.

Hunter, John D. *Memoirs of a Captivity Among the Indians of North America.* London, 1823.

Irving, Washington. *Astoria.* 2 vols. Philadelphia, 1836.

Irving, Washington. *The Rocky Mountains.* 2 vols. Philadelphia, 1837. Repr. Edgeley W. Todd, ed. Norman, 1961.

James, Edwin. *Account of an Expedition from Pittsburgh to the Rocky Mountains.* 2 vols. with atlas. Philadelphia, 1823. 3 vols. London, 1823. Repr. Reuben Gold Thwaites, ed. 4 vols. Cleveland, 1905.

James, Marquis. *The Raven, a Biography of Sam Houston.* Indianapolis, 1924.

James, Thomas. *Three Years among the Indians and Mexicans.* Waterloo, 1846. Repr. W. S. Douglas, ed. St. Louis, 1916. Repr. with introduction by A. P. Nasatir. Philadelphia, 1962.

Jewitt, John R. *Narrative of the Adventures and Suffering of John R. Jewitt.* Middletown, 1815. Repr. London, 1896. Repr. Boston, 1931.

Johansen, Dorothy O., and Gates, Charles M. *Empire of the Columbia.* New York, 1957.

Johnson. Overton, and Winter, W. H. *Route Across the Rocky Mountains.* Lafayette, 1846. Repr. Princeton, 1932.

Lavender, David. *Bent's Fort.* New York, 1954.

Lee, D., and Frost, J. H. *Ten Years in Oregon.* New York, 1844.

Leonard, Zenas. *Narrative.* Clearfield, 1839. Repr. W. F. Wagner, ed. Cleveland, 1904. Repr. John C. Ewers, ed. Norman, 1959.

Lewis, William S., and Phillips, Paul C. (eds.). *The Journal of John Work.* Cleveland, 1923.

Lord, Walter. *A Time to Stand.* New York, 1961.

Lumpkin, Wilson. *The Removal of the Cherokee Indians.* 2 vols. Savannah, 1907.

Luttig, John C. *Journal of a Fur Trading Expedition on the Upper Missouri, 1812-1813.* Stella M. Drumm, ed. St. Louis, 1920.

Lyman, George D. *Dr. John Marsh, Pioneer.* New York, 1930.

McDermott, John Francis (ed.). *Tixier's Travels on the Osage Prairies.* Norman, 1940.

MacKay, Douglas. *The Honourable Company.* Indianapolis, 1936.

Mackenzie, Alexander. *Voyages.* London, 1801. Repr. New York, 1922.

Maximilian, Prince of Wied. *Travels in the Interior of North America.* London, 1843. Repr. Reuben Gold Thwaites, ed. 3 vols. and atlas. Cleveland, 1931.

Merk, Frederick. *Fur Trade and Empire.* Cambridge, 1931.

Mofras, Duflot de. *Travels on the Pacific Coast.* Marguerite Eyer Wilbur, ed. 2 vols. Santa Ana, 1937.

Monaghan, Jay (ed.). *The Book of the American West.* New York, 1963.

Moore, Arthur K. *The Frontier Mind.* University of Kentucky, 1957. Repr. New York, 1963.

Morgan, Dale. *The Great Salt Lake.* Indianapolis, 1947.

Morgan, Dale. *Jedediah Smith and the Opening of the West.* Indianapolis, 1953.

Morgan, Lewis H. *The American Beaver and His Works.* Philadelphia, 1868.

Murray, Charles Augustus. *Travels in North America.* 2 vols. New York, 1839.

Myers, John Myers. *The Alamo.* New York, 1948.

Nasatir, A. P. *Before Lewis and Clark.* 2 vols. St. Louis, 1952.

Nevins, Allan. *Fremont, the West's Greatest Adventurer.* New York, 1928.

Nuttall, Thomas. *A Journal of Travels into the Arkansas Territory.* Philadelphia, 1821. Repr. Reuben Gold Thwaites, ed. Cleveland, 1905.

Palmer, Joel. *Journal of Travels over the Rocky Mountains.* Cincinnati, 1847. Repr. Reuben Gold Thwaites, ed. Cleveland, 1906.

Parker, Samuel. *Journal of an Exploring Tour Beyond the Rocky Mountains.* Ithaca, 1938.

Pattie, James O. *Personal Narrative.* Timothy Flint, ed. Cincinnati, 1831. Repr. Reuben Gold Thwaites, ed. Cleveland, 1905.

Paullin, Charles O., and Wright, John K. *Atlas of the Historical Geography of the United States.* Washington, 1952.

Paxon, Frederic L. *History of the American Frontier, 1763-1893.* Cambridge, 1924.

Pelzer, Louis. *Marches of the Dragoons.* Iowa City, 1917.

Perkins, James H. *Annals of the West.* Rev. by J. M. Peck. St. Louis, 1850.

Perrigo, Lynn I. *Our Spanish Southwest.* Dallas, 1960.

Perrin du Lac, Francis. *Travels Through the Two Louisianas.* London, 1807.

Phillips, Paul Chrisler. *The Fur Trade.* 2 vols. Norman, 1961.

Rich, E. E. (ed.). *Letters of John McLoughlin from Fort Vancouver. First Series, 1825-38.* Toronto, 1941.

Rich, E. E. (ed.). *Peter Skene Ogden's Snake Country Journals, 1824-25 and 1825-26.* London, 1950.

Richardson, Rupert Norval. *The Comanche Barrier to South Plains Settlement.* Glendale, 1933.

Richardson, Rupert Norval, and Rister, Carl Coke. *The Greater Southwest.* Glendale, 1934.

Riegal, Robert E. *America Moves West.* New York, 1930.

Robertson, David. *The Trial of Aaron Burr.* 2 vols. New York, 1875.

Robertson, James Alexander. *Louisiana under the Rule of Spain, France and the United States, 1785-1807.* 2 vols. Cleveland, 1911.

Robinson, Alfred. *Life in California.* New York, 1846. Repr. San Francisco, 1925.

Rollins, Philip Ashton. *The Discovery of the Oregon Trail: Robert Stuart's Narratives.* New York, 1935.

Ross, Alexander. *Adventures of the First Settlers on the Oregon or Columbia River.* London, 1849. Repr. Reuben Gold Thwaites, ed. Cleveland, 1904.

Ross, Alexander. *Fur Hunters of the Far West.* London, 1855. Repr. Kenneth A. Spaulding, ed. Norman, 1956.

Rucker, Maude A. (ed.). *The Oregon Trail and Some of its Blazers.* New York, 1930.

Russell, Osborne. *Journal of a Trapper.* Boise, 1921. Repr. Aubry L. Haines, ed. Portland, 1955.

Ruxton, George Frederick. *Adventures in Mexico and the Rocky Mountains.* London, 1847.

Ruxton, George Frederick. *Life in the Far West.* London, 1849. Repr. L. R. Hafen, ed. Norman, 1951.

Sabin, Edwin L. *Kit Carson Days.* 2 vols. New York, 1914. Rev. ed. 2 vols. New York, 1935.

Schurz, William Lytle. *The Manila Galleon.* New York, 1939. Repr. New York, 1959.

Stewart, George R. (ed.). *The Opening of the California Trail.* Berkeley, 1953.

Stewart, William Drummond. *Altowan.* New York, 1846.

Stewart, William Drummond. *Edward Warren.* London, 1854.

Stong, Phil. *Horses and Americans.* New York, 1939.

Terrell, John Upton. *Furs by Astor.* New York, 1963.

Sullivan, Maurice S. *The Travels of Jedediah Smith.* Santa Ana, 1934. Repr. Rufus Rockwell Wilson, ed. New York, 1936.

Thomas, Alfred B. *After Coronado.* Norman, 1935.

Thwaites, Reuben Gold. (ed.). *Original Journals of the Lewis and Clark Expedition.* 8 vols. New York, 1904-05. Repr. New York, 1954.

Townsend, John Kirk. *Narrative of a Journey Across the Rocky Mountains.* Philadelphia, 1839. Reprint Reuben Gold Thwaites, ed. Cleveland, 1905.

Traits of American Indian Life and Character. By a Fur Trader. London, 1853. Repr. San Francisco, 1933.

Turner, Frederick Jackson. *Rise of the New West, 1819-1829.* New York, 1906. Repr. with foreword by Ray Allen Billington. New York, 1962.

Turner, Frederick Jackson. *The Frontier in American History.* New York, 1920.

Turner, Frederick Jackson. *The Significance of Sections in American History.* New York, 1932. Repr. Gloucester, 1959.

Twitchell, Ralph E. *The Leading Facts of New Mexican History.* 2 vols. Cedar Rapids, 1911.

Victor, Frances Fuller. *The River of the West.* Hartford, 1870. Repr. Columbus, 1950.

Vinton, Stallo. *John Colter.* New York, 1926.

Wagner, Henry R. *The Plains and the Rockies.* San Francisco, 1921. Revised and extended by Charles L. Camp. San Francisco, 1937.

Wagner, Henry R. *The Cartography of the Northwest Coast of America to the Year 1800.* 2 vols. Berkeley, 1937.

Wakefield, John A. *History of the War Between the United States and the Sac and Fox Nations.* Jacksonville, Ill., 1834. Repr. Chicago, 1908.

Wandell, Samuel Henry, and Minnegerode, Meade. *Aaron Burr.* 2 vols. New York, 1927.

Washburn, Wilcomb E. (ed.). *The Indian and the White Man.* Garden City, 1964.

Watson, Douglas S. *West Wind; the Life Story of Joseph Reddeford Walker.* Los Angeles, 1934.

Webb, Walter Prescott. *The Great Plains.* New York, 1936.

Wheat, Carl I. *Mapping the Trans-Mississippi West, 1540-1861.* 5 vols. San Francisco, 1957-63.

Wheeler, O. D. *Trail of Lewis and Clark.* 2 vols. New York, 1904. Repr. with introduction by Frederick S. Dellenbaugh. New York, 1926.

Wilkes, Charles. *Narrative of the United States Expedition During the Years 1838, 1839, 1840, 1841, and 1842.* 5 vols. Philadelphia, 1844.

Williams, Joseph. *Narrative of a Tour from the State of Indiana to Oregon Territory.* Cincinnati, 1843. Repr. New York, 1921.

Wissler, Clark. *North American Indians of the Plains.* New York, 1922.

Wyman, Walker D. *The Wild Horse of the West.* Lincoln, 1963.

Young, F. G. (ed.). *Correspondence and Journals of Captain Nathaniel J. Wyeth, 1831-36.* Eugene, 1899.

Wyeth, John B. *Oregon: or a Short History of a Long Journey.* Cambridge, 1833. Reprint. Reuben Gold Thwaites, ed. Cleveland, 1905.

Index